Baedeker's
Historical Palestine

Baedeker's Historical Palestine

Handbook for Travellers

by
Karl Baedeker

Hippocrene Books Inc.
New York

David & Charles
Newton Abbot London

This is a facsimile edition of the Palestine excursions taken from Baedeker's Palestine and Syria, Fifth Edition.

1912

Leipzig: Karl Baedeker, Publisher
London: T. Fisher Unwin, 1 Adelphi Terrace, W.C.
New York: Charles Scribner's Sons, 153 Fifth Ave.

Hippocrene Books, Inc.
171 Madison Avenue
New York, NY 10016

First Hippocrene Edition, 1985
First David & Charles Edition, 1985

ISBN 0-88254-699-6 (United States)
ISBN 0-7153-8706-5 (Great Britain)
Printed in United States of America

PALESTINE

AND

SYRIA

WITH ROUTES THROUGH MESOPOTAMIA AND BABYLONIA AND THE ISLAND OF CYPRUS

HANDBOOK FOR TRAVELLERS

BY

KARL BAEDEKER

WITH 21 MAPS, 56 PLANS, AND A PANORAMA OF JERUSALEM

FIFTH EDITION, REMODELLED AND AUGMENTED

LEIPZIG: KARL BAEDEKER, PUBLISHER
LONDON: T. FISHER UNWIN, 1 ADELPHI TERRACE, W.C.
NEW YORK: CHARLES SCRIBNER'S SONS, 153 FIFTH AVE.

1912

CONTENTS.

LIST OF MAPS.

PLANS.

1. Approaches to Palestine.

The handbooks of the various steamship companies (see below) give full information as to the steamer-routes from England and the various Mediterranean ports. Particulars as to the overland routes (see below) from England to the Mediterranean will be found in *Bradshaw's Continental Railway Guide* (3*s*. 6*d*.). The Peninsular and Oriental Co. (see below) issues tickets for the sea-journey out and return overland, or *vice versâ*. Travellers from the United States may sail direct from New York to Gibraltar, Naples, or Genoa (weekly; fares $ 80-175). — Meals are included in the fare, consisting of breakfast (tea or coffee), luncheon (11-12 a.m.) and dinner (6-7 p.m.; on the French and Italian steamers wine is generally included). The Steward's Fee, which the passenger pays at the end of the voyage, amounts to 1-1½ fr. per day, but more is expected if unusual trouble has been given. — Return or Circular Tickets, issued at a reduced rate by some of the steamship companies are not to be recommended, as connections are not always certain on the Syrian lines, especially at Jaffa, owing to the difficulties of landing (comp. p. 6). Reduced Family Tickets, for three or more persons, are also issued.

Sea-routes and ports in the Mediterranean, see *Baedeker's Mediterranean*.

Palestine and Syria are generally reached from England viâ Egypt, either direct by steamer, or overland to the Mediterranean and thence by one of the numerous mail steamship-lines to Alexandria or Port Said, from which ports connecting lines ply to the Syrian coast (Jaffa, Beirût, etc.). From Alexandria express trains run to (3-3½ hrs.) Cairo, and thence to (ca. 4¼ hrs.) Port Said.

From Europe to Alexandria and Port Said.

a. Steamship Lines from England direct.

1. *Peninsular and Oriental Co.* (office, 122 Leadenhall St., E.C.). From Tilbury Dock (mail steamers) or Royal Albert Dock (intermediate steamers) every Frid. to Port Said in 12 days, viâ Gibraltar and Marseilles or Malta (fares 1st cl. 19*l*. or 17*l*., 2nd cl. 13*l*. or 11*l*.; from Marseilles 13*l*. or 12*l*., 9*l*. or 8*l*.).

2. *Orient Line* (28 Cockspur St., S.W., and 5 Fenchurch Ave., E.C.). From Tilbury Dock every second Frid. to Port Said viâ Gibraltar, Toulon, Naples, and Taranto (fares 1st cl. 19*l*., 2nd cl. 13*l*.; from Naples 9*l*., 7*l*.).

3. *North German Lloyd* (*Norddeutscher Lloyd*; 26 Cockspur St., S.W.). From Southampton ca. thrice monthly to Port Said viâ Genoa and Naples (fares 1st cl. 21*l*., 2nd cl. 14*l*.; from Genoa 346 fr., 247 fr.; from Naples 296 fr., 223 fr.).

4. *Bibby Line* (10 Mincing Lane, London, E.C., and 26 Chapel St., Liverpool). From Liverpool every fortnight to Port Said (and India) viâ Marseilles (fare 1st cl. 17*l*., from Marseilles 12*l*.).

b. From Mediterranean Ports and Constantinople.

Overland Routes from London. *Marseilles* is reached from London viâ Calais and Paris in 22½ hrs. by ordinary express (fares 1st cl. 6*l*. 15*s*. 2*d*., 2nd cl. 4*l*. 12*s*. 11*d*.) or in 20¼ hrs. by the 'P. & O. Marseilles Express' (on Thurs. only) or by the 'Calais-Mediterranean Express' (daily in winter; higher fares by these two). — *Genoa* is 25 hrs. and *Naples* 45 hrs. from London viâ Calais or Boulogne, Paris, and Turin (to Genoa, 7*l*. 4*s*. 8*d*.,

4*l.* 19*s.* 11*d.*; to Naples 8*l.* 18*s.* 2*d.*, 6*l.* 1*s.*). — *Venice* is 32½ hrs. from London viâ Paris and the Simplon (7*l.* 14*s.* 8*d.*, 5*l.* 7*s.*). — ***Brindisi*** is reached viâ Boulogne and Paris in 55 hrs. (9*l.* 6*s.* 7*d.*, 6*l.* 6*s.* 9*d.*) or in 45 hrs. by the 'P. & O. Brindisi Express' (on Frid. only; 9*l.* 10*s.* 2*d.*). — ***Trieste*** is 38 hrs. from London viâ Flushing and Cologne (7*l.* 19*s.* 8*d.*, 5*l.* 1*s.* 2*d.*). — *Constantinople* may be reached in ca. 70 hrs viâ Boulogne and Paris and thence by 'Orient Express' (1st cl. only, ca. 20*l.*), or viâ Dover and Ostend and thence by 'Ostend-Vienna Express' (1st cl. only, ca. 18*l.*), or in ca. 80 hrs. by ordinary express viâ Boulogne and Vienna (1st cl. ca. 14*l.*, 2nd cl. ca. 9*l.*).

From Marseilles by '*P. & O.*' or *Bibby Lines* (see p. 1) to Port Said, or by *North German Lloyd* weekly to Alexandria direct or viâ Bizerta (Tunis) in 5 days (fares 346 fr., 198 fr.). Also by vessels of the *Messageries Maritimes* (offices, 3 Place Sadi-Carnot, Marseilles) every Thurs. to Alexandria and Port Said (fares to either port 350 fr., 250 fr.), and thence to Beirût, calling at Jaffa in alternate weeks. The fortnightly Asiatic and African liners of the ***Messageries Maritimes*** (direct), ***German East African Line*** (viâ Naples), and ***Rotterdamsche Lloyd*** (direct) are also available for the voyage from Marseilles to Port Said.

From Genoa by the *Società Nazionale di Servizi Marittimi* (London office, 8 Leadenhall St., E.C.) every Mon. viâ Naples and Messina to Alexandria (314 fr. 20 c., 213 fr. 45 c.; from Naples 252 fr. 25, 172 fr. 75 c.) and Beirût; also monthly to Port Said viâ Naples. Steamers of the *North German Lloyd* to Port Said, see p. 1; also fortnightly viâ Naples and Corfu to Alexandria (fares from 346 or 198 fr.; from Naples 296 or 173 fr.). The Dutch *Nederland Line* steamers (from Amsterdam to Port Said viâ Southampton) call fortnightly at Genoa.

From Naples to Alexandria and Port Said by the *North German Lloyd* (see above and p. 1), the *German East African Line* (see above), and the *Società Nazionale* (see above); to Port Said also by the *Orient Line* (see p. 1).

From Venice by the *Società Nazionale* twice monthly viâ Brindisi to Alexandria (280 fr. 95 c., 191 fr. 30 c.; from Brindisi 198 fr. 25 c., 134 fr. 15 c.) and Port Said, going on to Jaffa and Beirût.

From Brindisi by '*P. & O.*' steamer (see p. 1) every Sun. midnight, in connection with the 'P. & O.' express. Fares (1st class only) from Brindisi to Port Said 9*l.*, from London (incl. railway and sleeping-car) 22*l.* 10*s.* 2*d.* The return-trains from Brindisi await the arrival of the steamer from Port Said. — To Alexandria by *Austrian Lloyd* (see below) twice weekly and to Alexandria and Port Said by the *Società Nazionale* twice monthly (see above).

From Trieste weekly in 5 days to Alexandria viâ Brindisi by *Austrian Lloyd* steamer (250 fr., 175 fr.; from Brindisi 200 fr., 135 fr.), going on thence viâ Port Said, Jaffa, Ḥaifâ, Beirût, etc. Or by 'accelerated line' of the same company also weekly to Alexandria in 3 days (360 fr., 250 fr.; from Brindisi 300 fr., 200 fr.).

From Constantinople by the ***Messageries Maritimes*** (see above) every fortnight to Smyrna and Beirût (fares 205 fr., 140 fr.), connecting there with steamers to Jaffa (fares from Beirût 30 fr., 25 fr.), Port Said (65 fr., 55 fr.), Alexandria (110 fr., 85 fr.), and Marseilles. From Constantinople to Alexandria, viâ Smyrna and the Piræus, weekly steamers of the *Compagnie Russe de Navigation à Vapeur* (200 fr., 140 fr.), the *Khedivial Mail Steamship and Graving Co.* (£E 8, £E 5), and the *Roumanian State Maritime Service* (240 fr., 135 fr.); in Alexandria the two first-mentioned lines make connection for Jaffa, Haifâ, Beirût, Tripoli, etc. Also fortnightly steamers of the *Comp. Russe* to Alexandria, calling at all the chief Palestine ports.

Subjoined are a few details concerning the above-mentioned European and Egyptian ports. In Alexandria, Marseilles, and Trieste the steamers lie to at the piers, and this is also sometimes the case in Constantinople. At the Italian ports, and generally at Port Said, the passengers are taken out to the steamers by small boats. The fare for this is 1-1½ fr., including luggage, but a bargain should be struck beforehand. Order is said to be often very badly maintained.

Brindisi (*Grand-Hôtel International*, at the harbour, first-class, R. 5-10, D. 6 fr.; *Albergo d'Europa*, *Alb. Centrale*, both in the Corso Garibaldi) is now a town of 22,000 inhab. and has resumed its old importance as a starting-point for travellers to the Orient. Comp. *Baedeker's Southern Italy.*

Genoa (*Grand-Hôtel Miramare*, above the main rail. station, first-class; *Grand-Hôtel de Gênes*, Piazza Deferrari; *Hôtel-Pension Bristol*, Via Venti Settembre; *Eden Palace*, at the Acquasola Park; *Savoy*, near the main rail. station, at all these R. from 5 or 6, D. 6 or 7 fr.; *Grand-Hôtel Isotta*, Via Roma 7) contains 163,200 inhab. and is the chief seaport of Italy. Visitors should see the palaces in the *Via Balbi*, *Via Cairoli*, and *Via Garibaldi*. They should also ascend to the *Castellaccio* (*View; cable-tramway). Comp. *Baedeker's Northern Italy.*

Marseilles (*Regina Hotel*, Place Sadi-Carnot; *Grand-Hôtel du Louvre et de la Paix*, *Grand-Hôtel Noailles et Métropole*, *Grand-Hôtel*, these three in the Rue Noailles; *Bristol*, Rue Cannebière, all of the first class; *Hôtel du Petit-Louvre; Hôt. de Genève; Hôtel de Russie et d'Angleterre*, near the station), with 517,500 inhab., is the second city and chief seaport of France. *La Cannebière*, beginning at the *Vieux Port*, and its prolongation, the *Rue Noailles*, have long been the chief pride of Marseilles. The best survey of the city is obtained from the church of *Notre Dame de la Garde*, to the S. of the Vieux Port (cable-tramway). Comp. *Baedeker's Southern France.*

Naples (*Bertolini's Palace Hotel*, high up in the Parco Grifeo; *Excelsior*, by the sea, both of the highest class; *Grand-Hôtel*, by the sea; *Hôtel Bristol*, *Parker's Hotel*, *Grand Eden Hotel*, *Macpherson's Hôt. Britannique*, these four high up in the Corso Vittorio Emanuele; *Grand-Hôtel Santa Lucia; Grand-Hôtel du Vésuve; Grand-Hôtel Victoria; Hôtel Royal des Etrangers; Grand-Hôtel de Londres*, all these also first-class), with more than 600,000 inhab., is the most populous city in Italy after Milan. The beauty of the Bay of Naples is celebrated. The tourist should not fail to walk in the grounds of the *Villa Nazionale*, to drive along the *Via Tasso* and the *Strada Nuova di Posilipo*, and to see the famous sculptures and Pompeian wall-paintings in the *Museo Nazionale*. The finest view is obtained from *San Martino* (cable-tramway). For details and for the excursions to *Pompeii*, *Sorrento*, *Capri*, and other points, see *Baedeker's Southern Italy.*

Venice (*Hôtel Royal-Danieli*, *Hôt. de l'Europe*, *Grand-Hôtel*, *Britannia*, these four first-class; *Grand-Hôtel d'Italie; Canal Hôtel et Monaco; Regina)*, a city of 148,500 inhab., was down to 1797 the capital of a powerful republic of the same name. The station is at the N.W. end of the Canal Grande; gondola hence to the *Piazzetta*, near which most of the hotels lie, 1 fr., with two rowers 2 fr. The chief sights are the *Piazza*, *Campanile*

(*View), and *Church of San Marco*, the *Doges' Palace*, and the *Canal Grande*. Comp. *Baedeker's Northern Italy*.

Trieste (*Excelsior Palace Hotel*, Riva del Mandracchio, R. from 4 *K*; *Hôtel de la Ville*, *Hôtel Volpich all'Aquila Nera*, both near the harbour; *Toniato*) is the chief seaport of Austria, with 229,500 inhabitants. The S. Railway Station (Süd-Bahnhof; restaurant) lies on the N. side of the town, to the E. of the piers of the Austrian Lloyd; the State Railway Station (Staats-Bahnhof) is on the S. side (cab 1 *K* 60 *h*, at night 2 *K*). Pleasant excursions to the château of *Miramar* (1/2 day), or to *Opčina* (2 hrs.; electric incline). Comp. *Baedeker's Austria-Hungary*.

Constantinople (*Tokatlian*, Grande Rue de Péra 180, with restaurant and café, R. from 6 1/2, D. 5 1/2, pens. from 15 fr.; *Pera Palace Hotel*, near the public garden of the Petits-Champs, R. from 10, D. 6 1/2, pens. from 20 3/4 fr.; *Bristol*, *Hôtel de Londres*, *Berliner Hof*, *Continental*, all four by the garden of the Petits Champs, R. from 4, 5, or 6 fr., D. 5, pens. from 12, 12 1/2, 14, or 15 fr.; *Hôtel Kroecker*, Rue Kabristan 36, R. from 4 fr.), the capital of Turkey, is a city of about 1,125,000 inhabitants. It includes the seaport of *Galata* and the European suburb of *Pera*, on the E. side of the Golden Horn; *Stambul*, to the W. of the Golden Horn; and *Scutari*, on the coast of Asia. The hotels are all in Pera, 1 1/2 M. from the station (carr. 4 1/2-5 fr.) and 1 M. from the landing-place of the steamers (disembarkation 2, carr. 2 1/4 fr.). — Passing visitors should ascend the *Tower of Galata*, drive across the *New Bridge* to the *Mosque of the Hagia Sophia* in Stambul, visit the *Museum*, walk through the *Great Bazaar* (with dragoman), and take a steamer-trip on the *Bosphorus*. Comp. *Baedeker's Mediterranean*.

Alexandria (*Savoy Palace Hotel; Metropole; Excelsior; Grand-Hôtel; Windsor; Canal de Suez*), a city of 377,000 inhab., is the chief seaport of Egypt, but offers little of interest to the stranger. Representatives of the hotels and of the chief tourist-agencies meet travellers on the steamer and relieve them of all trouble in passing to the station or to a hotel for a fee of 20-25 pi. (5 1/4-6 1/2 fr.; passport, see p. xxiii). — From the *Place Méhémet-Ali*, the centre of the European quarter, we drive to *Pompey's Pillar*, 88 ft. high, the dominant feature of Alexandria, dating from the 4th cent. A.D. Not far off are the *Egyptian Catacombs of Kôm esh-Shukâfa*, probably of the 2nd cent. A.D. (adm. 5 pi.). The *Museum of Graeco-Roman Antiquities* (mainly objects found in and near Alexandria) is also well worth a visit (open 9-12 & 3-5.30; adm. 2 pi.; closed on Thurs.).

Port Said (*Eastern Exchange Hotel; Savoy Hotel; Hôtel Continental;* passengers landed in boats, ca. 1 fr.), the flourishing town at the N. end of the Suez Canal, contains 50,000 inhabitants. At the harbour is a lighthouse, 175 ft. high, and on the W. mole is a colossal statue, by E. Frémiet, of *Ferdinand de Lesseps* (1805-94), the builder of the Suez Canal.

Cairo (*Shepheard's Hotel*, *Savoy*, *Semiramis*, all of the highest class; *Continental*. *Hôt. d'Angleterre*, *Hôt. National*, all these also first-class; *New Khedivial Hotel; Eden Palace;* cabs and omnibuses in waiting on the arrival at the main station in the N.W. part of the town), with ca. 655,000 inhab., is the largest city in the Arab world. The older quarters present an extraordinarily varied scene of a genuine Oriental character. Hurried visitors should drive (carr. 10 pi. per hr.) to the *Citadel* (visit to the *Mosques* of *Sultân Hasan* and *Mohammed 'Ali*), then back viâ the *Tombs of the Mamelukes* (1/2 day); or through the *Muski*, the main thoroughfare of the Oriental quarter, to the *Bazaars*, visiting the *Mosques* of *El-Azhar* and *El-Muaiyad*, and to the *Tombs of the Caliphs* (1/2 day). The mosques are all open about noon except on Friday. In the W. part of the town, near the Nile, is the *Egyptian Museum* (open 8.30-1 or 9-4.30; adm. 1, in winter 5 pi.; closed on Frid.). Beyond the river are the famous *Pyramids of Gîzeh* (1/2 day; electric tramway in ca. 1 1/4 hr., fare 4 or 2 pi.). Comp. *Baedeker's Egypt*.

I. JERUSALEM AND ITS ENVIRONS.

2. Jaffa.

Arrival. The steamer casts anchor outside the rock-girt harbour. The hotels (see below) and the tourist-offices (p. 7) send small boats to the ship, and the traveller should use these, rejecting the offers of all other boatmen, porters, and dragomans. The charge is 6-7 fr. a head, incl. luggage (upon which a sharp eye should be kept) and the drive to the hotel. In rough weather, the disembarkation is difficult, and as much as 20 fr. is then sometimes demanded from each person. If the wind blows very strongly from the W., landing is impracticable, and passengers must go on to Ḥaifâ (p. 229) or Beirût (p. 279). — *Passport* and *Customs Duties*, see pp. xxiii, xxiv. The boats land in front of the *Custom House*, which lies at the S. corner of the harbour. The various **Steamboat Offices** (Egyptian, Russian, Austrian, French, Italian) stand on the quay to the N. — The **Railway Station** (*Gare;* Pl. B, 1), in the N.E. part of the town, is about $1^1/_2$ M. from the harbour and $^1/_2$ M. from the German Colony. Travellers should beware of pickpockets, especially near the harbour.

Hotels (comp. p. xvi; bargaining advisable; previous notice desirable during the height of the travelling-season). — Hardegg's Jerusalem Hotel (Pl. a, B 1; German landlord), in the German Colony; Hôtel du Parc (Pl. b, B 1; landlords, *Hall Brothers*), adjoining the preceding; pension at these $12^1/_2$ fr., for a prolonged stay 10 fr., after the season 8 fr. (wine extra). Hotel Kaminitz (Pl. c; B, 1), Rue Boustrous (p. 10); Frank's Hotel (Pl. d, B 1; German landlord), in the German Colony, with restaurant.

Tourist Offices. *Thos. Cook & Son* (Pl. 1; B, 1); *Clark*, in the Hôtel du Parc (p. 6); *Dr. Immanuel Benzinger*, in Frank's Hotel (p. 6); *Hamburg-American Line*, *Agence Lubin*, both at the harbour.

Horses and Carriages (best obtained through the hotels or tourist-offices). Saddle-horse, 1 fr. per hr. Carriage from or to the railway station, 1 fr.; per drive, 1 beshlik (3½ pi.); ½ day 10, whole day 20 fr.; to Jerusalem, see p. 15; to Gaza, see p. 122; to Ḥaifâ, see pp. 230 and 235.

Post Offices. *Turkish* (Pl. 29; B, 1), Rue Boustrous (p. 10); *International Telegraph*, in the Post Office. The foreign post-offices are all on the quay: *Austro-Hungarian* (Pl. 32; A, 1), *German* (Pl. 31; A, 1), and *Russian* (Pl. 33; A, 2) to the S.W., *French* (Pl. 30; A, 1) to the N.E.

Vice-Consulates. British (Pl. 9; A, 1, 2), *N. Fiani;* United States, *J. Hardegg*, of the Jerusalem Hotel (p. 6); also French, German, etc.

Banks. *Anglo-Palestine Company* (Pl. 4b; A, 2), *Banque Ottomane* (Pl. B.O.; A, 2), both on the Gaza Road; *German Bank of Palestine* (Pl. 4a; A, 1), *Crédit Lyonnais* (Pl. 3; A, 1), both on the quay.

Physicians: *Dr. Keith* (English); *Dr. Lorch* (German); *Dr. Lin* (French) *Dr. Saad*, quarantine physician (with German diploma). — **Dentist**, *K. Lorch*. — Chemists, *Paulus*, *Wolfer*, *& Co.*, in the German Colony (p. 10).

European Firms. Commission & Forwarding Agents: *Aberle & Co.*, in the Gaza Road (Pl. A, 2); *P. Breisch*, *Jona Kübler*, these two on the quay. — Travelling Requisites: *Rabinowitz Brothers*, Gaza Road; *C. Besserer*, saddler, near the station. — Provisions: *Polemidis*, *Stephanidis*, *Kapellos*, all in the Gaza Road. — Wine: *Sarona & Jaffa Co.* (German; wines from the German Colonies), *Carmel Oriental Co.* (wines from the Jewish Colonies), both in the Gaza Road. — Nurseryman: *G. Egger* supplies bulbs and seeds of Syrian plants for exportation. — Photographers: *A. Soskin*, Station Road; *Sawabini*, Gaza Road. — *International Book Shop and Art Dealer*, Rue Boustrous.

Benevolent Institutions. *Church Missionary Society's Station*, with a hospital, two schools for boys, and one for girls (Pl. 17; A, 2); *London Jews Society*, see p. 10; *American Orphanage; French Hospital of St. Louis* (Pl. 22; A, 2), conducted by the Sisters of St. Joseph, who also have charge of an orphanage and school for girls (Pl. 16; A, 2); *German Hospital* and *Schools*, see p. 10; *Convent* and *Schools* of the *Frères des Ecoles Chrétiennes* (Pl. 15; A, 2); *Franciscan Convent* and *School* for boys (Casa Nuova; Pl. 7, A 2); *Italian Schools* for boys and girls. The *Jews* support a hospital (Sha'areih Zion), a school for girls, and three boys' schools (including a high school).

Anglican Church Services at the chapel of the *London Jews Society* (p. 10; Sun. 9.30 a.m.); services of the *Church Missionary Society* (see above; 3.30 p.m.), opposite the English Hospital (p. 10).

Jaffa or *Yâfâ*, Greek *Joppa*, the seaport of Jerusalem and the chief town of a Kaḍâ of the Liwa of Jerusalem (comp. p. lvii), contains about 50,000 inhab., including 30,000 Moslems, 10,000 Christians, and 10,000 Jews. The town has greatly increased within the last few decades, chiefly owing to the numerous pilgrims who flock here (15-20,000 yearly). Its trade is also considerable. The value of its exports in 1910 was 636,145*l.*, the chief items being oranges (235,605*l.*), beans and lupins (15,378*l.*), sesame, and vegetables. The chief imports (total 1,002,450*l.*) are cotton goods, flour, sugar, tobacco, rice, coffee, and cloth. In the same year the port was entered and cleared by 1514 vessels of 1,136,770 tons.

History. Jaffa was anciently a Phœnician colony in the land of the Philistines. The meaning of the ancient name *Japho* is doubtful; but the Hebrews translated it 'the beautiful'. According to an ancient myth Andromeda, the daughter of Cepheus and Joppa (daughter of Æolus), is said to have been chained to the rocks here, in order that she might be devoured by a huge sea-monster, but was released by Perseus. The prophet Jonah, too, is said to have just quitted Joppa when he was swallowed by the whale

(Jonah i. 3). Throughout the Roman period, and even down to the middle ages, the chains were shown with which Andromeda was bound to the rocks of the harbour. So, too, the huge bones of some marine monster were long an object of curiosity here. Jaffa is mentioned as a fortress in the list of cities overthrown by Thutmosis III. (p. lxxvii). In the days of Solomon it was the port for Jerusalem, to which Hiram, King of Tyre, undertook to send timber from Lebanon 'in floats', for the building of the Temple (2 Chron. ii. 16; comp. Ezra iii. 7). In the inscription relating to the victorious campaign of Sennacherib, the town is called Ya-ap-pu. The tomb-inscription of Eshmunazar (beginning of the 3rd cent. B.C.) mentions Jaffa as given to Sidon along with Dor by one of the Ptolemies.

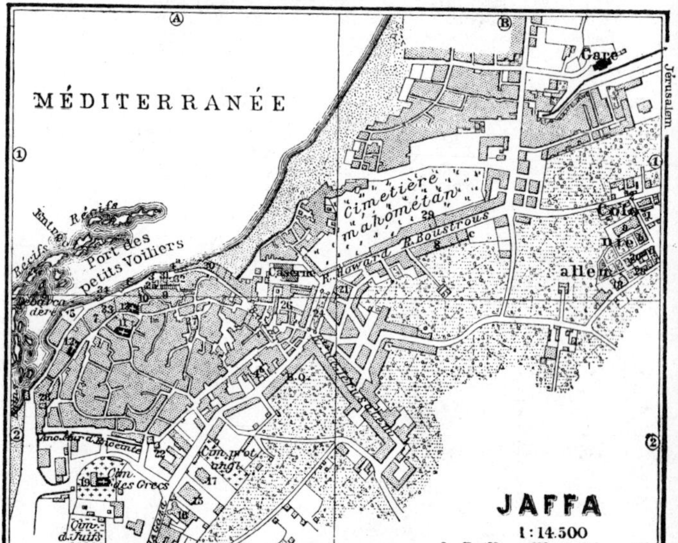

D'après un plan original du Dr Saad

Tourist Agency: 1. Cook, B, 1. — *Banks:* 3. Crédit Lyonnais, A, 1; B.O. Banque Ottomane, A, 2; 4a. German Bank of Palestine, A, 1; 4b. Anglo-Palestine Company, A, 2. — 5. *Passport Bureau*, A, 2. — 6. *Harbour Master*, A, 1. — 7. *Casa Nuova*, A, 2. — *Vice-Consulates:* 8. French, B, 1; 9. British, A, 1, 2; a. United States B, 1. — *Convents:* 11. Franciscan, A, 2; 12. Greek, A, 2; 13. Armenian, A, 2. — *Schools:* 15. Frères des Ecoles Chrétiennes, A, 2; 16. Sisters of St. Joseph (for girls), A, 2; 17. English (for girls), A, 2; 18. German Templars', B, 1. — *Churches:* 19. St. George's (Greek), A, 2; 20. German Protestant, B, 1. — 21. *Government Building* (Serâi; B, 1). — *Hospitals:* 22. French, A, 2; 23. German, B, 1. — 24. *Public Garden*, A, 2. — *Mosques:* 25. El-Bahr, A, 1; 26. El-Maḥmûdîyeh, A, 2; 27. Es-Serâi, A, 2. — 28. *Lighthouse*, A, 2. — *Post and Telegraph Offices:* 29. Turkish, B, 1; 30. French, A, 1; 31. German, A, 1; 32. Austro-Hungarian, A, 1; 33. Russian, A, 2. — 34. *Quarantine Station*, A, 1.

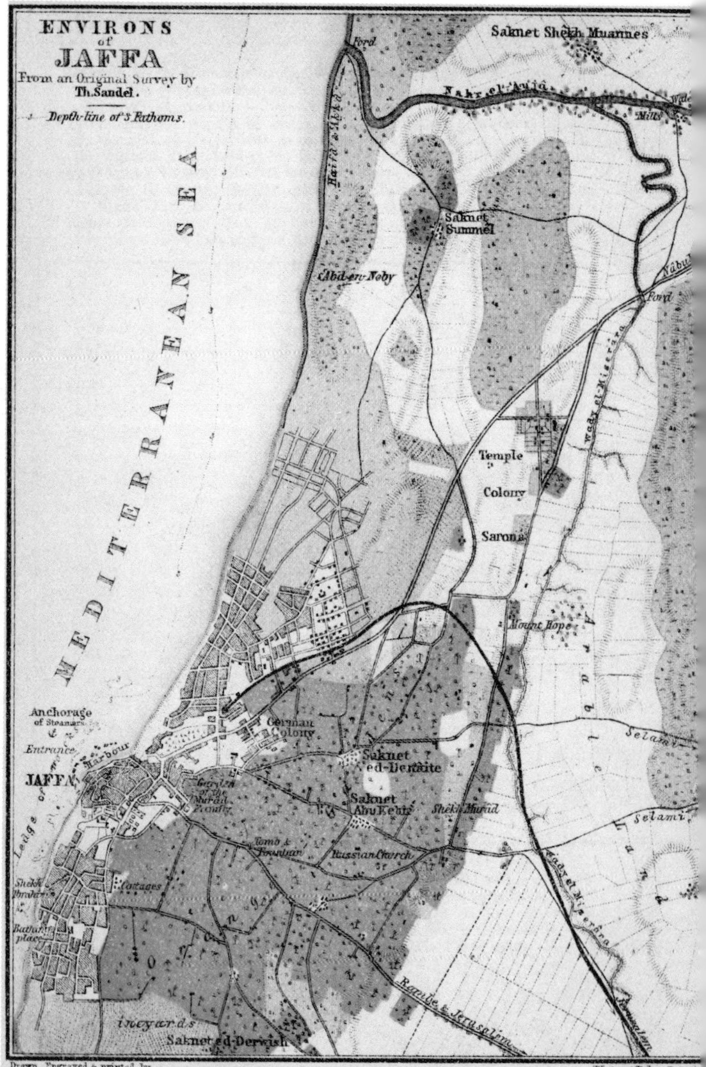

ENVIRONS
of
JAFFA
From an Original Survey by
Th. Sandel.
Depth-line of 3 Fathoms.
MEDITERRANEAN SEA
Sakmet Shekh Muannes
Ford
Mills
Saknet Summel
Abd-en-Neby
Ford
Temple
Colony
Sarona
Mount Hope
Anchorage
of Steamers
Entrance
Harbour
JAFFA
German
Colony
Saknet
ed-Derwish
Russian Church
Sheikh Murad
Cottages
Ramle & Jerusalem
Saknet ed-Derwish
Drawn, Engraved & printed by
1:50.000
Wagner & Debes Leipzig
0 500 1000 1500 2000
Paces
0 500 1000 1500
Yards

Jaffa was definitively brought under the Jewish yoke by the Maccabees (1 Macc. x. 74 et seq.). Christianity was introduced here at an early period (Acts ix. 36, etc.). During the Jewish war Joppa was destroyed; it was afterwards rebuilt, but was soon again destroyed by Vespasian as being a haunt of pirates. Several bishops of Joppa are mentioned as attending various church synods. The bishopric was restored by the Crusaders, and the town also became the seat of a count (1099). In 1126 the district of Joppa came into the possession of the Knights of St. John. The town was captured and destroyed by Melik el-ʿAdil, brother of Saladin, in 1187, and by Safeddin in 1191, recaptured by Richard Cœur-de-Lion, taken in 1197 by Melik el-ʿAdil, restored to the Christians in 1204, and finally destroyed in 1267 by Beybars. Towards the end of the 17th cent. the importance of Jaffa began to revive, and from that period dates the construction of the quay. In 1799 the place was taken by the French under Kléber.

The old town lies on the sea-coast, on the brow of a rocky hill 115 ft. in height. The streets are generally very narrow and dusty, and after the slightest fall of rain exceedingly dirty. From the landing-place (Débarcadère; Pl. A, 2) the chief business-street leads along the quay to its N.E. end and then bends to the right. The street then forks, the left branch traversing a large khân and passing along the N. side of the barracks (Caserne; Pl. A, 1) to the Serâi (p. 10). In a straight direction we reach the busy Arab *Bazaar* (Pl. A, 2), where the traveller will have an opportunity of noticing the purely Semitic type of the inhabitants. The *Mosque* (*Jâmiʿ el-Maḥmûdîyeh;* Pl. 26, A 2) to the left is of no interest; opposite its entrance we see an elegant *Fountain*, surrounded by ancient columns. The *Latin Hospice* (*Casa Nuova;* Pl. 7, A 2) was founded in 1654, from which period dates the tradition that it occupies the site of the *House of Simon the Tanner* (Acts ix. 43); but the site of Simon's house is now pointed out in an insignificant mosque near the *Fanar*, or lighthouse (Pl. 28; A, 2), on the S. side of the town, where, however, the view is the sole attraction (fee 1 pi.).

The new quarters, to the E., N.E., and S. of the old town, make a more favourable impression. The *Public Garden* (Pl. 24; A, 2) reached through the bazaar, with its clock-tower and several Arabian coffee-houses, is the starting-point of four great roads, one of which is that from the harbour, which we have just traversed. The Jerusalem Road leads to the S.E. through a new suburb, then between lofty cactus-hedges. After 12 min. we reach a handsome *Sebîl* or fountain, founded by *Abu Nebbût*, a former pasha, who is buried here. The road now forks, the turning to the right leading to Jerusalem, while that to the left brings us in 5 min. to the Russian settlement, where we are shown the site of the house of *Tabitha*, and her rock-tomb (Acts ix. 36). The top of the church-tower affords an admirable view of Jaffa and the Plain of Sharon, extending in clear weather to Mt. Carmel. — The Gaza Road (Pl. A, 2) passes through the S. suburb. On this road, to the left, are the English Protestant cemetery and the English school for girls (Pl. 17; A, 2); opposite, on the right, the French hospital (Pl. 22; A, 2); farther on, to the left, are the schools of the Frères des Ecoles

Chrétiennes (Pl. 15; A, 2) and of the Sisters of St. Joseph (Pl. 16; A, 2); to the right are the Greek church (Pl. 19; A, 2) and several cemeteries, then the English mission-house and hospital. To the W. of this road is the weli (p. lxxv) of *Sheikh Ibrâhîm* (fine view of the town). — The Rue Boustrous (road to Nâbulus) leads to the N., passing the *Barracks* (Caserne; Pl. A, 1), on the left, and the *Serâi*, or government-building (Pl. 21; B, 1), on the right. Beyond are the Turkish *Post and Telegraph Office* (l.; Pl. 29, B 1) and the Hotel Kaminitz (r.; p. 6). A few steps farther on a road to the left leads to the *Railway Station* (Gare; Pl. B, 1) and to the new N. suburb, which is inhabited mainly by Jews and Mohammedans.

The continuation of the Rue Boustrous leads through orange-gardens and past a fountain with an Arabic inscription (left) to the pleasant-looking houses of the **German Colony** (*Colonie Allemande*; Pl. B, 1). On the right, at the entrance to the colony, are the chapel and mission-house of the London Jews Society, and the Jerusalem Hotel, the Hôt. du Parc, and Frank's Hotel (p. 6). Beyond the last stands the new German Protestant Church (Pl. 20; B, 1). The colony was originally founded in 1856 by American settlers, but was afterwards abandoned, and purchased in 1868 by the 'German Temple' sect, which now numbers about 350 souls. There are two schools (Pl. 18; B, 1) and a hospital (Pl. 23; B, 1).

The constitution of the free religious community of the 'Temple' or 'Friends of Jerusalem' in 1860 was the result of a religious movement in Wurtemberg, mainly stimulated by *Chr. Hoffmann*. Starting from the principle that the task of Christianity is to embody the Kingdom of God on earth, they came to the conclusion that a really Christian social life was impossible on the basis of the current ideas of the Trinity, the Divinity of Christ, etc. On the contrary, they derived their religious and social programme from the Old Testament prophecies. They accordingly considered it to be their task, first of all to erect the ideal Christian community in the 'Land of Promise' and from this spot to begin regenerating the church and social life of Europe. The first colony was founded in Ḥaifâ in 1868, and the second almost simultaneously in Jaffa. The 'Temple' numbers some 1200 members in six colonies and has unquestionably done much to promote the colonization of the country.

About $1^1/_2$ M. to the N.E. of the town, on the road to Nâbulus (see above), lies **Sarona** (see Map, p. 9), another colony of the 'Temple'. The plain of *Sharon*, which extends along the seaboard between Joppa and Cæsarea, was famed in ancient times for its luxuriant fertility and pastures (Is. xxxv. 2, lxv. 10). Beneath the sand is excellent soil, and water is found everywhere. Vines thrive admirably (comp. p. liii). Apiculture is also pursued with success.

A beautiful excursion may be made along the Nâbulus road as far as the *Nahr el-'Aujâ* (carriage there and back, in 2-3 hrs., 10 fr.; sail-boat, $^1/_2$ day, 15 fr. or upwards according to the number of passengers). This river, next to the Jordan the largest in Palestine, rises near *Râs el-'Ain*, $10^1/_2$ M. to the N.E. of Jaffa, and drives a number of mills. Near *Mulebbis*, close by, is the Jewish colony *Petaḥ Tikweh*, the largest of the Jewish colonies in Judæa (pop. 1600), founded in 1878. Return on horseback along the coast (see Map).

Travellers interested in the Zionist movement may visit the following Jewish Colonies (comp. pp. liii, lxxxvii) to the S. of Jaffa (for Petaḥ

Tikweh, to the N.E., see p. 10). We follow the Jerusalem highroad (riding-horses and carriages, see p. 7) to (3/4 hr. on horseback) ***Mikweh Israel*** (p. 15) and (1 1/4 hr.) ***Rishon le-Zion*** (p. 15), whence a carriage-road leads to *Er-Ramleh* (2 hrs.; rail. station, p. 12). About 1 1/4 hr. to the S. of Rishon le-Zion lies the colony of *Wâdi el-Khanîn* (150 inhab.; founded in 1882), and 3/4 hr. to the S.E. that of *Rekhoboth* (600 inhab.), the latter, established in 1890, being the second-largest (in area) of the colonies in Judæa. Continuing to the S., we reach (3/4 hr.) ***Ekron*** (p. 13). Thence we proceed S.W. and, crossing the *Nahr Rûbîn* (p. 122; here called *Wâdi Katra*), arrive at (1 hr.) the settlement of *Katra*, founded in 1882, with 140 inhabitants. The southernmost of the colonies is (3 hrs. from Katra) *El-Kastînyeh* (pop. 100; founded in 1896). Thence we may return to (4 hrs.) Jaffa viâ *Yebna* (p. 122), or we may follow the carriage-road to (3 hrs.) ***Deir 'Abân*** (p. 14), where we join the railway.

From Jaffa to *Haifâ*, carriage-road, see pp. 237-235; to *Gaza* (also road), see p. 122.

3. From Jaffa to Jerusalem.

a. By Railway.

54 M. Two trains daily in each direction in 3 3/4 hrs., starting from Jaffa in the season ca. 7 a.m. & 2 p.m. and from Jerusalem at 7.40 a.m. & 1.30 p.m. Fares, 1st class 70 pi. 20 pa., 2nd class (corresponding to the 3rd class on European railways; not recommended) 25 piastres. In these fares one mejîdi = 20 piastres, one napoleon = 94 pi., 1*l.* = 124 pi., 1 Turkish pound = 108 piastres.

The line skirts the orange-gardens in the environs of Jaffa, with *Sarona* to the left, then turns S.E. and crosses the plain of *Sharon*, following the depression of the ***Wâdi Miserâra***. To the right lies *Mikweh Israel* (p. 15). Towards the E. the bluish mountains of Judæa come into view. On the right, close by, are (4 1/3 M.) *Yâzûr* and (6 M.) *Beit Dejan*; on the left, *Sâkiya*, then, farther to the E., *Kafr Anâ* (*Ono*, Nehem. xi. 35) and *El-Yehûdîyeh*, with the German Temple colony of *Wilhelma* (1902). The line passes through (8 M.) *Sâfirîyeh* (perhaps *Sariphaea*, an episcopal see in 530).

12 1/2 M. **Lydda**. — The STATION lies 3/4 M. to the S. of the town, on the road to Er-Ramleh (see next page).

Lydda, Arabic ***Ludd***, contains 7000 inhab., including 2000 Orthodox Greeks.

HISTORY. *Lôd* is first mentioned after the Exile (Ezra ii. 33; Neh. vii. 37). It became of some importance in the period of the Maccabees (Jos. Ant. xx. 6, 2), and in 145 B.C. it was detached from Samaria and included in Judæa (1 Macc. xi. 34, etc., where it is named *Lydda*). Under the Romans it was the capital of a district of Judæa, and after the fall of Jerusalem it became the seat of a rabbinical school. It contained a Christian community (Acts ix. 32) at an early period, and soon became the see of a bishop. In the Græco-Roman period it was called *Diospolis*, but its ancient name was retained in the episcopal lists. In 415 an ecclesiastical council was held at Lydda, at which Pelagius defended himself. In the 6th cent. we hear of a church built over the tomb of St. George at Lydda. In the following century this was destroyed by the Persians, but it was again built and existed until its second destruction by Caliph Hâkim Biamrillâh (p. lxxxiii) in 1010. Again rebuilt, it was once more destroyed by the Mohammedans in order not to interfere with the defence of the town against the Crusaders. The latter found a 'magnificent tomb' here, and in the second half of the 12th cent. erected a new church near the site of the old one, which, however, was destroyed with the town by Saladin in 1191. In 1271 Lydda was sacked by the Mongols, and since that period it has never recovered its former importance. — According to tradition, Mohammed declared that at the Last Day Christ would slay Antichrist at the gate of Lydda.

On the site of the just-mentioned church of the Crusaders (of which the two apses and a few arches and pilasters on the W. still subsist) stands the *Church of St. George*, which has been in the hands of the Greeks since 1870 (key kept by the sacristan of the Greek convent; fee 5 pi.). The square buttresses of the nave are adorned with small columns. The plan resembles that of the church of Sebasṭieh (p. 225). The ceiling has been restored with little taste. Below the altar is the crypt, which has also been restored (Revue Archéologique xix. 223 et seq.). The site of the earliest church (see p. 11) is now occupied by a small mosque.

From Lydda the train proceeds to the S., passing *El-Ḥadîtheh*, *Jimzû*, and *ʿAnnâbeh* on the left.

14½ M. **Er-Ramleh.** — The Railway Station is about ⅓ M. to the E. of the town, on the Jerusalem road. From the station to the 'Tower of Ramleh', ½ hr. — Accommodation at the *Franciscan Convent*, on the W. side of the town (p. 13).

Er-Ramleh contains fully 7000 inhab., about 2500 of whom are Christians, chiefly of the Greek faith. Schools are maintained by the Church Missionary Society and by the Franciscans and the Sisters of St. Joseph. There is also an Armenian Convent. The town is wretched and has no trade. The orchards around Ramleh are luxuriant; there are also sycamores and palm-trees. The fields yield rich crops. The climate is milder than that of Jerusalem, and more healthy than that of Jaffa.

History. The tradition that Ramleh occupies the site of the *Arimathaea* of the New Testament is a fabrication of the 13th century. The town was founded in 716 by the Omaiyade caliph Suleimân, the son of ʿAbd el-Melik. The truth of this statement is confirmed by the facts that the name of the town is of purely Arabic origin (*ramleh* signifying 'sand'), and that we find the name 'Ramula' applied to the place for the first time in the year 870. The place soon became prosperous, and was perhaps even larger than Jerusalem. Christians lived at Ramleh and had churches here before the time of the Crusades. In 1099 a bishopric of Ramleh was founded by the Crusaders. In 1177 the town was much damaged by a fire. Ramleh was twice captured by Saladin, and in 1266 it was finally wrested from the Franks by Beybars. The town continued to enjoy a share of its former prosperity down to the close of the 15th century.

On the E. side of the road to the rail. station is the *Chief Mosque (Jâmiʿ el-Kebîr)*, once a church of the Crusaders (12th cent.). Unbelievers are not always permitted to visit it, but the effect of the all-powerful bakshish may be tried (5 pi.; shoes must be taken off).

The church is one of the best-preserved of its period. On the W. side is a square minaret, which was probably once a Christian bell-tower. The principal entrance was on the W. side, but the W. front has now been covered by masonry; the entrance is on the N. side. The mosque is about 55 yds. long by 27 wide. The nave is loftier than the two aisles, from which it has been divided by two rows of pillars. Each pillar has three colonnettes with beautiful capitals. Above each row are seven arches, a plain cornice, and seven pointed windows. The windows in the aisles also have cornices.

The *Franciscan Convent* to the W. of the town, on the Jaffa road, occupies the traditional site of the house of Joseph of Arimathæa (Matt. xxvii. 59), to whom also the new church is dedicated. In 1799 Napoleon occupied a room here, which is still shown.

The most remarkable monument is the **Tower of Ramleh*, or *Jâmiʿ el-Abyaḍ*, the 'white mosque' (to the S.W. of the town).

The mosque was built by the founder of the town. The building was restored in the time of Saladin (1190), and Sultan Beybars also erected a dome and a minaret here (1268). An Arabic inscription over the door dates from the period of the Mameluke sultan, Moḥammed en-Nâṣir (1318). A later Mohammedan tradition is to the effect that forty companions of the prophet, or, if the Christian version is to be believed, forty Christian martyrs, repose in the subterranean vaults of the mosque.

The mosque, now in ruins, formed a square of which the sides were about 330 ft. long. The entrance was beautifully decorated. The court had pointed arcades on two sides. In the centre of the court are remains of a fountain. The whole area is undermined with vaults. In the 17th cent. a hospital or lunatic asylum *(mûristân)* was established here. — The tower recalls buildings erected by the Crusaders in the Romanesque Transition style (p. xcix). The pointed doorway and the elegant little windows of the five stories, especially on the S. side, are remarkably interesting. At the four corners are slender buttresses. The upper part of the tower tapers; the spire added in 1652 has fallen in. The *View from the top (110 steps) is magnificent (especially in the evening).

Towards the S. is a large olive-plantation; towards the E. are tombs and the town of Ramleh. Farther distant, towards the N. and S., stretches a beautiful fertile plain; in the distance to the W. is the silvery band of the Mediterranean; to the E. the blue mountains of Judæa. The most conspicuous of the neighbouring towns and villages is Lydda, to the N.E.; to the right of it is Beit Nebâla, and adjoining it, to the left beyond Lydda, is Deir Ṭarîf. Towards the E. lies Jimzû, to the right of which are Yâlô, Ḳubâb, and Lâṭrûn. In the extreme distance, to the E.S.E., En-Nebi Samwîl (p. 96) is said to be visible.

About 8 min. to the N. of Ramleh is situated the so-called *Cistern of St. Helena*, Arabic *Bîr el-ʿAneizîyeh* (comp. p. xcviii), consisting of six vaults, each 30 paces long and borne by fifteen pillars. The inscription is of Carmathian origin (comp. p. xciii). The cistern may be entered. It was probably constructed by Suleimân (p. 12).

Immediately after leaving Ramleh, the Railway crosses the road from Jaffa to Jerusalem and turns to the S. across the marshy plain, past (left) the small Arab village of (18 M.) *Nâʿaneh.* A little to the right (W.) of the railway lies *ʿAḳir* (*Ekron;* Josh. xiii. 3, etc.), one of the five chief cities of the Philistines, now a Jewish colony founded by Rothschild in 1884 (300 inhab.), with almost no traces of ruins. On a hill to the left (E.), near the village of *Abu Shûsheh*, are the ruins of **Gezer** (*Tell Jezer;* 755 ft.).

Gezer, mentioned in the letters found at Tell el-ʿAmarna (p. lxxvi), was an ancient Canaanitish city, not occupied by the Israelites (Josh. xvi. 10; Judg. i. 29). It was afterwards captured by Pharaoh and presented by him to Solomon, his son-in-law, as his daughter's dowry (1 Kings ix. 16). Gezer commanded one of the easiest passes between Jaffa and Jerusalem, and hence became an important fortress in the time of the Maccabees (1 Macc. iv. 15,

ix. 52, etc.). Gezer has been identified with the episcopal city of *Gadara* in Palæstina Prima and with the *Mont Gisart* of the Crusaders, who under Baldwin IV. here defeated Saladin in 1177 (Acad. des Inscrip., Comptes Rendus 1888, pp. 395 et seq.). Recent excavations by the Palestine Exploration Fund (1902-1909; now filled up again) have revealed five main epochs in the history of the town. The lowest stratum contains cave-dwellings, with flint implements (ca. 3000-2000 B.C.). The numerous Egyptian seals, rings, and other ornaments in the Caanitish stratum above this (2000-1000 B.C.) show how great was the influence of Egyptian culture at that remote period. Higher up, the periods of the Jewish city, before and after the Exile, were clearly distinguishable. Some of the caves used as graves contained numerous ancient weapons of bronze. On the saddle between the two heights lay the ancient sanctuary, with 'mazzeboth' or standing stones (comp. p. 185), and under its pavement were large clay-vessels containing the bodies of children, doubtless used in sacrifices. The clay-vessels discovered are in many instances closely allied to those from the island of Crete. — Comp. 'Bible Side-Lights from the Mound of Gezer: a Record of Excavation and Discovery in Palestine' (London; 1906) and 'The Excavations at Gezer' (3 vols.; London, 1911; *4l. 4s.*), both by *R. A. Stewart Macalister*.

25 M. **Sejed**; the station is situated in an insalubrious but fertile plain. From Sejed the line follows the depression of the *Wâdi eṣ-Ṣarâr* (the 'valley of Sorek'; Judg. xvi. 4), which is wide at its mouth, but afterwards narrows. *Beit ʿAṭâb*, situated on the top of the hills to the left, remains for some time in sight; farther on, also to the left, the weli of *Ṣarʿa* (the ancient *Zoreah*, Josh. xv. 33, xix. 14; Judg. xiii. 2). To the right lies the deserted village of *ʿAin Shems* (the ancient *Beth Shemesh*, 1 Sam. vi. 9; 1 Kings iv. 9), where excavations are now being carried on by the Palestine Exploration Fund. A megalithic wall, dating from the Israelite kingdom, with a well-preserved gate (S.) and quadrilateral bastions has been laid bare nearly in its whole circuit. Pottery of the same period as well as of pre-Israelite times (imported from Cyprus and Crete) has also been found. Farther to the S., on the hill, is *Beit el-Jemâl* (agricultural college of the Salesians).

$31^1/_2$ M. *Deir ʿAbân;* the station is about 3 M. distant from each of the three villages that are served by it: *Deir ʿAbân* (to the S., not visible), *Ṣarʿa* (see above), and *Artûf*, a colony of Bulgarian Jews (pop. 95), founded in 1896, a little below Ṣarʿa. Ṣarʿa and Artûf are seen on a hill to the left. The mountains now begin. Shortly after entering them we see high up in the rocks to the left the mouth of a grotto, the so-called *Samson's Cavern* (the story of Samson is localized in this district; Judg. xiii-xvi). The line passes along precipitous walls of rock and ascends the windings of the *Wâdi eṣ-Ṣarâr*. We pass ($38^1/_2$ M.) *Deir esh-Sheikh*, on a hill to the right, and ($40^1/_3$ M.) *ʿAḳûr*, on a hill to the left; beyond it, the *Wâdi Ḳalôniyeh* opens on the left. The line continues to follow the Wâdi eṣ-Ṣarâr. On a hill to the right is the village of (46 M.) *Bittîr*.

$47^1/_4$ M. **Bittîr**. — The *Baither* of Joshua xv. 59 in the Septuagint (*Beth-arabah* of Josh. xv. 61 in the A. V.), or *Bethar*, played an important part in the insurrection of Bar Cochba against the Romans (p. lxxxi). The latter succeeded in capturing it only after a siege of $3^1/_2$ years (A. D. 135), when a terrible massacre of the inhabitants ensued.

The Moslem village, with a copious spring, lies to the S.W. of the rail. station, between the *Wâdi Bittîr* and another valley. From the spring we ascend a steep path to a second terrace. Traces of walls, known as *Khirbet el-Yehûd*, or 'ruin of the Jews', prove that the place was once fortified. On the E. side are chambers in the rock and old cisterns, with some remarkable niches between them.

From Bittîr the line ascends the *Wâdi el-Werd* (valley of roses, p. 93) at a pretty steep gradient. *El-Welejeh* is on the left; farther on, (48 1/2 M.) Philip's Well (*'Ain el-Ḥanîyeh*, p. 93) and the villages of *'Ain Yâlô* (p. 93) and *Esh-Sherâfât* are seen on the right; then, on the left, *El-Mâliḥa* and *Ḳaṭamôn* (p. 70). *Beit Ṣafâfâ* and the monastery of *Mâr Elyâs* (p. 99) are visible on the right. Beyond Beit Ṣafâfâ the line runs straight across the plateau of *El-Buḳei'a*, which is probably identical with the valley of *Rephaim*, where the Philistines were defeated by David (2 Sam. v. 18, etc.). — We pass the Temple Colony (p. 70) and reach

54 M. *Jerusalem* (p. 19).

b. By Road.

40 M. Interesting route, 7-8 hrs. to drive and 11-12 hrs. to ride. — *Carriages* (see p. 7) during the season, 50-60 fr. (single seat, 10-15 fr.), and 5 fr. to the driver. — *Horses*, 12-15 fr. — We start early, so as to reach Jerusalem before night. Provisions should be taken. The usual halts are at *Ramleh* (3 1/4 hrs.' ride); at *Bâb el-Wâd* (6 1/2 hrs. from Jaffa; breakfast; p. 16); and again at *Ḳalôniyeh* (9 1/2 hrs. from Jaffa).

From Jaffa to the (12 min.) *Sebîl Abu Nebbût*, see p. 9. — After 1/4 hr. we pass, on the right, a farm called *Miḳweh Israel*, established by the Alliance Israélite in 1870, where Jews are taught agriculture. After a ride of 3/4 hr. from Jaffa, a watch-tower is seen rising on the right. It is the first of 17 which were built in 1860, to guard the route to Jerusalem. They are now mostly in ruins. We reach *Yâzûr* (left; beautiful retrospect) 1/4 hr. later, and farther on the *Weli Imâm 'Ali*, with its numerous domes; adjoining it is a well (*'Ain Dilb*). The road to Lydda diverges here to the left (see p. 18). After 20 min. the 2nd watch-tower is seen on the right. To the left we soon perceive *Sâḳiya* and *Beit Dejan* (p. 11). About 1 1/2 M. to the S. of the road lies *Rishon le-Zion*, Arabic *'Ayûn Ḳâra*, one of the most important of the Jewish colonies (900 inhab.), founded in 1882. *Sâfirîyeh* (p. 11) appears to the left 1/4 hr. later; then the 3rd watch-tower. Near (20 min.) the 4th watch-tower the tower of Ramleh becomes visible; fine view of the surrounding country. Farther on (20 min.) the village of *Ṣarafand* is seen on a hill to the right. In 1/2 hr. more we reach the 5th watch-tower and (11 1/2 M.) **Ramleh** (p. 12). At the entrance to the town we keep to the left; the road to the right leads to the tower.

Beyond Ramleh the route passes a Moslem cemetery with a large pond (*Birket el-Jâmûs*, or 'buffalo pond'), intersects the railway, and crosses (1/4 hr.) the small brook called *Nahr er-Ramleh*. 1/4 hr., the 6th watch-tower, on the left. The land is richly cultivated, but the plantations of trees soon disappear. In 25 min. more we reach the 7th watch-tower, 15 M. from Jaffa; on a hill to the N.E., *ʿAnnâbeh;* to the right is the hamlet of *Berrîyet er-Ramleh*, or 'outwork of Ramleh'. 1/2 hr., to the left, the insignificant ruin of *Kafr Tâb*, the ancient *Cafartoba* mentioned in the history of the Jewish war, with the weli of *Sheikh Suleimân;* on the right, to the S., *Abu Shûsheh* and beside it, the ruins of *Tell Jezer* (p. 13).

In 1/4 hr. more we reach (17 1/2 M.) *El-Ḳubâb* (*Cobe* of the Talmud), a village on a little hill, with many old cisterns. In descending beyond the village (8th watch-tower) we obtain a wide view of the plain; in front of us we see *Lâṭrûn*, *ʿAmwâs*, *Beit Nûbâ* (to the left or N.), *Yâlô*, and (on the hill) the two *Beit ʿUr.* 25 min., on the right, the 9th watch-tower (19 1/2 M.); 18 min. (5 1/2 hrs. from Jaffa), on the left, *Lâṭrûn* (20 1/2 M.) appears on a hill, with a Trappist convent and *ʿAmwâs* close by to the N.

Lâṭrûn. — This name, which was originally *Nâṭrûn*, was connected in the middle ages with the Latin 'latro', a robber. Hence arose the mediæval legend that this was the native place of the Penitent Thief ('Castellum Boni Latronis', who is said to have been called Dismas), or of both thieves. The ruins probably belong to the ancient fortress of *Nicopolis* (see below) and the partly preserved walls date from several different periods. The choir of a church is also said to be traceable.

ʿAmwâs. — The *Emmaus of the Old Testament* is frequently mentioned as a place of strategic importance in the time of the Maccabees (*e.g.* 1 Macc. iii. 40). It afterwards became the capital of a district of Judæa (Jos. Bell. Jud. ii. 20, 4; Pliny, Nat. Hist. v. 70); and an inscription mentions the 5th legion as encamped here in 68-70 A.D. The town was named *Nicopolis* from the beginning of the 3rd century. During the Christian period it was an episcopal see. In the early days of Islam several fierce skirmishes took place here. — The *Emmaus of the New Testament* can be identified with *ʿAmwâs* (about 175 stadia from Jerusalem) only if we accept the reading 160 stadia, found in some MSS. of Luke xxiv. 13. *Kalôniyeh* (p. 18), on the other hand, is only 34 stadia from Jerusalem. The most probable site is *El-Kubeibeh* (p. 96). Whether one of these two Emmauses is to be identified with Vespasian's military colony of the same name (30 stadia from Jerusalem; Jos. Bell. Jud. vii. 6, 6), and if so, which, cannot be determined (comp. ZDPV. xv. 172; xvi. 146; xvii. 224; also *Barnabé's* 'Deux Questions d'Archéologie Palestinienne', Jerusalem, 1902; Revue Bibl., 1903).

To the S. of the village is a famous spring to which healing properties were once attributed. The ruins, the property of the Carmelite Nuns of Bethlehem, perhaps belonged to a 6th cent. church.

The road skirts the hill on which Lâṭrûn lies. After 12 min. the 11th watch-tower rises on the left, and after 1/4 hr. more the 12th. We cross a small brook. A well, on the left, is called *Bîr Aiyûb* (Job's well). On a height, at some distance, rises the dilapidated house of *Deir Aiyûb* (Job's monastery). In 16 min. from the well we reach (24 M.) the narrow entrance to the *Wâdi (Imâm) ʿAli*, called *Bâb el-Wâd*, or gate of the valley (1050 ft.), on the left of which is the 13th watch-tower and on the right a café.

The road now enters the *Wâdi ʿAli* and leads in 1/2 hr. to the ruins of the mosque of Imâm ʿAli, situated at the junction of the valleys, and shaded by large trees. The route then reaches (25 min.; 27 1/2 M.) the village of *Sârîs*, on the right. The path next winds up the side of another valley, ascending the hill on which lie the ruins of the ancient *Sârîs*. At the top (12 min.) is discovered a beautiful view of the plain and the sea beyond. To the E. are Ṣûbâ and the ruin of Ḳasṭal (p. 18), while to the S. opens the bleak *Wâdi Sârîs*. After 25 min. we reach the top of a hill, and, a little farther, on (30 M.) *El-Ḳarya* or—

Abu Ghôsh. — The village is so called after a powerful village sheikh of that name, who was for many years at the beginning of the 19th cent. the terror of the whole district. It was formerly called *Ḳaryet el-ʿIneb (ʿEnab)*, or the town of grapes, a name which occurs for the first time in the 15th century. The present village does not occupy the site of the ancient town, which lay on the hill to the W., to the left of the road. Here are numerous cisterns and graves, and the foundations of a church with an apse have also lately been found. A Greek tradition places the *Emmaus* of the New Testament here (but comp. p. 16). Eusebius, as well as the Crusaders, appears to have here sought for *Kirjath-Jearim* (forest-town; 1 Sam. vii. 1), but the identification is very doubtful. — The **Church**, at present in possession of the French government, lies to the right of the road and has lately been restored by the Benedictines, who have also erected a small convent here. The three apses of the church are externally concealed by masonry. The nave is loftier and wider than the aisles, and is supported by three pilasters on each side; its arches rest on pillars of peculiar form, in which Vogüé detects Arabian influence. There is no transept. The walls of the church, particularly those of the apse, and those of the crypt likewise, were adorned with frescoes in the Byzantine style, and partly covered with mosaics, of which distinct traces still exist. The small spiral enrichments also occur in Arabian structures, whose architects borrowed them from Christian monuments of the 6-7th centuries. Under the whole length of the church runs a crypt. An opening in the floor of the crypt, near the centre, descends to a spring (Rev. Arch. xix. 223 et seq.). The theory that recognizes the building as originally a fort of Vespasian is improbable; still more so the identification of the site with Emmaus and the Crusaders' fortress of Fontenoide. — The church is mentioned for the first time in 1519 under the name of the church of St. Jeremiah. That name, however, was used in consequence of a mistaken identification of Ḳaryet el-ʿIneb with *Anathoth*, the birthplace of the prophet (p. 97). In an open space to the N. of the church is the tomb of the *Sheikh Abu Ghôsh*, with a sebîl (fountain).

The route skirts the outside of the village. We observe on a hill to the right (S.) the village of *Ṣûbâ*, with ancient rock-tombs. It has been wrongly identified by tradition since the 13th cent. with *Môdeïn* (1 Macc. ii. 1), the native place of the Maccabæan family. Môdeïn is now generally recognized in *El-Medieh*, a village with interesting rock-tombs, to the E.S.E. of Lydda, though even this identification is open to doubt (comp. 1 Macc. xiii. 27 et seq.). In 20 min. after leaving Abu Ghôsh (31 M. from Jaffa) we reach (on the right) a spring called *ʿAin Dilb*. On a hill to the left lies *Beit Naḳûbâ*. In 5 min. we come to a bridge across the valley; in the latter, farther to the S., we see the ruins of *Ḳebâla* (once perhaps a monastery). In 1/4 hr. more we attain the top of the hill, on

which the village of Ḳaṣṭal lies above us to the right. The name
is of Roman origin *(castellum)*. *En-Nebi Samwîl* is visible towards
the N., and, 1/4 hr. farther, *'Ain Kârim* in the distance towards the
S. (p. 94). We now descend by great windings into the *Wâdi Kalôniyeh* or *Wâdi Beit Ḥanînâ* (p. 96), frequently though erroneously
identified with the 'valley of Elah' (*i.e.* of terebinths) of 1 Sam.
xvii. 2 (comp. pp. 124, 113). About 20 min. farther on (91/2 hrs.
from Jaffa) is a bridge; close by is a café. On the hill to the left lies
Kalôniyeh, with the small Jewish colony of *Moza*, founded in 1890.
The name of Ḳalôniyeh is derived by some scholars from 'colonia';
but a place named *Koulon* is found in the Septuagint (Josh. xv. 59).
For the identification of Ḳalôniyeh with Emmaus, comp. p. 16. The
road now ascends the *Wâdi Beit Ḥanînâ* in long windings. En-Nebi
Samwîl is soon seen again; on the hill to the left, *Beit Iksâ*. On a
hill-slope, also to the left, lies *Liftâ*, with a large spring and the
stones of some very ancient buildings at the E. entrance to the
village. This place corresponds, perhaps, with *Nephtoah* on the con-
fines of Judah (Josh. xv. 9). After 3/4 hr. we pass, on our left,
the *Jewish Home for the Aged*, opposite to which stands the *Jewish
Lunatic Asylum*. The road to 'Ain Kârim (see p. 93) diverges here
to the right. Immediately beyond it, on the left, are the 15th watch-
tower and the weli of *Sheikh Bedr;* on the right the Greek Monastery
of the Cross (p. 92), Mâr Elyâs, and Bethlehem become visible. In
front of us is the glittering Dome of the Rock and behind it the tower
of the Mount of Olives, but the city itself is still hidden. Then
begin the houses of the Jewish colony; to the right is the large
hospital of the *Sha'areih Zedek*, and, farther on, to the left, is the
Town Hospital; opposite the latter (right) is a military post on the
site of the 16th watch-tower. We next perceive the extensive pile
of buildings belonging to the Russians, with its church of five domes.
The domes of the church of the Sepulchre, the tower of the German
church of the Saviour, etc., are also visible. A little farther on the
walls come in view, and in 20 min. more we reach the Jaffa Gate
(p. 33).

From Jaffa to Jerusalem viâ Lydda and Beit 'Ûr, 11 hrs. From Jaffa
to *'Ain Dilb* (1 hr.) by the Jerusalem Road, see p. 15. At this point our
route diverges to the left (S.E.). In 1/4 hr., on the left, we see the village
of *Sâkiya;* 17 min., on the right, *Beit Dejan.* 23 min., *Sâfiriyeh* (on the
left; p. 11); 1 hr., *Lydda* (p. 11); 50 min., *Jimzû* (*Gimzo*, 2 Chron. xxviii.
18), visible on a hill to the right. Farther on a path branches off to the
left; 2 hrs. 10 min., the ruins of *Umm Rûsh.* 1 hr., *Beit 'Ûr et-Taḥtâ*, halfway
up the mountain, on a low hill. 1 hr., *Beit 'Ûr el-Fôḳâ*, admirably situated on
the top of a mountain-spur between the two valleys. The 'lower' and the
'upper' Beit 'Ûr occupy the site of the *Beth-Horons* of antiquity (Josh. x.
10; xviii. 13, etc.). Solomon fortified the lower town (1 Kings ix. 17), and
here Judas Maccabæus defeated the Syrians under Nicanor (1 Macc. vii. 39).
A frequented road led in ancient days from Jerusalem to the coast viâ
these villages. In 1 hr. 40 min. we reach the top of the pass and see
El-Jîb and *En-Nebi Samwîl.* 23 min., *El-Jîb* (p. 97). Hence to *Jerusalem*,
see pp. 97, 215.

4. Jerusalem.

Arrival. The *Railway Station* (comp. Pl. C, 9) lies to the S. of the town, 3/4 M. from the Jaffa Gate (Pl. D, 5, 6). Carriage to the town, 2-5 fr. according to the season. The road to the town (Station Road, p. 69) leads past the British Ophthalmic Hospital (p. 70) to the Valley of Hinnom (p. 80), which it crosses by the embankment to the S. of the Birket es-Sulṭân, and then ascends along the W. side of the Zion suburb to the Jaffa Gate (comp. p. 33).

Hotels (comp. p. xvi). *Hôtel Fast (Pl. a, C, 4, 5; landlords, *A. Fast & Sons*), in the Jaffa Road; Grand New Hotel (Pl. c, D 5; landlord, *Morkos*), opposite the Citadel; Hôtel Hughes (Pl. d; C, 4), Jaffa Road; Hôtel Kaminitz (Pl. b; C, 4), in the same road. Pension at all the above, without wine, in the season 12-15 fr., at other times 8-10 fr. (by arrangement). Native wine 1-2 fr. per bottle, French red wine from 3 fr. — **Pensions.** Olivet House (Pl. e, C 2; landlord, *Hensman*), pens. 8-10 fr.; Williams (Pl. f; C, 1).

Hospices (comp. p. xvi). *Prussian Hospice of St. John* (Pl. g, F 4; superintendent, *Blankertz*), recommended for a prolonged stay (secure rooms in advance during the season); pension, incl. wine, 6 fr. — *German Catholic Hospice of St. Paul* (Pl. h, E 2; director, *Schmitz*). — *Empress Augusta Victoria Hospice*, on the Mount of Olives (p. 76), pens., without wine, 8-12 fr. — *Austrian Hospice* (Pl. i; F, 3). — *Casa Nuova* of the Franciscans (Pl. k; D, 4, 5). — *Notre Dame de France* (Pl. C, D, 3, 4; p. 68). — *Russian Hospice* (Pl. l, E, F, 5; p. 47). — All these are plainly but well fitted up, with clean beds (pens., incl. wine, 6-10 fr.).

Beer Houses and Cafés. *German Beer Room*, in the Jaffa Road; *A. Lendhold*, in the Temple Colony (brewery). — **Confectioner.** *Bacher*, in the Jaffa Road. — **Wine.** *Berner*, in the Jaffa Road; *Imberger*, in the Temple Colony; *Carmel Oriental Co.* (wines of the Jewish colonies), in the Jaffa Road.

Post Offices (comp. p. xxiv). *Turkish* (Pl. C, 5), *French* (Pl. C, 5), *German* (Pl. D, 5), *Russian* (Pl. B, 4), all in the Jaffa Road; *Austro-Hungarian* (Pl. E, 5, 6), opposite the Citadel (p. 33). — **International Telegraph**, in the Turkish post office.

Tourist Offices (comp. p. xii). *Thos. Cook & Son*, inside the Jaffa Gate; *F. Clark*, *Dr. I. Benzinger* (North German Lloyd), *Tadros*, *Agence Lubin*, all in the Jaffa Road; *Hamburg-American Line*, in Fast's Hotel (see above).

Dragomans (see p. xvii). *Dimitri Domian* (speaks English and German); *Karl Williams* (Engl., Ger., and French); *Hanna Auwad* (Engl., Fr., Ital.); *Rafael Lorenzo* (Fr., Ital.); *Joseph Lorenzo* (Engl., Ger., Fr., Ital.); *Francis Morkos* (Fr., Ital.); *Afif G. Atallah* (Engl., Fr., Ital.); *Kaiser* (Ger.); *Jos. Ibrâhîm* (Ger.); *Ibrâhîm As'ad Sa'id* (Engl., Ger.); *Shukrey Hishmeh* (Engl., Fr.); *Caesar Chaleel* (Engl., Fr.); *Selim Barakat* (Engl., Fr.); *Faraḥ Nasr* (Engl., Ger.).

Carriages and Horses. *Carriages* are always to be found at the Jaffa Gate, but for longer excursions they should be specially engaged at a tourist-office or a hotel. Per drive 1/4 mej., per hour 1/2 mej. Prices should be settled beforehand. — *Saddle Horse*, half-day 5, whole day 8 fr.; for longer tours according to bargain. A European saddle should be stipulated for (p. xx). — *Donkey*, half-day 2-3, whole day 4-5 fr.

Consulates (p. xxiv). British (Pl. 5; A, 1), *H. E. Satow;* United States (Pl. 13; A, 1), *W. Coffin;* Danish and Swedish (Pl. 6; A, 1), *G. Dalman;* Norwegian (see Map, p. 73), *L. W. Marcks;* Austro-Hungarian (Pl. 4; A, 2), *R. de Franceschi;* Belgian, *Dr. C. Mancini;* Dutch (Pl. 7; C, 5), *Dr. I. Benzinger;* French (Pl. 8; D, 4), *Gueyraud;* German (see Map, p. 73), *E. Schmidt;* Greek (Pl. 9; A, 3), *Raphaël;* Russian (Pl. 11; C, 3), *A. T. Kruglov;* Spanish (Pl. 12; A, 3), *A. Sanchez Vera.*

Bankers. *Anglo-Palestine Co.* (Pl. 1; D, 5), *Deutsche Palaestina-Bank* (Pl. 3; D, 5), *Crédit Lyonnais* (Pl. 2; D, 5), *Banque Ottomane* (Pl. D, 5), all in the Jaffa Road.

Physicians. *Dr. Heron*, physician of the British Ophthalmic Hospital; *Dr. Einsler*, oculist, see p. 70; *Dr. Grussendorf*, physician of the Hospital of the Deaconesses of Kaiserswerth; *Dr. Masterman*, physician of the Hospital of the London Jews Society; *Dr. Mancini*, physician of the Custodia Terræ Sanctæ; *Dr. Severin*, physician of the Russian Hospital; *Dr. Canaan*, medical officer of the city; *Dr. Nikola*, physician of the Greek Hospital; *Dr. V. Pascal*, physician of the Armenian patriarchate; *Dr. Wallach*, physician of the German Jewish Hospital. — **Dentist.** *Rezlaff*. — **Chemists.** *Gaïtanopoulos*, at the Jaffa Gate; *Pharmacie Municipale*, in the Jaffa Road; and at the *Hospitals*.

Baths. *Hydropathic Institution* (*Sanatorium;* Pl. B, C, 3).

Shops. Booksellers: *International Book and Art Dealers*, *The Palestine Educational Store* (also stationery), both in the Jaffa Road. — Photographs: *American Colony Store*, *Maroum*, *Boulos Meo*, *Afif Attallah* (see below), *Salman & Co.* (see below). The best are those of the *American Colony* and *Bonfils* of Beirût, and the coloured photographs of the *Photoglob* of Zürich. — Photographers (also photographic supplies): *Krikorian*, *Raad*, both in the Jaffa Road. — Antiquities: *N. Ohar*, Jaffa Road. — Provisions for trips into the country: *Artin Bekmesian*, Jaffa Road. — Travelling Requisites: *Schnerring*, saddler, Jaffa Road. — Tailor: *Eppinger*, Jaffa Road. — Dress Goods: *Imberger Brothers*, *F. & C. Imberger*, *Selim Meo*, *Rabinowitz*, *Nicodème*, all in the Jaffa Road. — Nurseryman: *J. Bacher*, in the German Colony, exporter of bulbs and seeds.

Favourite **Souvenirs** are rosaries, crosses and other ornaments in mother-of-pearl and olive-wood, vases and other objects in black 'stinkstone' from the Dead Sea, roses of Jericho, and dried wild flowers. Articles of this nature are annually exported to the value of 500,000 fr. Higher-class work is best bought from *Fr. Vester & Co.* (American Colony Store), *Boulos Meo*, *Shammas*, *A. Sfeir*, all at the Grand New Hotel (p. 19); *Afif Attallah Frères*, by the New Gate (p. 35); *Maroum*, at the Casa Nuova (p. 19); *Salman & Co.*, Jaffa Road; *Torazi*, in the Grand New Hotel (carpets and embroidery). A staple product of Jerusalem is carved work in olive-wood and oak (rulers, paper-weights, crucifixes, etc.; usually with the name 'Jerusalem' in Hebrew letters, or with the Jerusalem cross).

Forwarding Agents. *R. Aberle*, *P. Breisch.*

Churches, Convents, Charitable Institutions, Schools, etc. Roman Catholics. *Franciscans* (established in Jerusalem since the 13th cent.). Convent of St. Salvator (seat of the Custodian), with the Church of St. Salvator, school and orphanage for boys, seminary, industrial school, printing-office, and dispensary; Convent of the Holy Sepulchre; Convent of the Flagellation (comp. p. 49). — *Latin Patriarchate* (since 1847): Church of the Patriarchate; higher and lower seminary. — *Sisters of St. Joseph* (1848): boarding-school and orphanage for girls. — *Sisters of Zion* (1856): Convent and Church of 'Ecce Homo' (p. 49); boarding-school and orphanage for girls. — *Carmelite Nuns* (1873): Paternoster Church and Convent, on the Mount of Olives (p. 79). — *School Brethren* (1876): boys' school. — *White Fathers* (*Pères Blancs;* 1878): Convent and Church of St. Anne (p. 49), with higher and lower seminary for the United Greeks (p. 22). — *Soeurs du St. Rosaire* (1880): convent, school, and dispensary. — *Pères de Sion* (1884): Convent St. Pierre, with seminary and industrial school for Jews. — *Dominicans* (1884): Convent and Cathedral of St. Stephen (p. 87); Ecole Biblique (p. 23). — *Clarissines* (1884): Convent (p. 99). — *Franciscan Sisters* (1885): convent, school, and orphanage for girls (p. 34). — *Soeurs de St. Vincent de Paul* (1886): convent, orphanage for boys and girls, blind asylum, and home for the aged. — *Nuns of St. Carlo Borromeo* (German, 1887): school and orphanage. — *Assumptionists* (*Pères Augustins de l'Assomption;* 1887): Hospice Notre Dame de France (p. 19). — *Soeurs de Marie-Réparatrice* (1888): convent (p. 68). — *Lazarists* (German, 1900): hospice and boys' school. — *Benedictine Nuns* (*Soeurs Bénédictines du Calvaire*, 1890):

Legend for the Plan of Jerusalem.

Antonia, Castle of . . . . G 3
Banks, see p. 20.
Barracks . . . D, E, 6; G, 3, 4; G 4
Bazaar, Old (Sûḳs) and New F 5; E 5
Bezetha . . . . G, H. 2
Birket Ḥammâm el-Baṭraḳ. . . E 5
- Isra'în . . . . H 3
- Mâmilla . . . . . . A, 4, 5
- Sitti Maryam . . . . . . I 3
- es-Sulṭân . . . . . C, D, 7, 8
Caiaphas, House of . . . . . . E 8
Churches and Chapels: Abyssinian A 1. — Arab. Prot. C, 1, 2. — Christ Church E 6. — Notre Dame de France C, D, 3, 4. — Ch. of the Redeemer E 5. — Russian Cathedral B 3. — St. Anne's H 3. — St. George's Chapel C 7. — St. James's E 6. — St. Mary Magdalen's K 4. — St. Stephen's E 1. — Chapel of the Scourging G 3. — Ch. of the Holy Sepulchre E 4. — Ch. of the Tomb of the Virgin K 3.
Citadel (El-Kal'a) . . . . D 6
4-13. Consulates, see p. 19.
Conventa and Monasteries:
14. Abyssinian . . . . E 4
15. Armenian Catholic. . . F, 3, 4
16. Coptic, of the Holy Sepulchre . . . . . E 4
17. - , St. George . . . . D 5
18. Dervish . . . . G 4
19. Greek, of Abraham . . . E, 4, 5
20. - , Gethsemane . . . E 5
21. - , Panagia . . . . . E 4
22. - , Panagia Melæna . E 5
23. - , St. Basil . . . . . D 4
24. - , St. Caralambos . . E 4
25. - , St. Catharine . . . E 4
26. - , St. Demetrius. . . D 5
27. - , St. George (I). . . D 4
28. - , St. George (II) . . E 7
29. - , St. John the Baptist E 5
30. - , St. John Euthymius E 4
31. - , Archangel Michael D 4
32. - , St. Nicholas . . . D 4
33. - , St. Theodore . . . D 4
34. United Greek. . . . . . . D 5
35. Latin, St. Louis . . . D, E, 5
36. - , St. Salvator. . . . D 4
Armenian E, 6, 7. — Armenian Nunnery of Deir ez-Zeitûni E 7. — Armenian, of Mt. Zion E 8. — Dominican E 1. — Greek (Great) D, E, 4, 5. — Greek (New) E 3. — Greek, of the Cross, beyond A, 5, 6 (comp. Map of the Environs, p. 73). — Moslem F, 2, 3. — Sisters of St. Vincent B, C, 4, 5. — Sisters of Zion G 3. — Sœurs Réparatrices C 4. — Syrian E 6.
Cotton Grotto . . . . . . F, G, 2, 3
Dormitio. . . . . E 8
Fountain of the Virgin . . . . H 7
Garden of Gethsemane. . . . . K 4
Gates of the Town: Bâb el-'Amûd (Damascus Gate) E, 2, 3. — Bâb el-Jedîd (New Gate) C, D, 4. — Bâb el-Khalîl (Jaffa Gate) D, 5, 6. — Bâb el-Mughâribeh (Moghrebins' Gate) G, 6, 7. — Bâb en-Nebi Dâûd (Gate of Zion) E, 7, 8. — Bâb ez-Zâhireh (Herod's Gate) G 2. — Bâb Sitti Maryam (St. Stephen's Gate) I 3. — Valley Gate (ancient) E 9.
Goliath, Castle of . . . . C 4
Ḥammâm esh-Shifâ (Pool of Bethesda) . . . . G 5
Ḥaram esh-Sherîf . . . . . G-I, 3-6
Hospices, see pp. 19, 20, 22.
Hospitals: French (St. Louis) C 4. — Greek D 5. — Jewish (Rothschild's) A, 1, 2. — Russian B 3.
Jeremiah, Grotto of . . . . . F, 1, 2
Jewish Colonies: A 3; D 2. — (Montefiore's) C, 8, 9. Comp. also Map of Environs, p. 73.
El-Ma'muniyeh (ruin) . . . . . G 2
Mosques:
Kubbet eṣ-Ṣakhra (Dome of the Rock) . . . . H, 4, 5
Mesjid el-Aḳṣâ . . . . . . H, 5, 6
- el-Kurâmi. . . . . . . F 5
- el-Majâhidîn . . . . G, H, 3
37. Mosque of Sîdna 'Omar . . E 5
Mûristân . . . . E 5
En-Nebi Dâûd . . . . E 8
Patriarchates: Armenian E 7. — Greek D. E, 4. — Latin C, D, 5. — Syrian Catholic E 3.
Patriarch's Bath . . . . E 5
Post Offices, see p. 19.
Schools: Gobat's . . . . D, 8, 9
39. Of the Greek Patriarchate D 5
40. Latin Parochial, for boys D 4
Serâi F 4. — (Old) G 4.
Synagogues (S). . . . . . . E, F, 5-7
Tombs: Ancient D, E, 1, 2; I 7; K 2; K 4. — Near Karm esh-Sheikh G, H, 1. — Of the Kings, beyond E 1 (comp. Map, p. 73). — Of Absalom I 5. — Of Christ (acc. to Conder) E 2; (acc. to Gordon) E 1. — Of David (En-Nebi Dâûd) E 8. — Of Herod B 8. — Of St. James and Zacharias I 5.
Wailing Place of the Jews. . . G 5

convent and orphanage for United Greeks (see below). — *Benedictine Fathers* (*Pères Bénédictines de la Pierre qui Vire*, 1899): convent and seminary on the Mountain of Offence (p. 83) for the United Syrians (see below); Church and Convent of the Dormitio on the hill of Zion (p. 72), belonging to *German Benedictines from Beuron* (1906). — *Passionist Fathers* (*Pères Passionistes;* 1903): Convent near Bethany (p. 126). — *Salesians* (1904): Italian boys' school. — Hospitals: *Hôpital St. Louis* (p. 68; French, managed by the Sisters of St. Joseph); foundling hospital; home for the aged; hospital of the *Soeurs de Charité*. — Hospices: *Casa Nuova* (p. 19); *German Catholic Hospice of St. Paul* (p. 19); *Austrian Hospice* (p. 19); *Notre Dame de France* (p. 19). — The Oriental churches affiliated to the Roman Catholics are those of the *Maronites* (p. lxii); the *United Greeks* or *Greek Catholics* (p. lxii), with a church in the Patriarchate Building, the St. Veronica Chapel, the St. Anne Priests' Seminary of the Pères Blancs (p. 20), and the orphanage of the Benedictine sisters; the *United Syrians* (p. lxii), with a seminary (see above); and the *United Armenians*, with the church of Notre Dame du Spasme (p. 50), a chapel, a hospice, and a school.

English Protestant Community. The joint Protestant bishopric, supported by England and Prussia, under an arrangement due to Frederick William IV. of Prussia, was dissolved in 1887. Since then the British and German communities have been independent in religious matters. The English Protestant community is under the leadership of Bishop Blyth, consecrated in March, 1887, and is financially supported by the Jerusalem Bishopric Fund and the three English Missionary Societies working in Palestine. The community is mainly a missionary one, and comprises about 80 persons. The *Episcopal Residence* (p. 88), the *Collegiate Church of St. George* (services at 9 a.m. and 4.30 p.m.), the boys' and girls' schools connected with it, and an *Anglican Clergy House* or *College*, lie to the N. of the town. To the 'Church Missionary Society' belong the *Church of St. Paul* (p. 69; service in Arabic on Sun. at 9.30 a.m. and 3 p.m.), the *Bishop Gobat School* for boys (p. 70), founded by Bishop Gobat, a *Girls' Day School* and the *English College*, the last distinct from, though situated close to, the above-mentioned Anglican Clergy House. To the 'London Jews Society' belongs *Christ Church* (p. 35; English services on Sun. at 10 a.m. and also at 7.30 p.m. in summer and 4 p.m. in winter). Connected with the mission are a large hospital, schools for boys and girls, and an industrial school and printing-office. — The English *Knights of St. John* have an ophthalmic hospital on the Bethlehem road (p. 70).

German Evangelical Community. *Church of the Redeemer* (Pl. E, 5; p. 47; services in German on Sun. at 9.30 a.m., in Arabic at 3 p.m.); *Hospice of St. John* (p. 51); *Hospital* of the Deaconesses of Kaiserswerth (p. 69); the *Lepers' Hospital* (p. 70); the girls' orphanage *Talitha Cumi* (p. 69); the *Syrian Orphanage* for boys (p. 69; service in Arabic on Sun. at 9.30 a.m., in German at 6 p.m.), connected with a home for the blind and a day-school for Arab boys in the town; and the *Empress Augusta Victoria Foundation* (pp. 19, 76). — The German Evangelical Mission of the *Jerusalem-Verein* works in Bethlehem (p. 101), Beit Jâlâ (p. 100), and Beit Sâḥûr (p. 107).

Orthodox Greek Church (p. lxi). *Monastery of Helena and Constantine*, *Monastery of Abraham* (p. 45), *Monastery of Gethsemane* (p. 45), *Convents of St. Basil*, *St. Theodore*, *St. George*, *St. Michael*, *St. Catharine*, *St. Euthymius*, *St. Seetnagia*, *St. Spiridon*, *St. Caralombos*, *St. John the Baptist*, *Nativity of Mary*, *St. George* (a second of that name), *St. Demetrius*, *St. Nicholas* (containing a printing-office), and *Santo Spirito;* priests' seminary, girls' and boys' school, a hospital, etc.

To the Russian Mission belong the great 'Russian Buildings' in the Jaffa suburb (p. 69), the St. Mary Magdalen Church (p. 76), and the Russian buildings on the Mount of Olives (p. 78). The Russian Palestine Society has also a house for pilgrims (p. 69) and a nuns' hospice (p. 47).

Armenian Church (p. lxi). *Monastery* near the Gate of Zion (p. 35), with a seminary (Pl. E, 7), schools for boys and girls, and the *Church of St. James; Nunnery of Deir ez-Zeitûni* (p. 35); *Monastery of Mt. Zion* (p. 72).

Other Christian Churches and Convents. *Coptic Monastery* (p. 48); *Coptic Monastery of St. George*. — The *Jacobites* (p. lxi) have a bishop and a small church, which they regard as the house of John surnamed Mark (Acts xii. 12). — The *Abyssinians* have a monastery (p. 48), a hospice, a school, and a new church to the N.W. of the town (Pl. A, 1).

The Jews have three large synagogues (one belonging to the Sephardim, and two to the Ashkenazim, p. lxiii), besides more than 100 smaller houses of prayer (comp. p. 35). In addition to the numerous places of shelter for pilgrims and the poor (mostly founded by Montefiore, Rothschild, and the Alliance Israélite), the Jews have an asylum for the blind and a home for the aged (p. 18), and five hospitals: that of the *Ashkenazim* (Bikkur Cholim; p. 69), that of the *Sephardim* (Misgab Ladakh; p. lxiii), the Sha'areih Zedek (p. 18), the *Rothschild Hospital* (p. 69), and one for the insane (p. 18). They have, further, orphanages for the boys and girls of the Sephardim and the Ashkenazim, a boys' and a girls' school and an artisan school of the Alliance Israélite, the English Evelina de Rothschild School for Girls (Pl. C, 2), and the Bezalel School of Industrial Art. The Society for the Assistance of German Jews supports a school for boys and girls, a school of commerce, and a training-college for teachers.

Libraries and Scientific Institutions. — The Jerusalem Association Room of the *Palestine Exploration Fund* is at St. George's College (p. 22; hours, 8-12 and 2-6); visitors are welcome. — Library of the *Latin Patriarchate* (p. 35). — Library of the *Greek Patriarchate*, in the Great Greek Monastery (p. 34), containing 2736 Greek and other MSS., the oldest dating from the 10th and 11th centuries. — *Jewish Central Library* (20,000 vols.). — *Musée Biblique des Pères Blancs* in St. Anne's Church (p. 49). — *Musée de Notre Dame de France* (p. 68). — *Municipal Museum.* — The *Ecole Pratique d'Etudes Bibliques*, founded in 1890, in the Dominican Monastery (p. 87), and conducted by Fathers H. Vincent, M. I. Lagrange, and others, issues the 'Revue Biblique', mentioned at p. c. A pension is connected with the school. — *American School of Oriental Study and Research in Palestine*, founded in 1900 (library open to visitors). — *German Archaeological Institute*, founded in 1900, and supported by the German Protestant churches. Director, Prof. Dalman. — *Model of the Haram esh-Sherif* (Place of the Temple), by Dr. Schick, at the house of Frau Schoeneke (comp. p. 51). — *Exhibition of Pictures by the Painter Bauernfeind* (d. 1904), at the house of Frau Bauernfeind, in the German Colony.

Distribution of Time, see pp. xiii, xiv.

Jerusalem (Hebrew *Yerushalayim*, Lat. and Greek *Hierosolyma*, Arabic *El-Kuds*) lies in 31° 46′ N. lat. and 35° 13′ E. long., upon the S. part of a badly watered and somewhat sterile plateau of limestone, which is connected towards the N. with the main range of the mountains of Palestine and surrounded on all the other sides by ravines. The actual site of the city is also marked by various elevations and depressions. The Temple hill is 2440 ft., the hill to the N. of it 2525 ft., the W. hill 2550 ft., and the N.W. angle of the present city-wall 2590 ft. above the level of the Mediterranean.

The town proper is enclosed by a wall 38½ ft. in height, forming an irregular quadrangle of about 2½ M. in circumference; it has eight gates, one of which has been walled up for centuries (see p. 63). The two chief streets, beginning at the Jaffa Gate on the W. (p. 33) and at the Damascus Gate on the N. (p. 85), intersect in the middle of the town and divide it into four quarters: the Moslem on the N.E., the Jewish on the S.E. (p. 35), the Armenian on the S.W. (p. 35), and the Græco-Frankish on the N.W. (comp. Map at p. 73). The streets are ill-paved and crooked, many of them being blind alleys, and are excessively dirty after rain. Some of them are vaulted over.

The houses are built entirely of stone; all the surfaces are so arranged as to catch the rain-water and conduct it to the cistern in the court. The rooms, covered with flat domes and each having its own entrance, are grouped round the court; the passages and staircases are left open to the air. The water of the cisterns is quite wholesome when clear; other sources of water are the Fountain of the Virgin (p. 83) and Job's Well (comp. p. 84). The new aqueduct (comp. pp. 108, 109) serves exclusively for the Ḥaram esh-Sherîf and a few fountains.

Of the more recent suburbs, the most important is the Jaffa quarter on the N.W. (p. 68), in which the houses are more like those of Europe. Here also are several large churches, convents, hospices, charitable institutions, and the like. It is probable that nearly the half of the present population of the city is settled in the suburbs.

According to a recent estimate the Population numbers at least 70,000, of whom about 10,000 are Moslems, 45,000 Jews, and 15,000 Christians. The Christians include 4000 Latins (*e. g.* Roman Catholics), 250 United Greeks, 50 United Armenians, 7000 Orthodox Greeks, 1000 Armenians, 150 Copts, 100 Abyssinians, 100 Syrians, and 1600 Protestants. The number of *Jews* has greatly risen in the last few decades, in spite of the fact that they are forbidden to immigrate or to possess landed property. The majority subsist on the charity of their European brethren, from whom they receive their regular *khalûka*, or allowance, and for whom they pray at the holy places. Sir Moses Montefiore, Baron Rothschild, and others, together with the Alliance Israélite and the Society for the Assistance of German Jews, have done much to ameliorate the condition of their poor brethren at Jerusalem by their munificent benefactions. The most powerful religious community is that of the Orthodox Greeks. The Russian Mission is concerned with national and political ends as well as with ecclesiastical affairs. The strong Armenian colony dates its importance from the middle of the 18th century. The Latins have attained their present influential position mainly through the exertions of the Franciscans. The office of patriarch, which was suppressed in 1291, was restored in 1847. Associated with the patriarch is the 'Custodian of the Holy Land', the head of the Franciscan order in Palestine, Syria, and Egypt. The British and American inhabitants of Jerusalem are about 150 in number. German Templars (pp. 10 and 70) number about 400, chiefly tradesmen and workmen, the German Evangelical community about 200.

Government. Jerusalem is the residence of a ***Muteṣarrif*** of the first class, immediately subject to the Porte (see p. lvii). The organs of government are the ***Mejlis idâra*** (executive council; president, the governor) and the ***Mejlis belediyeh*** (town-council; president, the mayor). In both these councils the recognized confessions (Greeks, Latins, Protestants, Armenians, and Jews) have representatives. — The garrison consists of a battalion of infantry.

History. Egyptian sources (p. lxxvi) testify that *Urusalim* held a prominent place among the cities of S. Palestine as early as 1400 B.C. The town was distinguished as a stronghold when David captured it (2 Sam. v. 6-10). He selected it for his residence and built the *City of David*. Solomon did much to beautify the city and erected a magnificent palace and temple (p. 51) on the E. hill. He also built *Millo* (1 Kings ix. 24; xi. 27), a kind of bastion or fort in the N.E. part of the town. During his reign Jerusalem first became the headquarters of the Israelites. After the division of the kingdom it became the capital of Judah. As early as Rehoboam's reign, the city was compelled to surrender to the Egyptian king Shishak, on which occasion the Temple and palace were despoiled of part of their golden ornaments. About one hundred years later, under King Jehoram, the Temple was again plundered by Arabian and Philistine tribes (2 Chron. xxi. 17). Sixty years later Jehoash, King of Israel, having defeated Amaziah of Judah, entered the city in triumph (2 Kings xiv. 13, 14). Uzziah, the son of Amaziah, re-established the prosperity of Jerusalem. During this period, however, Jerusalem was visited by a great earthquake.

On the approach of Sennacherib the fortifications were repaired by Hezekiah (2 Chron. xxxii. 5), to whom also was due the great merit of providing Jerusalem with water. Probably the only spring at Jerusalem was the fountain of *Gihon* on the E. slope of the Temple hill, outside the city-wall (now called the Fountain of the Virgin, p. 83). By means of a subterranean channel Hezekiah conducted the water of the spring to the pool of Siloam (2 Kings xx. 20; see p. 83), which lay within the walls. Cisterns and reservoirs for the storage of rain-water were also constructed. The pools on the W. side of the city (Birket Mâmilla, p. 68; Birket es-Sulṭân, p. 70) were probably formed before the period of the captivity, as was also the large reservoir to the N. of the Temple plateau (Birket Isra'în; p. 68), in the formation of which advantage was taken of a small valley, whose depth was at the same time destined to protect the site of the Temple on the N. side. A besieging army generally suffered severely from want of water, as the issues of the conduits towards the country could be closed, while the city always possessed water in abundance. The valleys of Kidron and Hinnom must have ceased to be watered by streams at a very early period.

Hezekiah on the whole reigned prosperously, but the policy of his successors soon involved the city in ruin. In the reign of Jehoiachin it was compelled to surrender at discretion to King Nebuchadnezzar. Again the Temple and the royal palace were pillaged, and a great number of the citizens, including King Jehoiachin, the nobles, 7000 'men of might', 1000 craftsmen and their families, were carried away captive to the East (2 Kings xxiv. 15 et seq.). Those who were left having made a hopeless attempt under Zedekiah to revolt against their conquerors, Jerusalem now had to sustain a long and terrible siege (1 year, 5 months, and 7 days). Pestilence and famine meanwhile ravaged the city. The defence was a desperate one, and every inch of the ground was keenly contested. The Babylonians carried off all the treasures that still remained, the Temple of Solomon was burned to the ground, and Jerusalem was in great part destroyed.

When the Jews returned from captivity, they once more settled in Jerusalem, the actual rebuilding of which was the work of Nehemiah (p. lxxix). He re-fortified the city, retaining the foundations of the former walls, although these now enclosed a far larger space than was necessary for the reduced population (p. 31).

The city opened its gates to Alexander, and after his death passed into the hands of the Ptolemies in the year 320. It was not till the time of Antiochus Epiphanes (175-164) that it again became a theatre of bloodshed. On his return from Egypt, Antiochus plundered the Temple. Two years afterwards he sent thither a chief collector of tribute, who razed the walls and established himself in a stronghold in the city. This was the *Akra*, the site of which is disputed. As according to Josephus (Bell. Jud. v. 4, 1) it was situated on the hill on the slopes of which the lower town also lay, it must probably be located to the S. of the Temple. Some authorities place it, however, to the N.W. of the Temple.

Judas Maccabæus (p. lxxx) recaptured the city, but not the Akra, and he fortified the hill of the Temple. But after the battle of Beth-Zachariah (p. 112), Antiochus V. Eupator caused the walls of 'Zion' to be taken down (1 Macc. vi. 61 et seq.), in violation, it is said, of his sworn treaty. Jonathan, the Maccabæan, however, caused a stronger wall than ever to be erected (1 Macc. x. 11). He constructed another wall between the Akra, which was still occupied by a Syrian garrison, and the city, whereby, at a later period, under Simon (B.C. 141), the citizens were enabled to reduce the garrison by famine (1 Macc. xiii. 49 et seq.). Under John Hyrcanus, the son of Simon, Jerusalem was again taken by the Syrians (under Antiochus VII. Sidetes) in 134. The walls were demolished, but after the fall of Antiochus VII. Hyrcanus restored them, at the same time fortifying the *Baris* (p. 27) in the N.W. angle of the Temple precincts and pulling down the Akra.

Internal dissensions at length led to the intervention of the Romans. Pompey besieged the city, and again the attacks were concentrated against the Temple precincts. The quarter to the N. of the Temple, as well as the Gate of St. Stephen, do not appear to have existed at that period. The moat on the N. side of the Temple was filled up by the Romans on a Sabbath; they then entered the city by the embankment they had thrown up, and, exasperated by the obstinate resistance they had encountered, committed fearful ravages within the Temple precincts. In this struggle, no fewer than 12,000 Jews are said to have perished. To the great distress of the Jews, Pompey penetrated into their inmost sanctuary, but he left their treasures untouched. These were carried off by Crassus a few years later. — Internal discord at Jerusalem next gave rise to the incursion of the Parthians, B. C. 40.

In B.C. 37 Herod, with the aid of the Romans, captured the city after a gallant defence, which so infuriated the victors that they gave orders for a general massacre. Herod, who now obtained the supreme power, embellished and fortified the city, and above all, he rebuilt the Temple (p. 52). He then re-fortified the Baris (p. 26) and named it *Antonia* in honour of his Roman patron. He also built himself a sumptuous palace on the N.W. side of the upper city. This building is said to have contained a number of halls, peristyles, inner courts, and richly decorated rooms. On the N. side of the royal palace stood three large towers of defence, named the *Hippicus*, *Phasaël*, and *Mariamne* respectively (comp. p. 33). According to Roman custom, Herod also built a theatre at Jerusalem, and at the same time a town-hall and the Xystus, a space for gymnastic games surrounded by colonnades. At this period Jerusalem, with its numerous palaces and handsome edifices, the sumptuous Temple with its colonnades, and the lofty city-walls with their bastions, must have presented a very splendid appearance. The wall of the old town had sixty towers, and that of the small suburb to the N. of it fourteen; but the populous city must have extended much farther to the N., and we must picture to ourselves in this direction numerous villas standing in gardens. Such was the character of the city in the time of Christ, but in the interior the streets, though paved, were narrow and crooked. The population must have been very crowded, especially on the occasion of festivals. Josephus states that on one occasion the Roman governor caused the paschal lambs to be counted, and found that they amounted to the vast number of 270,000, whence we may infer that the number of partakers was not less than 2,700,000, though this statement is probably much exaggerated.

After the death of Christ, Agrippa I. at length erected a wall which enclosed the whole of the N. suburb within the precincts of the city. This wall was composed of huge blocks of stone, and is said to have been defended by ninety towers. The strongest of these was the *Psephinus* tower at the N.W. angle, which was upwards of 100 ft. in height, and stood on the highest ground in the city (2570 ft. above the sea-level; comp. p. 35). From fear of incurring the displeasure of the Emperor Claudius, the wall was left unfinished, and it was afterwards completed in a less substantial style. Comp. p. 32.

At this time there were two antagonistic parties at Jerusalem: the fanatical Zealots under Eleazar, who advocated a desperate revolt against the Romans, and a more moderate party under the High Priest Ananias. Florus, the Roman governor, having caused many unoffending Jews to be put to death, a fearful insurrection broke out in the city. Herod Agrippa II. and his sister Berenice endeavoured to pacify the insurgents and to act as mediators, but were obliged to seek refuge in flight. The Zealots had already gained possession of the Temple precincts. After a terrible struggle they succeeded in capturing the upper city and the castle of Herod. Cestius Gallus, an incompetent Roman general, now besieged the city, but when he had almost achieved success he gave up the siege, and withdrew towards Gibeon. His camp was there attacked by the Jews and his army dispersed. The Zealots then proceeded to organize an insurrection throughout the whole of Palestine.

The Romans now despatched their able general Vespasian with 60,000 men to Palestine. This army first quelled the insurrection in Galilee (A. D. 67), and it was not till after a great part of Palestine had been conquered that he advanced against Jerusalem. Events at Rome compelled him, however, to entrust the continuation of the campaign to his son Titus. Within Jerusalem itself bands of robbers had in the meantime taken possession of the Temple, and summoned to their aid the Idumæans (Edomites), the ancient hereditary enemies of the Jews. The moderate party, with Ananias, its leader, was practically annihilated, and no fewer than 12,000 persons of noble family are said to have perished on this occasion. When the Romans approached Jerusalem there were no fewer than four parties within its walls. The Zealots under John of Giscala occupied the castle of Antonia and the court of the Gentiles, while the robber party under Simon of Gerasa held the 'upper city'; Eleazar's party was in possession of the inner Temple and the court of the Jews; and, lastly, the moderate party was also established in the upper part of the city. At the beginning of April, A. D. 70, Titus had assembled six legions (each of about 6000 men) in the environs of Jerusalem. He posted the main body of his forces to the N. and N.W. of the city, while one legion occupied the Mt. of Olives. On April 23rd the besieging engines were brought up to the W. wall of the new town (near the present Jaffa Gate); on May 7th the Romans effected their entrance into the new town. Five days afterwards Titus endeavoured to storm the second wall, but was repulsed; but three days later he succeeded in taking it, and he then caused the whole N. side of the wall to be demolished. He now sent Josephus, who was present in his camp, to summon the Jews to surrender, but in vain. Titus thereupon caused the city-wall, 33 stadia in length, to be surrounded by a wall of 39 stadia in length. Now that the city was completely surrounded, a terrible famine ensued. At length, on the night of July 5th, the castle was stormed. The Jews still retained possession of the gates of the Temple, though by degrees the colonnades of the Temple were destroyed by fire; yet every foot of the ground was desperately contested. At last, on August 10th, a Roman soldier is said to have flung a firebrand into the Temple, contrary to the express commands of Titus. The whole building was burned to the ground, and the soldiers slew all who came within their reach. A body of Zealots, however, contrived to force their passage to the upper part of the city, and it was not till September 7th that it was burned down. Jerusalem was now a heap of ruins; those of the surviving citizens who had fought against the Romans were executed, and the rest sold as slaves.

At length, in 130, the Emperor Hadrian (117-138) erected a town on the site of the Holy City, which he named *Ælia Capitolina*, or simply *Ælia*. Hadrian also rebuilt the walls, which followed the course of the old walls in the main, but were narrower towards the S., so as to exclude the greater part of the W. hill and of Ophel. Once more the fury of the Jews blazed forth under Bar Cochba (132), but after that period the history of the city was for centuries buried in profound obscurity, and the Jews were prohibited under severe penalties from setting foot within its walls.

With the recognition of Christianity as the religion of the state a new era begins in the history of the city. Constantine permitted the Jews to return to Jerusalem, and once more they made an attempt to take up arms against the Romans (339). The Emperor Julian the Apostate favoured them in preference to the Christians, and even permitted them to rebuild their Temple, but they made a feeble attempt only to avail themselves of this permission. At a later period they were again excluded from the city.

As an episcopal see, Jerusalem was subordinate to Cæsarea. An independent patriarchate for Palestine was established at Jerusalem by the Council of Chalcedon in 451. Pilgrimages to Jerusalem soon became very frequent, and the Emperor Justinian erected a hospice for strangers, as well as several churches and monasteries in and around Jerusalem. In 570 there were in Jerusalem hospices with 3000 beds. Pope Gregory the Great and several of the western nations likewise erected buildings for the accommodation of pilgrims, and, at the same time, a thriving trade in relics of every description began to be carried on at Jerusalem †.

In 614 Jerusalem was taken by the Persians and the churches destroyed, but it was soon afterwards restored, chiefly with the aid of the Egyptians. In 628 the Byzantine emperor Heraclius again conquered Syria. In 637 the city was captured by the Caliph ʽOmar

† The mosaic map of Palestine discovered at Mâdebâ (p. 152; comp. ZDPV. xxviii. 120 et seq.), which contains the oldest known plan of Jerusalem, probably dates from this period (6th cent.). The walls of the city are represented as protected by strong towers. The chief gate (the present Damascus Gate) is to the N.; inside this is an open space containing a large column (p. 86). From the gate itself a colonnaded street runs to the S., traversing the entire city. A few of its columns are still extant (p. 47), at the point where the propylæa of the basilica rise above the Holy Sepulchre, immediately to the W. of the street. Other columns have also been found on the Assumptionists' concession on Mount Zion (p. 72). The great Church of Zion (p. 72) stood at the S. end of the street.

after a gallant defence. The inhabitants, who are said to have numbered 50,000, were treated with clemency, and permitted to remain in the city on payment of a poll-tax. The Caliph Harûn er-Rashîd is even said to have sent the keys of the Holy Sepulchre to Charlemagne. The Roman-German emperors sent regular contributions for the support of the pilgrims bound for Jerusalem, and it was only at a later period that the Christians began to be oppressed by the Moslems. The town was named by the Arabs *Beit el-Maḳdis* ('house of the sanctuary'), or simply *El-Ḳuds* ('the sanctuary').

In 969 Jerusalem fell into possession of the Egyptian Fatimites; in the second half of the 11th cent. it was involved in the conflicts of the Turcomans. During the First Crusade the Christian army advanced to the walls of Jerusalem on June 7th, 1099. Robert of Normandy and Robert of Flanders were posted on the N. side; on the W. Godfrey and Tancred; on the W., too, but also on the S., was Raymond of Toulouse. When the engines were erected, Godfrey attacked the city, chiefly from the S. and E.; Tancred assaulted it on the N., and the Damascus Gate was opened to him from within. On July 15th the Gate of Zion was also opened, and the Franks entered the city. They slew most of the Moslem and Jewish inhabitants, and converted the mosques into churches.

In 1187 (Oct. 2nd) Saladin captured the city, treating the Christians, many of whom had fled to the surrounding villages, with great leniency. Three years later, when Jerusalem was again threatened by the Franks (Third Crusade), Saladin caused the city to be strongly fortified. In 1219, however, Sultan Melik el-Muʿaẓẓam of Damascus caused most of these works to be demolished, as he feared that the Franks might again capture the city and establish themselves there permanently. In 1229 Jerusalem was surrendered to Emp. Frederick II., on condition that the walls should not be rebuilt, but this stipulation was disregarded by the Franks. In 1239 the city was taken by Emir David of Kerak, but four years later it was again given up to the Christians by treaty. In 1244 the Kharezmians took the place by storm, and it soon fell under the supremacy of the Aiyubides. Since that period Jerusalem has been a Moslem city. In 1517 it fell into the hands of the Osmans.

Topography of Ancient Jerusalem (comp. adjoining Plan). The earliest city occupied the S. part only of the present city; but on the S. it extended beyond the present city-wall to the edge of the rocky plateau, where remains of the old fortifications have been discovered (p. 70). The E. scarp of the plateau was once much more abrupt than it is at present. Through the accumulation of the rubbish of thousands of years, the lowest part of the *Kidron Valley* (p. 80) is now 30 ft. farther to the E. than it used to be, while at the S.E. corner of the Temple Hill it was formerly 36 ft. deeper than it now is. The actual site of the city was also much less level than at present; what is now recognizable only as a

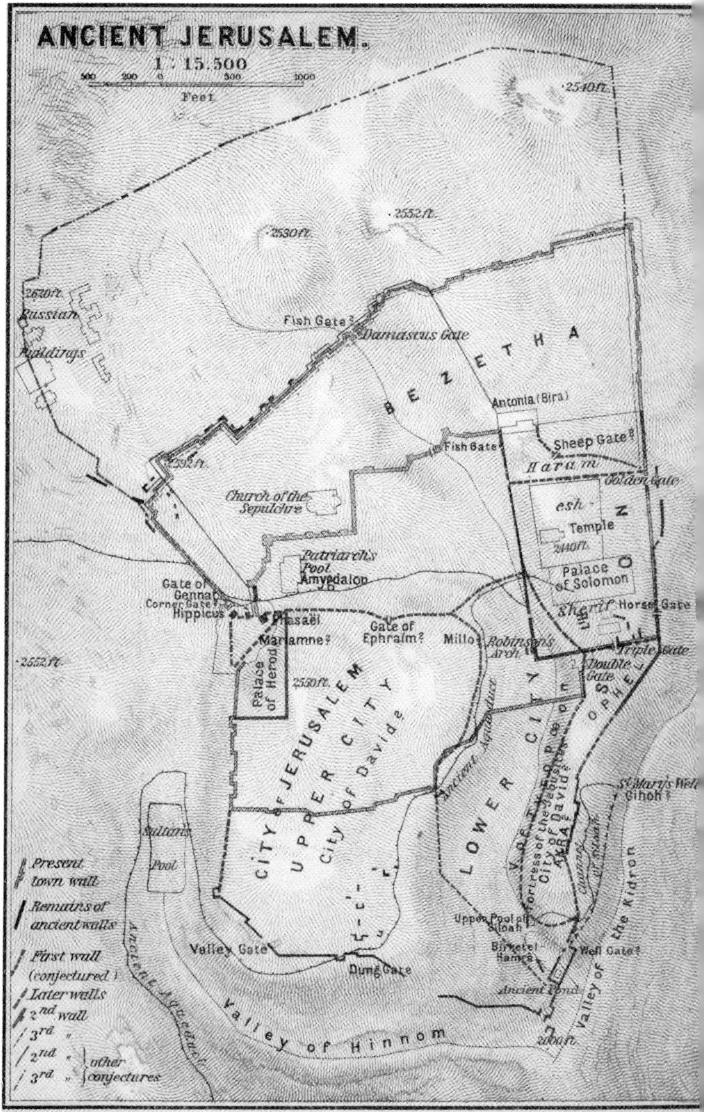

Engraved & printed by Wagner & Debes, Leipzi

shallow depression was formerly a distinct valley, running from the vicinity of the present Damascus Gate first towards the S.E. and then towards the S. This depression (p. 50), called by Josephus *Tyropoeon*, *i.e.* Valley of Dung (wrongly translated the Cheesemongers' Valley), but not mentioned in the Bible, attained a depth of about 60 ft. below the present level (p. 66) and separated the narrow and abrupt E. hill from the W. hill, which was 110 ft. higher. Both hills were also cross-sectioned by other depressions.

Tradition, probably with justice, places the City of David on the W. hill and accordingly calls this *Mt. Zion* (2 Sam. v. 7). Several authorities, however, look for it on the E. hill. In his stronghold David also kept the national shrine, the ark. When Solomon built the Temple on the E. hill and also removed his royal residence to it, the name of Zion was likewise transferred thither; this is the dwelling-place of the Lord (Yahweh) referred to by Biblical writers (Joel iii. 21; Micah iv. 2; Isaiah viii. 18). It is hence easily understood how Zion became later a romantic name for the whole city. On the other hand, however, early literary references clearly distinguish Mt. Zion from the city of Jerusalem (Isaiah x. 12). The name of *Moriah* also occasionally occurs as the religious designation of the Temple Hill (Gen. xxii. 2; 2 Chron. iii. 1). The level surface required for the Temple and Palace of Solomon was provided by massive substructures. The Temple lay on the site of the present Dome of the Rock (p. 53), the Palace immediately to the S. of it (Ezek. xliii. 7, 8), approximately on the site of the Aḳṣâ Mosque (p. 59), where the rock forms a broad ridge. The Palace thus lay below the Temple (comp. 2 Kings xi. 19).

The First Wall, that of David and Solomon, enclosed the old part of the town. Beginning on the W. at the *Furnace Tower* (which perhaps stood on the site later occupied by the *Tower of Hippicus*), it followed the upper verge of the W. hill on the W. and S. sides, thus enclosing the modern suburb of Zion (comp. p. 70). In the W. part of the S. side were probably two gates, *viz.* the *Valley Gate* and the *Dung Gate*. The E. part of the wall was then carried in a double line across the Tyropœon, at the mouth of which was the 'Well Gate', probably identical with the 'Gate between two Walls'. From the Pool of Siloam (p. 83) the wall ascended the hill northwards to the wall of the Temple. In the *Ophel* quarter, which lay to the S.E. of the present Ḥaram, was the *Water Gate* and farther to the N. was the *Horse Gate*. From the Hippicus the N. wall ran E. in an almost straight line to the Temple. Immediately to the S. of this N. wall stood the palace of Herod, the Xystus, and the bridge which crossed the Tyropœon to the Temple.

The Second Wall also dates from the period of the early kings; it was rebuilt by Nehemiah. On the W., S., and E. it corresponds with the First Wall, but it diverges from it to the N.W. at the Hippicus, thus enclosing more ground to the N., the only direction in which the city could be extended. Josephus here placed the *Gennat Gate* (*i.e.* Garden Gate, perhaps the 'Corner Gate' of the Bible). Thence the wall made a curve to the N.E., interrupted by the *Gate of Ephraim*, the *Old Gate*, and the *Fish Gate*, and impinging on the N.W. angle of the Temple precincts. Here rose the *Bira*, a strong bastion called *Baris* by Josephus and afterwards named *Antonia* (comp. p. 27). This part of the N. wall was further strengthened by the towers of *Hananeel* and *Mea*, the exact positions of which are still undetermined. On the direction assigned to this second wall depends the question of the genuineness of the 'Holy Sepulchre'. A number of authorities believe that the wall took much the same direction as the present town-wall, in which case it would have included what is now called the 'Holy Sepulchre', which, therefore, could not be genuine (p. 35). Others hold that the wall and moat ran round the E. and S. sides of Golgotha, so that the Sepulchre lay outside the city-wall. To the S.E. of the Baris lay the *Sheep Gate*, and in its vicinity (John v. 2) the Pool of Bethesda (p. 68).

With regard to the situation of the THIRD WALL, topographers likewise disagree. Those who hold that the second wall corresponded to the present town-wall (see above) must look for the third wall far to the N. of it. The opinion now generally accepted is that this wall occupied nearly the same site as the present N. town-wall of Jerusalem; there are still clear traces of an old moat round the present N. wall, and this view appears to be confirmed by the statement of the distances given by Josephus (4 stadia to the royal tombs, 7 stadia to the Scopus), who, however, is not always accurate.

Literature (comp. p. c). The best works on Jerusalem include *George Adam Smith's* 'Jerusalem: The Topography, Economics, and History from the Earliest Times to A. D. 70' (2 vols.; London, 1907 & 1908; 24*s.*); *Col. C. R. Conder's* 'The City of Jerusalem' (London, 1909; 12*s.*); *Selah Merrill's* 'Ancient Jerusalem' (New York; 1908); *Barclay's* 'City of the Great King'; *Besant & Palmer's* 'Jerusalem, the City of Herod and Saladin' (5th edit., London, 1908); *Warren's* 'Underground Jerusalem' (London; 1876); *Wilson & Warren's* 'Recovery of Jerusalem' (London; 1871); *D. S. Margoliouth's* 'Cairo, Jerusalem, and Damascus' (New York; 1908); *Sir C. M. Watson's* 'Jerusalem' ('Mediæval Towns Series', London, 1912; 4*s.* 6*d.*); *Tobler's* 'Denkblätter' (2nd edit., Constance, 1856) and 'Topographie von Jerusalem' (Berlin; 1854); *Spiess's* 'Das Jerusalem des Josephus' (Berlin; 1881); *Bliss & Dickie's* 'Excavations at Jerusalem' (London; 1898); *Père Vincent's* 'Underground Jerusalem' (Engl. trans.; London, 1911); *Glaisher's* 'Meteorological Observations at Jerusalem'; *Mommert's* 'Topographie des Alten Jerusalem' (4 vols.; Leipzig, 1902-1907; 27 *M* 50 pf.); *Zimmermann's* maps (Bâle; 1876); *Schick & Benzinger's* maps of Jerusalem and its environs (p. cii); *Kuemmel's* 'Karte der Materialien zur Topographie des Alten Jerusalem' (2 sheets on a scale of 1:2500; Halle, 1906; 18 *M*). For closer investigation the Jerusalem volume of the English Palestine Survey, with plans, is indispensable. *Miss A. Goodrich-Freer's* 'Inner Jerusalem' (1904), *Hanauer's* 'Walks about Jerusalem' (1910), and *Laurence Hutton's* 'Literary Landmarks of Jerusalem' (1895) may also be mentioned.

Jerusalem, to most travellers, is a place of overwhelming interest, but, at first sight, many will be sadly disappointed in the modern town. It would seem, at first, as though little were left of the ancient city of Zion and Moriah. It is only by patiently penetrating beneath the modern crust of rubbish and decay, which shrouds the sacred places from view, that the traveller will at length realize to himself a picture of the Jerusalem of antiquity, and this will be the more vivid in proportion to the amount of previously acquired historical and topographical information at his command. He will, however, be obliged to confess that the material and moral decline of the city forms but a melancholy termination to the stupendous scenes once enacted here. The combination of wild superstition with the merest formalism which everywhere forces itself on our notice, and the fanaticism and jealous exclusiveness of the numerous religious communities of Jerusalem form the chief modern characteristics of the city — the Holy City, once the fountain-head from which the knowledge of the true God was wont to be vouchsafed to mankind. Jerusalem, the centre of the three great religions of the world, is not at all a town for amusement, for everything in it has a religious tinge, and from this point of view, the impressions the traveller receives in Jerusalem are anything but pleasant. The native Christians of all sects are by no means equal to their task, the bitter war which rages among them is carried on with very foul weapons, and the contempt with which the orthodox Jews and Mohammedans look down on the Christians is only too well deserved.

a. The Western and Southern Quarters.

The W. entrance of Jerusalem is formed by the **Jaffa Gate** (Pl. D, 5, 6), called by the Arabs *Bâb el-Khalîl*, *i.e.* Gate of Hebron. The street leading from the railway station (p. 69) reaches the town here; and the spot always presents an animated concourse of pilgrims, travellers, donkey-drivers, and the like. In 1907 a clock-tower in the modern Arabian style was built on the top of the old gate-tower. As in all the old city-gates of Jerusalem (pp. 48, 85), the gateway forms an angle in passing between its towers. A portion of the adjacent city-wall was removed in 1898 to form a road for the German Emperor. — To the S.E. of the gate rises **El-Ḳalʿa** or the **Citadel** (Pl. D, 6), also mistakenly called (since the middle ages) the '*Castle of David*' (comp. p. 31). This building, which dates in its present form from the beginning of the 14th cent., with some additions of the 16th cent., consists of an irregular group of towers standing upon a massive substructure rising at an angle of about 45° from the bottom of the moat. The N.E. tower, the almost solid lower part of which consists of large drafted blocks, with rough surfaces (p. xcvi), probably corresponds to the '*Phasaël Tower*' of Herod's palace (p. 27) and offers the finest example of the ancient wall-towers of Jerusalem.

The David Street, running towards the E. from the Jaffa Gate (at first under the name of *Sueiḳat ʿAllân*; Pl. D, E, 5), between the

Citadel and the Grand New Hotel (p. 19), descends in a series of steps, crosses the Street of the Christians (see below), and is prolonged as the Bazaar Street (*Ḥâret el-Bizâr;* Pl. E, F, 5) to the S. of the Mûristân (p. 45). At this point is the market for grain and seeds, while the Crown Prince Frederick William Street diverges to the left. Farther on the street crosses the three lanes of the Old Bazaar (p. 47). Its E. continuation (Ṭarîḳ Bâb es-Silseleh) ends at the Es-Silseleh Gate of the Ḥaram esh-Sherîf (p. 65).

At the *Greek Monastery of St. John* (Pl. 29; E, 5), which has accommodation for 500 pilgrims, we turn to the N. and enter the STREET OF THE CHRISTIANS (*Ḥâret en-Naṣâra;* Pl. E, 5, 4), the chief approach to the Church of the Holy Sepulchre. It is lined on both sides with shops. Beyond the Monastery of St. John, on the right, is a covered passage leading to the New Bazaar (p. 47); farther on in the Street of the Christians is the large *Bath of the Patriarch* (Pl. E, 5; *Ḥammâm el-Baṭraḳ*). Opposite, to the left, is an Arab coffee-house with a balcony.

From another balcony at the back of this café we obtain the best survey of the **Patriarch's Pool** (*Birket Hammâm el-Baṭraḳ;* Pl. E, 5), an artificial reservoir, 80 yds. long (N. to S.) and 48 yds. wide, the construction of which is ascribed to King Hezekiah. Josephus calls it *Amygdalon*, or the 'tower-pool'. The bottom lies only 10 ft. below the level of the Street of the Christians. At the S.E. corner its coping consists of hewn blocks. On the W. side part of the rock has been removed, in order that a level surface might be obtained. On the N. it is bounded by the so-called *Coptic Khân* (Pl. E, 5), under which is a wall supposed to indicate the original extension of the reservoir on this side. In summer the reservoir is either empty or contains a little muddy water only. It is supplied from the Mâmilla pool (p. 68), and the water is chiefly used for filling the '*Bath of the Patriarch*' (see above).

Farther on a covered passage diverges to the right from the Street of the Christians, descends a few steps, and comes out on the space in front of the Church of the Holy Sepulchre (p. 45). To the left stands the **Great Greek Monastery** (Pl. D, E, 4, 5), called *Deir er-Rûm el-Kebîr*, entered from the *Ḥâret Deir er-Rûm*, which ends to the N. at the Street of the Christians. It is a building of considerable extent and an interesting example of Jerusalem architecture, being first mentioned in 1400 as the monastery of St. Thecla. The monastery includes five churches, the chief of which is that of St. Thecla. The churches of Constantine and Helena are on the E. side of the Street of the Christians. The monastery also possesses a valuable library (p. 23).

At the N. end of the Street of the Christians we take the turning to the left (W.). Here are the Girls' Orphanage of the Franciscan Sisters (r.; Pl. 38, E 4), the *Greek Patriarchate* (l.), and the Latin Parochial School for Boys (Pl. 40; D, 4). Farther on, to the right, are the Greek Convents of the *Archangel Michael* (Pl. 31) and *St. George* (Pl. 27), and, on both sides of the covered street, the ***Franciscan Convent of Our Saviour*** (Pl. 36). The street to the left (S.) leads to the Casa Nuova (p. 19). We turn to the right, passing the Greek

Convents of *St. Theodore* (l.; Pl. 33) and *St. Basil* (r.; Pl. 23). The next street to the right leads to the *New Gate* or *Bâb el-Jedîd* (Pl. C, D, 4). At the N.W. corner of the wall stands the building of the *Frères des Ecoles Chrétiennes*, or *School Brethren*, with the remains of the so-called **Tower** or **Castle of Goliath** (Arabic *Kaṣr Jâlûd;* Pl. C, 4). The oldest relics of the castle consist (in the S. part) of the substruction of a massive square tower (perhaps the '*Psephinus*' of Josephus; p. 27); four courses of large smooth-hewn stones are still recognizable. The centre of the building is occupied by four large pillars of huge drafted blocks. — To the S.E. lies the *Latin Patriarchate* (Pl. C, D, 5), containing a church, a seminary, and an extensive library (p. 23). Continuing towards the S.E., and passing the boys' school of the Greek Patriarchate and the Greek Hospital (Pl. D, 5), we find ourselves again at the Jaffa Gate (p. 33).

To the S. and S.E. of the Citadel (p. 33) extends the **Armenian Quarter** (Pl. D, E, 6, 7). In the N. part of this quarter, opposite the Citadel, stands the English *Christ Church* (Pl. E, 6; comp. p. 22). Proceeding towards the S., we reach the **Great Armenian Monastery** (Pl. E, 6, 7), the extensive buildings of which are said to have room for several thousand pilgrims. The old convent-church, the **Church of St. James (Pl. E, 6)**, is well worth a visit. The nave and aisles, of equal height, are separated by graceful pillars; the dome is formed by two intersecting semicircular arches. The walls are lined with porcelain tiles to the height of 6 ft., above which they are covered with paintings. The W. aisle contains the chief sanctuary, *viz.* the prison in which James the Great was beheaded (Acts xv. 2). The monastery includes a printing-office, a seminary, a large hospice for pilgrims, schools for boys and girls, and a small museum. The large garden, stretching along the city-wall, contains numerous imposing trees and offers a fine view of the upper part of the Valley of Hinnom (p. 69). The lane skirting the garden on the E. ends on the S. at the *Zion Gate* (p. 73). A little farther to the E. is the Armenian nunnery of *Deir ez-Zeitûni* (Pl. E, 7), the interesting old church of which is regarded by the Armenians as the house of Annas, the father-in-law of Caiaphas.

The dirty **Jewish Quarter** (Pl. E, F, 6, 7; comp. p. 23) contains numerous *Synagogues* (marked S upon the Plan), hucksters' booths, and taverns, but offers no object of interest to the traveller.

b. The Church of the Holy Sepulchre.

The Church of the Holy Sepulchre is open free before 11.30 a.m. and after 3 p.m., but by paying a bakshish of 1 fr. to the Moslem custodians the visitor will be allowed to remain in the building after 11.30 o'clock. An opera-glass and a light are indispensable. A bright day should be chosen, as many parts of the building are very dark. — Moslem guards, appointed by the Turkish government, sit in the vestibule (p. 39) for the purpose of preserving order among the Christian pilgrims and of keeping the keys. The office of custodian is hereditary in a Jerusalem family. Down to the beginning of the 19th cent. a large entrance-fee was exacted from every visitor. — Comp. *Sir Charles W. Wilson's* 'Golgotha and the Holy Sepulchre' (London, Palestine Exploration Fund, 1910; 6*s*.).

The ***Church of the Holy Sepulchre** (Arab. *Kenîset el-Kiyâmeh*, *i.e.* 'Church of the Resurrection'; Pl. E, 4), with its conspicuous dome, surmounted by a gilded cross, occupies a site which has been held sacred for many centuries and probably corresponds to the *Golgotha* (Aramaic *gulgolta*, skull) of the New Testament. According to the Bible (Matt. xxviii. 11; Hebr. xiii. 12) Golgotha lay outside

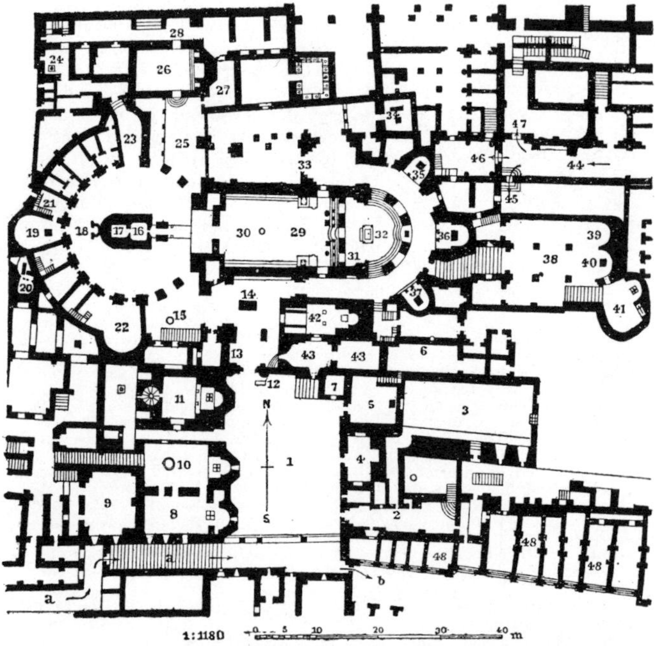

a. *Entrance from the Street of the Christians.* b. *Path to the Mûristân.* 1. *Quadrangle.* 2. *Monastery of Abraham.* 3. *Greek Shops.* 4. *Armenian Chapel of St. James.* 5. *Coptic Chapel of Michael.* 6. *Abyssinian Chapel.* 7. *Chapel of St. Mary of Egypt* (below) and *Chapel of the Agony of the Virgin* (above). 8. *Greek Chapel of St. James.* 9. *Chapel of St. Thecla.* 10. *Chapel of Mary Magdalen.* 11. *Chapel of the Forty Martyrs.* 12. *Tomb of Philip d'Aubigny.* 13. *Post of the Moslem custodians.* 14. *Stone of Unction.* 15. *Place from which the Women witnessed the Anointment.* 16. *Angels' Chapel.* 17. *Chapel of the Holy Sepulchre.* 18. *Chapel of the Copts.* 19. *Chapel of the Syrians.* 20. *Chamber in the Rock.* 21. *Passage to the Armenian Gallery.* 22. *Original S. Apse.* 23. *Passage to the Cistern.* 24. *Cistern.* 25. *Antechamber of next chapel.* 26. *Chapel of the Apparition.* 27. *Latin Sacristy.* 28. *Latin Convent.* 29. *Greek Cathedral ('Catholicon').* 30. *'Centre of the World'.* 31. *Seat of the Patriarch of Jerusalem.* 32. *Choir.* 33. *North Aisle of the Church of the Crusaders.* 34. *Chapel (Prison of Christ).* 35. *Chapel of St. Longinus.* 36. *Chapel of the Parting of the Raiment.* 37. *Chapel of the Derision* 38. *Chapel of the Empress Helena.* 39. *Altar of the Penitent Thief.* 40. *Altar of the Empress.* 41. *Chapel of the Invention of the Cross.* 42. *Chapel of the Raising of the Cross.* 43. *Chapel of the Nailing to the Cross.* 44. *Entrance from the Bazaar.* 45. *Abyssinian Monastery.* 46. *Entrance to the Coptic Monastery.* 47. *Entrance to the Cistern of St. Helena.* 48. *Greek Hospice.*

the city-wall, but the course of the second city-wall is still a matter of dispute (comp. p. 32). Some explorers now look for Golgotha to the N. of the town (comp. p. 87). Bishop Eusebius of Cæsarea (314-340 A.D.), the earliest ecclesiastical historian, records that during the excavations in the reign of *Constantine* the sacred tomb of the Saviour was, 'contrary to all expectation', discovered. Later historians add that Helena, Constantine's mother (d. ca. 326), undertook a pilgrimage to Jerusalem, and that she there discovered the Cross of Christ. Two churches were consecrated here in 336: — the Church of the Holy Sepulchre (also called the Anastasis, because Christ here rose from the dead), consisting of a rotunda, in the middle of which was the sepulchre surrounded by twelve columns, and a Basilica dedicated to the sign of the Cross. A few remains of the atrium of the latter still exist (see pp. 47, 48).

In 614 the buildings were destroyed by the Persians. In 616-626 Modestus, abbot of the monastery of Theodosius, built a new Church of the Resurrection (Anastasis), a new Church of the Cross (Martyrion), and a Church of Calvary. From a description by Arculf in 670 it appears that an addition had been made to the holy places by the erection of a church of St. Mary on the S. side. In the time of Caliph Mâmûn (p. 53) the patriarch Thomas enlarged the dome over the Anastasis. In 936, 969, and 1010 the holy places were damaged either by fire or the Moslems. In 1055 a church again arose, but this building seemed much too insignificant to the Crusaders, who therefore erected a large Romanesque church which embraced all the holy places and chapels (beginning of the 12th cent.). In spite of the numerous alterations and additions that have since been made, there still subsist many remains of the two main parts of this building, — *viz.* the circular church over the Holy Sepulchre on the W. and a church with a semicircular choir on the E. New acts of destruction were perpetrated in 1187 and 1244, but in 1310 a handsome church had again arisen, to which in 1400 were added two domes. During the following centuries complaints were frequently made of the insecure condition of the dome of the sepulchre. At length, in 1719, a great part of the church was rebuilt. In 1808 the church was almost entirely burned down. The Greeks now contrived to secure to themselves the principal right to the buildings, and they, together with the Armenians, contributed most largely to the erection of the new church of 1810, which was designed by a certain Komnenos Kalfa of Mitylene. The dilapidated dome was restored by architects of various nationalities in 1868, in pursuance of an agreement made with the Porte by France and Russia.

In front of the main portal of the church, on the S. side, is an Outer Court, or *Quadrangle* (Pl. 1, on opposite page), dating from the period of the Crusades, as is evidenced by the immured columns to the left, adjoining the staircase, and by a piece of vaulting in the

W. archway (p. 34). Remains of bases of columns on the ground show that a porch also stood here. The court is paved with yellowish slabs of stone, and is always occupied by traders and beggars. Almost in front of the door of the Holy Sepulchre is the gravestone of Philip d'Aubigny, an English Crusader (Pl. 12; d. 1236; inscription). [For the buildings on the S. and S.E. sides of this square, see pp. 45 et seq.]

From the court the first door on the right (S.E.) leads to the *Monastery of Abraham* (Pl. 2; p. 45). Ascending a staircase to the left, we reach a small terrace above the Armenian Chapel of St. James (Pl. 4; see below), where an olive-tree, surrounded by a wall, marks the spot where Abraham discovered the ram when about to sacrifice Isaac (Gen. xxii). A small door and stair to the E. lead to the *Church of the Apostles* (above Pl. 3), with the altar of Melchizedek. A vestibule to the N. leads to the *Church of Abraham* (above the Chapel of the Archangel Michael, Pl. 5). A round hollow in the centre of the pavement indicates the spot where Abraham was on the point of sacrificing Isaac (comp. pp. 44, 48). This chapel is the only spot within the precincts of the Holy Sepulchre where Anglican clergy have been allowed to celebrate the Holy Eucharist. The scene of Abraham's sacrifice was placed in this neighbourhood as early as the year 600. — Two other doors on the E. side of the quadrangle lead respectively into the Armenian *Chapel of St. James* (Pl. 4), with a crypt underneath, and the Coptic *Chapel of the Archangel Michael* (Pl. 5). From the latter a staircase leads E. to the *Abyssinian Chapel* (Pl. 6) belonging to the convent mentioned at p. 48. — The building in the N.E. corner of the quadrangle contains two stories, each of which has pointed arches similar to those on the façade of the main edifice. The interior is now occupied by chapels. Below is the Greek *Chapel of St. Mary of Egypt* (Pl. 7). This Mary, it is said, was mysteriously prevented from entering the church until she had invoked the image of the mother of Jesus. Above is the *Chapel of the Agony of the Virgin* (p. 44), which is reached by the staircase to the right of the E. portal.

The chapels to the W. of the quadrangle belong to the Greeks. The *Chapel of St. James* (Pl. 8), sacred to the memory of the brother of Christ, is handsomely fitted up; behind it is the *Chapel of St. Thecla* (Pl. 9). The *Chapel of Mary Magdalen* (Pl. 10) marks the spot, where, according to Greek tradition, Christ appeared to Mary Magdalen for the third time. The *Chapel of the Forty Martyrs* (Pl. 11) stands on the site of the monastery of the Trinity, which was formerly the burial-place of the patriarchs of Jerusalem; it now forms the lowest story of the Bell Tower.

The *Bell Tower*, erected about 1160-80 in the N.W. corner of the quadrangle, has flying buttresses and large Gothic arched windows, above which were two rows of louvre-windows, the lower row only of which has been preserved. The tower originally stood detached from the church, according to the custom of S. Europe, but was afterwards partly incorporated with it. The upper part of the tower has been destroyed; but we know from old drawings that it consisted of several blind arcades, each with a central window, above which were pinnacles and an octagonal dome.

The FAÇADE of the Church is divided into two stories. There are two portals (of which that to the E. has been walled up), each with a corresponding window above it. Both portals and windows are surmounted by depressed pointed arches, which are adorned with a border of deep dentels, and over these again runs a moulding of elaborately executed waved lines, which are continued to the extremity of the wall on each side. A similar line of moulding, executed in egg and leaf work, separates the one story from the other. The pointed tympanum over the W. portal, originally covered with mosaic, is adorned in the Arabian style with a geometrical design of hexagons. The columns adjoining the doors, probably taken from some ancient temple, are of marble: their capitals are Byzantine, finely executed, and the bases are quite in the antique style. The imposts of the columns, adorned with oak-leaves and acorns, are continued to the left and right in the form of a moulding. The lintels of both doors are decorated with *Reliefs* of great merit, which were probably executed in France in the second half of the 12th century.

The *Relief over the W. Portal* represents scenes from Bible history. In the first section to the left is the Raising of Lazarus: Christ with the Gospel, and Mary at his feet; Lazarus rises from the tomb; in the background spectators, some of them holding their noses! In the second section from the left, Mary beseeches Jesus to come for the sake of Lazarus. In the third section begins the representation of Christ's entry into Jerusalem. He first sends the disciples to fetch the ass; and two shepherds with sheep are pourtrayed. The disciples bring the foal and spread out their garments; in the background appears the Mt. of Olives. Then follows the Entry into Jerusalem. (The missing fragment, showing Christ upon the ass, is now in the Louvre.) The small figures which spread their garments in the way are very pleasing. A man is cutting palm-branches. A woman carries her child on her shoulder as they do in Egypt at the present day. In the foreground is a lame man with his crutch. The last section represents the Last Supper: John leans on Jesus' breast; Judas, on the outer side of the table, and separated from the other disciples, is receiving the sop. — The *Relief over the E. Portal* is an intricate mass of foliage, fruit, flowers, nude figures, birds, and other objects. In the middle is a centaur with his bow. The whole has an allegorical meaning: the animals below, which represent evil, conspire against goodness.

The **Interior of the Church of the Holy Sepulchre** consists now, as it did in the time of the Crusaders (p. 37), of two main parts, the circular domed building to the W. (p. 40), and the rectangular church with nave and aisles to the E. (p. 42). These two were originally separated. In entering from the S. we first reach a vestibule (Pl. 13; p. 36) in which the Moslem custodians sit. From this we pass into the S. aisle of the second of the above-mentioned churches. Immediately in front of us, surrounded by numerous lamps and colossal candelabra, is the '*Stone of Unction*' (Pl. 14), on which the body of Jesus is said to have lain when it was anointed by Nicodemus (John xix. 38-40), while about 33 ft. to the W. of it is a second stone (Pl. 15), which marks the spot whence the women are said to have witnessed the anointment.

Before the period of the Crusades a separate 'Church of St. Mary' rose over the place of Anointment, but a little to the S. of the present spot; when, however, the Franks enclosed all the holy places within one building, the Stone of Unction was removed to somewhere about its present site. The stone has often been changed, and has been in possession of numerous different religious communities in succession. In the 15th cent. it belonged to the Copts, in the 16th to the Georgians (from whom the

Latins purchased permission for 5000 piastres to burn candles over it), and afterwards to the Greeks. Over this stone Armenians, Latins, Greeks, and Copts are entitled to burn their lamps. The present stone, a reddish yellow marble slab, 7 ft. long and 2 ft. broad, was placed here in 1808. — To the S. of the Stone of the Women is a flight of steps leading to the Armenian Chapel.

The ROTUNDA OF THE SEPULCHRE, which we now enter, dates in its present form from 1810. The dome is borne by eighteen pillars connected by arches, and enclosing the sepulchre itself. The supports of the pillars belong to the original structure, which consisted of twelve large columns, probably divided into groups of three by piers placed between them. Round these pillars ran a double colonnade, and the enclosing wall had three apses (comp. p. 41). The present ambulatory is divided by cross-vaulting into two stories. The dome, which is 65 ft. in diameter, is made of iron, and consists of two concentric vaults, the ribs of which are connected by iron braces. Above the opening in the middle is a gilded screen covered with glass. The outer dome is covered with lead, while the inner dome is lined with painted tin. [The upper story of the ambulatory is reached through the Greek Monastery, see p. 34.]

In the centre of the rotunda, beneath the dome, is the CHAPEL OF THE HOLY SEPULCHRE, a building 26 ft. long and 17½ ft. wide, consisting of a hexagonal W. part and an E. addition. It was reconstructed of marble in 1810. In front of the E. side of it there is a kind of antechamber provided with stone benches and large candelabra. From this we enter the so-called *Angels' Chapel* (Pl. 16), 11 ft. long and 10 ft. wide, the thick walls of which contain flights of steps leading to the roof. Of the fifteen lamps burning in this chapel five belong to the Greeks, five to the Latins, four to the Armenians, and one to the Copts. In the middle lies a stone set in marble, which is said to be that which covered the mouth of the sepulchre and was rolled away by the angel. — Through a low door we next enter the *Chapel of the Holy Sepulchre* (Pl. 17) properly so called, 6½ ft. long by 6 ft. wide. [Here is the 14th Station of the Via Dolorosa, p. 51.] From the ceiling, which rests upon marble columns, hang forty-three lamps, of which four belong to the Copts, while the rest are equally divided among the other three sects. In the centre of the N. wall is a relief in white marble, representing the Saviour rising from the tomb. This relief belongs to the Greeks, that on the right of it to the Armenians, and that on the left to the Latins. On the inside of the door is the inscription in Greek, referring to the architect Kalfa (p. 37). The tombstone, which is covered with marble slabs and now used as an altar, is about 5 ft. long, 2 ft. wide, and 3 ft. high. The upper slab is cracked. Mass is said here daily.

According to Luke xxiii. 53, the grave of Jesus was a rock-tomb, probably a kind of niche-tomb (p. xcvi). In the course of Constantine's search for the Holy Sepulchre (comp. p. 37) a cavern in a rock was discovered, and a chapel was soon erected over the spot. In the time of the Crusaders the sanctuary of the Sepulchre was of a circular form. At that period there were already two cavities, the outer of which was the angels' chapel while the inner contained the niche-tomb. A little later we hear of a polygonal building, artificially lighted within. It is impossible to decide definitely whether the mouth of the tomb, which was overlaid with marble at a very early period, is in the natural rock or in an artificial mound. After the destruction of the place in 1555 the tomb was uncovered, and an inscription with the name of Helena (?), and a piece of wood supposed to be a fragment of the Cross were found. The whole building was restored in 1719, and was little injured by the fire of 1808.

Immediately beyond the Holy Sepulchre (to the W.) is a small chapel (Pl. 18) which has belonged to the Copts since the 16th century.

The pillars in the W. ambulatory are connected by transverse partition-walls with the strong enclosing wall dating from the great building of the Crusaders. The small chapels thus created belong to different religious communities; those on the W., the N., and the S. (Pl. 19, 23, 22) still possess their old apses. The plain *Chapel of the Syrians* (Pl. 19), on the W., is usually entered through the adjoining room on the N. (Pl. 21), from which a staircase leads up to the Armenian part of the gallery. A door in the S. wall of the chapel leads into a rocky chamber (Pl. 20). By the walls are first observed two 'sunken tombs' (p. xcvi), one of which is about 2 ft. and the other $3^1/_2$ ft. long, and both 3 ft. deep, having been probably destined for bones. In the rock to the S. are traces of 'shaft tombs', $5^1/_2$ ft. long, $1^1/_2$ ft. wide, and $2^1/_2$ ft. high. Since the 16th cent. tradition has placed the tombs of Joseph of Arimathæa and Nicodemus here. — The northernmost chapel (Pl. 23) is adjoined by a passage leading between the dwellings of officials to a deep cistern (Pl. 24), from which good fresh water may be obtained.

From the N.E. side of the ambulatory we enter an antechamber (Pl. 25) which tradition points out as the spot where Jesus appeared to Mary Magdalen (John xx. 14, 15). The place where Christ stood is indicated by a marble ring in the centre, and that where Mary stood by another near the N. exit from the chamber. To the left is the only organ in the church, which belongs to the Latins. — We now ascend by four steps to the *Chapel of the Apparition* (Pl. 26), dating from the 14th cent., the principal chapel of the Latins. Legend relates that Christ appeared here to his mother after the resurrection, and the central altar is dedicated to her. The N. altar contains various relics. [The door on the N. side forms the approach to the Latin Convent; see next page.] Behind the S. altar, immediately to the right of the entrance, is shown a fragment of the Column of the Scourging, preserved in a latticed niche in the wall.

The column was formerly shown in the house of Caiaphas (p. 72), but was brought here at the time of the Crusaders. Judging from the narratives of different pilgrims, it must have frequently changed its size and colour, and a column of similar pretensions is shown in the Church of Santa Prassede, at Rome, whither it is said to have been taken in 1223. There is a stick here which the pilgrims kiss after pushing it through a hole and touching the column with it. — One legend relates that the Chapel of the Apparition occupies the site of the house of Joseph of Arimathæa.

On the E. side of the antechamber is the entrance to the *Latin Sacristy* (Pl. 27), where we are shown the sword, spurs, and cross of Godfrey de Bouillon, antiquities of doubtful genuineness. These are used in the ceremony of receiving knights into the Order of the Sepulchre, which has existed since the Crusades. The sword is 2 ft. 8 in. long and has a simple cruciform handle 5 in. in length. Behind the Sacristy is the *Convent of the Franciscans* (Pl. 28), with the steps leading up to the Latin half of the galleries.

The RECTANGULAR PART OF THE CHURCH, to which we now turn, belongs in its essential features to the Frankish church built by an architect named Jourdain between 1140 and 1149. It consists of a nave and aisles, with an ambulatory and semicircular apse towards the E. The pointed windows, the clustered pillars, and the groined vaulting bear all the characteristics of the French transition style, with the addition of Arabian details. The original effect of the building, particularly the simple and noble form of the choir, has been, however, seriously disfigured by smaller structures erected round and against it. According to tradition, the church occupies the site of the garden of Joseph of Arimathæa. — The main entrance was on the W. side, opposite the Holy Sepulchre, where the large 'Arch of the Emperor' still stands. Through this we enter the —

GREEK CATHEDRAL (Pl. 29), the so-called *Catholicon*, in the nave of the church of the Crusaders. It is separated from the aisles by partition-walls between the pillars, and is lavishly embellished with gilding and painting. In the W. part of the church, which is covered by a dome resting on the pointed arches, stands a kind of cup containing a flattened ball, covered with network, which is said to occupy the *Centre of the World* (Pl. 30), a fable of very early origin. Of the two episcopal thrones, that to the N. is designed for the Patriarch of Antioch, that to the S. for the Patriarch of Jerusalem (Pl. 31). The choir (Pl. 32) with the high-altar is shut off by a wall in the Greek fashion, and a so-called Iconoclaustrum thus formed, in which the treasures of the church are sometimes shown to distinguished visitors. They include a bone of St. Oswald, King of Northumbria (d. 642). — We return through the Arch of the Emperor and turn to the right into the —

North Aisle (Pl. 33). Between the two huge piers on the N. side are remains of the 'Seven Arches of the Virgin', which formed one side of an open court existing in the time of the Crusaders. — In the N.E. corner is a dark chapel which was shown as early as the beginning of the 12th cent. as the *Prison of Christ* (Pl. 34) and of the two thieves before the Crucifixion. On the right of the entrance is an altar with two round holes, said to be the stocks in which the feet of Jesus were put during the preparations for the Crucifixion (comp. p. 50). Through the holes we see two impressions on the stone, which are said to be the footprints of Christ (comp. the adjoining picture). This legend, of Greek origin, dates from the end of the 15th century.

The old Frankish retro-choir, to the E. of the Greek Cathedral, has three apses cut out of its thick outside wall. The first of these apses is called the *Chapel of St. Longinus* (Pl. 35). Longinus, whose name is mentioned in the 5th cent. for the first time, was the soldier who pierced Jesus' side; he had been blind of one eye, but when some of the water and blood spurted into his blind eye it recovered its sight. He thereupon repented and became a Christian. The chapel of this saint appears not to have existed earlier than the end of the 16th century. It belongs to the Greeks. The next chapel is that of the *Parting of the Raiment* (Pl. 36), and belongs to the Armenians. It was shown as early as the 12th century. — The third is the *Chapel of the Derision*, or of the *Crowning with Thorns* (Pl. 37), belonging to the Greeks, and without windows. About the middle of it stands an altar shaped like a box, which contains the so-called *Column of Derision*. This relic, which is first mentioned in 1384, has passed through many hands and frequently changed its size and colour since then. It is now a thick, light-grey fragment of stone, about 1 ft. high. — Between the 1st and 2nd chapels is a door, through which the canons are said formerly to have entered the church.

Between the second and third chapels, 29 steps lead us down to a chapel 65 ft. long and 42 ft. wide, situated 16 ft. below the level of the Sepulchre. This is the *Chapel of St. Helena* (Pl. 38), belonging to the Armenians, and here once stood Constantine's basilica. In the 7th cent. a small sanctuary in the Byzantine style was erected here by Modestus, and the existing substructions date from this period. The dome is borne by four thick columns of reddish colour (antique monoliths), surmounted by clumsy cubic capitals. According to an old tradition, the columns used to shed tears. The pointed vaulting dates from the 12th century. The chapel has two apses, of which that to the N. (Pl. 39) is dedicated to the Penitent Thief and that to the S. (Pl. 40) to the Empress Helena. The seat on the right, adjoining the altar in the S.E. corner, is said to have been occupied by the Empress while the cross was being sought for; this tradition, however, is not older than the 15th century. In the 17th cent. the Armenian patriarch, who used to occupy this seat, complains of the way in which it was mutilated by pilgrims. In the middle ages the chapel was regarded as the place where the Cross was found. Some explorers take it to be a piece of the old city moat.

Thirteen more steps descend to what is properly the *Chapel of the Invention* (i. e. *Finding*) *of the Cross* (Pl. 41); by the last three steps the natural rock makes its appearance. The (modern) chapel, which is really a cavern in the rock, is about 24 ft. long, nearly as wide, and 16 ft. high, and the floor is paved with stone. On its W. and S. sides are stone ledges. The place to the right belongs to the Greeks, and here is a marble slab in which a cross is inserted. The altar (l.) belongs to the Latins. A bronze statue of the Empress Helena, of life-size, represents her holding the cross. The pedestal is of the colour of the rock and rests on a foundation of green serpentine. On the wall at the back is a Latin inscription with the name of the founder.

On the S. side of the ambulatory adjoining the chapel of the Derision is a flight of steps ascending to the chapels on **Golgotha,** or *Mt. Calvary* (Pl. 42, 43). The pavement of these chapels lies $14^1/_2$ ft. above the level of the Church of the Sepulchre. It is uncertain whether this corresponds to the Mt. Calvary enclosed in Constantine's basilica. In the 7th cent. a special chapel was erected over the holy spot, which, moreover, was afterwards alleged to be the scene of Abraham's trial of faith (pp. 38, 48). At the time of the Crusaders the place, notwithstanding its height, was taken into the aisle of the church. The chapels were enlarged in 1810.

We first enter the *Chapel of the Raising of the Cross* (Pl. 42), which belongs to the Greeks. It is $42^1/_2$ ft. long and $14^1/_2$ ft. wide, and is adorned with paintings and valuable mosaics. In the E. apse is shown an opening lined with silver, where the Cross is said to have been inserted in the rock: this was the 12th Station of the Cross (Via Dolorosa, comp. p. 51). The sites of the crosses of the thieves are shown in the corners of the altar-space, each 5 ft. distant from the Cross of Christ (doubtless much too near). They are first mentioned in the middle ages. The cross of the penitent thief was supposed to have stood to the S., that of the impenitent thief to the N. About $4^1/_2$ ft. to the S. of the Cross of Christ is the famous *Cleft in the Rock* (Matt. xxvii. 51), now covered with a brass slide and lined with slabs of red Jerusalem marble. When the slide is pushed aside, a cleft of about 10 inches in depth only is seen. A deeper chasm in rock of a different colour was formerly shown. The cleft is said to reach to the centre of the earth! Behind the chapel is the refectory of the Greeks.

The altar of the 'Stabat' between the two chapels (13th Station: the spot where Mary received the body of Christ on the descent from the Cross), and the adjoining chapel on the S., the *Chapel of the Nailing to the Cross* (Pl. 43), belong to the Latins. Christ is said to have been disrobed and nailed to the Cross here (10th and 11th Stations). The spots are indicated by pieces of marble let into the pavement, and an altar-painting represents the scene. Through a screen on the S. we look into the *Chapel of the Agony of the Virgin* (above Pl. 7), which belongs to the Latins. It is only 13 ft. long and $9^1/_2$ ft. wide, but is richly decorated. The altar-piece represents Christ on the knees of his mother. This chapel is at the top of the staircase outside the E. portal of the Church (p. 38).

The following points may also be mentioned. Beneath the Chapel f the Nailing to the Cross (Pl. 43) lies the office of the Greek Archimandrite, and towards the N., under the Chapel of the Raising of the Cross (Pl. 42), the *Chapel of Adam*, belonging to the Greeks. A tradition relates that Adam was buried here, that the blood of Christ flowed through the cleft in the rock on to his head, and that he was thus restored to life. Eastwards, and a little to the right of the altar, a small brass door covers a split in the rock which corresponds with the one in the chapel above. — Before reaching the W. door of the chapel, we observe, on the right and left, stone ledges on which originally (until 1808) were the monuments of *Godfrey of Bouillon* and *Baldwin I.* The bones of these kings had already been dispersed by the Kharezmians (p. lxxxv), and the Greeks removed the monuments also in order to put an end to the claims of the Latins to the spot.

During the Festival of Easter, the Church of the Sepulchre is crowded with pilgrims of every nationality, and is the scene of much disorder. On Palm Sunday, the Latins walk in procession, holding palm-branches brought from Gaza (p. 119), which are consecrated on Palm Sunday and distributed among the people. On Maundy Thursday they celebrate a grand mass and walk in procession round the chapel of the Sepulchre, after which the 'washing of feet' takes place at the door. The Franciscans celebrate Good Friday with a mystery play, and with the nailing of a figure to a cross. Late on Easter Eve a solemn service is performed; pilgrims with torches shout Hallelujah, while the priests move round the Sepulchre singing hymns. The festivals of the Greeks follow the old Julian calendar, which is 13 days behind ours. As their Easter also falls on the Sunday after the first full moon of spring, it may occur either before or after ours. One of their most curious ceremonies is the so-called Miracle of the Holy Fire, which strangers may witness from the galleries of the church. The wild and noisy scene begins on Good Friday. The crowd passes the night in the church in order to secure places. On Easter Eve a procession of the superior clergy moves round the Sepulchre, all lamps having been carefully extinguished in view of the crowd. Some of the priests enter the chapel of the Sepulchre, while others pray and the people are in the utmost suspense. At length, the fire which has come down from heaven is pushed through a window of the Sepulchre, and there now follows an indescribable tumult, everyone endeavouring to be the first to get his taper lighted. The sacred fire is carried home by the pilgrims. It is supposed to have the peculiarity of not burning human beings, and many of the faithful allow the flame to play upon their naked chests or other parts of their bodies. The Greeks declare the miracle to date from the apostolic age, and it is mentioned by the monk Bernhard as early as the 9th century. Caliph Ḥâkim (p. lxxxiii) was told that the priest used to besmear the wire by which the lamp was suspended over the sepulchre with resinous oil, and to set it on fire from the roof.

c. East and South Sides of the Church of the Holy Sepulchre.

The quadrangle in front of the Church of the Holy Sepulchre is bounded on the S.E. by the Greek *Monastery of Abraham* (p. 38; Pl. 19, E, 4, 5), with an interesting old cistern of great size, and on the S. by the ruined *Mosque of Sîdna 'Omar* (Pl. 37; E, 5), with a square minaret built in 1417, and by the small Greek *Monastery of Gethsemane* (Pl. 20; E, 5). The last two buildings are in the N.W. corner of the **Mûristân** (Pl. E, 5), a large open space covering an area of 170 yds. long and 151 yds. broad. Here stood in the middle ages the inns and hospitals of the Frankish pilgrims, in particular those of the *Knights of St. John.*

The earliest hospice for pilgrims was erected by Charlemagne. More important, however, were buildings erected by the merchants of Amalfi, who enjoyed commercial privileges in the East, including the churches of *Santa Maria Latina* (1030) and *Santa Maria Minor*. Adjoining the latter the Benedictines afterwards erected a hospital dedicated to St. John Eleëmon of Egypt. This hospice was at first dependent on the other, but

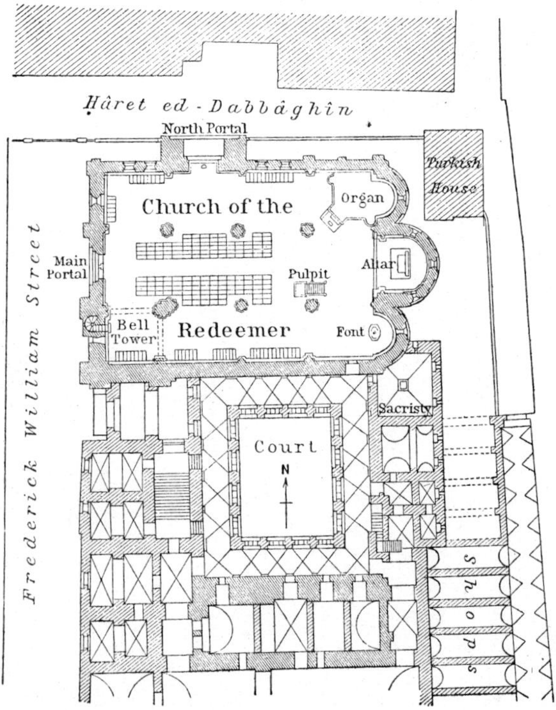

after the capture of Jerusalem by the Crusaders in 1099 it attained under its director Gerardus an independent importance. This new order of the *Hospitallers*, or *Knights of St. John*, distinguished by a black mantle with a white cross on the breast, soon assumed the character of an ecclesiastical order and selected John the Baptist as their patron instead of the Egyptian saint. Raymond de Puy, the commander of the order, caused several important buildings to be erected in 1130-40, but the Knights of St. John had to leave Jerusalem in 1187. *Saladin* (p. lxxxiv) granted the property of the Hospitallers as an endowment (wakf) to the Mosque of ʿOmar. In 1216 Shihâb ed-Dîn, nephew of Saladin, converted the hospital-church into a hospital, the Arabic-Persian name of which, *Mûristân*, was transferred to the whole plot of ground. The hospice, which the Moslems allowed to subsist, was still at the beginning of the 14th cent. capable of containing 1000 persons. At a later date the buildings were suffered to fall into decay. In 1869, on the occasion of the visit of the Crown Prince of Prussia, the Sultan presented the E. half of the Mûristân to Prussia.

The entrance to the Mûristân is in the lane Ḥâret ed-Dabbâghîn, running to the E. from the quadrangle in front of the Church of the Sepulchre (comp. the Plan opposite).

In the N.E. corner of the Mûristân, on the site of the old church of *Santa Maria Latina*, rises the German Protestant CHURCH OF THE REDEEMER (*Erlöserkirche;* Pl. E, 5), consecrated on Oct. 31st, 1898, in presence of Emperor William II. and the Empress Augusta Victoria (key kept by sacristan). It follows the lines of the ancient church as closely as possible. The foundations, which rest upon the solid rock, are in some places 46 ft. below the ground. The present *Main Portal* is on the W. side. Adjacent is the *Belfry*, which affords an extensive panorama. The old main portal, facing the Ḥâret ed-Dabbâghîn, is now the *North Portal* of the new church. The sculptures on the great arch of the door recall the occidental art of the 12th century.

Among these are representations of the months (much damaged). January, on the left, has disappeared; 'Feb', a man pruning a tree; 'Ma'; 'Aprilis', a sitting figure; 'Majus', a man kneeling and cultivating the ground; (Ju)'nius'; (Ju)'lius', a reaper; 'Augustus', a thresher; (S)'epten'(ber), a grape-gatherer; (Octob)'er', a man with a cask; (November), a woman standing upright. Above, between June and July, is the sun (with the superscription 'sol'), represented by a half-figure holding a disc over its head. Adjacent is the moon ('luna'), a female figure with a crescent. The cornice above these figures bears medallions representing leaves, griffins, etc.

On the S. the church is adjoined by the two-storied *Cloisters* of the former convent, surrounding a square court containing some fragments of marble columns (see p. 29). To the S. of this again is the old *Refectory* (entrance to the Cloisters and the Refectory by the church). On the W. side of the Cloisters, next the Crown Prince Frederick William Street, is the *Evangelical Hospice of the Mûristân*, with a flight of steps brought hither from a building of Saladin.

In the W. half of the Mûristân, belonging to the Greek Patriarchate, is the handsome *New Bazaar* (Pl. E, 5; comp. p. 34).

On the E. side the Mûristân is bounded by the old CHIEF BAZAAR of Jerusalem, consisting of three parallel streets (Pl. F, 5; *Sûḳ el-Laḥḥâmîn, Sûḳ el-'Aṭṭârîn, Sûḳ el-Khawâjât*), connected by transverse lanes and containing several khâns. — Opposite the N.E. corner of the Mûristân, next to the Greek Monastery of Abraham, lies the *Hospice of the Russian Palestine Society* (Pl. 1; E, F, 5), with an old gateway and remains of old walls, which belong to the Atrium of Constantine's Basilica (see next page).

We follow the N. continuation of the Bazaar St., along the E. side of the Russian hospice, but just short of the vaulted-over portion of it turn to the left, and ascend the steps by the Russian hospice. Above, in a small street which leads W. to the E. side of the Church of the Holy Sepulchre, on the right and just to the N. of the Russian hospice, is a new Coptic hospice. On its groundfloor may be seen the N. continuation of the Atrium of Constantine's Basilica (see p. 47), discovered in 1907. The threshold and side-posts of the old gateway are still extant. The road once passing through this gateway led direct to the Holy Sepulchre.

We continue to follow the small street farther to the W., until it ends at a column (9th station of the Via Dolorosa, p. 51) and three doors. Through the door to the left (45 on ground-plan at p. 36) we enter the court of the **Abyssinian Monastery** (Pl. 14; E, 4), in the middle of which rises the dome above the Chapel of St. Helena (p. 43). The court is surrounded by several miserable huts. Here also an olive-tree is shown, said to mark the spot where Abraham found the ram when about to sacrifice Isaac (comp. pp. 38, 44). In the background, to the S., a wall of the former refectory of the canons' residence becomes visible here. (Chapel, see p. 38.)

The door directly before us (46 on ground-plan at p. 36) leads to the **Monastery of the Copts** (Pl. 16, E 4; *Deir es-Sulṭân*, Monastery of the Sultan). It has been fitted up as an episcopal residence, and contains cells for the accommodation of pilgrims. The church, the foundations of which are old, has been entirely restored.

The third (r.; 47 on ground-plan at p. 36) of the three doors mentioned above leads to the *Cistern of St. Helena* (key with the porter of the Coptic Monastery; fee for one person 3 pi., for a party more in proportion). A winding staircase of 43 steps, some of which are in a bad condition, descends to the cistern; at the bottom is a handsome balustrade hewn in the rock. The water is bad and impure. The cistern perhaps dates from a still earlier period than that of Constantine.

d. From the Gate of St. Stephen to the Church of the Holy Sepulchre. Via Dolorosa.

The question of the direction of the *Via Dolorosa*, or *Street of Pain*, along which Jesus carried the Cross to Golgotha, depends upon the situation assigned to the *Praetorium*, or dwelling of Pilate. In the 4th cent. the supposed site of that edifice was shown near the Bâb el-Kaṭṭânîn (p. 53), and in the 6th cent. it was occupied by a Basilica of St. Sophia. By the early Crusaders it was instinctively felt that the Prætorium should be sought for on the W. hill, in the upper part of the town, and they erected there a church of St. Peter. At a later period, however, that holy place was transferred by tradition to the spot where it is now revered, and the so-called 'Holy Steps' ('Scala Santa') were removed to the church of San Giovanni in Laterano at Rome. The present Via Dolorosa is not expressly mentioned till the 16th century. From the reports of pilgrims it is evident that the sites of the fourteen Stations (see p. 49) were often changed.

The **Gate of St. Stephen** (*Bâb Sitti Maryam;* Pl. H, I, 3), situated on the E. side of the town, on the way to the Mt. of Olives (p. 73), is said to be that through which Stephen was taken out to be stoned (Acts vii. 58; see pp. 72, 74, 87). The name 'Gate of Our Lady Mary', as it is called by the native Christians, refers to the propinquity of the Tomb of the Virgin (p. 74). The present gate probably dates from the time of Solimân (p. 85). The passage through it, however, has been formed in a straight direction, whereas originally the gate was built at an angle with the thoroughfare. On each side, over the entrance, is a stone lion in relief. The gate-keepers show a footprint of Christ, preserved in the guard-house.

Within the gate, in the STREET OF THE GATE OF THE VIRGIN (*Ṭarîḳ Bâb Sitti Maryam;* Pl. G, H, 3), a doorway on the N. leads to the **Church of St. Anne** (Pl. H, 3), which is said to occupy the site of the house of Joachim and Anna, the parents of the Virgin Mary (comp. p. 244). It is first mentioned in the 7th cent., was afterwards connected with a nunnery, and was rebuilt about the middle of the 12th century. Saladin converted it into a richly-endowed school, and hence it is to this day known by the Moslems as *Eṣ-Ṣalâḥîyeh.* In 1856 it was presented by the Sultan to Napoleon III., and it is now in possession of the White Fathers (p. 20). The main entrance, on the W. side, consists of three pointed portals.

The interior is 120 ft. long and 66 ft. wide; the nave is 42 ft., the aisles 24 ft. high. The pointed vaulting rests upon two rows of pillars. Above the centre of the transept rises a tapering dome, which was probably restored by the Arabs. The apses are rounded inside and polygonal outside. A flight of 21 steps in the S.E. corner descends to a crypt, which is almost entirely hewn in the rock, and consists of two parts. This is said by tradition to have been the birthplace of the Virgin. The graves of SS. Joachim and Anne are also shown here (comp. p. 75). Traces of ancient paintings have been discovered in the crypt. A *Convent* and *Seminary* have been built on the land belonging to the church, and in the course of their construction an ancient rock-hewn pool was discovered, with chambers and traces of a mediæval church above it. The plan of Jerusalem in the Mâdebâ mosaic (p. 152) shows that as early as the 6th cent. the *Pool of Bethesda* was sought for here (comp. p. 68). — The small *Museum* of Biblical objects is interesting (adm. 50 c.).

We now proceed towards the W. along the Street of the Gate of the Virgin, and at the point where the street is vaulted over observe some ancient relics, traditionally said to be part of the *Castle of Antonia* (Pl. G, 3; p. 27). Farther on, to the right, is the Franciscan *Chapel of the Scourging* (Pl. G, 3), built in 1838. Below the altar is a hole in which the column of the scourging is said to have stood, but during the last few centuries the place of the scourging has been shown in many different parts of the city. Adjoining the Chapel of the Scourging are a new convent and church.

At this point begins the **Via Dolorosa,** the 14 Stations of which are indicated by tablets. The *First Station* is in the barracks (Pl. G, 3) which rise on the site of the Castle of Antonia (see above) and are now believed to occupy also the site of the Prætorium (comp. p. 48). The *Second Station*, below the steps ascending to the barracks, marks the spot where the Cross was laid upon Jesus.

At the imposing building of the *Sisters of Zion* (Pl. G, 3) the street is crossed by the so-called *Ecce Homo Arch*, marking the spot where, according to a 15th cent. tradition, Pilate uttered the words: 'Behold the man!' (John xix. 5). The arch is probably part of a

Roman triumphal arch; the N. side-arch now forms the choir of the *Church* of the Sisters of Zion. This church is partly built into the rock, and in the vaults beneath it we may trace the Roman pavement to the full breadth of the larger arch. Under the convent are several deep rocky passages and vaults leading towards the Ḥaram. — Opposite the church, on the S. side of the street, are a small mosque and a monastery of dervishes (Pl. 18; G, 4); the outer wall of the monastery contains a niche, said to be connected with the Virgin Mary. — Adjoining the buildings of the Sisters of Zion is a new Greek hospice. In the basement of this building may be traced the continuation of the above-mentioned Roman pavement. In the artificial rocky scarp, running from E. to W., are hewn various chambers, one of which is shown as the prison of Jesus, with the stocks in which he was exhibited to the multitude (comp. p. 42). Below the Roman pavement have been found remains of an earlier and rougher pavement.

We may now descend the street to the point where it is joined by that from the Damascus Gate (p. 85), and here we see a trace of the depression of what was once the Tyropœon valley (p. 31). To the right is the *Austrian Pilgrims' Hospice* (Pl. i, F 3; p. 19). On the left are the *Hospice of the United Armenians* (Pl. 15; F, 4) and their Church of Notre Dame du Spasme (ancient mosaic pavement). Close by is a broken column, forming the *Third Station*, near which Christ is said to have sunk under the weight of the Cross.

The Via Dolorosa now runs S. along the Street of the Damascus Gate, in which, to the right, is situated the traditional *House of the Poor Man* (Lazarus). Farther to the S. we see a mediæval house with a small bay window, projecting over the street and known since the 15th cent. as the *House of the Rich Man* (Dives). The house is built of stone of various colours. An inscription in a lane diverging to the left marks the *Fourth Station*, where Christ is said to have met his mother. At the next street coming from the right the Via Dolorosa again turns to the W., and now joins the *Ṭarîḳ el-Alâm* (*Ṭarîḳ es-Serâi;* Pl. F, 4), or route of suffering, properly so called. Here, at the corner, is the *Fifth Station*, where Simon of Cyrene took the Cross from Christ. A stone built into the next house to the left has a depression in it said to have been caused by the hand of Christ. We now ascend the street for about 100 paces, and, near an archway, come to the *Sixth Station*. To the left is the *House (and Tomb) of St. Veronica* (chapel of the United Greeks, recently restored; below is an ancient crypt). Veronica is said to have wiped off the sweat from the Saviour's brow at this spot, whereupon his visage remained imprinted on her handkerchief. (This handkerchief is shown as a sacred relic in several European churches.)

The last part of the street is vaulted. Where the street crosses the Khân ez-Zeit (Pl. F, 4) is the *Seventh Station*, called the *Porta Judiciaria*, through which Christ is said to have left the town, and

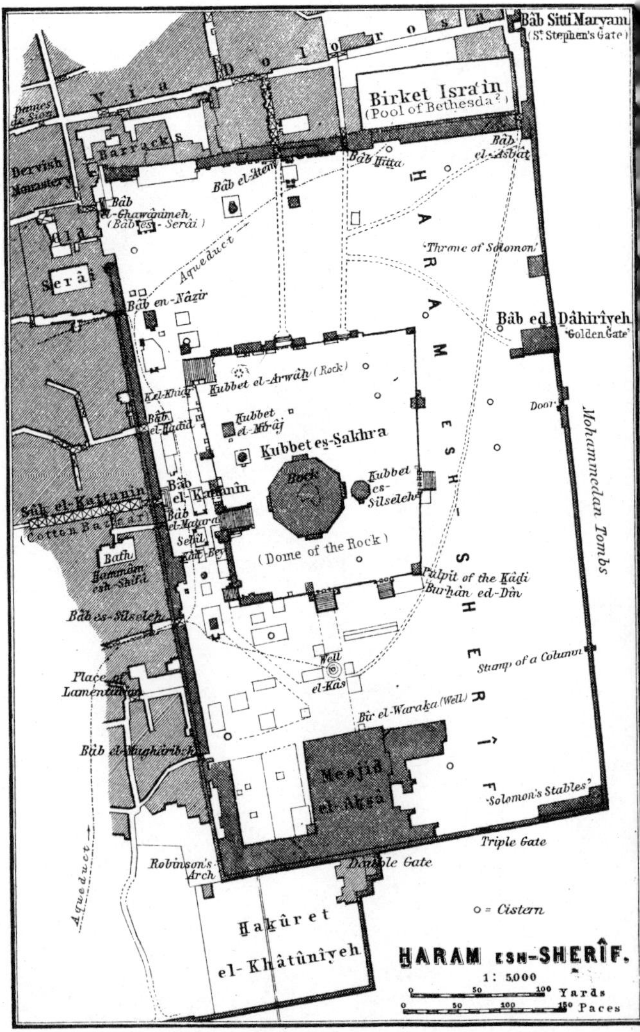
Bâb Sitti Maryam
(St. Stephen's Gate)
Via Dolorosa
Dames de Sion
Birket Isra'în
(Pool of Bethesda?)
Barracks
Dervish Monastery
Bâb el-Atem
Bâb Hitta
Bâb el-Asbât
Bâb el-Ghawânimeh
(Bâb es-Serâi)
Aqueduct
'Throne of Solomon'
Serâi
Bâb en-Nâzir
HARAM ESH-SHERÎF
Bâb ed Dâhirîyeh
'Golden Gate'
Kubbet el-Arwâh (Rock)
Kubbet el-Mi'râj
Kubbet es-Sakhra
Bâb el-Hadîd
Door
Mohammedan Tombs
Rock
Kubbet es-Silseleh
Bâb el-Kattanîn
Sûk el-Kattanîn
(Cotton Bazaar)
Bâb el-Matara
Sebîl
Kait-Bey
(Dome of the Rock)
Bath
Hammâm esh-Shifâ
Pulpit of the Kâdi Burhân ed-Dîn
Bâb es-Silseleh
Well
el-Kâs
Stump of a Column
Place of Lamentation
Bîr el-Waraka (Well)
Bâb el-Mughâribeh
Mesjid el-Aksâ
'Solomon's Stables'
Triple Gate
Robinson's Arch
Double Gate
○ = Cistern
Hakûret el-Khâtûnîyeh
HARAM ESH-SHERÎF.
1 : 5,000
0 50 100 Yards
0 50 100 150 Paces

where he fell a second time. Close by is a modern chapel containing an ancient column, said to be connected with the Gate of Justice. Passing the Prussian *Hospice of St. John* (Pl. g, F 4; p. 19), we observe about thirty paces farther on (l.) a black cross in the wall of the Greek monastery of *St. Caralombos* (Pl. 24; E, 4). This is the *Eighth Station*, where Christ is said to have addressed the women who accompanied him. — The Via Dolorosa proper ends here. The *Ninth Station* is in front of the Coptic monastery (p. 48), where Christ is said to have again sunk under the weight of the Cross. The next four stations are in the Golgotha chapels of the Church of the Sepulchre (p. 44). The *Fourteenth and Last Station* is by the Holy Sepulchre itself (p. 40).

e. The Ḥaram esh-Sherîf (Place of the Temple).

For a Visit to the Ḥaram esh-Sherîf the permission of the Turkish authorities and the escort of a soldier are necessary. Both these are obtained through the traveller's consul, and the kavass of the consulate also joins the party. Each member of a party pays 4-5 fr. to the kavass (a single visitor 8-10 fr.), who is then responsible for all expenses (fees, tips, etc.). — On Friday and during the time of the Nebi-Mûsâ festival (*i.e.* Easter Week) entrance is entirely prohibited to strangers.

Literature: *M. de Vogüé*, 'Le Temple de Jérusalem' (Paris, 1864; 100 fr.); *C. Schick*, 'Beit el-Makdas' (Jerusalem, 1887); 'Die Stiftshütte, der Tempel in Jerusalem und der Tempelplatz der Jetztzeit' (Berlin, 1896; 15 *M*); *Chipiez et Perrot*, 'Le Temple de Jérusalem' (Paris, 1889; 100 fr.); *R. Hartmann*, 'Der Felsendom in Jerusalem' (Strassburg, 1909; 4½ *M*); *W. Shaw Caldecott*, 'The Second Temple in Jerusalem' (London, 1909). — The large *Model of the Ḥaram esh-Sherîf* by Dr. Schick (at Mrs. Schoeneke's) is well worth seeing (p. 23).

The ancient site of the Temple, now called the **Ḥaram esh-Sherîf** (Pl. G-I, 4-6) or 'chief sanctuary', is the most interesting part of Jerusalem. It is occupied by numerous buildings and is surrounded by walls; on the N. and W. are a few houses, with open arcades below them. This area has been a place of religious sanctity from time immemorial. Here David erected an altar (2 Sam. xxiv. 25). This was also the site chosen by Solomon for the erection of his palace and the Temple, which, to judge from the formation of the ground, must have occupied pretty much the same site as the present 'Dome of the Rock' (comp. p. 31). The tenacity with which religious traditions have clung to special spots in the East, defying all the vicissitudes of creeds down to the present day, also confirms this view. The sacred rock probably bore the altar of burnt offerings (p. 56), while the Temple itself stood to the W. of it. *Solomon's Temple* consisted of the 'sanctuary' and the 'holy of holies', the latter to the W. of the former, and in the form of a cube. The porch of the sanctuary, to the right and left of which stood the two pillars of *Jachin* and *Boaz* (1 Kings vii. 21), opened on the court which contained the altar of burnt offerings, the 'molten sea' (a large basin), the 'bases', and the lavers (1 Kings vii. 27 et seq.). For many years after Solomon's death the work was continued by his successors. The *Second Temple*, which the Jews erected under very adverse circumstances after their return from exile, was far inferior in magnificence to its predecessor, and no trace of it now remains. All the more magnificent was the *Third Temple*, that of Herod. The erection of this edifice was begun in B.C. 20, but it was never completely carried out in the style originally projected. After the destruction of Herod's Temple in 70 A.D. Hadrian erected here a large temple of Jupiter, containing statues of that god and of himself (or of Castor and Pollux?). Coins of the period show that this building was adorned with twelve columns. The earliest pilgrims found the temple and the equestrian statue of the emperor still standing, near the 'Holy Rock' (p. 56). There is a great controversy as to what buildings were afterwards erected on this site. Mohammed, who asserted that he had visited the spot (comp. p. 57), professed great veneration for the ancient temple, and before he had finally broken off his relations with the Jews, he even commanded the faithful to turn towards Jerusalem when praying. The Caliph 'Omar found the spot covered with heaps of rubbish, which the Christians had thrown there in derision of the Jews. To this day the Ḥaram of Jerusalem is regarded by the Moslems as the holiest of all places after Mecca. The orthodox Jews never enter it, as they dread the possibility of committing the sin of treading on the 'Holy of Holies'. — The excavations of 1911, undertaken by some Englishmen at various points of the Place of the Temple in the hope of finding treasure, were fruitless.

We possess an account of the **Herodian Temple** by the Jewish writer *Flavius Josephus*, who accompanied Titus to Rome and there wrote a history of the Jewish war and his books on Jewish antiquities (Ant. xv. 11; Bell. Jud. i. 21; v. 5). To the Herodian period belong the imposing substructions on the S. side of the Ḥaram, in which direction the Temple platform was at that time much extended, and also the enclosing walls, which were constructed out of gigantic blocks of stone (p. 64). The entire area was surrounded by double rows of monolithic columns; on the S. side the colonnade was quadruple, and consisted of 162 columns. There were four gates on the W. side and two on the S. side. 'Solomon's Porch' (John x. 23) was probably on the E. side, but it is uncertain whether there was a gate here. In the middle lay the great Court of the Gentiles, which always presented a busy scene. A balustrade enclosed a second court, lying higher, where notices were placed prohibiting all but Israelites from entering this Inner Court. One of these notices in the Greek language was discovered among the supposed ruins of the Castle of Antonia in the street of the Gate of the Virgin (p. 49). The E. section of the forecourt of the Israelites was specially set apart for the women, while the adjoining higher portion, separated from it by a railing, was reserved for the men. Inside the latter and enclosed by another railing was the Court of the Priests, with the Temple proper and the great sacrificial altar of unhewn stones. A richly decorated corridor ascended thence by twelve steps to the Sanctuary, or 'holy place' strictly so called, which occupied the highest ground on the Temple area. The sanctuary was surrounded on three sides (S., W., N.) by a building 20 ells in height, containing 3 stories, the upper story rising to 10 ells beneath the top of the 'holy place', so that space remained for windows to light the interior of the sanctuary. Beyond the gate was the curtain or 'veil', within which stood the altar of incense, the table with the shew-bread, and the golden candlestick. In the background of the 'holy place' a door led into the small and dark Holy of Holies, a cube of 20 ells. The Temple was built of magnificent materials, and many parts of it were lavishly decorated with plates of gold. On the N. side two passages led from the colonnades of the Temple to the castle by which the sacred edifice was protected. It was thence that Titus witnessed the burning of the beautiful building in the year A.D. 70.

The Ḥaram is entered from the town by seven gates, *viz.* (beginning from the S.) the *Bâb el-Mughâribeh* (gate of the Moghrebins; p. 66), *Bâb es-Silseleh* (chain-gate; p. 65), *Bâb el-Mutawaḍḍâ*, or *Maṭara* (gate of ablution), *Bâb el-Ḳaṭṭânîn* (Pl. G, 4, 5; gate of the cotton-merchants), *Bâb el-Ḥadîd* (iron gate), *Bâb en-Nâẓir* (Pl. G, 4; custodian's gate), also called *Bâb el-Ḥabs* (prison gate), and lastly, towards the N., *Bâb es-Serâi* (gate of the seraglio), also called the *Bâb el-Ghawânimeh* (named after the family of Beni Ghânim). — The W. side of the Ḥaram is 536 yds., the E. 518 yds., the N. 351 yds., and the S. 309 yds. in length. The surface is not entirely level, the N.W. corner being about 10 ft. higher than the N.E. and the two S. corners. Scattered over the entire area are a number of *Masṭabas* (raised places) with *Miḥrâbs* (prayer-recesses; p. lxxv), and there are also numerous *Sebîls* (fountains) for the religious ablutions. It is planted with cypresses and other trees. — Visitors are usually conducted first through the Bâb el-Ḳaṭṭânîn (see above), and past the *Sebîl Ḳâït Bey* (p. 58) to the *Meḥkemet Dâûd* (p. 57).

The ***Dome of the Rock**, or **Kubbet eṣ-Ṣakhra**, formerly erroneously called by the Franks the Mosque of ʿOmar, is said by Arab historians to have been built by ʿAbd el-Melik. A Cufic inscription in the interior of the building mentions the year 72 of the Hegira (691 A.D.) as the date of its erection, but names as its builder ʿAbdallâh el-Imâm el-Mâmûn, who ruled 813-833 A.D. From this discrepancy, and from the different colour of this part of the inscription, we must assume that the name of el-Mâmûn was substituted at a later period for that of el-Melik. ʿAbd el-Melik was moved by political considerations to erect a sanctuary on this spot, as admission to the Kaaba in Mecca was at that time refused to the Omaiyades (p. lxxxii). Mâmûn probably restored the building, a supposition which receives confirmation from the inscription on the doors (p. 54). A second restoration took place in the year 301 of the Hegira (913 A.D.). The resemblance to Byzantine forms need not surprise us, as at that time the Arabs were practically dependent on Greek architects. — The Crusaders took the building for the oldest Temple of Solomon, and the Templars erected several churches in Europe on this model (at London, Laon, Metz, etc.). The polygonal outline of this shrine is even to be seen in the background of Raphael's celebrated 'Sposalizio' in the Brera at Milan.

The Dome of the Rock stands on an irregular platform 10 ft. in height, approached by three flights of steps from the W., two from the S., one from the E., and two from the N. side. The steps terminate in elegant arcades, called in Arabic *Mawâzîn*, or scales, because the scales at the Day of Judgment are to be suspended here. These arcades afford a good view of the entire Ḥaram. The building forms an octagon, each of the sides of which is 66 ft. 7 in. in length. The lower part of it is covered with marble slabs, while the part from the window-sills upward is covered with porcelain-tiles in the Persian style *(Kâshâni)*. This porcelain incrustation, which was added by Solimân the Magnificent in 1561, is very effective, the subdued blue contrasting beautifully with the white, and with the green and white squares on the edges. Passages from the Koran, beautifully inscribed in interwoven characters, run round the building like a frieze. In each of those sides of the octagon which are without doors are seven, and on each of the other sides are six windows with low pointed arches, the pair of windows nearest the angle being walled up in each case. The present form of the windows is not older than the 16th century; formerly seven lofty round-arched windows with a sill and smaller round-arched openings were visible externally on each side. A porch is supposed to have existed here formerly. Mosaics have also been discovered between the arcades.

The Gates, which face the four cardinal points of the compass, are square in form, each being surmounted with a vaulted arch. In front of each entrance there was originally an open, vaulted porch, borne by four columns. Subsequently the spaces between the columns were built up. The S. Portal, however, forms an exception, as there is here an open porch with eight engaged columns. The W. entrance is a modern structure of the beginning of the 19th century. The N. Portal is called *Bâb el-Jenneh*, or gate of paradise; the W., *Bâb el-Gharb*, or W. gate; the S., *Bâb el-Ḳibleh*, or S. gate; and the E., *Bâb Dâûd* or *Bâb es-Silseleh*, gate of David, or chain gate. On the lintels of the doors are inscriptions of the reign of Mâmûn, dating from the year 831, or 216 of the Hegira. The twofold doors dating from the time of Solimân, are of wood, covered with plates of bronze attached by means of elegantly wrought nails, and have artistically executed locks.

The Interior of the edifice is 58 yds. in diameter, and is divided into three concentric parts by two series of supports. The first series, by which the outer octagonal aisle is formed, consists of eight hexagonal piers and sixteen columns. The shafts of the columns are marble monoliths, and differ in form, height, and colour. They have all been taken from older edifices, probably from the temple of Jupiter mentioned at p. 52. The capitals are likewise of very various forms, dating either from the late-Romanesque or the early-Byzantine period, and one of them formerly bore a cross. To secure a uniform height of 20 ft., large Byzantine blocks which support small arches are placed above the capitals. These blocks or 'dosserets' are connected by so-called 'anchors', or broad beams consisting of iron bars with wooden beams beside and beneath them. These are covered beneath with copper-plates in repoussé. On the beams lie marble slabs, which project like a cornice on the side next the external wall, but are concealed by carving on that next the rotunda. Under the ends of the beams are placed foliated enrichments in bronze. While the pilasters are covered with slabs of marble, dating from the period of Solimân, the upper part of the wall is intersected by arches and adorned with mosaics. The rich and variegated designs of these mosaics consist of fantastic lines intertwined with striking boldness, and frequently of garlands of flowers, and are all beautifully and

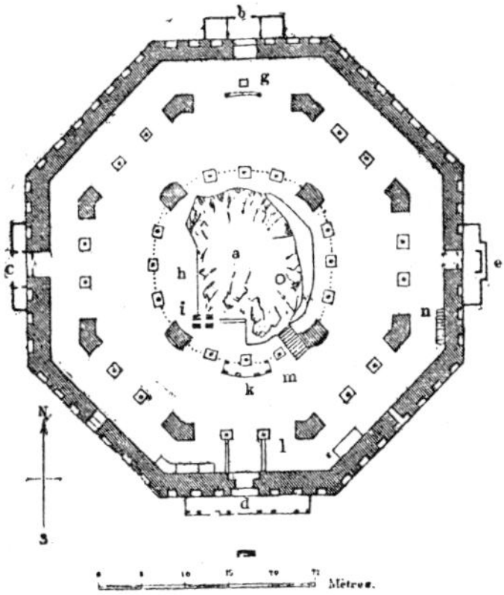

a. *Es-Ṣakhra* (the Sacred Rock).
b. *Bâb el-Jenneh* (Gate of Paradise).
c. *Bâb el-Gharb* (W. Gate).

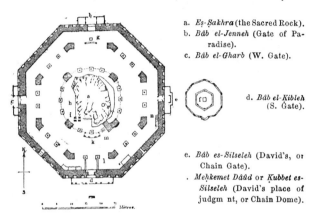

d. *Bâb el-Kibleh* (S. Gate).

e. *Bâb es-Silseleh* (David's, or Chain Gate).
. *Mehkemet Dâûd* or *Ḳubbet es-Silseleh* (David's place of judgm nt, or Chain Dome).

elaborately executed. Above them is a broad blue band, bearing very ancient Cufic inscriptions in gold letters. These are verses of the Koran bearing reference to Christ: —

Sûreh xvii. 111: Say—Praise be to God who has had no son or companion in his government, and who requires no helper to save him from dishonour; praise him. Sûreh lvii. 2: He governs heaven and earth, he makes alive and causes to die, for he is almighty. Sûreh iv. 169: O ye who have received written revelations, do not be puffed up with your religion, but speak the truth only of God. The Messiah Jesus is only the son of Mary, the ambassador of God, and his Word which he deposited in Mary. Believe then in God and his ambassador, and do not maintain there are three. If you refrain from this it will be better for you. God is One, and far be it from him that he should have had a son. To him belongs all that is in heaven and earth, and he is all-sufficient within himself. Sûreh xix. 34 et seq.: Jesus says — 'Blessings be on me on the day of my birth and of my death, and of my resurrection to life.' He is Jesus, the son of Mary, the word of truth, concerning whom some are in doubt. God is not so constituted that he could have a son; be that far from him. When he has resolved upon anything he says 'Let it be', and it is. God is my Lord and your Lord; pray then to him; that is the right way.

Here, too, is an inscription of great historical importance, which we have already mentioned at p. 53.

A second aisle is formed by a second series of supports arranged in a circle, on which also rests the dome. These supports consist of four massive piers and twelve monolithic columns. These columns also are antique; their bases were covered with marble in the 16th century. The arches above them rest immediately on the capitals. — The drum under the dome is richly adorned with mosaics on a gold ground, and its upper part contains 16 windows. The mosaics are by Byzantine artists of the 10-11th centuries. The flower-vases with grapes and ears of corn recall Christian representations in which these devices are used as emblems of the Last Supper.

The Dome erected by Ḥâkim in 1022, on the site of the original dome which had fallen in six years previously, consists of two wooden vaults placed one inside the other. The innermost of these, 37½ ft. high and 66 ft. in diameter, is in the form of a stilted hemisphere, while the outer hemisphere, 98 ft. high, is somewhat flattened. A flight of steps ascends between the two vaults, and at the top is a trap-door giving access to the crescent, which is 16 ft. higher. The stucco incrustation of the inner dome, with its rich painting upon a blue ground, was restored by Saladin in 1189, and its colouring was revived in 1318 and 1830.

The window-openings are closed with thick slabs of plaster perforated with holes and slits of various shapes, wider inside than outside. These perforations have been glazed on the outside with small coloured glass plates, forming a variety of designs. When the doors are closed, the effect of the colours is one of marvellous richness, but the windows shed a dim light only on the interior, and the darkness is increased, firstly by regular glass windows framed in cement, secondly by a wire lattice, and lastly by a porcelain grating placed over them outside to protect them from rain. The lower windows bear the name of Solimân and the date 935 (*i.e.* 1528). Saladin caused the walls to be covered with marble, and they were restored by Solimân. — The pavement consists of marble mosaic and marble flagging.

The wrought-iron screen connecting the columns of the inner row is a French work of the end of the 12th cent., when the Crusaders converted the mosque into a 'Templum Domini' and fitted it up for the Christian form of worship. The *Holy Rock* (Pl. a) is surrounded by a coloured wooden screen. The best view of it is obtained from the high bench by the N.W. gate of the screen. The Rock is 58 ft. long and 44 ft. wide, and rises about 4-6½ ft. above the surrounding pavement. It may have been the site of the great altar of burnt-offering (p. 51), and traces of a channel for carrying off the blood have been discovered in the rock. The Ark of the Covenant cannot have stood here, as the 'holy of holies' was altogether too small to contain a rock of this size. There is a hollow under the rock (Pl. m) to which 11 steps descend on the S. side, and no doubt excavations, if permitted, would show that this was a cistern. The round slab of stone in the middle rings hollow. The Crusaders erected an altar on the rock and made it accessible by steps of which traces are still visible. A fragment is also visible of the two walls with which they enclosed the choir.

According to the Talmud, the Holy Rock covers the mouth of an abyss in which the waters of the Flood are heard roaring. Abraham and Melchizedek sacrificed here, Abraham was on the point of slaying Isaac here, and the rock is said to have been anointed by Jacob. It was regarded as the centre of the world, and as the 'stone of foundation' (*eben shatyâ*), that is, the spot upon which the Ark of the Covenant stood. On the destruction of Jerusalem, Jeremiah is said to have concealed the Ark beneath the rock (but according to 2 Macc. ii. 5 in a cave in Mount Nebo), and, according to Jewish tradition, it still lies buried there. Jesus is said to have discovered the great and unspeakable name of God (*shem*) written upon the rock, and was enabled to work his miracles by reading it. The Moslems carried these traditions further. According to them the stone hovers over the abyss without support. In the hollow below it small benches are shown as the places where David, Solomon, Abraham (left), and Elijah were in the habit of praying. The Moslems maintain that beneath this rock is the *Bîr el-Arwâḥ*, or well of souls, where the souls of the deceased assemble to pray twice weekly. Some say that the rock rests upon a palm watered by a river of paradise; others assert that it is the gate of hell. Mohammed declared that one prayer here was better than a thousand elsewhere. He himself prayed here, to the right of the holy rock, and from hence he was translated to heaven on the back of El-Burâḳ, his miraculous steed. In the ceiling is shown an impression of his head; and on the W. side is shown the mark of the hand of the angel (Pl. h) who restrained the rock in its attempt to follow the prophet to heaven. The rock is said to have spoken on this occasion, as it did afterwards when it greeted ʿOmar, and it therefore has a 'tongue', over the entrance to the cavern. At the last day the Kaaba of Mecca will come to the Ṣakhra, for here will resound the blast of the trumpet which will announce the judgment. God's throne will then be planted upon the rock.

A number of other marvels are shown in the Dome of the Rock. In front of the N. entrance there is let into the ground a slab of jasper (*Balâṭat el-Jenneh*, Pl. g), said to have been the cover of Solomon's tomb, into which Mohammed drove nineteen golden nails; a nail falls out at the end of every epoch, and when all are gone the end of the world will arrive. One day the devil succeeded in destroying all but three and a half, but was fortunately detected and stopped by the angel Gabriel. — In the S.W. corner (Pl. i), under a small gilded tower, is shown the footprint of the prophet, which in the middle ages was said to be that of Christ. Hairs from Mohammed's beard are also preserved here, and on the S. side are shown the banners of Mohammed and ʿOmar. — By the prayer-niche (Pl. l) adjoining the S. door are placed several Korans of great age, but the custodian is much displeased if they are touched by visitors.

Outside the E. door of the mosque, the *Bâb es-Silseleh*, or *Door of the Chain* (which must not be confounded with the entrance-gate of the same name, p. 53), rises the elegant little *Ḳubbet es-Silseleh*, or 'dome of the chain', also called *Meḥkemet Dâûd* (Pl. f), David's place of judgment. The creation and decoration of this building seem to belong to the same period as those of the Dome of the Rock. According to Moslem tradition, a chain was once stretched across this entrance by Solomon, or by God himself. A truthful witness could grasp it without producing any effect, whereas a link fell off if a perjurer attempted to do so. This structure consists of two concentric rows of columns, the outer forming a hexagon, the inner an endecagon. This remarkable construction enables all the pillars to be seen at one time. These columns also have been taken from older buildings and are chiefly in the Byzantine style. The pavement is covered with beautiful mosaic, and on the S. side (facing Mecca) there is a large recess for prayer. Above the slightly sloping flat roof rises a hexagonal drum surmounted by the dome, which is slightly curved outwards. The top is adorned with a crescent.

About 20 yds. to the N.W. of the Ṣakhra rises the *Ḳubbet el-Miʿrâj*, or Dome of the Ascension, erected to commemorate Mohammed's miraculous nocturnal journey from Mecca to Jerusalem (p. 59). According to the inscription, the structure was rebuilt in the year 597 of the Hegira (*i.e.* 1200). It is interesting to observe the marked Gothic character of the windows, with their recessed and pointed arches borne by columns. Close by is an ancient font, now used as a water-trough. Farther towards the N.W. is the *Ḳubbet en-Nebi* (dome of the prophet), a modern-looking building over a subterranean mosque built in the rock. This mosque is not shown to visitors. There is also a very small building called the *Ḳubbet el-Arwâḥ* (dome of the spirits), which is interesting from the fact that the bare rock is visible below it. Beside the flight of steps on the N.W., leading down from the terrace, is the *Ḳubbet el-Khiḍr* (St. George's Dome). Here Solomon is said to have tormented the demons.

More to the S. we observe below, between us and the houses encircling the Ḥaram, an elegant fountain-structure, called the *Sebîl Ḳâït Bey*, which was erected by the Mameluke sultan Melik el-Ashraf Abu'n-Naṣer Ḳâït-Bey (1468-96). Above a small cube, the corners of which are adorned with pillars, rises a cornice and above this an octagonal drum with sixteen facets; over this again a dome of stone, the outside of which is entirely covered with arabesques in relief.

At the S.E. angle of the terrace is a pulpit in marble, called the 'summer pulpit' or *Pulpit of Ḳâḍi Burhân ed-Dîn* from its builder (d. 1456). A sermon is preached here every Friday during the fast of the month Ramaḍân (p. lxxi). The horseshoe arches supporting the pulpit, and the slender columns, above which rise arches of trefoil form, present a good example of Arabian art.

The other buildings on the terrace are unimportant, consisting of Koran schools and dwellings. Objects of greater interest are the cisterns with which the rock is deeply honeycombed, especially to the S.W. of the Dome of the Rock. Numerous holes through which the water was drawn are visible on the surface.

Passing the pulpit, and descending a flight of twenty-one steps towards the S., we soon reach a large round basin *(El-Kâs)*, probably once fed by a conduit from the pools of Solomon (p. 108). To the E. of this, in front of the Aḳṣâ, there is a cistern hewn in the rocks known as the *Sea*, or the *King's Cistern*, which was also supplied from Solomon's pools. This reservoir is mentioned by Tacitus. It was probably constructed before Herod's time. It is upwards of 40 ft. in depth, and 246 yds. in circumference. A staircase hewn in the rock descends to these remarkably spacious vaults, which are supported by pillars of rock. Below the N.E. corner of the Aḳṣâ mosque is another large cistern called the *Bîr el-Waraḳa*, or leaf fountain. A companion of ʿOmar, having once let his pitcher fall into this cistern, descended to recover it, and discovered a gate which led into an orchard. He there plucked a leaf, placed it behind his ear, and showed it to his friends after he had quitted the cistern. The leaf came from paradise and never faded. The orifice of the cistern is in the Aḳṣâ Mosque, to the left of the entrance (Pl. 8, p. 60).

The ***Aḳṣâ Mosque** *(Mesjid el-Aḳṣâ)*, the 'most distant' shrine (*i.e.* from Mecca), to which God brought the prophet Moḥammed from Mecca in one night (Sûreh xvii. 1), is said to be an ancient holy place of Proto-Islam, and to have been founded only forty years after the foundation of the Kaaba by Abraham. The probability, however, is that it was originally a basilica erected by the Emperor Justinian in honour of the Virgin Mary. Procopius, who has described the buildings of Justinian, states that artificial substructions were necessary in this case. The nave, in particular, rests on subterranean vaults. The building was of so great width that it was difficult to find beams long enough for the roof. The ceiling was borne by two rows of columns, one above the other. ʿOmar converted the church into a mosque. ʿAbd el-Melik (p. 53) caused the doors of the Aḳṣâ to be overlaid with gold and silver plates. During the caliphate of Abu Jaʿfar el-Manṣûr (758-775) the E. and W. sides were damaged by an earthquake, and in order to obtain money to repair the mosque the precious metals with which it was adorned were converted into coin. El-Mahdi (775-785), finding the mosque again in ruins in consequence of another earthquake, caused it to be rebuilt in an altered form, its length being now reduced, but its width increased. In 1060 the roof fell in, but was speedily repaired. With the exception of a few capitals and columns, there is little left of Justinian's building, but the ground-plan of the basilica has been maintained. The mosque is 88 yds. long and 60 yds. wide, not reckoning the annexes. Its principal axis rests perpendicularly on the S. enclosing wall of the Ḥaram.

The Porch (Pl. 1, p. 60), consisting of seven arcades, was erected by Melik el-Muʿaẓẓam ʿIsâ (d. 1227), and was restored at a later period; the roof is not older than the 15th century. The central arcades show an attempt to imitate the Gothic style of the Franks, but the columns, capitals, and bases do not harmonize, as they are taken from ancient buildings of different styles.

The Interior, with its nave and triple aisles, presents a striking appearance. The original plan has single aisles only, the E. aisle, as in the case of the mosque of the Omaiyades at Damascus (p. 316), being adjoined by the court of the mosque. The great transept with the dome, which perhaps belongs to the restoration of El-Mahdi, gave the edifice a cruciform shape. This, however, was afterwards obliterated by the two rows of lower aisles added on the E. and W. In their present form, however, the outer aisles belong to a later restoration. The piers are of a clumsy square form, and the vaulting is pointed.

The *Nave* and its two immediately adjoining aisles are less elegant than the outer aisles, but show greater originality. The columns of the nave were taken from the church of Justinian, but have been shortened, and therefore look somewhat clumsy. The capitals, some

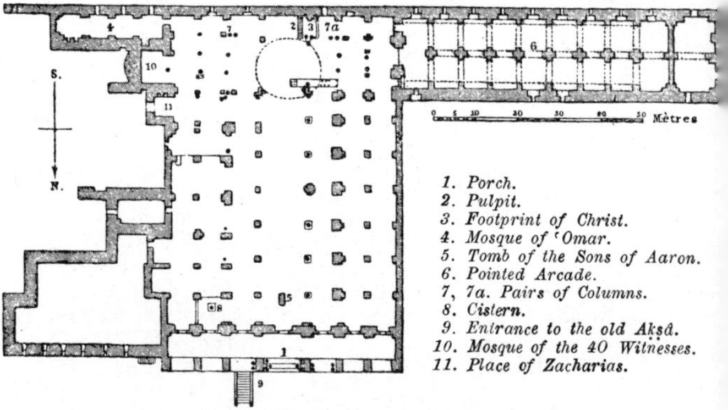

of which still show the form of the acanthus leaf, perhaps date from the 7th century. The wide arches above them are of later date, and here again we find the wooden 'anchor', or connecting beam between the arches, which is peculiar to the Arabs. Above the arches is a double row of windows, the higher of which look into the open air, the lower into the aisles. The nave has a lofty timber roof, rising high above all the others. The two immediately adjoining aisles have similar roofs, the gables of which, curiously enough, are at right angles to the main axis of the building. The outer aisles are covered with groined vaulting under flat terrace-roofs.

The *Transept* is also constructed of old materials, and according to an inscription was restored by Saladin in 583 (1187). The columns are antique and vary in form and material and even in height. The fine mosaics on a gold ground in the drum of the dome date from Saladin's restoration, and are said to have been brought from Constantinople. To the same period belongs the prayer-niche on the S. side, flanked with its small and graceful marble columns. The coloured band which runs round the wall of this part of the mosque, about 6 ft. from the ground, consists of foliage, in Arabian style.

The Cufic inscriptions are texts from the Koran. — The Dome is constructed of wood, and covered with lead on the outside; within, it is decorated in the same style as the dome of the Ṣakhra. An inscription records the name of the Mameluke sultan Moḥammed Ibn Kilâûn as the donor or restorer of these decorations in 728 (1327). — On the W. the transept is adjoined by the so-called '*White Mosque*' (Pl. 6), designed for the use of women. This consists of a long double colonnade with pointed vaulting, and was erected by the Knights Templar, who resided here. The Templars called the Aḳṣâ the *Porticus*, *Palatium*, or *Templum Salomonis*.

Among the chief features of the interior are the following. In the floor of the nave, not far from the entrance, is the *Tomb of the Sons of Aaron* (Pl. 5), covered with mats. The *Stained Glass Windows* date like those of the Dome of the Rock from the 16th cent., but are not so fine. The wretched paintings on the large arch of the transept were executed in the 19th century. — Adjoining the prayer-niche we observe a *Pulpit* (Pl. 2) beautifully carved in wood and inlaid with ivory and mother-of-pearl. It was executed in 564 (1168) by an artist of Aleppo by order of Nûreddîn. On the stone behind this pulpit is shown the *Footprint of Christ* (Pl. 3), which appears to have been seen by Antonio of Piacenza, one of the earliest pilgrims. On each side of the pulpit we observe a pair of columns close together (Pl. 7 and 7a), now connected by iron screens. Of these, a legend, also occurring elsewhere, asserts that no one can enter heaven if he cannot pass between them. — The graves of the murderers of St. Thomas of Canterbury (Thomas Becket), dating from the original Christian church (p. 59), are still pointed out near the main entrance.

The *Mosque of 'Omar* is said to have stood on the site of the S.E. annex (Pl. 4). The so-called *Mosque of the Forty Witnesses* (Pl. 10) is the apse of an earlier Christian church. To the N. of this (Pl. 11) is the place where Zacharias is said to have been slain (p. 82). There is a handsome rose-window here dating from the time of the Crusaders.

The S. side of the Ḥaram rests almost entirely upon massive vaulted **Substructions**, dating in their original form from a very early period, though the present walls belong to later restorations. A flight of 18 steps, to the E. of the entrance of the Aḳṣâ mosque, descends to the central portion of these substructions. The vaults are borne by rectangular piers; the middle row of these stands under the E. side of the nave of the mosque, and so may possibly have been erected when the mosque was enlarged towards the E. Towards the S. end is a chamber at a somewhat lower level, the four flat arches of which rest in the centre against a short and thick column, with a Byzantine capital. This formed the vestibule of the old *Double Gate* to the S., which is constructed of large blocks of stone belonging to the Jewish period, and is now walled up. The lintels of the gate are still in position, but the E. one is broken and supported by columns added at a later period. This double gate is supposed to be the '*Huldah Portal*' of the Talmud, and we may therefore assume that Christ frequently entered the Temple from this point, particularly on the occasion of solemn processions, which advanced from the Well Gate of the Pool of Siloam (p. 83) to the doors of the Temple. It is now a Moslem place of prayer, and is therefore covered with straw matting.

The vaults under the S.W. corner of the Ḥaram are inaccessible, but we may proceed through a children's school to Barclay's Gate (p. 66).

The entrance to the South Eastern Substructions is in the S.E. corner of the Ḥaram area. A staircase descends to a small Moslem *Oratory*, where a horizontal niche, surmounted by a a dome borne by 4 small columns, is pointed out as the '*Cradle of Christ*'. The mediæval tradition that this was the dwelling of the aged Simeon, and that the Virgin spent a few days here after the Presentation in the Temple, seems to rest on the fact that in ancient days the Hebrew women used to resort to this building to await their confinement, a custom also commemorated in the 'Basilika Theotokos' (of the Mother of God), which stood here in pre-Islamic times.

From this point we descend into the spacious substructions, known as '*Solomon's Stables*', which were probably erected in the Arabian period on the site of some earlier substructions. The drafted stones of the piers are ancient. Many Jews sought refuge in these substructions on the capture of Jerusalem by the Romans. At the time of the Crusades they served as stables for the horses of the Frankish kings and the Templars, and on the angles of the piers may be seen the holes to which the horses were tethered. There are in all 13 galleries, the vaulting of which is borne by 88 piers arranged in 12 parallel rows. They extend 91 yds. from E. to W. and 66 yds. from S. to N. Towards the N. they extend beyond the limits of the Aḳṣâ mosque, but this part of them has not yet been carefully investigated. In the sixth gallery, counting from the E., there is a small closed door in the S. wall called the '*Single Gate*', where the 'Cradle of David' used to be pointed out. A door at the end of the 13th gallery opens to the W. upon another triple series of substructions, 53 ft. in width by 23 ft. in height. The series terminates on the S. by a *Triple Gate* (blocked up), resembling the Double Gate (p. 61). The foundations only are preserved (exterior, see p. 67); the arches are almost elliptical in shape. Fragments of columns are built into the walls here, and an entire column is visible about 20 yds. from the gate. Farther on, about 132 yds. from the S. wall, the style in which the gallery is built, especially in the upper parts, becomes more modern.

Under both the Triple Gate and the Single Gate there are various passages hewn in the rock and several water-courses, but these have not yet been efficiently investigated.

We now again ascend to the plateau of the Ḥaram, and proceed to investigate the **Enclosing Wall** (interior side). The upper parts of the East Wall are entirely modern. The top, which is reached by a flight of steps, affords an admirable view of the valley of the Kidron (Valley of Jehoshaphat) with its tombs immediately below, and of the Mt. of Olives. We find here the stump of a column built in horizontally and protruding beyond the wall on both sides. A small building (a place of prayer) has been erected over the inner end.

A Mohammedan tradition, also accepted by the Jews, asserts that all men will assemble at the Last Judgment in the valley of Jehoshaphat (p. 80), when the hills on both sides will recede. From this prostrate column a thin wire-rope will then be stretched to the opposite Mt. of Olives. Christ will sit on the wall, and Mohammed on the mount, as judges. All men must pass over the intervening space on the rope. The righteous, preserved by their angels from falling, will cross with lightning speed, while the wicked will be precipitated into the abyss of hell. The idea of a bridge of this kind occurs in the ancient Persian religion.

A little farther on we reach the **Golden Gate**, which the Arabs call *Bâb eḍ-Ḍâhirîyeh*, the N. arch being known as the *Bâb et-Tôbeh*, or gate of repentance, and the S. arch the *Bâb er-Raḥmeh*, or gate of mercy. It resembles the double gate mentioned at p. 61, and probably stood on the site of the 'Shushan' gate of the Herodian Temple. The name rests upon a misunderstanding. The 'Beautiful Gate' (θύρα ὡραία), mentioned in the Acts of the Apostles (iii. 2), mistranslated in Latin as the 'porta aurea', was certainly in the inner forecourt of the Temple. Antonius Martyr still distinguishes between the 'portes précieuses' and the Golden Gate. The gate in its present form dates from the 7th century after Christ. In 810 the Arabs built it up entirely with the exception of one small opening. The monolithic door-posts to the E., said to have been presented by the Queen of Sheba to Solomon, have been converted into pillars, which now rise 6 ft. above the top of the wall (on the outside; see p. 67). The arched vaulting is borne by a large central pillar, with pilasters on each side of it (not visible from without). The whole structure was restored in 1892. The roof affords an excellent survey of the whole of the Temple plateau.

The interior consists of a large arcade with six flat vaults, which rest on two columns in the middle. The elaborate architectonic decoration belongs to a late Byzantine period. — In 629 Heraclius entered the Temple by this gate. At the time of the Crusades the gate used to be opened for a few hours on Palm Sunday and on the festival of the Raising of the Cross. On Palm Sunday the great procession with palm-branches entered by this gate from the Mt. of Olives. The patriarch rode on an ass, while the people spread their garments in the way, as had been done on the entry of Christ. Among the Moslems there still exists a tradition that on a Friday some Christian conqueror will enter by this gate. According to Ezekiel (xliv. 1, 2), the gate on the E. side of the Temple precincts was kept closed from a very early period.

The modern mosque to the N. of the Golden Gate is known as the *Throne of Solomon*, from the legend that Solomon was found dead here. In order to conceal his death from the demons, he supported himself on his seat with his staff, and it was not till the worms had gnawed the staff through and caused the body to fall that the demons became aware that they were released from the king's authority. Here we observe many shreds of rags suspended from the window-gratings by pilgrims (p. lxxv). The subterranean chambers under the mosque and farther on (inaccessible) appear to have been built in Herodian times to make the surface level. — At the N.E. corner of the Ḥaram are preserved the ruins of a massive old tower. The gate here is called the *Bâb el-Asbâṭ*, or gate of the tribes.

We now skirt the North Wall. From the windows under the arcades, we see, far below us, the Birket Isra'în (p. 68). To the left are several places of prayer. We soon reach the next gate on the right, called the *Bâb Ḥiṭṭa*, or *Bâb Ḥoṭṭa*, following which is the *Bâb el-ʿAtem*, or gate of darkness, also named *Sheref el-Anbiyâ* (honour of the prophets), or *Gate of Devadâr*. This, perhaps, answers to the *Tôdi* gate of the Talmud. To the left is a fountain fed by Solomon's pools; near it to the W. are two small mosques, the W. one of which is called *Ḳubbet Sheḳîf eṣ-Ṣakhra*, from the piece of rock which, it is said, Nebuchadnezzar broke off from the Ṣakhra and the Jews brought back again. At the N.W. angle of the Temple area the ground consists of rock, in which has been formed a perpendicular cutting 23 ft. in depth, and above this rises the wall. The foundations of this wall appear to be ancient, and they may possibly have belonged to the fortress of Antonia (p. 27). There are now barracks here (p. 49). At the N.W. corner rises the highest minaret of the Ḥaram.

Having examined the whole of the interior of these spacious precincts, we now proceed to take a walk round the **Outside of the Wall,** which will enable us better to realize the character of the substructions. The different periods of building are easily distinguishable. At a depth of 35-55 ft. below the present surface, and at a still greater depth, are layers of blocks with rough unhewn exterior, fitted to each other without the aid of mortar (comp. p. xcvi). These, like the courses of drafted blocks with smooth exterior, probably belong to the Herodian period. The courses of smoothly hewn but undrafted blocks may be ascribed to the time of Justinian. The ordinary masonry of irregularly shaped stones is modern. The wall is not perpendicular, but batters from the base, each course lying a little within that below it. On the N.W. side of the temple area (but difficult of access) the exterior of the wall shows remains of buttresses (like the temple wall in Hebron, p. 115).

We leave the Ḥaram by the second gate on the N.W. side (*Bâb en-Nâẓir;* Pl. G, 4), and follow the lane in a straight direction which leads between the *Old Serâi* (at present a state-prison, Pl. G, 4), on the right, and the *Cavalry Barracks* (Pl. G, 4), on the left, to the transverse street called *El-Wâd* (Pl. F, G, 4, 5), which comes from the Damascus Gate. At the corner to the right is a handsome fountain. We turn to the S. into this cross-street, leaving on the right the present *Serâi* (Pl. F, 4), on the site of the former Hospital of St. Helena; on the left we pass a lane which leads to the Ḥaram. We thus arrive at the covered-in *Sûḳ el-Ḳaṭṭânîn* (Pl. G, 5) or cotton-merchants' bazaar, now deserted.

About halfway through the bazaar to the right, is the entrance to the **Ḥammâm esh-Shifâ** (Pl. G, 5), an old and still used healing-bath, which has been supposed to be the Pool of Bethesda (comp. p. 68). A stair ascends 34 ft. to the mouth of the cistern, over which stands a small tower. The shaft is here about 100 ft. in depth (*i.e.* about 66 ft. below the surface of the earth). The basin is almost entirely enclosed by masonry; at the

S. end of its W. wall runs a channel built of masonry, 100 ft. long, 3½ ft. high, and 3 ft. in width, first to the S., then to the S.W. The water is bad, being rain-water which has percolated through impure earth.

The El-Wâd street ends on the S. at the David Street (*Ṭarîḳ Bâb es-Silseleh;* Pl. F, G, 5; comp. p. 34), which runs from W. to E. on a kind of embankment formed of subterranean arches. In Jewish times a street led over the deep valley here (the *Tyropoeon*, p. 31) to the upper city; one of the large arches on which it rests is named '*Wilson's Arch*' after the late director of the English survey. This well-preserved arch is 22 ft. in height and has a span of 49 ft. Below it is the *Burâḳ Pool*, named after the winged steed of Mohammed, which the prophet is said to have tied up here. Whilst making excavations under the S. end of Wilson's Arch, Sir Charles Warren discovered a water-course at a depth of 44 ft. (a proof that water still trickles through what was formerly a valley), and at length, at a depth of about 50 ft., he found the wall of the Temple built into the rock. We follow the David Street to the E. towards the Ḥaram. To the left is a handsome fountain; to the right is the so-called '*Meḥkemeh*' or *Court House* ('House of Judgment' on Plan), a cruciform arcade with pointed vaulting, which was built in 1483. At the S. end is a prayer-recess, and in the centre is a fountain, fed by the water-conduit of Bethlehem. — The David Street ends at the *Bâb es-Silseleh*, or Gate of the Chain (Pl. G, 5; p. 53); near it are a basin which resembles a font, and a new well of the conduit (restored in 1901), which runs under the gate (p. 24).

We now return along the David St. towards the W., taking the first narrow *Transverse Lane* leading to the left (S.) between two handsome old houses. That on the right, with the stalactite portal, was a boys' school at the period of the Crusades; that to the left, called *El-'Ajemîyeh*, was a girls' school, but has been used as a boys' school since the time of Saladin. Descending this lane for 4 min. and keeping to the left, we reach the ***Wailing Place of the Jews** (*Kauthal Ma'arbê;* Pl. G, 5), situated beyond the miserable dwellings of the Moghrebins (Moslems from the N.W. of Africa). The celebrated wall which bears this name is 52 yds. in length and 59 ft. in height. The nine lowest courses of stone consist of huge blocks, only some of which, however, are drafted; among these is one (on the N.) 16½ ft. long and 13 ft. wide. Above these are fifteen courses of smaller stones. It is probable that the Jews as early as the middle ages were in the habit of repairing hither to bewail the downfall of Jerusalem. A touching scene is presented by the figures leaning against the weather-beaten wall, kissing the stones, and weeping. The men often sit here for hours, reading their well-thumbed Hebrew prayer-books. The Spanish Jews, whose appearance and bearing are often refined and independent, present a pleasing contrast to their brethren of Poland. The Wailing Place is most frequented on Friday after 4 p.m.

On Friday, towards evening, the following litany is chanted: —

Leader: *For the palace that lies desolate:* — Response: *We sit in solitude and mourn.*

L. *For the temple that is destroyed:* — R. *We sit*, etc.
L. *For the walls that are overthrown:* — R. *We sit*, etc.
L. *For our majesty that is departed:* — R. *We sit*, etc.
L. *For our great men who lie dead:* — R. *We sit*, etc.
L. *For the precious stones that are burned:* — R. *We sit*, etc.
L. *For the priests who have stumbled:* — R. *We sit*, etc.
L. *For our kings who have despised Him:* — R. *We sit*, etc.

Another antiphony is as follows: —

Leader: *We pray Thee, have mercy on Zion!* — Response: *Gather the children of Jerusalem.*

L. *Haste, haste, Redeemer of Zion!* — R. *Speak to the heart of Jerusalem.*

L. *May beauty and majesty surround Zion!* — R. *Ah! turn Thyself mercifully to Jerusalem.*

L. *May the kingdom soon return to Zion!* — R. *Comfort those who mourn over Jerusalem.*

L. *May peace and joy abide with Zion!* — R. *And the branch (of Jesse) spring up at Jerusalem.*

To the S. of the Wailing Place is an ancient gate, called the *Gate of the Prophet* or (after the discoverer) *Barclay's Gate.* The fanaticism of the Moghrebins prevents travellers from seeing this unless accompanied by a guide who knows the people. (For the approach from the interior of the Ḥaram, see p. 62.) The upper part of it consists of a huge, carefully hewn block, $6^1/_2$ ft. thick and over 19 ft. long, now situated 10 ft. above the present level of the ground. The threshold lies 48 ft. below the present surface, and a path cut in steps has been discovered in the course of excavations.

In the S. part of the Moghrebin quarter is a large open space (Pl. G, 6), bounded on the E. by the Temple wall, here about 58 ft. high. It is composed of gigantic blocks, one of which, near the S.W. corner, is 26 ft. long and $2^1/_2$ ft. high, and that at the corner $27^1/_2$ ft. long. It is sometimes difficult to distinguish the joints from clefts caused by disintegration. The whole S.W. corner was built during the Herodian period.

About 13 yds. to the N. of the corner, we come upon the remains of a huge arch, called *Robinson's Arch* after its discoverer. The arch is 50 ft. in width; it contains stones of 19 and 26 ft. in length, and about three different courses are distinguishable. To the W., at a distance of $13^1/_2$ yds., Warren found the corresponding pier of the arch; and about 42 ft. below the present surface there is a pavement upon which lie the vault-stones of Robinson's arch. This pavement further rests upon a layer of rubbish 23 ft. in depth, containing the vaulting-stones of a still earlier arch. The general opinion is that Robinson's Arch is the beginning of a viaduct, mentioned by Josephus (Bell. Jud. vi. 6, 2, etc.), which led from the Temple over the Tyropœon to the Xystus (comp. p. 65), but excavations on the W. side have not yet brought to light a corresponding part of the bridge there. Some authorities (ZDPV. xv. 234 et seq.) therefore believe that Robinson's Arch is the 'staircase gate' mentioned by Josephus (Ant. xv. 11, 5) as the entrance to the 'royal portico'.

From this point we see only the W. part of the South Wall of the Ḥaram, extending as far as the 'Double Gate' (see p. 61). We pass through the *Dung Gate* or *Moghrebins' Gate* (*Bâb el-Mughâribeh;* Pl. G, 6, 7), and turn to the E., keeping as close as possible to the wall. The rock here rapidly falls from the S.W. corner of the area towards the E. from a depth of 59 ft. to 87 ft., and then rises again towards the E. In other words, the Tyropœon valley (p. 31) runs under the S.W. angle of the Temple plateau, so that the S.W. corner of the Herodian Temple stood not on the Temple hill itself, but on the opposite slope. At the bottom of this depression, at a depth of 23 ft. below the stone pavement, Warren discovered a subterranean canal, probably of a late-Roman period. A a depth of 39 ft. there is another pavement, of earlier date. A wall still more deeply imbedded in the earth consists of large stones with rough surfaces. The rock ascends to the Triple Gate (p. 62), where it lies but a few feet below the present surface. Thence to the S.E. corner the wall sinks again for a depth of 100 ft., while the present surface of the ground descends only 23 ft. The gigantic blocks above the surface of the ground in this S.E. angle attract our attention. Some are 16-23 ft. in length and 3 ft. in height. The wall at the S.E. corner is altogether 156 ft. in height, of which only $77^1/_2$ ft. are now above ground. — In the course of his excavations Warren discovered a second wall at a great depth, running from the S.E. corner towards the S.W., and surrounding Ophel (Pl. H, 6), the quarter to the S.E. of the Ḥaram.

On the East Side of the wall of the Ḥaram lies much rubbish, and the rock once dipped much more rapidly to the Kidron valley (comp. pp. 30, 31) than the present surface of the ground does. The Golden Gate (p. 63) stands with its outside upon the wall, but with its inside apparently upon rock. The different periods of building are easily distinguishable. The wall, along which are placed numerous Moslem tombstones, here extends to a depth of 29-39 ft. below the surface. Outside of the Ḥaram wall Warren discovered a second wall, possibly an ancient city-wall, buried in the débris. The whole of the N.E. corner of the Temple plateau, both within and without the enclosing

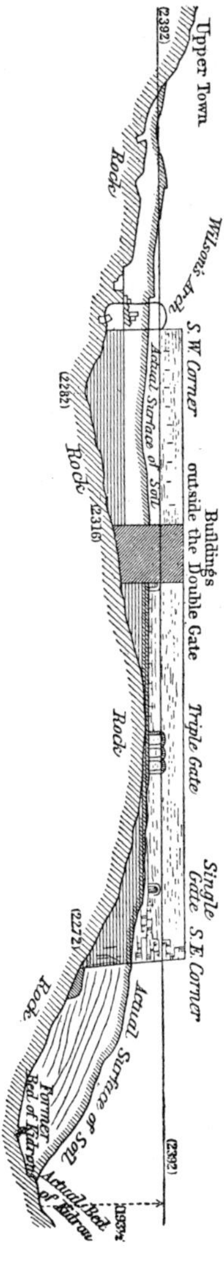

wall, is filled with immense deposits of débris, some of which was probably the earth removed in levelling the N.W. corner.

Under the North Part of the Haram there was originally a small valley running from N.W. to S.E.; the N.E. corner of the wall reaches to a depth of 118 ft. below the present level of the ground. In the valley lay the *Birket Isra'în* ('pool of Israel'; Pl. H, 3), now filled up with rubbish. It was formerly regarded as the *Pool of Bethesda* (comp. p. 49). Early pilgrims call it the 'Sheep Pool' (Piscina Probatica), as it was erroneously supposed that the 'Sheep Gate' (John v. 2) stood on the site of the present gate of St. Stephen. It was fed from the W., and could be regulated and emptied by a channel in a tower at the S.E. corner. In a cistern near the S.W. end of the pool Warren found a double set of vaulted substructions, one over the other, and to the N. of these an apartment with an opening in the N. side of the wall of the Haram.

We return to the town through the *Gate of St. Stephen* (p. 48).

f. Western and Southern Suburbs.

Two broad roads start from the space in front of the *Jaffa Gate* (Pl. D, 5, 6; p. 33), which always presents an animated scene: that to the S. leads past the railway station to Bethlehem and Hebron, that to the N.W. to Jaffa.

The Jaffa Road (Pl. A-D, 2-5), which is the favourite promenade of the natives on Friday and Sunday, runs through the Jaffa Suburb, which is the headquarters of the European population, containing nearly all the consulates, several Christian churches, convents, and hospitals, the Russian Colony, and several Jewish settlements. Near the gate lie the banks mentioned at p. 20 and the German post-office. The first road (Pl. C, 5) diverging to the left from the Jaffa Road leads past the French and Turkish post-offices to the **Mâmilla Pool** (*Birket Mâmilla;* Pl. A, 4, 5), which lies at the beginning of the valley of Hinnom, in the middle of a Moslem burial-ground. It is 97 yds. long from E. to W., and 64 yds. wide from N. to S., and 19 ft. in depth. It is partly hewn in the rock, but the sides are also lined with masonry. It is empty except in winter, when it is filled with rain-water, which is discharged into the Patriarch's Pool (p. 34). The name has never been satisfactorily explained, and its identification with the 'upper pool' of the Old Testament or with the 'Serpent's Pool' of Josephus, is very problematical. — Continuing along the Jaffa Road, we reach (l.) the Hôtel Fast (Pl. a; C, 4, 5) and (r.) the Kaminitz Hotel (Pl. b; C, 4). Beyond the latter a street diverges to the right, which leads past the convent of the *Soeurs Réparatrices*, the *St. Louis Hospital*, the New Gate (p. 35), and the pilgrims' hospice of *Notre Dame de France* (with an Augustine church; Pl. C, D, 3, 4), then skirts the N. city-wall and reaches the Damascus Gate (p. 85).

Farther on the Jaffa Road passes (l.) the Hôtel Hughes (Pl. d; C, 4) and (r.) the *Public Garden* (Pl. B, C, 3, 4). A few paces down a small side-road to the right bring us to the S.E. entrance of the large **Russian Buildings** (Pl. A-C, 2, 3). Inside the enclosing wall to the left are the hospital, with its dispensary, and the mission-house, with the dwellings of the priests and rooms for wealthier pilgrims. To the right is the *Russian Consulate* (p. 19). In the centre, amid various large hospices for men and women, stands the handsome *Cathedral* (Pl. B, 3), the interior of which is richly decorated. Divine service generally takes place about 5 p.m. (best viewed from the gallery; good vocal music). In the open space behind the church lies a gigantic column (40 ft. by 5 ft.), cut out of the solid rock but, owing to a fracture, never completely severed from its bed. — Outside the Russian enclosure, opposite its N. gate, stands the *Hospice of the Russian Palestine Society* (Pl. A, B, 2).

The Jaffa Road now leads through several *Jewish Settlements* (comp. Map at p. 73). To the S. of the road is the attractive *Talitha Cumi* (Mark v. 41: 'Damsel, I say unto thee, Arise!'), an orphanage for Arab girls managed by the Kaiserswerth deaconesses. On an eminence to the S. is the *Convent of St. Pierre*, with an industrial school and seminary for Arab boys (founded by P. Ratisbonne). Farther out, to the N., is *Schneller's Syrian Orphanage* (p. 22), where Arab boys are trained by German teachers.

The street skirting the E. side of the Russian enclosure leads to the Olivet House Pension (p. 19), the Evelina de Rothschild school (p. 23), the Arab-Protestant *Church of St. Paul* (Pl. C, 1, 2), and other buildings of the English Mission (p. 22). Farther on the road forks. In a straight direction it passes through the Jewish colony of Mea Shârim. To the right it leads past the Hill of Ashes (on the way to En-Nebi Samwîl; p. 96) to the residence of the English bishop (p. 88) and to the road to the Mount of Olives (p. 76). — On the cross-road beyond the Church of St. Paul, leading to the Jaffa Road, are the *German Rectory* and *School* (r.; Pl. B, 1), the *United States Consulate* (r.; Pl. 13, A 1) with the *Rothschild Hospital* opposite, the girls' school of the French *Sisters of St. Joseph* (r.), the *German Hospital* (opposite the last), the new building of the Jewish hospital *Bikkur Cholim* (p. 23), the church of the *Christian Missionary Alliance*, and the *German Consulate* (all to the left), and lastly the *Hospital of the London Jews Society* (right).

The Station Road, leading S. from the Jaffa Gate to Bethlehem and Hebron (p. 99), descends into the *Valley of Hinnom* (Pl. C, D, 9; p. 84). [At the S.W. corner of the Citadel (p. 33) the road to the Zion Suburb diverges to the left (p. 70).] The middle part of the Valley of Hinnom lies N. and S. and was used probably in an early Jewish period for the construction of an imposing reservoir, which now, however, has been partly filled in. The present name of this pool, **Birket es-Sulṭân** (Pl. C, D, 8), refers to Solimân, who restored the basin in the middle of the 16th century. The pool is 185 yds. long and 73 yds. broad, and is enclosed by strong walls, between which the ground was excavated till it reached the rock at a depth of 36-42 ft. The rubbish in the W. part of the pool is now covered with gardens. A cattle-market is held here on Friday.

The road skirts the E. side of the Pool of the Sultan and crosses the Valley of Hinnom by the embankment to the S. The valley turns here to the S.E. Farther on, the road passes the *Jewish Colony* founded by Montefiore, with its large hospice (Pl. C, 8, 9), and then forks. The left (E.) branch, passing the *British Ophthalmic Hospital* (p. 22), is the road to the *Railway Station* and to Bethlehem (p. 99), while the branch to the right (W.) leads to the **German Colony of the Temple.** This flourishing colony is named *Rephaim*, from the plain (p. 15), and is the seat of the Temple Society (pp. 10, 24).

The road leads hence to the S.W., through the Colony, passing its cemetery, and brings us in 12 min. to the Greek buildings at *Katamôn*, among which are a small church called *Mâr Sim'ân* (St. Simeon) and the summer-residence of the patriarch. The church is said to stand on the site of the house of Simeon (Luke ii. 25), who recognized the Infant Jesus as the Messiah. Fine view.

A few minutes to the W. of the Temple Colony lies the **Lepers' Hospital,** maintained by the Moravian Brothers under the name of 'Jesus-hilfe' (physician, *Dr. Einsler;* 50-60 patients). Leprosy (Lepra) is a chronic, infectious disease caused by the Lepra bacillus, which affects the skin, the nerves, and the bones. Two forms of leprosy are recognized: tubercular (lepra nodosa), in which festering sores are developed, and smooth leprosy (lepra anæsthetica), in which the skin turns ashen-gray or reddish-brown in colour, and which ends with the mortification of one limb after another. The disease, though not at first infectious, becomes so on long and frequent intercourse. It was a disease of somewhat frequent occurrence among the Israelites, and the Biblical regulations regarding it are of a very rigorous character (Levit. xiii, xiv). There are now about 70-80 lepers in Jerusalem. Hideously repulsive leprous beggars from the Turkish Leprosy Hospital (p. 82) are still met with on the Jaffa Road, especially on the way to the Mount of Olives.

The road diverging from the Bethlehem road to the left, at the S.W. corner of the citadel (see p. 69), leads to the so-called Zion Suburb, which occupies the rocky plateau to the S. of the present city-wall, and contains the *Burial Places* of the Latins, Armenians, Greeks, and other Christians. At the S.W. corner of the city-wall the road forks. The branch straight on leads to the *Bishop Gobat School* (Pl. D, 8, 9; p. 22) for boys, while the branch to the left leads between the burial-places to En-Nebi Dâûd (p. 71).

The Zion Suburb was certainly enclosed by the wall of David and Solomon, and is traditionally identified with the Stronghold of Zion ('City of David', 2 Sam. V. 7; comp. p. 31). Traces of the earliest wall are visible near Bishop Gobat's School. To the N. of the school is a point where the rock has evidently been artificially cut away. In the vicinity are some old cisterns. The dining-room of the school stands upon a cube of rock which formerly bore a tower. The rocky escarpment here projects 16 yds. towards the W., and in the angle are remains of a square trough and mangers cut in the rock. To the E. the escarpment continues towards the *Protestant Cemetery*, where a tower-platform projects on the right. To the N.E. of the cemetery are the remains of a third tower; also 36 steps in the rock, and an old reservoir for water.

The large congeries of buildings known as **En-Nebi Dâûd** ('Prophet David'; Pl. E, 8) contains on the first floor the so-called *Coenaculum*, or *Chamber of the Last Supper*, and in its subterranean chambers the so-called *Tomb of David*, which is held in especial reverence by the Moslems. The present form of the buildings is

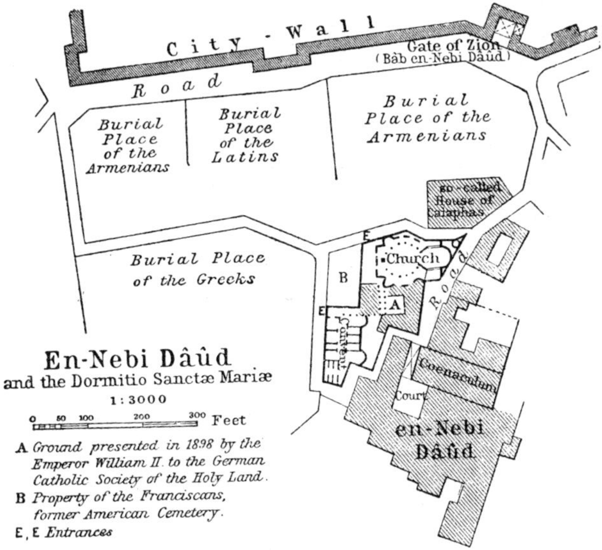

due mainly to the Franciscans, who established themselves 'on Zion' in 1333. During the following century, however, their possessions were much circumscribed, and in 1547 they were wholly supplanted by the Moslems, who are still in possession and often refuse admission to Christians (fee 1-2 fr.). The gate is on the N. side. The Cœnaculum is part of an old church, the pointed vaulting of which, dating from the 14th cent., rests upon two columns in the middle, and on half-pillars with quaint capitals built into the walls. Under the centre window is a niche for prayer. A stone in the N. wall marks the Lord's seat. In the S.W. corner of the room a staircase descends to a lower room (no admission), in the middle of which is shown the place where the table *(sufra)* of the Lord is said to have stood. Visitors are also refused admission to the tomb of David, but a modern copy of his sarcophagus is shown in an upper room.

The *Church of the Apostles* on Zion (also called the 'Church of Zion' and 'Mother of Churches') is mentioned as early as the 4th cent., before the erection of the Church of the Holy Sepulchre. It stood on the site of the house of John whose surname was Mark (Acts xii. 12 et seq.), where the earliest Christians assembled. The scene of the Last Supper (Mark xiv. 15) and of the Descent of the Holy Ghost (Acts ii. 1 et seq.) was also laid on this spot. The 'column of scourging' (see below and p. 41) was likewise shown here. The scene of the Virgin's death was also at a later period (7th cent.) transferred hither, and the spot has been identified with the scene of St. Stephen's martyrdom (8th cent.; comp. pp. 48, 74, 87). About 1130 the Crusaders built a new *Church of Zion*, or of *St. Mary*, consisting of two stories. The lower had three apses, an altar on the spot where Mary died, and another on the spot where Jesus appeared 'in Galilee'. The washing of the apostles' feet was also said to have taken place here, while the upper story was considered the scene of the Last Supper. — The *Tomb of David* formed one of the holy places in the church of Zion so far back as the Crusaders' period, and it is possible that ancient tombs still exist beneath the building. As David and his descendants were buried in 'the city of David' (1 Kings ii. 10, etc.), the expression was once thought to mean Bethlehem, and their tombs were accordingly shown near that town from the 3rd to the 6th century. The earliest Christians, however, who were doubtless aware of the site of David's tomb, appear to place it in Jerusalem (Acts ii. 29), where by that time Hyrcanus and Herod had robbed the tombs of all their precious contents. According to Nehemiah iii. 16 and Ezekiel xliii. 7, we are justified in seeking for the tombs of the kings on the Temple mount, above the pool of Siloam.

The plot of ground of the Dormitio Sanctæ Mariæ (Pl. E, 8; dormitio = 'the sleep of death'), situated to the N. of the Nebi-Dâûd, was presented in 1898 by the Emperor William II. to the German Catholic Society of the Holy Land. The *Church of the Virgin (Marien-Kirche)*, erected in 1901-1910 from plans by Heinrich Renard, is a structure in the Romanesque style, with a choir and crypt. On the S. side of the church is the *Zion Convent* of the Dormitio, occupied by Benedictines from Beuron (adm. on application).

The way to the Gate of Zion leads past the *Armenian Monastery of Mount Zion* (Pl. E, 8), which, according to the legend, is on the site of the *House of Caiaphas* (see below). The tombs of the Armenian patriarchs of Jerusalem in the quadrangle should be noticed. The small church is decorated with paintings, and has an altar containing the 'angel's stone', with which the Holy Sepulchre is said to have been closed. A door to the S. leads into a chamber styled the prison of Christ, from which the Arabs call the building *Habs el-Mesîh*. The spot where Peter denied Christ, and the court where the cock crew, are also shown.

The tradition as regards this incident has undergone alteration. According to the Pilgrim of Bordeaux (ca. 333), the house of Caiaphas stood on the road from the city-gate to Zion (Cœnaculum). Here also the 'column of scourging' was shown, its site being transferred later to the Church of the Apostles (see above). In the 5th cent. the site of the house of Caiaphas, in which St. Peter denied his Master (Matt. xxvi. 66 et seq.), was occupied by a Church of St. Peter; compare the account of the pilgrim Theodosius (ca. 530). In consequence of a misunderstanding of the Biblical story the house of Caiaphas and the prison of Christ were shown during the 12th cent. at the Prætorium (p. 48). In the same century the grotto where St. Peter wept after denying Christ (Luke xxii. 62) was also identified and marked by the church called 'St. Peter in Gallicantu'. The exact site of this church, however, is now unknown. Of late the Assumptionist Fathers

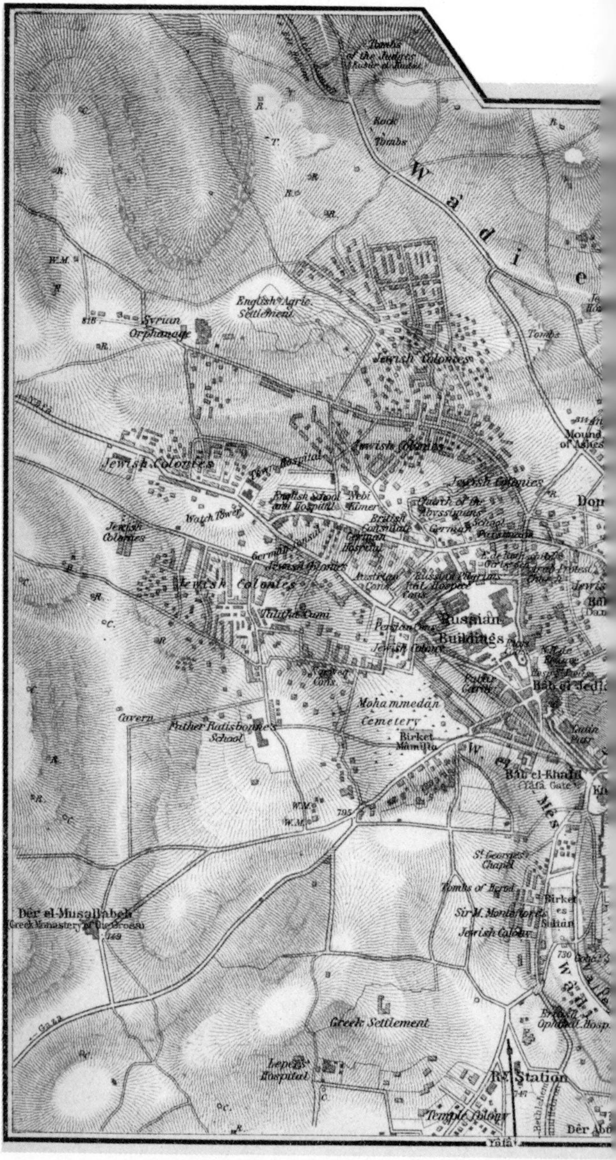

Tombs of the Judges
Rock Tombs
Wâdi e
English Agric. Settlement
Syrian Orphanage
Jewish Colonies
Tombs
Mound of Ashes
Jewish Colonies
Watch Tower
English School and Hospital
Nebi Akâsheh
British Consulate
German School
German Consul
German Hospital
Jewish Colonies
Austrian Cons.
Russian Pilgrims
Russian Buildings
Talitha Cumi
Persian Cons.
Jewish Colony
Mohammedan Cemetery
Birket Mâmilla
Cavern
Father Ratisbonne's School
Bâb el-Jedîd
Bâb el-Khalîl
Yâfâ Gate
St George's Chapel
Tombs of Herod
Sir M. Montefiore's
Jewish Colony
Birket es Sultân
Dêr el-Musallabeh
Greek Monastery of the Cross
Greek Settlement
Lepers' Hospital
Rly. Station
Temple Colony
British Ophthal. Hosp.
Gaza
Yâfâ
Dêr Abû

Heights in Metres

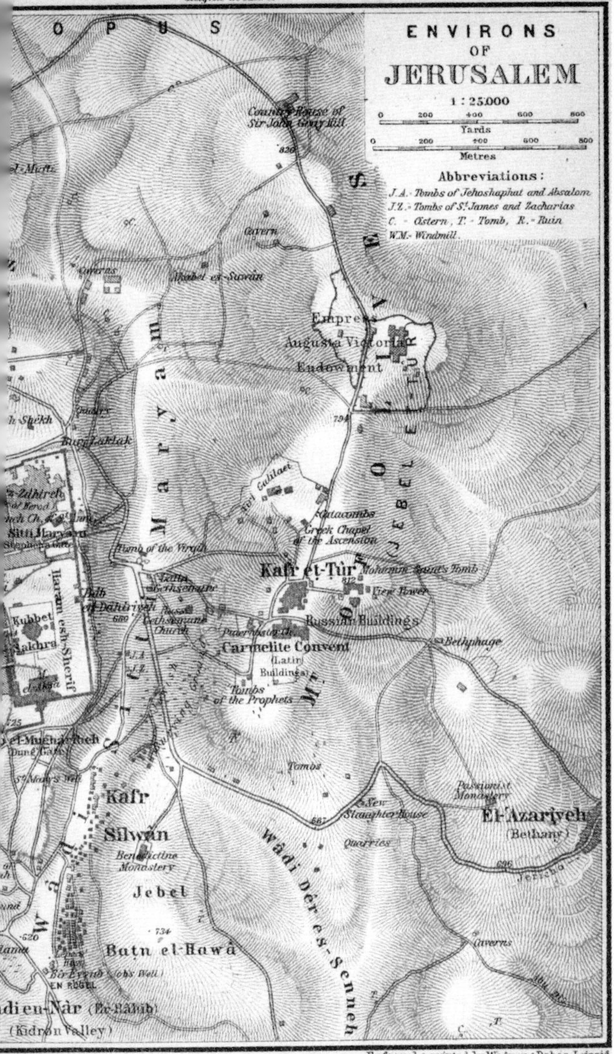

Engraved & printed by Wagner & Debes, Leipzig.

claim to have found it on their property to the S.E. of the Cœnaculum, where excavations have brought to light some interesting rocky caves and tombs. — The 'angel's stone' is not heard of till the 14th cent., since which period it has been differently described and probably renewed.

A few paces to the N. we reach the **Gate of Zion** (Arab. *Bâb en-Nebi Dâûd*, gate of the prophet David; Pl. E, 7, 8), situated in a tower of the town-wall. According to the inscription it was built in 947 (1540-41). A stone built into the E. side-wall of the gateway bears a Latin inscription of the time of Trajan and originally belonged to a monument in honour of Jupiter Serapis. From the top of the battlements we may enjoy a fine view of the hills beyond Jordan.

Through the Armenian quarter back to the Jaffa Gate, see p. 35.

5. Environs of Jerusalem.

a. The Mount of Olives.

The *Mount of Olives* is closely connected with the last earthly days of Jesus Christ. In full view of the Temple on the hill opposite he here announced its coming destruction to his disciples (Mark xiii. 1, 2). It was from the Mt. of Olives that he rode into the city on an ass, amid the jubilation of the people, who expected him to restore the earthly kingdom of the Messiah (Matt. xxi; Mark xi; Luke xix; John xii). After the Last Supper he repaired with his disciples to the quiet Garden o Gethsemane (p. 75), and there, through the treachery of Judas, he was arrested in the course of the night (Matt. xxvi. 36-56; Mark xiv. 43; Luke xix. 29 and xxii. 39; John xviii. 1). The tradition that the Ascension took place on the Mt. of Olives is, however, at variance with the assertion of St. Luke (xxiv. 50) that 'he led them out as far as Bethany'.

The EXCURSION may be made either on foot or by carriage (fare 10-12 fr.; to the top of the hill 3/4 hr.). Drivers who wish to combine this excursion with that to Gethsemane and the valley of the Kidron (comp. p. 76) should order the carriage to meet them at the Garden of Gethsemane. As the view of the Jordan valley is finest in the evening, while Jerusalem is best seen in the light of the rising sun, the hill should certainly be visited twice.

The **Mt. of Olives** *(Mons Oliveti*, Arab. *Jebel eṭ-Ṭûr)*, or *Mt. of Light*, as it is sometimes called, runs parallel with the Temple hill, but is somewhat higher. It consists mainly of chalky limestone. The Mt. of Olives, in its broadest sense, includes the Mt. of Offence (Pl. K, 8, 9; pp. 82, 83) to the S., and the Scopus (p. 76) to the N. The Mt. of Olives proper is divided into four eminences by low depressions. The highest point, to the N. ('Viri Galilæi', p. 77), is 2680 ft. above the sea-level. The slopes are cultivated, but the vegetation is not luxuriant. The principal trees are the fig and carob, and here and there are a few apricot, terebinth, and hawthorn trees. The paths are stony, and the afternoon sun very hot.

PEDESTRIANS start at *St. Stephen's Gate* (Pl. H, I, 3; p. 48), outside which the Mt. of Olives route keeps straight on.

Immediately beyond the gate a path to the right descends to the lower valley of the Kidron (comp. p. 81), while to the left diverges a fair path by which pedestrians or riders may reach the Empress Augusta Victoria Endowment (ca. 1/2 hr.; p. 76). The latter route passes the pond named *Birket Sitti Maryam* (Pl. I, 3), *Birket el-Asbâṭ* ('Dragon Pool'), or *Cistern of Hezekiah*, for which last, however, there is no authority. The pond, which is doubtless of mediæval construction, is 32 yds. long, 25 yds. wide, and 13 ft. deep; in the corners are remains of stairs, and in the S.W. corner is a niche where the water is drawn off into a channel for the supply of the *Bath of Our Lady Mary (Ḥammâm Sitti Maryam)*. Farther on, near the *Burj Laḳlak* or *Storks' Tower* (Pl. H, 1), we turn to the right and then take the first path to the left, passing a quarry. Finally we follow the path leading E.

The Mt. of Olives road now descends, passing a rock where the stoning of St. Stephen is said to have taken place (comp. pp. 48, 72, 87), to the bottom of the valley, which we cross by the *Upper Bridge* (Pl. I, 3).

To the left of the road, beyond the bridge, is the church of the **Tomb of the Virgin** (*Kenîset Sitti Maryam;* Pl. K, 3), where, according to the legend, she was interred by the apostles, and where she

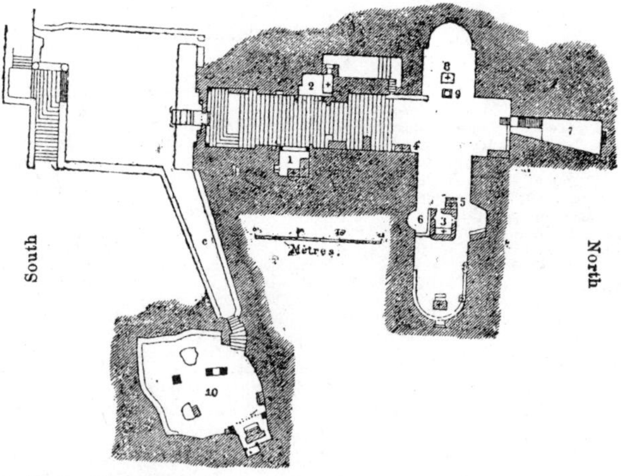

1. Tomb of Mary's Parents. 2. Joseph's Tomb. 3. Sarcophagus of May. 4. Altar of the Greeks. 5. Altar of the Armenians. 6. Prayer Recess of the Moslems. 7. Vaults. 8. Altar of the Abyssinians. 9. Cistern. 10. Cavern of the Agony.

lay until her 'assumption'. A church was erected here in the 5th cent. but was repeatedly destroyed. Its present form is due to *Milicent* (d. 1161), daughter of King Baldwin II. The chapel now belongs to the Greeks, the Latins having a slight share in the ownership.

A flight of steps descends to the space in front of the church; to the right is the passage leading to the Cavern of the Agony (p. 75). The only part of the church above ground is the *Porch*. The arches of the portal rest on four marble columns. A handsome *Staircase* of 47 marble steps descends immediately within the portal, passing a walled-up door (perhaps the entrance to the tomb of Milicent) and two side-chapels. That on the right (Pl. 1) contains two altars and the tombs of Joachim and Anne, the parents of the Virgin. The transference of these tombs hither from the church of St. Anne seems to have taken place in the 15th cent., but the traditions regarding them have since been frequently varied (comp. p. 49). The chapel to the left (Pl. 2) contains an altar over the alleged tomb of Joseph. The flight of steps ends at the *Church*, which lies 35 ft. below the level of the porch and is 31 yds. long, from E. to W., and 6½ yds. wide. The E. wing, which is much longer than the W., has a window above. In the centre of this wing is the so-called *Sarcophagus of Mary* (Pl. 3), a lofty sarcophagus in a small square chapel, resembling that in the Church of the Holy Sepulchre and probably, like that, covering a rock-tomb. There are also altars belonging to the Greeks (Pl. 4) and to the Armenians (Pl. 5). To the S. of the tomb is a prayer-recess of the Moslems (Pl. 6), who for a time had a joint right to the sanctuary. 'Omar himself is said once to have prayed here, in '*Jezmânîyeh*' (Gethsemane). Opposite the stairs, to the N., are vaults of little importance (Pl. 7). The W. wing contains an altar of the Abyssinians (Pl. 8), in front of which is a cistern (Pl. 9) with fairly good water, considered by the Greeks and Armenians to be a specific against various diseases.

On our return to the upper forecourt we follow the passage (Pl. c; p. 74), which finally leads us into the so-called *Cavern of the Agony* ('Antrum Agoniæ'; Pl. 10), where the sweat of Jesus 'was as it were great drops of blood falling down to the ground' (Luke xxii. 44). The cavern, hewn in the rock, is about 18 yds. long, 9½ yds. broad, and 12 ft. high, and is lighted by a small opening above. The grotto is whitewashed at places, and the ceiling, borne partly by natural pillars and partly by masonry, still bears traces of old frescoes, particularly on the E. The cavern, now belonging to the Franciscans, contains three altars and several stone benches. In the middle ages it was believed to be the spot where Jesus was taken captive.

A few paces from the Tomb of the Virgin, towards the S., on the opposite side of the road leading to the Mt. of Olives, is situated the **Garden of Gethsemane** (Pl. K, 4), a word signifying 'oil-press'. The garden, still a quiet and secluded spot, is surrounded by a wall and forms an irregular square, with a diameter of 70 paces. It belongs to the Franciscans. The earliest account of the place dates from the 4th cent.; and in this case tradition tallies with the Bible narrative. At one time it contained several churches. The entrance is by a very low door on the E. side, *i.e.* the side next the Mt. of Olives. A rock immediately to the E. of this door marks the spot where Peter, James, and John slept (Mark xiv. 32 et seq.). A few paces to the S. of this spot, the fragment of a column in the wall indicates the traditional place where Judas betrayed Jesus with a kiss. The garden contains eight venerable olive-trees, which are said to date from the time of Christ; their trunks have split with age and are shored up with stones. The olive-oil yielded by the trees is sold at a high price, and rosaries are made from the olive-stones.

DRIVERS from Jerusalem to Gethsemane follow the road to Jericho (see p. 125), which skirts the N. side of the town-wall to the E. as far as the *Burj Laklak* (p. 74). Here it turns S.E. and rapidly descends to the upper bridge in the Kidron valley (p. 74). — At the Garden of Gethsemane the road turns S. and passes to the W. of the Garden. The road to the Kidron valley (see p. 81) diverges to the right a little farther on.

Three routes lead from the garden of Gethsemane to the (1/4 hr.) top of the Mt. of Olives, one of which starts from the S.E. and another from the N.E. corner, the latter soon again dividing. At this point, about thirty paces from the garden, there is situated, on the right, a light-grey rock, which has been pointed out since the 14th cent. as the place where the Virgin on her assumption dropped her girdle into the hands of St. Thomas. Close by is a small Russian hospice. Several Christian graves were found here, one of which yielded some silver coins of King Baldwin. — The steep path to the right leads direct to Kafr eṭ-Ṭûr (p. 78). To the right, above this path, is a separate Gethsemane Garden belonging to the Greeks; the *Church of St. Mary Magdalen* (Pl. K, 4), surmounted by seven domes and adorned in the interior with paintings, was built in 1888 by Emp. Alexander III. About halfway up, a ruin on the left has been shown since the 14th cent. as the spot where 'when he was come near, he beheld the city, and wept over it' (Luke xix. 41; Latin inscription on the wall to the right). The spot commands a beautiful view of the city. Even the Moslems once regarded the scene of the *Weeping of Christ* as holy, and a mosque stood here in the 17th century.

The CARRIAGE ROAD TO THE MOUNT OF OLIVES leads viâ the *Damascus Gate* (Pl. E, 3; p. 85) or the 'Hill of Ashes' (p. 89), to the house of the English bishop (Tombs of the Kings; p. 88). It then crosses the flat upper part of the Kidron Valley, here named the *Wâdi el-Jôz* (Valley of Nuts), with the Jewish Colonies to the left, while to the right, in the valley, are some rock-tombs, including the 'Grave of Simon the Just', a Jewish place of pilgrimage. Beyond the valley the road to Nâbulus (p. 215) diverges to the left, while that to the Mount of Olives ascends in a wide curve to the top of the *Scopus* (Arabic *Meshârif*), where Titus and his legions encamped during the siege of Jerusalem. This point affords the best idea of the rocky ridge upon which the city lies. The N. city-wall resembles a mediæval fortress. Farther on our road makes a sweep to the S.E., passing the country-house of Sir John Gray Hill, and ascends towards the S. to the top of the Mount of Olives and the —

Empress Augusta Victoria Endowment (open Mon. & Thurs. 4-6 p.m., Tues. & Frid. 9.30-11 a.m., fee 50 c.; ascent of the church-tower 50 c.). This consists of a large hospice and convalescent home under the protection of the Order of St. John, built in the Romanesque style and opened in 1910. In the court are bronze statues of Emp. William II. and the Empress, by A. Wolff (1910). The

Tower (197 ft.) of the *Church of the Ascension* affords a magnificent *PANORAMA (adm., see p. 76). Beyond the Kidron valley extends the Ḥaram esh-Sherîf, where the Dome of the Rock and the Aḳṣâ Mosque are especially imposing. The hollow of the Tyropœon (p. 31) is distinguishable between the Temple hill and the upper part of the town. To the left of the Church of the Holy Sepulchre and the more distant Latin Patriarchate rises the tower of the Protestant Church of the Redeemer (p. 47). Farther to the right, in the distance, is the large Russian building in the W. suburb. — Towards the N. is seen the upper course of the valley of the Kidron, decked with rich verdure in spring, beyond which rises the Scopus. — The view towards the E. is striking. The clearness of the atmosphere is so deceptive that the blue waters of the Dead Sea seem quite near our eye, though really 15½ M. distant and no less than 3900 ft. below our present standpoint. The blue heights which rise beyond the deep chasm are the mountains of Moab (p. xlix). To the extreme S. of the range, a small eminence crowned by the village of El-Kerak (p. 154) is visible in clear weather. On the E. margin of the Dead Sea are seen two wide openings; that to the S. is the valley of the river Arnon (Môjib), and that to the N. the valley of the Zerḳâ Mâʿîn. Farther to the N. rises the Jebel Jilʿâd (Gilead). Nearer to us lies the valley of the Jordan (El-Ghôr), the course of the river being indicated by a green line on a whitish ground. — Towards the S.E. we see the road to Jericho; to the left some of the houses of Bethany; high up, beyond Bethany, the village of Abu Dîs; farther to the left, the Chapel of the Meeting (p. 126); below, in the foreground, the chapel of Bethphage (p. 80). Quite near us rises the 'Mountain of Offence', beyond the Kidron that of 'Evil Counsel', and farther distant, to the S., is the 'Frank Mountain', with the heights of Bethlehem and Tekoah. To the S.W., on the fringe of hills which bounds the plain of Rephaim on the S., lies the monastery of Mâr Elyâs, past which winds the road to Bethlehem. This town itself is concealed from view, but several churches are visible.

Footpath to St. Stephen's Gate, see pp. 74, 73.

The road leads S. along the ridge of the Mount of Olives to the so-called **Viri Galilæi** (Arab. *Karem eṣ-Ṣaiyâd*, 'the vineyard of the hunter'), with a chapel and other buildings, belonging to the Greeks. It owes its first name to a tradition of the 13th cent., that the 'men of Galilee' were addressed here, on the spot marked by two broken columns, by the two men in white apparel after the Ascension (Acts i. 11). The passage Matt. xxvi. 32 was also interpreted to mean that Christ had appeared here 'in Galilee'.

Towards the S. traces of a *Christian Burial Ground* were discovered (remains of the wall, fragments of columns, mosaic pavement with 15 graves beneath it). Under the present E. wall of the area an extensive burial-place, consisting of *Jewish and Christian Rock Tombs* (possibly the Peristereon of Josephus), was found. The antiquities are preserved in the bishop's house.

The road ends at the village of *Kafr eṭ-Ṭûr*, a group of poor stone cottages on the W. side of the two central summits. The inhabitants are sometimes rather importunate.

We now proceed to the E. to the **Russian Buildings.** In the garden, which is surrounded by a high wall, is a handsome *Church*, erected after the design of the old church, the remains of which were found here. A stone in front marks the scene of the Ascension according to the believers of the Greek Church. From the platform of the adjoining *Tower* (214 steps) we have a view similar to that from the tower mentioned at p. 77.

Eastwards, behind the church, is the *House of the Archimandrite*. Some interesting mosaics, discovered in building this house, have been retained in one of the rooms; beneath this room is a sepulchral chamber. There are similar mosaics in the vaulted chambers and tomb discovered to the S. of the house. The mosaics contain Armenian inscriptions of the 9th and 10th centuries: all of them are relics of an Armenian monastery.

The **Chapel of the Ascension,** on a site long accepted by Occidental tradition but dating in its present form only from 1834-35, lies in

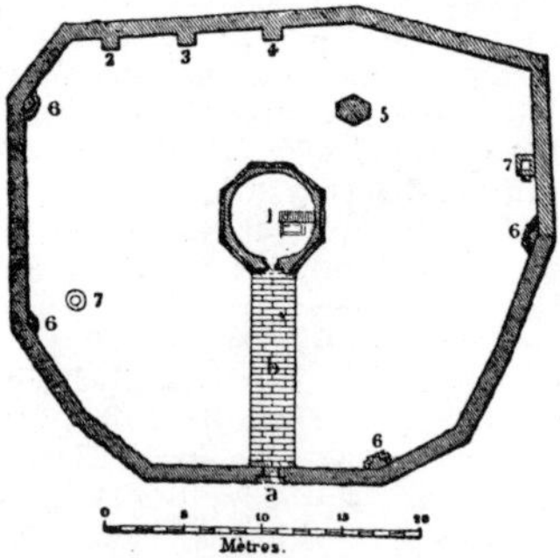

a. Entrance.
b. Paved Path.
1. Chapel of the Ascension.
2. Altar of the Armenians.
3. Altar of the Copts.
4. Altar of the Syrians.
5. Altar of the Greeks.
6. Remains of Columns.
7. Cisterns.

the village itself, adjoining a Dervish monastery, which was originally an Augustine abbey. The scene of the Ascension was located on the Mt. of Olives as early as 315. Constantine erected a roofless circular building over the spot. In the 7th cent. there was a church here, which had been built by Modestus (p. 37), but was destroyed in the 11th century. A church mentioned in 1130 was also destroyed. The chapel now belongs to the Moslems, who also consider this a sacred spot, but Christians are permitted to celebrate mass in it on certain days. A door (Pl. a) admits us to a court, in the centre of which is the chapel of irregular octagonal shape, 21 ft. in diameter, over which rises a cylindrical drum with a dome. The chapel has been rebuilt according to the original model, but the pointed arches over the corner-pilasters were formerly open instead of built up. The capitals and bases of the columns are of white marble and have probably been brought from older buildings. In an oblong marble enclosure is shown the impression of the right foot of Christ, turned southwards. Since the time of the Frankish domination this footprint has been so variously described, that it must have been frequently renewed since then.

In the S.W. corner of the monastery of the dervishes is a door leading to the *Vault of St. Pelagia* (Arab. *Râhibet Bint Ḥasan*). The door opens into an ante-room, whence steps descend to a tomb-chamber, now a Moslem place of prayer, and generally closed.

The Jews place here the tomb of the prophetess *Huldah* (2 Kings xxii. 14), and the Christians the dwelling of St. Pelagia of Antioch, who did penance here for her sins in the 5th cent., and wrought miracles even after her death. The tradition as to Pelagia dates from the Crusaders' period.

To the S. of the village of Kafr eṭ-Ṭûr, beyond the divergence of the routes to Bethany (see p. 80) on the left, and Gethsemane (see p. 76) on the right, lie the **Latin Buildings**, consisting of a *Carmelite Nunnery*, the Church of the Creed, and the Church of the Lord's Prayer. The low-lying *Church of the Creed* is so situated that the roof forms a terrace only slightly raised above the surface of the ground. Of the pointed arches at the sides, only two at the N. end are still preserved. According to the account of Eusebius, the Empress Helena erected a church upon the Mount of Olives 'over the grotto in which Jesus initiated his disciples into the secrets of his doctrines'. In the 15th cent. a 'Church of St. Mark' stood here. According to mediæval tradition, it was here that the apostles drew up the Creed. The *Church of the Paternoster*, or

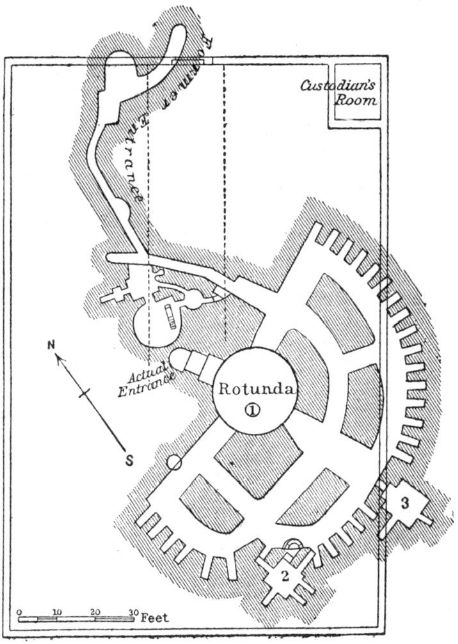

Lord's Prayer, to the E. of the Church of the Creed, was originally erected, in consequence of a sermon by Peter the Hermit, on the spot where, according to mediæval tradition, Christ taught his disciples the Lord's Prayer. The present building was erected in 1868 at the cost of the Princess La Tour d'Auvergne. In the vestibule are a leaden sarcophagus, many fragments of marble, and other antiquities found in the course of building. To the W. is the Hall of the Lord's Prayer. In the passage round the handsome court are tablets inscribed with the Lord's Prayer in 32 different languages. On the S. side is the tomb of the princess, with a lifesize marble effigy.

The road leads on to the S.W. to the so-called **Tombs of the Prophets,** a series of old rock-tombs which are greatly revered by the Jews and now belong to the Russians. No charge is made for admission, but the custodian expects a gratuity of 10-15 centimes. The arrangement of the tombs is shown on the ground-plan at p. 79. The passages are partly filled up, and the wall of the outermost contains several shaft-tombs (p. xcvi). To the S.W., at a somewhat higher level, is a side-chamber (Pl. 2) containing five tombs; another side-chamber (Pl. 3) has been left unfinished. Greek inscriptions found here make it highly probable that this was a burial-place of the 4-6th cent., while the central rotunda may have been a cistern. Pl. 1 shows the opening in the ceiling.

On the road to Bethany (comp. p. 79), about 1/2 M. to the E. of the Latin Buildings, are the remains of a chapel of the Crusaders discovered in 1876. The Franciscans have built a new chapel on the site. The stone with frescoes and inscriptions found here shows that the Crusaders regarded this as the site of *Bethphage*, where the disciples found the ass on which Jesus rode into Jerusalem (Matt. xxi. 1; Mark xi. 1; Luke xix. 29). The stone is also known as the 'Stone of Meeting' and is supposed to mark the spot where Jesus met Martha (see p. 126); this identification was made as early as the time of the Pilgrim Silvia (ca. 385). — It is a walk of 20 min. to reach *Bethany* (p. 126) from the chapel.

b. The Valley of the Kidron and the Valley of Hinnom.

The valleys enclosing Jerusalem on the E., S., and W. are wide and shallow in their upper parts, but contract and fall off rapidly toward the S. The *Valley of the Kidron* or *Kedron*, now called *Wâdi Sitti Maryam*, or 'Valley of St. Mary', to the E. of the city, contained water in winter during the time of Christ, but is now entirely dry (comp. p. 30). At Gethsemane its floor is 150 ft. below the Haram, but at Job's Well (p. 84) it is 200 ft. lower. In contradistinction to the Temple Hill, this valley was regarded as unclean. The name of '*Valley of Jehoshaphat*' is of early origin, having been already applied to this valley by the venerable Pilgrim of Bordeaux (ca. 333), but the tradition that this gorge will be the scene of the Last Judgment, founded on a misinterpretation of a passage in the book of Joel (iii. 2), is probably of pre-Christian origin. The Moslems, who have also adopted this tradition (comp. p. 63), accordingly bury their dead on the E. side of the Haram esh-Sherîf, while the Jews have their cemetery on the W. side of the Mt. of Olives. — The name of VALLEY OF HINNOM is attached to the valley to the S. and W. (Arabic *Wâdi er-Rabâbi*), especially to its lower part. The Hebrew name is *Gê Ben Hinnom*, 'the valley of Ben Hinnom' (Josh. xv. 8). In this neighbourhood lay *Tophet*, the 'place of fire', where the Israelites sometimes sacrificed children to Moloch (Jer. vii. 31; 2 Kings xxiii. 10). Even at a later period the valley was an object of detestation to the Jews, whence the word *Gehenna*, used in the New Testament, a contraction of Gehinnom, came to signify hell among both the Jews and the Mohammedans. The name 'Valley of Fire', at present applied to the lower part of the valley of the Kidron (*Wâdi en-Nâr*), may perhaps have some connection with these ancient idolatrous rites.

The excursion may be made either on foot or on horseback.

Just outside the *Gate of St. Stephen* (Pl. H, I, 3; p. 48) we follow a road diverging to the right from the route to the Mount of Olives (p. 73). This leads us past the Moslem graves below the E. wall of the Haram (Golden Gate, p. 67) to the S.E. corner, beyond which we take the first turning to the left and proceed across the *Lower Kidron Bridge* (Pl. I, 5) to the Tomb of Absalom.

Those who combine this excursion with the visit to the Mount of Olives diverge to the right from the Jericho road (Pl. K, 4; p. 76) to the S. of Gethsemane. The whole slope above this road is covered with Jewish graves. The first tomb we come to on this route, to the left of the road, is the so-called —

Tomb of Absalom (Arab. *Tanṭûr Fir'aun*, 'cap of Pharaoh'; Pl. I, K, 5). The lower part of this strange-looking monument consists of a large cube, $19^1/_2$ ft. square and 21 ft. high, hewn out of the solid rock. Above this rises a square superstructure of large stones, terminating in a low spire which widens a little at the top like an opening flower. The whole monument rises to a height of 48 ft. above the surrounding rubbish. The rock-cube is first mentioned in 333 A.D., but it was not till the 16th cent. that it was exclusively connected with Absalom (based on 2 Sam. xviii. 18). The prominent Ionic capitals of the half-columns and corner-pilasters, the frieze, and the Doric architrave point to the Græco-Roman period as the date of its construction. The tomb-chamber in the interior, now filled with rubbish, may be possibly of earlier origin, but in this case the decorations, with their grotesque mixture of Greek and Egyptian forms, were presumably added at a much later time. In memory of Absalom's disobedience, it used to be customary with the Jews to pelt this monument with stones.

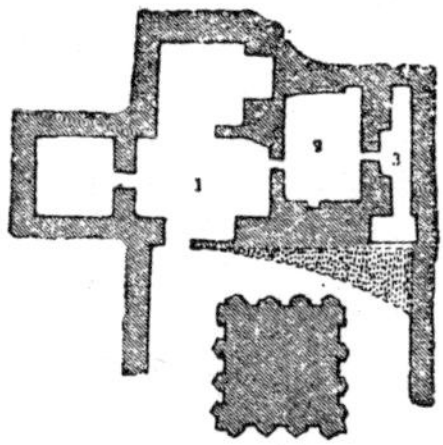

A

On the above Plan the Tomb of Absalom is marked with *A*. The so-called **Tomb of Jehoshaphat,** to the E. of it, is entirely choked with rubbish. The main chamber (Pl. 1) shows traces of a coat of mortar and of frescoes, which suggest that it was once used as a Christian chapel. It may possibly be the chapel which enclosed the tomb of St. James in the time of the Franks.

A little farther to the S. is the **Grotto of St. James** (Pl. I, K, 5; entrance to the left of the Pyramid of Zacharias, p. 82), a rock-tomb probably also dating from the Græco-Roman period, in which, according to a tradition of the 6th cent., St. James is said to have lain concealed without food from the taking of Jesus until the Resurrection. The tradition that this grotto is his tomb is not earlier than the 15th century. The vestibule of the tomb (Pl. 1) is open towards the valley (W.) for a space of 16 ft. The front part of the ceiling is borne by two Doric columns 7 ft. in height (Pl. a), adjoining which are two side-pillars incorporated with the rock. Above these runs a Doric frieze with triglyphs; over the cornice is a Hebrew inscription. Through a second antechamber (Pl. 2), we enter a chamber (Pl. 3) with three shaft-tombs, beyond which we ascend by several steps to a small chamber (Pl. 4). To the N. of No. 2 is a chamber (Pl. 5) containing three shaft-tombs, and to the S. of it is a passage (Pl. 6) with a shelf of rock, to which steps ascend; above the shelf are four shaft-tombs. — From the vestibule of the Grotto of St. James a passage (Pl. 7) leads southwards to the **Pyramid of Zacharias** (Pl. I, K, 5), erected according to the Christians in memory of the Zacharias mentioned by St. Matthew (xxiii. 35; comp. p. 61), but according to the Jews in memory of the Zechariah of 2 Chron. xxiv. 20. This monument, which is 29½ ft. high and 16½ ft. square, is entirely hewn in the rock. On the S. side are still seen the holes which probably supported the scaffolding of the masons. Between the square corner-pillars are placed half-columns with Ionic capitals, which again seem to point to the Græco-Roman period. Above runs a bare cornice, over which rises a pyramid.

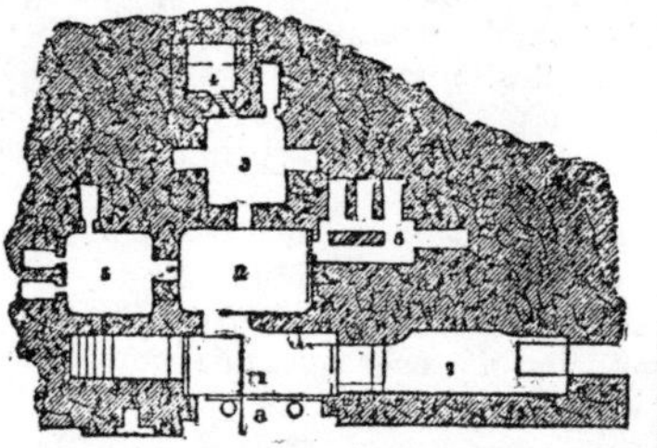

A little farther to the S. we reach the village of **Siloah** (Arab. *Kafr Silwân;* Pl. H, I, 7-9), the houses of which cling to the steep hillside. Many ancient rock-tombs here are used either as dwellings or as stables. At the entrance to the village there is another monument cut out of the rock, known as the 'Tomb of Pharaoh's Daughter'; over the entrance are the remains of an inscription in ancient Hebrew letters. This monument dates from a period before the Exodus; the cornice with hollow moulding is evidence of Egyptian influence. In the lower part of the cliff is a series of entrances to tombs. The inhabitants of Silwân, who are all Moslems, are notorious for their thievish propensities. They live chiefly by farming and cattle-breeding, and some of them bring water (on the backs of donkeys) from the Fountain of the Virgin into the town for sale. To the S. of Siloah lies the *Leper Hospital* of the Turkish Government, managed by the Sœurs de Charité (comp. p. 70). — From the village we may ascend in 7-8 min. to the top of the *Jebel Baṭn el-Hawâ*, or **Mountain**

of Offence (Pl. K, 8, 9), considered part of the Mount of Olives group (comp. p. 73). Its name *(Mons Offensionis, Mons Scandali)* is derived from 2 Kings xxiii. 13, as the Vulgate, rightly or wrongly, localized here the scene of Solomon's idolatrous practices. On the summit is a *Benedictine Convent*, with a seminary of the United Syrians. The view includes the *Wâdi Kattûn* on the E., and the Valley of the Kidron, on the W. and S.

From the N. part of the village of Siloah a road descends to the W. to the neighbouring (5 min.) **Fountain of the Virgin** (Pl. H, 7), Arab. *'Ain Sitt Bedrîyeh, 'Ain Sitti Maryam*, or *'Ain Umm ed-Derej* (fountain of steps). The name is derived from a legend of the 14th cent. to the effect that the Virgin once drew water or washed the swaddling-clothes of her Son here. It is probably identical with the spring of *Gihon*, where the faithful followers of David anointed Solomon as King (1 Kings i. 38). We descend by sixteen steps through a vault to a level space, and by fourteen steps more to the water. The basin is $11^1/_2$ ft. long and 5 ft. wide, and the bottom is covered with small stones. The spring is intermittent. In the rainy winter season the water flows from three to five times daily, in summer twice, and in autumn once only. This is accounted for as follows. In the interior of the rock there is a natural reservoir, in which the water collects. This reservoir is connected with the basin by a syphon-shaped passage, which, acting by a natural law, empties the reservoir into the basin whenever the water in the former reaches the highest level of the syphon-like outlet.

Efforts were made at a very early period to make the waters of this spring available for the inhabitants of the city. Perhaps the earliest of these is the canal, discovered by Schick in 1891 and not yet fully excavated, which conveyed the water along the surface of the ground to the Pool of Siloam (see below). This channel is perhaps referred to in the phrase of Isaiah (viii. 6), 'the waters of Shiloah that go softly'. As this channel would be of little use in time of war, a subterranean passage was constructed (probably also in the time of one of the early kings) from within the walls to a perpendicular shaft above the spring. An attempt to deprive enemies of the water was made by the construction of the subterranean *Siloah Canal*, which is very probably a work of Hezekiah (2 Kings xx. 20). This channel is of very rude construction and now at places very low and narrow. Curiously enough, it is not straight, but has several windings, and there are a number of small *culs de sac* in its course, apparently showing that the unskilled workmen had frequently lost the right direction. The distance in a straight line is 366 yds., but by the rocky channel 583 yds. The vertical shafts are also interesting. As the water frequently fills the passage quite unexpectedly, it is dangerous to attempt to pass through it. — In 1880 the oldest Hebrew inscription we possess (now in Constantinople) was found at the S. orifice of this channel in the rock. It contains a brief account of the construction of this channel, 1200 ells long, and, among other details, mentions that the workmen began the boring from both ends. In consequence of this discovery, the channel was again examined, and the spot was found (near the middle) where the picks of the diggers met.

The **Pool of Siloam** or **Siloah** (Arab. *'Ain Silwân;* Pl. G, H, 9) lies a little farther down the valley, near the mouth of the above-mentioned channel, and was in antiquity enclosed within the city-wall (Well Gate, see p. 31). It is 52 ft. long and 19 ft. wide. Excavations have here revealed a bath-house and the remains of a basilica, while close by, to the N.W., have been discovered parts of the old wall, a flight of steps cut in the rock, a paved street, etc. The bath is, perhaps, of the Herodian period; the basilica, which is first mentioned in 570 A.D., commemorated the healing of the man blind from his birth (John ix. 7). To the S. of the small upper pool lies the larger *Lower Pool of Siloam* (*Birket el-Ḥamrâ*, or 'the red pool'; probably the 'king's pool' of Neh. ii. 14), which belongs to the Greeks and has been filled up by them. To the S. of the large pool stands an old mulberry-tree, enclosed by stones for its protection, and mentioned for the first time in the 16th cent., where the prophet Isaiah is said to have been sawn asunder in presence of King Manasseh. The tradition of this martyrdom is alluded to by some of the fathers of the church.

A road hence leads farther down the valley, reaching in a few minutes the junction of the valleys of Jehoshaphat and Hinnom (350 ft. below the Ḥaram), and a ruined mosque adjoined by the spring called **Job's Well** (*Bîr Aiyûb;* comp. the Map, p. 73). The well is 125 ft. deep and seldom dries up. The water is considered excellent. When springs burst forth below the well after the winter rains, it is thought to presage a fruitful year, and gives occasion for a general festivity.

The name is derived from a late and senseless Moslem legend. An equally valueless tradition arose in the 16th cent. to the effect that the holy fire was concealed in this well during the captivity and was rediscovered by Nehemiah. Probably we are here standing on the brink of the well of '*En Rogel* ('fullers' spring'), mentioned in 1 Kings i. 9. The modern *Ez-Zaḥweileh* has of late been supposed identical with the 'stone of *Zoheleth*', but the fullers' spring would then have to be placed nearer the Fountain of the Virgin. The question cannot be answered until it has been settled whether Job's well is of ancient or modern date.

We now turn to the W. and enter the VALLEY OF HINNOM (p. 80; *Wâdi er-Rabâbi*). To the N.W. rise the steep slopes of the so-called Suburb of Zion (p. 70). To the S. is *Jebel Abu Tôr*, a hill also called by the Franks the *Mount of Evil Counsel*, according to a legend of the 14th cent., to the effect that Caiaphas possessed a country-house here, where he consulted with the Jews how he might kill Jesus. [A path leads to the top from Job's Well, but it is more easily ascended from the Bethlehem road.] The soil is well cultivated at places, though plentifully sprinkled with small stones.

The slope of the Jebel Abu Tôr is honeycombed with rock-tombs, the low entrances of which, many of them ornamented, are approached by rock-hewn steps; a few of them have stone doors. The tombs invariably contain a number of vaults for different families. Some of them were occupied by hermits from the early Christian period down to the middle ages, and afterwards by poor families and cattle. The largest is the so-called —

Apostles' Cave, in which, according to a tradition of the

16th cent., the apostles concealed themselves during the Crucifixion. It is now used as a chapel for the Greek convent adjoining it.

Above the entrance is a frieze of which eight sections have been preserved. The forecourt was adorned with frescoes, of which only scanty traces remain. Beyond the chapel itself are two other chambers, the innermost of which contains several shaft-tombs and also two vaulted shelf-tombs, which are pointed out as the tombs of Caiaphas and Annas.

The roof of the convent commands a beautiful view of the junction of the Hinnom Valley with that of the Kidron.

Two adjacent burial-places are supposed to mark *Aceldama*, or the **Field of Blood,** mentioned in Matt. xxvii. 8. As the Bible does not inform us where the 'field of blood' lay, various other sites have also been identified with it. The Greeks connect the name with the large burial-place below the Apostles' Cave (see p. 84).

Through the entrance-door, the lowest stones of the columns of which are old, we enter the *Vestibule*. A door adorned with mouldings and gable leads hence to the *Main Chamber*, on a somewhat lower level. The ceiling of this chamber is vaulted in a dome-like manner. On each side it is adjoined by a smaller chamber, each of which contains two vaulted niche-tombs with human bones in them. Passages in the rear wall lead to the right and left to other *Chambers* with niche-tombs in the walls. The chamber to the left also contains a curious grave sunk in the floor and reproducing the shape of the human body. The whole arrangement recalls that of the Tombs of the Kings (p. 88).

The grave which Occidental tradition takes to be the site of the Field of Blood (comp. above) lies a little to the W. and farther up the valley. It was visited by pilgrims at an early period, and appears in a map of the 13th cent. as 'carnelium' (*i.e.* charnel-house). The Arabs call the spot *El-Ferdûs* (Paradise). The structure is formed of a large half-open grotto, walled up in front and roofed over with masonry. The interior may be entered by a gap in the wall. In the centre is a massive pillar and in the rocky sides are shaft-tombs. The floor is covered with a layer of bones about 6 ft. thick, above which is a covering layer of sand and rubbish. On the W. wall of the interior are crosses and Armenian inscriptions.

A little farther on we reach the Ophthalmic Hospital of the Knights of St. John, whence we may return to the Jaffa Gate by the road described at pp. 70, 69.

c. North Side of the City.

The *Cotton Grotto*, the *Grotto of Jeremiah*, and the *Tombs of the Kings* (p. 88) may be reached by carriage, but the *Tombs of the Judges* are best approached on horseback. A ticket of admission to the Cotton Grotto (1 fr.) is obtained at the American Colony Store or through the dragoman or the landlord of the hotel. It is necessary to take a light when visiting the different caverns.

We leave the town by the **Damascus Gate** (*Bâb el-ʿAmûd;* Pl. E, 3), which ranks with the Jaffa Gate as one of the most important entrances to the city. According to the inscription it stands on the site of an older gate, built, or at least restored, by Solimân in the year 944 of the Hegira (beginning 10th June, 1537) and is a fine example of the architecture of the 16th century. It consists of two towers between which is visible the upper part of an ancient arch. The passage between the towers forms two angles. On the side next the city the gateway is enclosed by two thin columns, above which is a pointed pediment with the inscription mentioned at p. 85. The battlements are surmounted by small tapering columns. The Mâdebâ mosaic map (p. 152) shows that in the 6th cent. there was an open space within the gate on which stood a large column. It is to this column that the Arabic name, 'gate of the column', refers. The tower of the gate commands a celebrated view.

Under the towers there still exist subterranean chambers, that under the E. tower being built of large blocks. A reservoir and a fragment of wall (running from E. to W.) constructed of drafted blocks have also been discovered here. Outside the gate we can still clearly see on our right (E.) ancient courses of drafted blocks; when the gateway was rebuilt the Turks had grooves cut in the blocks to make them look more modern. The rushing of a subterranean water-course is said to have been frequently heard below the Damascus Gate, and it is not improbable that one may exist here. In the 12th cent. the gate was called St. Stephen's Gate (see p. 87).

The open space (Pl. E, 2) in front of the Damascus Gate is the point where four roads meet. On the left is the road leaving the Jaffa Road at the Kaminitz Hotel, which skirts the city-wall to the right (E.) and is continued to the upper valley of the Kidron (comp. pp. 68, 76). The road to the N.W. leads to the Jewish colonies to the N. of the Jaffa Suburb, and the road to the N. is the road to the Mount of Olives and Nâbulus (comp. pp. 76, 215).

In the rock to the right of the Kidron Valley road, about 100 paces to the E. of the Damascus Gate, and 19 ft. below the wall, is the entrance to the so-called **Cotton Grotto** (Pl. F, 2, 3), rediscovered in 1852. This cavern is called the linen grotto *(Mughârat el-Kettân)* by Moslem authors, and it corresponds to the 'royal grottoes' of Josephus (Bell. Jud. v. 4, 2). It is an extensive subterranean quarry, stretching 214 yards in a straight line below the level of the city, and sloping considerably down towards the S. On the sides are still seen niches for the lamps of the quarrymen. The rocky roof is supported by huge pillars. The blocks were separated from the rock by means of wooden wedges, which were driven in and wetted so as to cause them to swell; and traces of this mode of

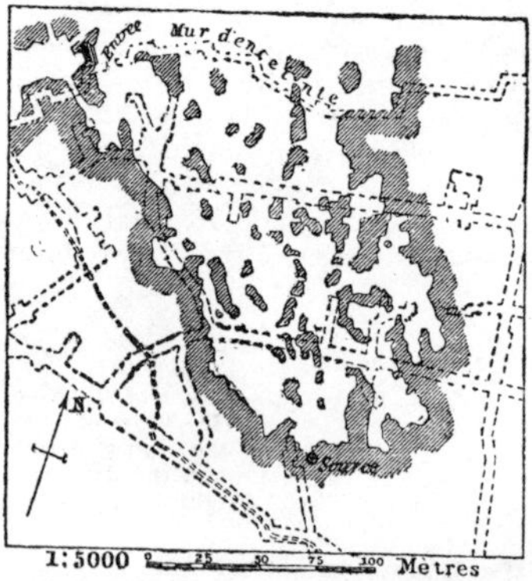

working the quarry are still distinguishable. We possess no clue as to the period when the quarry was used. On one of the walls was a kind of cherub in the Assyrian style (a four-footed being with a human head), which is now in the Louvre. There is a trickling spring on the right side.

Opposite the Cotton Grotto, and a little to the N. of the road, is the so-called **Grotto of Jeremiah** (*El-Edhemîyeh*; Pl. F, 2; fee 6 pi.). This was probably also an old quarry originally connected with the Cotton Grotto and afterwards separated from it by the removal of the intervening rock in order to increase the strength of the fortifications. We first enter a small garden, in which fragments of columns are scattered about. Passing through a place of prayer we are conducted into a cavern towards the E., and then into a second, circular in shape, about 40 paces long and 35 wide, and supported by a pillar in the centre. To the S.W. we are shown the tomb of the Sultan Ibrâhîm, and beyond it a lofty rock-shelf, with a tomb, which since the 15th cent. has been called the tomb of Jeremiah. The prophet is said to have written his Lamentations here. These caverns were once inhabited by Moslem santons or monks. In the S.E. angle of the court there are an entrance and a descent of 7 steps to a vault borne by a short, thick column, beyond which a passage like a door leads to the N. We find here a large and handsome cistern, with its roof supported by a massive pillar, and lighted from above. Steps lead down to the surface of the water.

We return to the Damascus Gate and take the *Nâbulus Road* (p. 86), which leads to the N. The large new building at the corner, with a church and a school, is the *Hospice of St. Paul* (p. 19), completed in 1910, the property of the Cologne Roman Catholic Society of the Holy Land. The roof affords a fine view. — The first side-road to the right leads in a few steps to a garden containing a niche-tomb (p. xcvi) hewn in the rock. Some English authorities, including General Gordon, who visited Jerusalem in 1882, three years before his death at Khartûm, regard the hill immediately above the Grotto of Jeremiah as the true Golgotha (comp. pp. 35, 37), and believe this niche-tomb to be the *Grave of Jesus* (Pl. E, 1; adm. 1/2 fr.).

Adjacent is the large **Dominican Monastery** (Pl. E, 1), with which the archæological school mentioned at p. 23 is connected. Its grounds contain several rocky tombs similar to those just described, and two churches erected over the remains of two older *Churches of St. Stephen.* It is not known at what date the site of the stoning of St. Stephen was transferred by tradition to this spot (comp. pp. 48, 72, 74). In 460 the Empress Eudoxia built a large church in honour of St. Stephen to the N. of the city, but this appears to have been destroyed when the Arabs besieged Jerusalem in 637 (p. 29). About the 8th cent. a humbler church and a monastery were raised here by the Greeks. The Crusaders found this church in ruins and restored it, but it was again pulled down by Saladin during the siege of 1187 (p. 30). The easternmost of the two present churches occupies the site of the basilica of Eudoxia. Mosaic pavements, the altar-slab, and fragments of columns were discovered, and the positions of the apse, the columns, and the aisles were quite distinct. From the nave a few steps descend to an underground altar. The church has been rebuilt on the old plan. — The smaller church to the W. stands on the ruins of the Crusaders' Church and was partly built with the remains of the basilica.

Beyond the Dominican Monastery the road forks. The branch to the left leads to the Tombs of the Judges (p. 90) and En-Nebi Samwîl (p. 96). We follow the right branch (to Nâbulus and the Mt. of Olives, see p. 76) and beyond the *House of the English Bishop* (p. 22) take the cross-road to the right. A few more paces bring us to the so-called —

Tombs of the Kings (Arab. *Ḳubûr es-Salâṭîn;* fee to the custodian 5 pi., more for a party). A rock-hewn staircase of 24 steps, 9 yds. wide, leads down into the tombs in an E. direction. We here observe channels cut in the rock for conducting water to the cisterns below; these cross the staircase at the 10th and 20th steps and lead down beside the wall to the right. At the foot of the staircase we observe the beautiful cisterns, which have now been repaired; the smaller is on the right; straight before us is a much larger one, with a double-arched entrance in the wall of the rock. The roof is slightly vaulted and supported by a pillar. At the corner of each cistern are steps for drawing water. On the left is a round-arched passage which leads hence through a rocky wall, nearly 12 ft. thick, down three steps into an open court hewn in the rock at a depth of about 26 ft., 87 ft. long and $80^1/_2$ ft. wide. To the W. we perceive the richly hewn portal of the rock-tombs. The portal has been widened to 39 ft.; like that of St. James's Grotto (see p. 82), it was formerly divided by two columns into three openings. Some of the mouldings of the portal are still in good preservation, consisting of a broad girdle of wreaths, fruit, and foliage. In the vestibule (Pl. l) are remains of columns, capitals, and fragments of sarcophagi. We cross over a round cistern (k) and descend a few steps; on our left is an angular passage (b) with a movable rolling stone (c) by which the entrance to the tomb could be closed. The chamber (a) is about $6^1/_2$ yds. square, and from it four entrances, two to the S., one to the W., and one to the N., lead to tomb-chambers. The S.E. chamber (Pl. d) contains benches in three of its walls and shaft-tombs in two (E. and S.; p. xcvi). In the N.W. angle of this chamber four steps descend into a lower chamber (d^1) with three shelf-tombs. The second chamber (e) has a depression in the middle, three shaft-tombs on the S., and three on the W.; this chamber also has a subsidiary chamber (f), and on the ground lie fragments of the lid of a handsome sarcophagus. To the W. of the vestibule is a chamber (g) containing shelf-tombs and also (on each of three of its walls) two shaft-tombs. Between each pair of the latter is a passage leading to a small chamber with three shelf-tombs. From the N. wall of the N. chamber a passage leads farther down to a larger apartment (h), in which are a vaulted shelf-tomb on the left, and a double shelf at the back. The chamber (i) to the right of

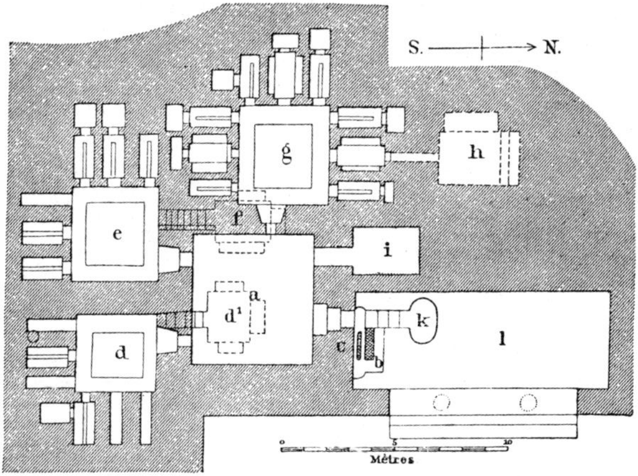

the principal entrance once contained a richly decorated sarcophagus (now in the Louvre). The different chambers bear distinct traces of having once been closed by properly fitted stone doors.

These catacombs are revered by the Jews, who from a very early period have called them the *Cavern of Zedekiah*, or the *Tomb of the rich Kalba Sabua*, a noble who lived at the time of the Roman siege. It is most probable, however, that this is the tomb of *Queen Helena of Adiabene*, which, according to Josephus (Ant. xx. 4, 3), was situated here. This queen, with her son Izates, became converted to Judaism and for some time resided at Jerusalem. Helena and Izates were buried in a handsome tomb, situated three stadia from Jerusalem, which was so famous that Pausanias compares it with the tomb of Mausolus. Izates had twenty-four sons, and hence the extent of the tomb. A sarcophagus, found by De Saulcy, bore an inscription (in which the name of *Queen Zaddo* occurs) in Syriac and Hebrew characters, a proof that this Jewish queen belonged to a Syrian royal family, *viz.* that of Adiabene. These vaults were understood to be tombs as early as the 14th cent., and they were sometimes referred by tradition to the early kings of Judah, whence they are still called 'tombs of the kings' (comp. p. 72).

The Tombs of the Judges lie about 35 min. from the Damascus Gate, on the road to En-Nebi Samwîl (comp. p. 88), which skirts the so-called 'Hill of Ashes' and is joined by the road from the Jaffa Suburb (Church of St. Paul, p. 69). They are reached from the Tombs of the Kings by following the cross-road diverging to the N.W. from the Nâbulus road and keeping the direction of the conspicuous minaret of En-Nebi Samwîl.

The myth that the Judges of Israel are buried in the so-called **Tombs of the Judges** *(Ḳubûr el-Ḳuḍât)* is of comparatively modern origin. They have also been called Tombs of the Prophets *(Ḳubûr el-Anbiyâ)*. Other authorities assign them to members of a later Jewish court of justice. The entrance is in the rocks to the right of the road. A forecourt, $6^{1}/_{2}$-7 ft. wide, has been hewn in the rock; the vestibule is 13 ft. wide, open in front, and provided with a gable. In the pediment is a ring from which pointed leaves extend in the form of rays. There is also a pediment over the portal leading into the tomb-chamber. The portal was once capable of being

I. Tombs on level of ground. II. Basement. III. Upper series of tombs.

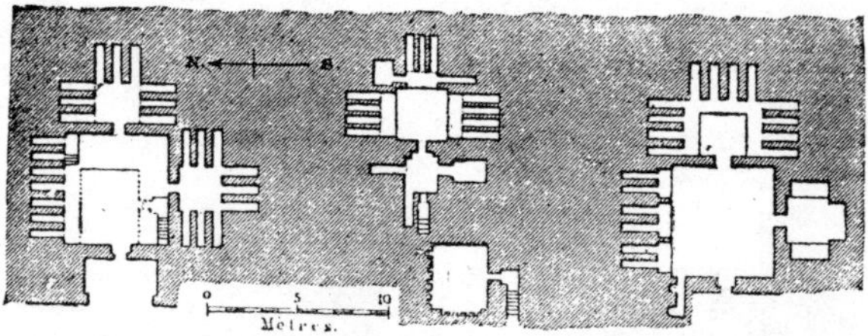

closed from within. The S.E. and N.W. corners of the first tomb-chamber are imbedded in rubbish. On the left (N.) side of it are seven shaft-tombs, above which, at irregular distances, are three vaulted shelf-tombs (Pl. III); and at the back of these there are two other shaft-tombs. In the W. wall is a niche. Adjoining this first chamber on the E. and S. (Pl. I) are two others on about the same level, and two on a lower level (Pl. II). On each of three sides of the E. chamber are three shaft-tombs on a level with the ground (Pl. I), and 3 ft. above these (Pl. III) are four more of the same kind. The S. chamber has on each of three sides three shaft-tombs, and above these a long vaulted shelf-tomb. From the first chamber a passage, with three shaft-tombs, descends to the N.E. chamber, which contains five shaft-tombs on the N., five on the S., and three on the E. side. The subterranean side-chamber to the S.W. was originally a quarry.

There are other rock-tombs in the vicinity, but none of so great extent. There is, however, an interesting tomb about 5 min. to the N.E. of the Tombs of the Judges, and about 5 min. to the E. of them is an admirably preserved wine-press with a cistern.

II. JUDÆA, THE COUNTRY EAST OF THE JORDAN, SOUTHERN PALESTINE, AND THE PENINSULA OF SINAI.

6. From Jerusalem to the Monastery of the Cross, Philip's Well, and Bittîr.

2¼ hrs. From Jerusalem to the *Monastery of the Cross* 20 min.; thence to *Philip's Well* 1½ hr., and thence to *Bittîr* 25 minutes. Horses and donkeys, see p. 19. From Bittîr the return may be made by railway.

The road leads from the Jaffa Gate to the Moslem burial-ground with the *Birket Mâmilla* (p. 68), where a road to the German Colony diverges to the left (comp. Map, p. 73). Our road ascends parallel with the cemetery-wall, passing an ancient windmill, beyond which it descends into the valley containing the Greek Monastery of the Cross (Arab. *Deir el-Muṣallabeh*).

Monastery of the Cross. — History. The foundation of the monastery is attributed to the Empress Helena; according to another tradition it was founded by Mirian (265-342), first Christian ruler of Georgia, one of the three kings depicted over the inner portal of the church. It is at any rate certain that it was founded before the introduction of Islam. It was rebuilt in the middle of the 11th century. At the period of the Crusades the monastery was the property of the Georgians (Grusinians), from whom, however, it was taken by Beybars (1260-77) and fitted up as a mosque. The Georgians recovered it in 1305, and it was restored in 1644 by Leontatian, one of their kings. The monastery at a later date became, like the other Georgian monasteries, loaded with debt. It has suffered much from the hands of the Arabs, who plundered it and murdered the monks more than once, as evidenced by the traces of a great pool of blood in the nave. Hence, too, the high wall without windows and the iron-mounted wicket, which is characteristic of the older Oriental monasteries

The monastery is of irregular quadrangular form. Its buildings embrace several large and irregular courts, and are fitted up partly

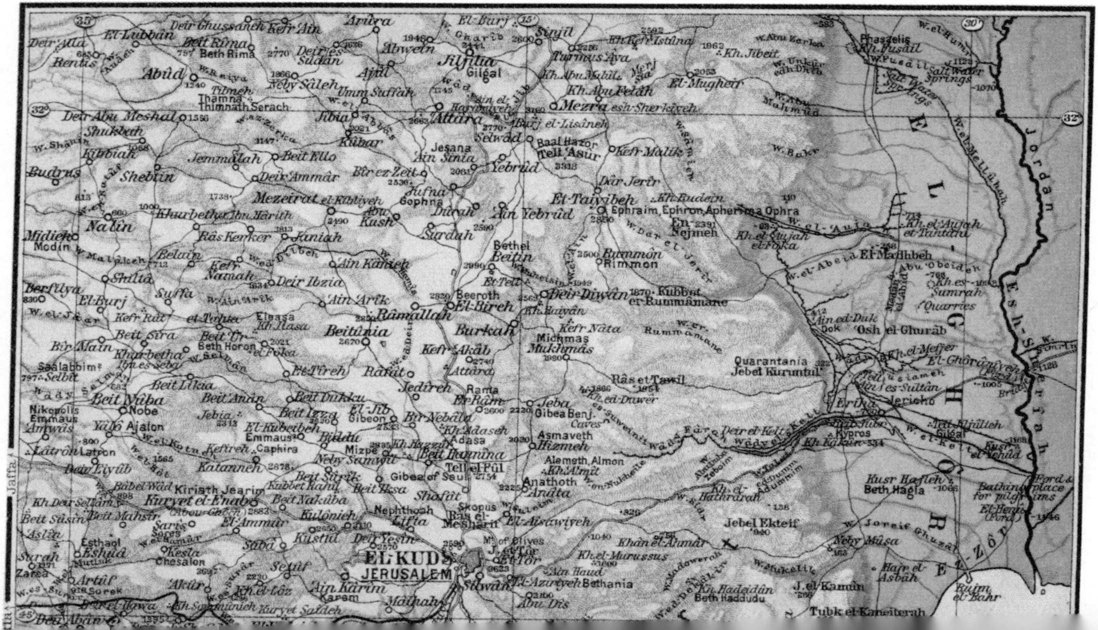

Jordan
E L G H Ô R
EL-KUDS
JERUSALEM
Jericho
Bethel
Ramallah
El-Bireh
Jaffa

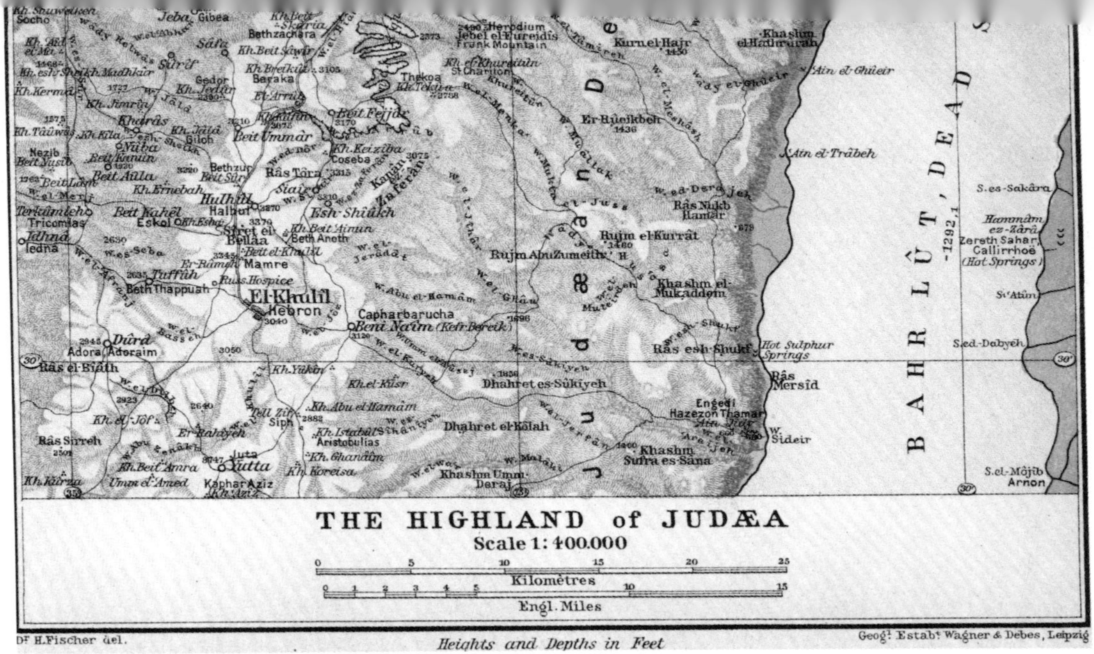
THE HIGHLAND of JUDÆA
Scale 1: 400.000
Kilometres
Engl. Miles
Dr H. Fischer del.
Heights and Depths in Feet
Geogl. Estabt. Wagner & Debes, Leipzig
BAHR LÛT, DEAD S
-1292,1
Socho
Jeba
Gibea
Bethzachara
Herodium
Jebel el Fureidîs
Frank Mountain
Kurmel Hajr
Thekoa
Beit Fejjâr
Er-Rûeikbeh
'Ain el-Ghûeir
'Ain el-Trâbeh
Ras Nukb Hamar
Rujm el Kurrât
Rujm Abu Zumeitir
Khashm el-Mukaddem
Beit Ummâr
Baraka
Gedor
Kharâs
Giloh
Nûba
Beit Ûla
Halhul
Halbul
Bethzur
Beit Sûr
Râs Tôra
Coseba
Zaferân
Esh-Shiûkh
Beit Kahel
Eskol
Tricomias
Idhnâ
Iedna
Mamre
Beth Aneth
Beth Thappuah
Russ. Hospice
El-Khulil
Hebron
Caphar barucha
Beni Naîm (Kefr Bereik)
Dûra
Adora
Adoraim
Râs el-Biâth
Râs esh-Shukf
Hot Sulphur Springs
Râs Mersîd
Engedi
Hazezon Thamar
W. Sideir
Dhahret es-Sûkiyeh
Dhahret el-Kôlah
Khashm Sufra es-Sâna
Khashm Umm Deraj
Tell Zîf
Siph
Aristobulias
Juta
Yutta
Kaphar Aziz
Umm el-'Amed
Râs Sirreh
S. es-Sakâra
Hammâm ez-Zârâ
Zereth Sahar
Callirrhoë
(Hot Springs)
S. ed-Dabyeh
S. el-Môjib
Arnon

in the European style. The *Church*, consisting of nave and aisles, dates from the Byzantine period. The dome is borne by four large pillars, and the vaulting and arches are pointed. The paintings on the walls, some of them of a rude character, were retouched in 1643. The interesting mosaic pavement is ancient. The principal shrine of the monastery is behind the high-altar, where a round aperture, lined with marble, marks the spot where the tree from which Christ's cross was formed is said to have grown. This tradition gives the monastery its name, which is more properly the 'monastery of the place of the cross'. The tradition is probably very ancient, although not traceable further back than the Crusades, and never entirely recognized by the Latins. Among later myths may be mentioned that of Adam being buried, and that of Lot having lived here. Connected with the monastery is a large seminary for priests. The library is now incorporated with the Patriarchal Library at Jerusalem (p. 23).

The road from the Monastery of the Cross to Philip's Well descends the little valley of the monastery to its junction with the *Wâdi ʿAmmâr*, which in turn leads us down to the ($^1/_2$ hr.) *Wâdi el-Werd*, or 'Valley of Roses'. Through this last valley run the railway to Jaffa and the old caravan-route to Gaza. We ride down the valley alongside the railway. In $^1/_4$ hr. we observe, to the right, *El-Mâliḥa*, and above us, to the left, *Esh-Sherâfât*. We cross the railway, and 12 min. farther on we reach the spring of *ʿAin Yâlô*, anciently *Ajalon* (but not the *Ajalon* mentioned in Josh. x. 12). By the spring are several remains of marble columns. To the N. of ʿAin Yâlô are some remarkable artificial hills *(rujûm)*. In 5 min. more the *Wâdi Aḥmed* opens on the left, which brings us in $^1/_4$ hr. to —

Philip's Well *(ʿAin el-Ḥanîyeh)*. The spring bubbles forth from beneath a niche in the wall, with Corinthian columns on each side. At the back is a small pointed window, now walled up. The building is a ruin; remains of columns and hewn stones still lie scattered about. The tradition that ʿAin el-Ḥanîyeh was the spring in which Philip baptized the Eunuch of Ethiopia (Acts viii.36) dates from 1483, before which the scene of that event was placed near Hebron (p. 112).

From Philip's Well to Bittîr the road descends the *Wâdi el-Werd*. After 20 min. the village of *El-Welejeh*, with its vineyards and nursery-gardens, lies on our right. A few minutes beyond the spot where the Valley of Roses enters the *Wâdi Bittîr* lies *Bittîr* (p. 14).

From Bittîr to *ʿAin Kârim* (p. 94) viâ *El-Welejeh*, $1^1/_4$ hr.
From Bittîr to *Bethlehem* (p. 101), $1^3/_4$ hr.

7. From Jerusalem to ʿAin Kârim.

4 M. Carriage (p. 19) in 1 hr.; there and back half-a-day.

We follow the Jaffa road as far as the Jewish lunatic asylum (p. 18). Here our road diverges to the S.W. (left). We soon see the Monastery of the Cross to the left, and then, to the right, the village of *Deir Yâsîn*, with its gardens. From the top of the hill the carriage-road leads in great windings down to ʿAin Kârim. During the descent we have a beautiful view of the village; below us, the Franciscan monastery and church, with the village behind; a little to the right, on an eminence, is the large establishment of the Sisters of Zion: convent, girls' school, and girls' educational institution (founded by Father Ratisbonne). On the hill to the left (S. of the village) are the Russian buildings and a Latin chapel; below in the valley, between this hill and the village, is the beautiful St. Mary's Well.

ʿAin Kârim *(St. John)* is much visited by Greek and Latin pilgrims. The village contains ca. 2000 inhab., of whom 300 are Latins, 200 Orthodox Greeks (incl. 150 Russians), and the rest Moslems.

ʿAin Kârim is probably the *Karem* of the Septuagint (Josh. xv. 60). The tradition which assigns to this spot the birthplace of John the Baptist (Luke i. 39) is of no great antiquity. Before the time of the Crusades there was much uncertainty as to the site, old ecclesiastical writers mentioning Machærus (Mukaur, p. 153), Bethlehem, Hebron, and Jerusalem. In the 4th cent. we hear of a church of Zacharias in the environs of Jerusalem, and in the 6th cent. the birthplace of the Baptist was described as lying five Roman miles distant from that city. In the 9th cent. 'Mount Carmel' (*i. e.* Kârim) is mentioned for the first time in this connection, and this identification has prevailed since the time of the Crusades. Down to the 15th cent. the tradition, however, remained uncertain as regards such details as the exact birthplace and the spot where the Virgin visited Elizabeth (see p. 95).

The castellated Latin *Monastery of St. John* belongs to the Franciscans. Travellers can be accommodated on bringing letters of recommendation from the secretary of the Salvator monastery in Jerusalem. The dome-covered *Church of St. John*, which is enclosed by the monastery on three sides, peeps prettily above the walls. It consists of nave and aisles; the elegant dome is borne by four pillars. The high-altar is dedicated to Zacharias, and the S. chapel to the memory of the Virgin's visit to Elizabeth. Adjoining the organ is a picture representing the Baptist in the desert, copied from Murillo. On the left (N.) of the altar seven steps descend to a *Crypt*, the alleged birthplace of the Baptist, where five bas-reliefs in white marble, representing scenes from his life, are let into the black walls. A grotto in front of the entrance to the church contains a fine mosaic (6th cent.?), with a Greek inscription ('Greeting, oh ye martyrs in the Lord!'); adjoining are two rock-tombs.

According to tradition this is the spot on which stood the house of Zacharias, John the Baptist's father. — After this church had long been used by the Arabs as a stable, the Marquis de Nointel, ambassador of Louis XIV., prevailed upon the Sultan to restore it to the Franciscans; and these indefatigable monks rebuilt the monastery, and purged and restored the church. The older part of the building is earlier than the Crusaders' period.

Following the carriage-road we reach (4 min.) the *Spring of ʿAin Kârim*, which was associated in the 14th cent. with the supposed visit of the Virgin and called *St. Mary's Well*. Over the spring is a mosque with a minaret. — A road leads from the spring towards the W.

along the slope of the S. hill, which belongs to the Russians. Here are numerous houses with pretty gardens, occupied by nuns, a *Russian Church of St. John*, and a bell-tower. — A little higher up (5 min. from the spring) stands the Latin chapel of *Mâr Zakaryâ*, marking the alleged site of the summer-dwelling of Zacharias, where the Virgin visited Elizabeth (Luke i. 39). In the right wall of the chapel is shown a piece of stone which yielded when Elizabeth, during her flight from Herod, laid the infant John on it. Beside the chapel are a small Franciscan monastery and a tower commanding a good view.

As early as the 5th or 4th cent. a convent and a church of two stories stood here. The apse of the upper church is still to be seen above the chapel and other fragments of masonry also still exist. In the 14th cent. the site belonged to the Armenians, but it was purchased by the Franciscans in 1679.

Following the road leading W. from the spring to the Wâdi Beit Ḥanînâ or Wâdi Ḳalôniyeh (p. 18), we reach in 1 hr. the spring **ʿAin el-Ḥabîs.** The *Grotto of St. John*, to which steps hewn in the rock ascend, lies close to the spring. It belongs to the Latins. On the side next the valley there are two apertures in the wall of rock, leading to a kind of balcony, whence we survey the Wâdi Ṣâṭâf and the village of Ṣûbâ. The place is called by the Christians the *Wilderness of St. John*, although it is now well planted, and was cultivated in ancient times also, if we may judge from the traces of garden-terraces.

Since the end of the 12th cent. tradition has here placed the 'wilderness' in which the Baptist dwelt (Luke i. 80). The altar in the grotto is said to stand on the spot where he slept. At the same period a church and convent stood here, the ruins of which are still extant. From other passages, however (Luke iii. 3, etc.), it is obvious that by the 'wilderness' the region near Jordan is meant.

From ʿAin Kârim to Philip's Well (1¼ hr.). We ride for some distance along the Jerusalem road. At the point where this bears to the left we leave it and ascend the side of the narrow valley towards the S.E. Halfway up we leave on our left the path which leads by *El-Mâliḥa* and keep to the right (S.E.) After ½ hr. we arrive at the top, which commands a splendid view. Continuing in the same direction, we descend a small dale, and arrive in ½ hr. at the *Wâdi el-Werd*. Thence we descend the valley to (¼ hr.) *Philip's Well* (p. 93).

8. From Jerusalem to En-Nebi Samwîl and El-Ḳubeibeh (Emmaus).

Comp. Map, p. 92.

2½ hrs. From Jerusalem to *En-Nebi Samwîl* 1¾ hr., thence to *El-Kubeibeh* ¾ hr. Horses, see p. 19. — The View from *En-Nebi Samwîl*, the highest mountain near Jerusalem, is worth seeing. The Crusaders called the mountain *Mons Gaudii*, or Mountain of Joy, because it was their first halting-point that commanded a view of Jerusalem.

From Jerusalem to the Tombs of the Judges (ca. 35 min.), see p. 89. The road descends steeply into the valley (8 min.). Following the downward course of the valley, we arrive in 13 min. at the

Wâdi Beit Ḥanînâ (p. 18), deriving its name from the village of *Beit Ḥanînâ* (*Ananiah*, Neh. xi. 32), on the spur rising between the two valleys which unite here. We now cross the wide bed of the brook, which is full of boulders, and ascend to the N.W. in the side-valley which opens exactly opposite. After 25 min. we reach a small plain; to the left, on the crest of the hill, is the ruin of *Khirbet el-Jôz*, or *Khirbet el-Burj*, dating from the Crusaders' period, and supposed in the middle ages to have been the château of Joseph of Arimathæa. The village of *En-Nebi Samwîl* is reached in 20 min. more. Before we enter it we see, on the right of the road, two reservoirs hewn in the rock; the spring which supplies them is more to the north.

The village of **En-Nebi Samwîl,** 5 min. below the summit of the mountain of that name (2935 ft.), consists of a few houses and of a ***Mosque*** which contains the traditional tomb of the Prophet Samuel ('En-Nebi Samwîl'), revered alike by Jews, Christians, and Moslems. The tomb is shown reluctantly, but the traveller loses little if he fails to see it. He should not, however, fail to ascend the *Minaret* for the sake of the magnificent *View (fee 1 fr. each person). To the right, to the N. of El-Jîb, rises the hill of Râmallâh (p. 216); in front of it, below, lies the village of Bîr Nebâlâ; to the E., Beit Ḥanînâ; and farther E., the hill of Tell el-Fûl (p. 216). Beyond these, in the distance, rise the blue mountains to the E. of Jordan; to the S.E. are Jerusalem and the Mount of Olives; adjoining these, on the hill to the S., is Mâr Elyâs; above it rises the round summit of the Frank Mountain (p. 110); a little to the right is Bethlehem. The village of Beit Iksâ lies quite near us to the S.; to the S.S.W. is Liftâ, and to the W.N.W., Biddu. Ramleh and Jaffa lie farther to the W.; the Dead Sea and the Mediterranean are also visible in clear weather.

The great antiquity of the site of En-Nebi Samwîl is shown by its walls, which are partly hewn in the rock, and by the fine large blocks of building-stone outside the mosque on the N.E. side. It is usually identified with the ancient fortress of *Mizpah*, the famous city of Benjamin. King Asa of Judah fortified it against Israel (1 Kings xv. 22). Tradition points out En-Nebi Samwîl as the birthplace, residence, and burial-place of the prophet Samuel, and it is recorded that the Emperor Justinian (d. 565) caused a well to be dug here in the monastery of St. Samuel. The Crusaders regarded the place as the ancient *Shiloh* (comp. p. 218), and built a church over 'Samuel's Tomb' in 1157, of which the transept and the N. wing are still preserved. In the 16th cent. a handsome and much-frequented pilgrimage-shrine stood here.

From the summit of the mountain we descend to the S.W. and then turn directly to the W. We remain on the height and thus skirt the valleys which descend towards the S. (left). After 35 min. we reach the village of *Biddu*, where the Crusaders gained their first glimpse of Jerusalem (the road by *Beit Nûbâ* and *Biddu* is a very old one; traces of the pavement are still visible). **El-Ḳubeibeh** is reached in 1/4 hr. more. The tradition of the middle ages identifies this village with the *Emmaus* of the New Testament, its distance from Jerusalem (about 64 stadia) agreeing with this probability; comp. p. 16. The village contains numerous ruins. The new *Church of the*

Franciscan Monastery stands on the still plainly-visible foundations of an old Crusaders' church (100 ft. long by 50 ft. broad), with a nave and aisles. The church is said to stand on the spot where Jesus broke bread with the two disciples (Luke xxiv. 30). Some antiquities have also been dug up. — The German Catholic Palestine Society also has a small hospice and a chapel.

Return Route to Jerusalem ($2^1/_2$ hrs.). We return to *Biddu* (see p. 96). Three roads meet here; we take the central one, which leads us along the valley past the spring *ʿAin Beit Sûrîk* (above us, on the right, is the village of the same name). In $^3/_4$ hr. we pass the ruins of *Khirbet el-Lôzeh* on our right; in 20 min. more the valley unites with the *Wâdi Beit Ḥanînâ*; on the right are the ruins of *Beit Ṭulmâ* (road on the right to *Ḳalôniyeh* in 20 min.). We cross the valley, ascend straight on to the S.E., and in 10 min. reach the Jaffa road. Thence to the Jaffa Gate 1 hr. (see p. 18).

From El-Kubeibeh to Jerusalem viâ El-Jîb ($3^3/_4$ hrs.). Beyond Biddu we follow an old Roman road to the N.E. and in 40 min. reach **El-Jib**, a small village on an isolated hill, the ancient *Gibeon* (Josh. ix. 3 et seq.; 1 Kings iii. 4 et seq.). The houses are built among old ruins, and there is a large building that seems to have been a castle. On the E. slope of the hill, about 100 paces from the village, is a large reservoir with a spring, and there is a second farther down, perhaps the pool mentioned in 2 Sam. ii. 13. Fine view. From El-Jîb we proceed to the S.E., passing *Bîr Nebâlâ*, viâ ($1^1/_4$ hr.) *Beit Ḥanînâ* (p. 96) and ($^3/_4$ hr.) *Shaʿfât*. In 7 min. more we join the Nâbulus road. Thence to the (40 min.) Damascus Gate, see p. 215.

9. From Jerusalem to ʿAnâtâ, ʿAin Fâra, Jebaʿ, and Makhmâs.

Comp. Map, p. 92.

$3^1/_4$ hrs. From Jerusalem to *ʿAnâtâ* $^1/_2$ hr.; thence to *ʿAin Fâra* 1-$1^1/_4$ hr.; thence to *Jebaʿ* $^3/_4$ hr.; thence to *Makhmâs* 50 minutes. Horses, see p. 19.

From the Damascus Gate along the Mount of Olives road to the vicinity of Sir John Gray Hill's Villa, see p. 76. To the N. of this point we turn to the left, avoiding the road to the right, which leads to the village of *El-ʿÎsâwîyeh*, perhaps the ancient *Nob* (Isaiah x. 32). The path next descends gradually to the N. to the village of ʿAnâtâ.

ʿAnâtâ corresponds to the ancient *Anathoth*, in the territory of Benjamin, the birthplace of Jeremiah (Jerem. i. 1; xi. 21-23). It seems to have been fortified in ancient times, and fragments of columns are built into the houses of the present village. A little to the right of the road, at the very entrance to the village, we observe the ruins of a large old building, probably a church, with a mosaic pavement. The view from the top of the broad hill on which the village lies embraces the mountains of ancient Benjamin towards the E., part of the Dead Sea, and a number of villages on the hills to the W. and N. This is the district mentioned in Isaiah's description of the approach of the Assyrians under Sennacherib (x. 28, 30).

The road (guide now necessary) leads us towards the N.E., and in $^3/_4$ hr. skirts the *Wâdi Fâra* (magnificent view). After 20 min. more we descend precipitously into the valley a little below the **'Ain Fâra**, a spring with abundant water. The vegetation in the bottom of the valley remains green and fresh even in summer, the brook in some places running underground; numerous relics of aqueducts, bridges, and noble buildings are visible. High up on the steep rocky sides are ancient habitations of hermits (ascent difficult).

Following a small side-valley which issues a little below the spring, we ascend in a N.W. direction to ($^3/_4$ hr.) Jeba'.

Jeba', a village with the shrine of the *Nebi Ya'kûb* ('Prophet Jacob'), is the ancient *Geba* of the tribe of Benjamin (Is. x. 29), and commands the Pass of Makhmâs. The view is extensive, especially towards the N., where the villages of *Burka*, *Deir Dîwân*, and *Eṭ-Ṭaiyibeh* are situated. The last, a Christian village, is perhaps *Ophrah* of Benjamin (Josh. xviii. 23; 1 Sam. xiii. 17). To the N.E. *Rammôn* is visible.

Geba is not to be confused with the adjacent Gibeah of Benjamin ('Gibeah of Saul', 'Gibeah of God'), which has been identified with Tell el-Fûl (p. 216). Geba and Gibeah seem, however, to have been confounded even in the Old Testament; thus Geba of Benjamin is evidently meant in 1 Sam. xiii. 16 and 1 Sam. xiv. 16 instead of Gibeah (comp. also 1 Sam. x. 5).

From Jeba' the route now descends to the N.E. into the *Wâdi es-Suweinîṭ* (35 min.); another valley also opens here to the N. The village of **Makhmâs** (400 inhab.), on a hill $^1/_4$ hr. to the N.E., contains nothing of interest except a cavern with columbaria, or receptacles for cinerary urns. Farther down the Wâdi es-Suweinîṭ contracts between lofty cliffs and forms a ravine, answering to the description of the 'passage of Michmash' in 1 Sam. xiv. 4, 5. The two 'sharp rocks' there mentioned may also be identified, and may be reached by a détour of $^1/_2$ hr. (recommended).

From Makhmâs to Beitîn viâ Deir Dîwân ($1^3/_4$ hr.). We ascend towards the N. to the tableland along the E. side of a narrow, but deep valley which runs into the Wâdi es-Suweinîṭ. At the point where we obtain a view of the valley there are several rock-tombs on the W. slope. After 35 min. the village of *Burka* lies opposite, to the W.N.W., and that of *Kudeira* farther to the N. After $^1/_4$ hr., tombs and quarries. We next reach ($^1/_4$ hr.) the large village of **Deir Dîwân,** loftily situated, and enclosed by mountains.

The city of *'Ai (Hai)* lay near Deir Dîwân, but its exact site is uncertain. 'Ai is described as having lain to the E. of Bethel (Gen. xii. 8). It was captured by Joshua (Josh. viii). Isaiah (x. 28) calls it Aiath. After the captivity it was repeopled by Benjamites.

From Deir Dîwân the road leads through a hollow to the (20 min.) top of *Tell el-Ḥajar*, and then traverses a beautiful, lofty plain. To the N.E. we see the hill of *Rimmon*, now *Rammôn* (Judges xx. 45-47). Farther on we pass the ruins of *Burj Beitîn*. On the opposite side of a fertile valley we perceive the village of *Beitîn*, which we reach in 20 min. more (p. 217).

10. From Jerusalem to Bethlehem.

Comp. Map, p. 92.

5 M. Good ROAD. — *Carriages* (12 fr.) and *Riding Horses*, see p. 19. The excursion may also be made on foot. — Half-a-day will suffice for Bethlehem itself, but travellers who go on to Solomon's Pools require a whole day (comp. p. 108).

From the Jaffa Gate to the Ophthalmic Hospital of the English Knights of St. John, see pp. 69, 70. At the top of the hill a road to the left ascends to the barren summit of the *Mount of Evil Counsel* (p. 84), which commands a good survey of the S. side of Jerusalem. The ruins of an Arab village on the hill are traditionally called the Country House of Caiaphas. To the S. of the *Weli Abu Tôr* is the tree on which Judas is said to have hanged himself; all its branches extend horizontally towards the E. Tradition has, however, several times changed the position of this tree. — Farther on, to the left of the road, is a large *Convent of Clarissine Nuns*.

The lofty and well cultivated plain extending hence towards the S. is called *El-Bukeiʿa* (p. 15). The plain sinks towards the W. to the *Wâdi el-Werd* (p. 93). On the right, at the entrance to this valley, we first observe the village of *Beit Ṣafâfâ*, and then that of *Esh-Sherâfât*, at some distance. On an eminence close by, to the right, is the Greek settlement called *Ḳaṭamôn* (p. 70). Farther on ($2^1/_2$ M. from Jerusalem), to the left of the road, a cistern is pointed out as the traditional *Well of the Magi*, where they are said to have again seen the guiding star (Matt. ii. 9). Mary also is said to have rested here on her way to Bethlehem, whence its ancient name *Kathisma* (seat), preserved in the modern name *Bîr Kadîsmû*.

We ascend a hill to (3 M.) the monastery of **Mâr Elyâs**, very pleasantly situated (l.) on the saddle of the hill. On the left of the road lies a *Well* from which the Holy Family is said once to have drunk. The view from the terrace of the monastery is very fine. To the S. lies Bethlehem, to the N. Jerusalem, beyond which rises En-Nebi Samwîl, while the blue mountain-range to the E. of Jordan is seen to great advantage.

The monastery was erected at an unknown date by a Bishop Elias, whose tomb was shown in the monastery church down to the 17th cent., and was rebuilt during the Frank régime (1160) after its destruction by the infidels. Shortly afterwards the tradition was invented that the place was connected with the prophet Elijah, and the events described in 1 Kings xix. 3 et seq. were even localized in a depression in the rock (to the right of the road, opposite the monastery-door), which was said to have been made by the prophet's body.

Beyond the monastery the road leads to the right, skirting a valley which descends to the E. and reaches to the Dead Sea. In front of us, beyond the valley towards the S.E., the round summit of the Frank Mountain (p. 110) comes in sight, and towards the S., Bethlehem. On the right (S.S.W.) lies the village of *Beit Jâlâ* (p. 100). After 10 min. we reach *Ṭanṭûr*, a settlement of the Roman

Catholic Maltese Order, beautifully situated on a hill to the right and containing a hospital and chapel. Here is shown the *Field of Peas*, so called from the legend that Christ once asked a man what he was sowing, to which the reply was 'stones'. The field thereupon produced peas of stone, some of which are still to be found on the spot. To the left is a fine view of the Dead Sea.

After 10 min. (4½ M. from Jerusalem) we see on our right the **Tomb of Rachel** (*Ḳubbet Râḥîl*). The dome of the tomb closely resembles those of the innumerable Moslem welis, and the white-washed sarcophagus is modern. The entrance to the forecourt is on the N. side. The tomb is revered by Moslems, Christians, and Jews, and is much visited by pilgrims, especially of the last-named faith. The walls are covered with the names of these devotees. The tomb is generally closed (key with the chief rabbi in Jerusalem).

According to 1 Sam. x. 2 et seq., and Jer. xxxi. 15, the tomb of Rachel was on the border of Benjamin, near Ramah (Er-Râm, p. 216). Traces of a conformable spot (based on old tradition) have been discovered about 1½ M. to the N.E. of *Ḳasṭal* (p. 18). In the time of Christ, however, the tomb was located near Bethlehem and the passage in Jeremiah was regarded as applying to Bethlehem. This view was already shared by the author of the erroneous gloss ('that is Bethlehem') in Gen. xxxv. 19 and xlviii. 7, placed after the name of *Ephrath*, near which Rachel died; and also by the writer of Micah v. 2. Throughout the whole of the Christian period the tradition has always attached to the same spot, and for many centuries the supposed tomb was marked by a pyramid of stones, of which the number was said to have been twelve, corresponding with the number of the tribes of Israel. The monument appears to have been altered in the 15th cent., since which time it has been repeatedly restored.

The whole district was famous in antiquity for its fertility, and its careful cultivation and luxuriant vegetation still present a strong contrast to the environs of Jerusalem and the deserts to the E. and S.E. of Bethlehem (comp. p. 170). To the right of the road, on the opposite slope of the valley, we see the large Christian village of **Beit Jâlâ**, situated in the midst of extensive olive-orchards, to which a road turns off immediately beyond the Tomb of Rachel.

Beit Jâlâ, which, perhaps, corresponds with *Giloh* (Josh. xv. 51; 2 Sam. xv. 12), contains about 4500 inhab., most of whom are Orthodox Greeks (with a church). There are 700-800 Latins, with a seminary of the Latin Patriarchate and a school, and 160 Protestants, with a school and a small church maintained by the German Jerusalem Society.

Beyond the Tomb of Rachel the road divides; the branch straight on leads to Hebron (p. 108). We, however, turn to the left, and in a few minutes reach the first houses of Bethlehem. From the point where the road bends to the right a narrow path straight on brings us to the (2 min.) so-called *David's Well* (water unwholesome). Since the 15th cent. tradition has associated this spot with the narrative in 2 Sam. xxiii. 14-17. Close beside the well a necropolis has been discovered with inscriptions in red pigment (mostly names of the deceased). In the vicinity is a fine mosaic pavement with a Greek inscription (Psalms cxviii. 19), probably the remains of an ancient monastery founded by Paula (p. 106).

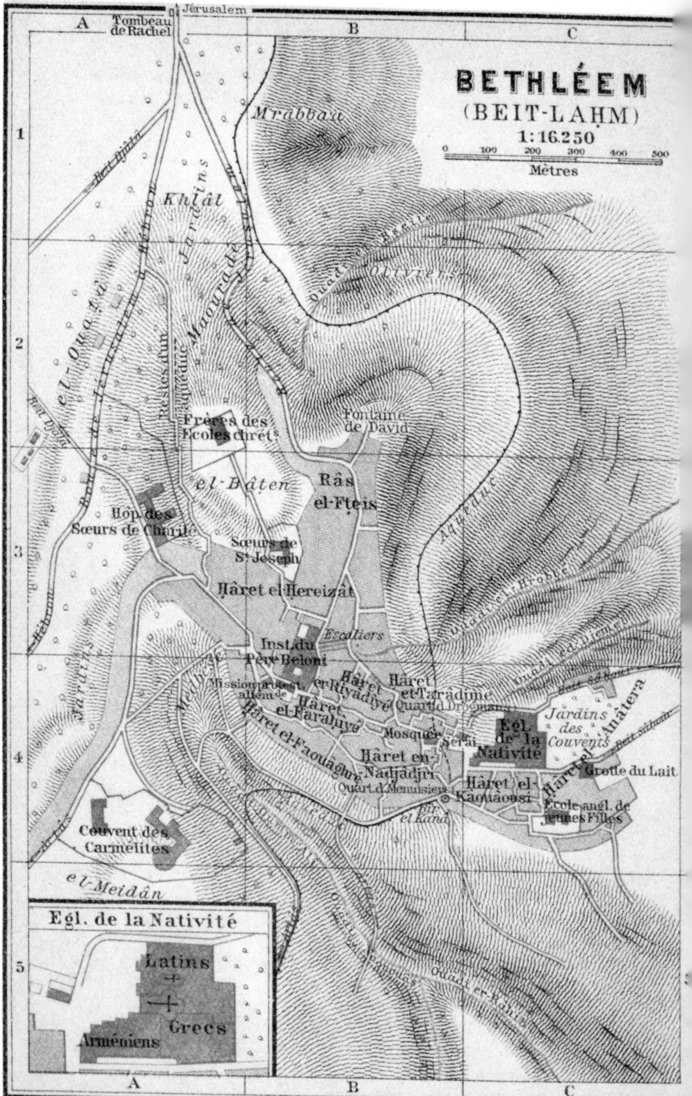
BETHLÉEM
(BEIT-LAHM)
1:16.250
Mètres
Jérusalem
Tombeau de Rachel
M'rabbaa
Khlâl
Frères des Écoles chréts
Fontaine de David
el-Bâten
Râs el-Fteis
Hôp. des Sœurs de Charité
Sœurs de St Joseph
Hâret el-Hereizât
Escaliers
Inst. du Père Beloni
Hâret et-Tarâdime
Mosquée
Serai
Egl. de la Nativité
Jardins des Couvents
Grotte du Lait
Hâret en-Nadjâdjri
Quart. d. Menuisiers
Hâret el-Kaouâousi
École angl. de jeunes Filles
Couvent des Carmélites
el-Meidân
Egl. de la Nativité
Latins
Grecs
Arméniens
Aqueduc
Ouadi er-Rahib
Beit Sâhûr

D'après L. Palmer

Wagner & Debes, Leipz

Bethlehem (2550 ft.), the home of David and the birthplace of Jesus Christ, now contains about 11,000 inhab., nearly all of whom are Christians. The two ridges upon which the town lies are bounded on the N. by the *Wâdi el-Hrobbeh* (Pl. C, 4), on the S. by the *Wâdi er-Râhib* (Pl. B, 5), and on the W. and E. by two shallower depressions. The W. hill is connected with the E. hill by a short saddle. — On the square in front of the church are the Serâi (Pl. B, C, 4), with the Turkish Post and Telegraph Office, some shops, and a small Arab hotel (landlord, *Dabdub*), where nightquarters may be obtained if necessary.

The name of *Bêt Lehem* ('place of bread', or more generally 'place of food'; Arab. *Beit Lahm*) has existed without change during thousands of years. Bethlehem is the scene of the beautiful idyl of the book of Ruth, but it was specially famous as the home of the family of David. Not only that monarch but also other celebrated members of the family, Joab, Asahel, and Abishai, once resided here (2 Sam. ii. 13, 18, 32). It was not, however, until the Christian period, when it began to attract pilgrims, that Bethlehem became a place of any size. Constantine erected a magnificent basilica here in 330 (p. 103), and Justinian caused the walls to be rebuilt. Many monasteries and churches were soon erected, and it is spoken of as a flourishing place about the year 600. On the approach of the Crusaders the Arabs destroyed Bethlehem, but the Franks soon rebuilt the little town and founded a castle near the monastery. In 1244 the place was devastated by the Kharezmians (p. lxxxv), and in 1489 it was again destroyed. For a time the place lost much of its importance, but within the last three centuries it has gradually recovered. Quarrels between the Christians and the Moslems frequently caused bloodshed, and the inhabitants were even occasionally molested by the Beduins. The Moslems were expelled by the Christians in 1831, and after an insurrection in 1834 their quarter was destroyed by order of Ibrâhîm Pasha; there are now only about 300 Moslems in the place.

The inhabitants live chiefly by agriculture and breeding cattle, besides which they have for several centuries been occupied in the manufacture of rosaries, crosses, and other fancy articles in wood, mother-of-pearl, coral, and stinkstone (lime mixed with bitumen) from the Dead Sea. The vases made of the last-named material, however, are very fragile. A visit to one of the workshops will prove interesting. Bethlehem is also the market-town of the Beduins in the neighbourhood.

Comp. *Palmer*, Das jetzige Bethlehem: ZDPV. xvii (1894), 89 et seq.

The town is divided into eight districts. The Latins possess a *Franciscan Monastery* (comp. Pl. A, 5) here with a hospice, boys' school, and pharmacy, and a new church (on the slope of the hill, at the back of the large church); they have also a *Convent of the Sisters of St. Joseph* (Pl. B, 3), with a girls' school and an orphanage. In the S.W. quarter is the French *Convent of the Carmelite Sisters* (Pl. A, 4), a building in the style of the Castle of Sant'Angelo at Rome, with a church and a seminary; on the hill in the N. suburb is the large *Boys' Home and Industrial School of Father Beloni* (Pl. B, 3, 4), with a church; to the N.W., near the Hebron road, is a *Hospital of the Sisters of Charity* (Pl. A, 3); and on the highest point to the N. is a school of the '*Frères des Ecoles Chrétiennes*' (Pl. A, 2). The Greeks have a *Monastery of the Nativity*, the *Churches of St. Helen* and *St. George*, a school for boys, and another for girls. The Armenians also have a large *Monastery*. The three monasteries together form the fortress-like building at the S.E. end of the town (comp. Pl. A, 5). The number of **Protestants** is about 60. There are also a school for girls (Pl. C, 4) and a seminary for female teachers of the English Church Missionary Society, and a German Protestant institution (Pl. B, 4), with a church (p. 107), an orphanage to the W. of the town on the way to Arṭâs (p. 110), and a medical mission.

The large ***Church of the Nativity** (Pl. C, 4), erected over the traditional birthplace of Christ, lies in the E. part of the town, and is the joint property of the Greeks, Latins, and Armenians.

The tradition which localizes the birth of Christ in a cavern near Bethlehem extends back as far as the 2nd century (Justin Martyr). As an

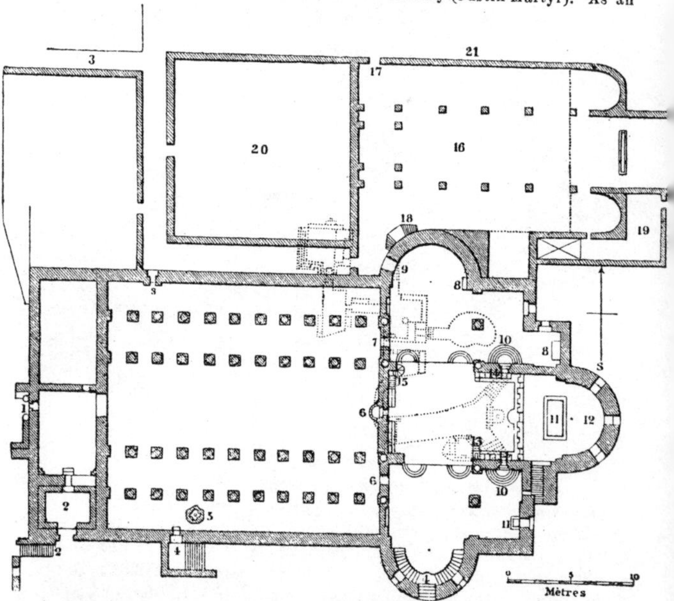

1. *Principal Entrance.* 2. *Entrance to the Armenian Monastery.* 3, 3. *Entrances to the Latin Monastery and Church.* 4, 4. *Entrances to the Greek Monastery.* 5. *Font of the Greeks.* 6, 6. *Entrances of the Greeks to the Choir.* 7. *Common Entrance of the Greeks and Armenians to the Choir.* 8, 8. *Armenian Altars.* 9. *Entrance to the Church of St. Catharine (Latin).* 10, 10. *Steps leading to the Grotto of the Nativity* (comp. Plan, p. 104). 11, 11. *Greek Altars.* 12. *Greek Choir.* 13. *Throne of the Greek Patriarch.* 14. *Seats of the Greek Clergy.* 15. *Pulpit.* 16. *Latin Church of St. Catharine.* 17. *Entrance to the Latin Monastery.* 18. *Stairs to the Grottoes* (comp. Plan, p. 104). 19. *Latin Sacristy.* 20. *Schools of the Franciscans.* 21. *Latin Monastery.*

The dotted lines in the above Plan indicate the situation of the grottoes under the church (comp. Plan, p. 104).

insult to the Christians, Hadrian is said to have destroyed a church which stood on the sacred spot, and to have erected a temple of Adonis on its site, but this story is not authenticated. It is certain that a basilica was erected here by order of the Emperor Constantine. The assertion that the present church is the original structure is based on the simplicity of its style and the absence of characteristics of the buildings of the subsequent era of Justinian. Other authorities consider it beyond question that the building underwent considerable restoration in the days of Justinian (527-565). In any case, it is not only extremely old, but specially interesting as an example of the earliest Christian style of architecture. In the year 1010 the church is said to have miraculously escaped destruction by the Moslems under Ḥâkim, and the Franks found the church uninjured. Throughout the accounts of all the pilgrims of the middle ages there prevails so remarkable a unanimity regarding the situation and architecture of the church, that there can be little doubt that it has never been altered. On Christmas Day, 1101, Baldwin was crowned king here, and in 1110 Bethlehem was elevated to the rank of an episcopal see. The church soon afterwards underwent a thorough restoration, and the Byzantine emperor Manuel Comnenos (1143-1180) munificently caused the walls to be adorned with gilded mosaics. The church was covered with lead. In 1482 the roof, which had become dilapidated, was repaired, Edward IV. of England giving the lead for the purpose, and Philip of Burgundy the pine-wood. At that period the mosaics fell into disrepair. Towards the end of the 17th cent. the Turks stripped the roof of its lead, in order to make bullets. On the occasion of a restoration of the church in 1672 the Greeks managed to obtain possession of it. The Latins were again admitted to a share of the proprietorship of the church through the intervention of Napoleon III. in 1852. — Comp. 'The Church of the Nativity at Bethlehem', by *W. Harvey* and others, edited by *R. Weir Schultz* (London, 1911; 30*s*.).

In front of the principal entrance on the W. side lies a large paved space, in which traces of the former atrium of Constantine's basilica have been discovered. From the atrium three doors led into the vestibule of the church; but of these the central one (Pl. 1) only has been preserved, and it has long been reduced to very small dimensions from fear of the Moslems. The portal is of quadrangular form, and the simply decorated lintel is supported by two brackets. The porch is dark, and is divided by walls into several chambers. Being no higher than the aisles, its roof is greatly overtopped by the pointed gable of the church. The side-doors leading into the church are also walled up.

The Interior of the church is characterized by the grand simplicity of the structure. It consists of a nave and double aisles, and of a wide transept and a semicircular apse, which are unfortunately concealed by a wall erected by the Greeks in 1842. The floor is paved with large slabs of stone. The aisles are lower than the nave and only $4^1/_2$ and 4 yds. in width. The nave and aisles are separated from each other by four rows (11 to a row) of monolithic columns of reddish limestone, with white veins. The base of each column rests on a square slab. The capitals are Corinthian, but show a decline of the style; at the top of each is engraved a cross. The columns, including capitals and bases, are 19 ft. high. Above the columns are architraves. In the aisles these architraves bear the wooden beams of the roof. The aisles were not, as elsewhere, raised to the height of the nave by means of an upper gallery, but walls were erected to a height of about 32 ft. above the architraves of the inner row of columns for the support of the roof-beams of the nave. These form a pointed roof, which was once richly painted and gilded. Unfortunately very little has been preserved of the mosaics of Comnenos (p. 103). The lowest row on the S. (right) side consists of a series of half-figures of the ancestors of Christ, of which seven only, representing the immediate ancestors of Joseph,

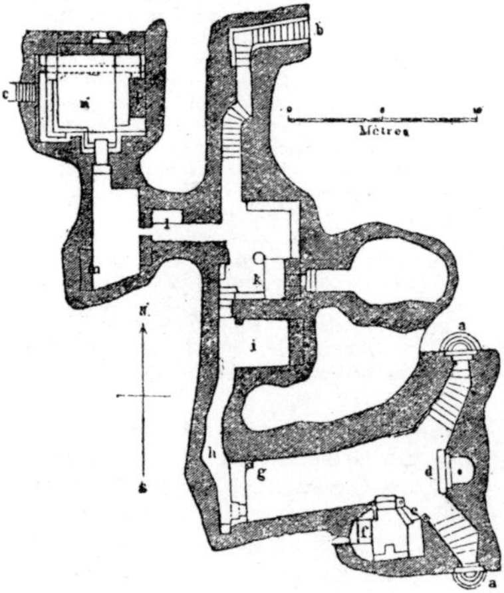

a, a. *Stairs to the Crypt*, descending from the Greek choir of the church of the Nativity (see Plan, p. 102). b. *Stairs to the Crypt*, from the Latin Church of St. Catharine. c. *Stairs now closed.* d. *Place of the Nativity.* e. *Manger of the Latins.* f. *Altar of the Adoration of the Magi.* g. *Spring of the Holy Family.* h. *Passage in the Rock.* i. *Scene of the Vision commanding the Flight into Egypt.* k. *Chapel of the Innocents.* l. *Tomb of Eusebius.* m. *Tomb of St. Jerome.* n. *Chapel of St. Jerome.*

are now distinguishable; above these, interspersed with fantastic foliage, are arcades, containing altars concealed by curtains, on which books of the Gospels are placed. The Greek inscription above contains an extract from the resolutions of the Council of Constantinople (381; concerning the Godhead of the Holy Ghost), and still higher are two crosses. On the N. (left) side, in the spaces between the fantastic plants, are representations of the interior of the churches of Antioch and Sardica, and a third church, with altars and books of the Gospels. Here, too, are inscriptions relating to the resolutions of Councils. The drawing is very primitive, being without perspective.

Three passages (Pl. 6, 6, 7) lead us into the transept, which is of the same width as the nave. The four angles formed by the intersection of the transept with the nave are formed by four large piers, into which are built pilasters and half-columns corresponding to the columns of the nave. The transepts terminate in semicircular apses. The aisles are prolonged to the E. beyond the transept, to the right and left of the choir; they are of unequal length and have rectilinear instead of apsidal terminations. The mosaics in the transept, some only of which are now distinguishable, chiefly represent the history of Christ. The S. apse of the transept contains a very quaint representation of the Entry into Jerusalem. In the N. apse is a representation of the scene where Christ invites Thomas to examine his wounds. The apostles here are without the nimbus. A third fragment represents the Ascension, but the upper part is gone. Here again the apostles are without the nimbus; in their midst is the Virgin between two angels.

Two flights of steps (Nos. 10, 10 on the large ground-plan, p. 102; 'a, a' on the plan at p. 104) descend into the CHAPEL OF THE NATIVITY, which is situated below the choir and is lighted by 32 lamps. It is 40 ft. long (from E. to W.), 12 ft. wide, and 10 ft. high. The pavement is of marble, and the walls, which are of masonry, are lined with marble. Under the altar in the recess to the E., a silver star (Pl. d) is let into the pavement, with the inscription '*Jesus Christus natus est hic de Virgine Maria*'. Around the recess burn 15 lamps, of which 6 belong to the Greeks, 5 to the Armenians, and 4 to the Latins. The recess still shows a few traces of mosaics. This sacred spot was richly decorated as early as the time of Constantine, and even with the Moslems was in high repute at a later period. — Opposite the recess of the Nativity are three steps (Pl. e) descending to the CHAPEL OF THE MANGER. The manger, in which, according to tradition, Christ was once laid, is of marble, the bottom being white, and the front brown; a wax-doll represents the Infant. The form of the chapel and manger of Bethlehem have in the course of centuries undergone many changes; and a cradle-like manger is shown as the original in the church of Santa Maria Maggiore in Rome, to which it was probably brought about the year 750. In the same chapel, to the E., is the *Altar of the Adoration of the Magi* (Pl. f), belonging to the Latins. The picture is quite modern. — At the end of the subterranean passage towards the W. we observe a round hole (Pl. g) on the right, out of which water is said to have burst forth for the use of the Holy Family. In the 15th cent. the tradition was invented that the star which had guided the Magi fell into this spring, in which none but virgins could see it.

The entrance to the N. part of the grotto, which belongs to the Latins, is from the Church of St. Catharine (see below). We leave the grotto by the N. steps (No. 10 on the ground-plan, p. 102), and continue past the Armenian Altars (Nos. 8, 8 on the ground-plan, p. 102) to the N. apse of the transept, where a door (No. 9 on the ground-plan, p. 102) leads into the CHURCH OF ST. CATHARINE (No. 16 on the ground-plan, p. 102). Here Christ is said to have appeared to St. Catharine of Alexandria and to have predicted her martyrdom. The church is probably identical with a chapel of

St. Nicholas mentioned in the 14th century. It is handsomely fitted up and in 1881 was entirely re-erected by the Franciscans. — On the N. and W. is the *Monastery of the Franciscans*, which looks like a fortress with its massive walls.

Some steps in the S.W. corner of the church (No. 18 on ground-plan, p. 102; 'b' on ground-plan, p. 104) descend into the *Chapel of the Innocents* (Pl. k), where, according to a tradition of the 15th cent., Herod caused several children to be slain, who had been brought here for safety by their mothers. — Five steps lead hence to a second *Chapel* (Pl. i; fitted up in 1621), where Joseph is said to have been commanded by the angel to flee into Egypt. Other Scriptural events were also associated by tradition with this spot.

We return to the Chapel of the Innocents (Pl. k) and enter the passage to the left, containing the altar and tomb of *Eusebius of Cremona* (Pl. l), of which there is no mention before 1556. A presbyter named Eusebius (not to be confounded with Eusebius, Bishop of Cremona in the 7th cent.) was a pupil of St. Jerome, but that he died in Bethlehem is unlikely. Farther on is the *Tomb of St. Jerome* (Pl. m), in a chapel hewn in the rock. The tomb of the great Latin Church Father, who was born in Dalmatia about 340 and died at Bethlehem in 420, has been shown on this spot for about three centuries. St. Jerome is chiefly famous for his translation of the Bible into Latin (the Vulgate), for which his knowledge of Hebrew specially fitted him. Opposite the tomb of St. Jerome, on the E., the tombs of his pupil *Paula* and her daughter *Eustochium* (formerly on the S. side of the church) have been shown since 1566. — A little farther to the N. is the large *Chapel of St. Jerome* (Pl. n), in which he is said to have dwelt and to have written his works. It was originally hewn out of the rock, but is now lined with masonry. A window looks towards the cloisters. A painting here represents St. Jerome with a Bible in his hand. The chapel is mentioned for the first time in 1449, and the tomb of the saint (see above) was also once shown here.

To the S. of the basilica are the *Armenian* and the *Greek Monastery*. The tower of the Greek Monastery affords a beautiful View of Bethlehem and its environs, particularly towards the S. and E., into the Wâdi er-Râhib, and towards Tekoah and the Frank Mountain.

From the open space in front of the basilica a street leads S.E., between houses, the Greek Monastery, and its dependencies. After 5 min. we come (r.) to the so-called *Milk Grotto*, or *Women's Cavern*, a natural rocky cavern about 16 ft. long, 10 ft. wide, and 8 ft. high. The tradition from which it derives its name is that the Holy Family once sought shelter or concealment here, and that a drop of the Virgin's milk fell on the floor of the grotto. For many centuries both Christians and Moslems have entertained a superstitious belief that the rock of this cavern has the property of increasing the milk of women and even of animals, and to this day round cakes mixed with dust from the rock are offered to pilgrims.

The view from the platform of the *German Protestant Church* includes the large Carmelite Monastery to the W., the village of Beit Jâlâ (p. 100) to the N.W., and Arṭâs (p. 110) and the mountains of Judæa to the S.; the towers of the vineyards should be noticed (Matt. xxi. 33).

In order to visit the so-called *Field of the Shepherds*, we may continue to follow the road which led us to the Milk Grotto towards the E., descending in 7 min., to a chapel dedicated to St. Joseph which occupies the site of a small church of earlier date. Here, according to a mediæval tradition, stood the *House of Joseph*, in which he had his dream (Matt. i. 20). In 5 min. more we reach the village of *Beit Sâḥûr en-Naṣârâ* (*i.e.* 'of the Christians'). The first mention of it is by pilgrims in the 16th cent.; perhaps it is the *Ashur* of 1 Chron. ii. 24. It has about 1800 inhabitants, mostly Orthodox Greeks, with a few Latins and Moslems. There are several grottoes with flint tools and cisterns here. The highest cistern, situated in the middle of the village, is famous as the scene of a traditional miracle: the inhabitants having refused to draw water for the Virgin, the water rose in the well of its own accord. The dwelling of the shepherds is now placed here (Luke ii. 8). The key of the Grotto of the Shepherds must be obtained at the Greek monastery here *(Deir er-Rûm)*. — We then ride on towards the E. through a small, well-cultivated plain, called by tradition the *Field of Boaz* (Ruth ii. 3 et seq.). After 10 min. we reach the **Field of the Shepherds,** in the middle of which is the *Grotto of the Shepherds* (Arab. *Deir er-Ra'wât, i. e.* Convent of the Shepherds), a cavern now converted into a chapel and probably originally used as a cistern. A very old tradition makes this the spot where the angels appeared to the shepherds. The subterranean chapel, to which 21 steps descend, contains some paintings, shafts of columns, and a few traces of a mediæval mosaic pavement. Around lie some ruins which perhaps belong to the small mediæval church of '*Gloria in Excelsis*'. An attempt has been made to identify the site of this church with the ruin of *Khirbet Ṣiyâr el-Ghanam*, about 650 yds. to the N., but it is questionable whether the latter ruins could once have been a church with nave and two aisles (as is asserted).

The *Tower of Edar* (Gen. xxxv. 21) or *Tower of Flocks*, in the Field of the Shepherds, was known to Paula (p. 106). Arculfus (ca. 670) relates that a fine church stood there and that the tombs of the shepherds were shown in the rock. At the time of the Crusades the church long lay in ruins.

From Bethlehem viâ Arṭâs to the *Pools of Solomon* (50 min.), see pp. 110, 109; to the *Monastery of Mâr Sâbâ*, see p. 136; to *Engedi*, see p. 171.

11. From Jerusalem to the Pools of Solomon and the Frank Mountain.

Comp. Map, p. 92.

CARRIAGE ROAD as far as the *Pools of Solomon*, 8 M. (carriages and saddle-horses, see p. 19); thence with guide viâ Khareitûn to the *Frank Mountain* 3 hrs.; from the Frank Mountain to *Bethlehem* $1^1/_2$ hr.; thence back to Jerusalem $1^1/_4$ hr. — By starting early from Jerusalem the traveller may accomplish the round trip in one day, although by so doing no time is left for a visit to Bethlehem (nightquarters, see p. 101). Provisions and lights should be taken. If the traveller wishes to see the Pools only, he can do this best when visiting Bethlehem (p. 101) or Hebron (p. 113).

From the Jaffa Gate to the *Tomb of Rachel* ($1^1/_4$ hr.), see pp. 99, 100. Thence we follow the Hebron road (p. 100), from which a few yards farther on a road diverges to the right to Beit Jâlâ (p. 100).

Beyond Bethlehem, on the left, is the German orphanage for Armenian children. After about 50 min., at the point where the road bends, we observe on the right the Greek monastery *Deir el-Khaḍr*, with an asylum for the insane, close to the village of *El-Khaḍr*. A few minutes farther on is *Ḳal'at el-Burak*, or 'castle by the pools', erected in the 17th cent. for protection against the Beduins. We here obtain the key for the spring *'Ain Ṣâliḥ*, which rises on the hill about 110 yds. to the W., and is supposed by the Christians, curiously enough, to be the *Sealed Fountain* of the Song of Solomon (iv. 12). The well-house contains two dark chambers, in the innermost of which the water bubbles forth from the wall. The water of the different streams is conducted by the main pipe of the new water-system of Jerusalem past the pools. The overflow of the spring is conveyed by the old conduit to a point below the uppermost pool. Thence it flows by an iron pipe to rejoin the main conduit. There is a second fountain a little to the S. of the castle, the water of which flows in the old conduit mentioned above.

The so-called ***Pools of Solomon** *(El-Burak)*, situated in a small valley at the back of the castle, served as a reservoir for the old aqueduct of Jerusalem (p. 109). They owe their name to the supposition that the gardens of Solomon were in the Wâdi Arṭâs (p. 109), and to an arbitrary interpretation of Eccles. ii. 6, where pools for irrigation purposes are mentioned. According to Josephus, Pilate built (or repaired) a conduit with money taken from the Temple treasury, and an attempt has been made to connect this with Solomon's Pools (comp. p. 109). As a matter of fact, there is really no evidence whatever as to the date of the construction of the reservoir. There are three pools, at intervals of 52-53 yds. from each other, the second being about 19 ft. above the first, and the third the same height above the second. At the lower (E.) end of each pool a wall is built across the valley, as is the case with the Sultan's Pool (p. 70). The *Highest Pool* is 127 yds. long, 76 yds. wide at the top and 79 yds. below, and at the lower (E.) end 25 ft.

deep. It is partly hewn in the rock, and partly enclosed by masonry, buttresses being used for the support of the walls. A staircase descends in the S.W. corner. The *Central Pool* is 141 yds. long, 53 yds. wide at the top and 83 yds. below, and 38 ft. deep. It is almost entirely hewn in the rock, and stairs descend in the N.W. and N.E. corners. In the N.E. corner is the mouth of a conduit from ʿAin Ṣâliḥ (see p. 108). The E. wall of the reservoir is very thick, and is strengthened by a second wall with a buttress in the form of steps. To the left of the road are seen remains of the old conduit (see p. 108 and below). The *Lowest Pool*, the finest of the three, is 194 yds. long, 49 yds. wide at the top and 69 yds. below, and at places 48 ft. deep. It is partly hewn in the rock, and partly lined with masonry. Stairs descend in the S.E. and N.E. corners. The inner walls are supported by numerous buttresses. On the S. side there is a conduit for the reception of rain-water. The lower wall (E.) is built of large blocks in the form of steps, and is penetrated by a passage leading to a chamber. Similar chambers, but inaccessible, exist in the lower masonry of the other pools. In the chamber of the lowest pool rises the third spring, *ʿAin Farûjeh*, and a little to the E. of it, another spring, *ʿAin ʿAṭân*, issues from a little valley to the S. The two springs unite and join the new Jerusalem aqueduct (p. 108) below the third pool.

These springs, however, did not suffice for the water supply of ancient Jerusalem. Two other large Conduits met at the pools and allowed their water to flow into them. One of these conduits runs above the first pool and was carried through the valley of ʿ*Aṭân* by a tunnel. Farther on it runs to the S. along the W. slope of the *Wâdi Deir el-Benât* (Valley of the Nunnery), then for 3/4 hr. along the bottom of the *Wâdi el-Biyâr* (Valley of Springs), or *Wâdi el-Fuheimish*, in a channel cut in the rock and with openings in the top, and finally flows into the spring *Bîr ed-Derej* (Spring of the Steps). The other conduit, a channel 2½ ft. wide, begins in the *Wâdi el-ʿArrûb* (p. 112), crosses the slope of the hills, and flows into the middle pool. The total length of its remarkable windings, amounting to about 47 M., corresponds with the statement of Josephus (400 stadia). — From the pools the water was carried to the city in two different conduits. The higher of these conveyed the water from *ʿAin Sâliḥ* and the aqueduct of the *Wâdi el-Biyâr* along the N. slope of the *Wâdi el-Burak* (Valley of the Pools). It was partly hewn in the rock, partly constructed of masonry. The conduit descends near Rachel's Tomb and then rises again: here the water ran in stone siphon-pipes. The lower conduit, still in a state of complete preservation, conveyed water to the city from all the pools and springs in great windings about 20 M. long. One arm of the conduit was connected, no doubt under Herod's government, with the Arṭâs spring, and conducted to the Frank Mountain. The main arm passed Bethlehem and Rachel's Tomb on the S. By the bridge over the Valley of Hinnom the upper and lower conduits met, and ran along the S. slope of the W. hill of Jerusalem towards the temple. The upper conduit is the more artificial construction, and is no doubt the older.

We descend the *Wâdi Arṭâs* towards the E. (carriage-road), where at several points the conduit is open to view. After 10 min. we observe on the opposite side of the valley, to our right, a conical hill with ruins and rock-tombs, probably the site of the ancient *Etam* (1 Chron. iv. 3), the name of which is still preserved in ʿAin ʿAṭân

(p. 109). In 7 min. more we see to the right below us the rather forlorn village of **Arṭâs**, chiefly inhabited by Moslems, with a convent and church of the Sisters of Notre Dame du Jardin.

FROM ARṬÂS TO BETHLEHEM. The road continues to follow the conduit. After 8 min. a view of the town is obtained in front; in 1/4 hr. more the foot of the hill is reached, and the ascent is made in 10 minutes.

Farther on the road descends the valley. After 20 min. a small lateral valley descends from Bethlehem on the left, while the main valley, along which the road now continues, curves to the S.E. Our route frequently crosses the stony bed of the brook. After 1/4 hr. we observe the ruins of mills on the rock to the right. After 1/2 hr. we leave the Wâdi Arṭâs and ascend a lateral valley to the right (S.W.). After 10 min. this valley makes a sharp bend to the left (S.); another lateral valley descends from the right (N.W.).

Proceeding farther up the valley to the S., we come in 3/4 hr. to *Khirbet Teḳû'a*, the ancient **Tekoah**, on the summit of a long hill, 2790 ft. above the level of the sea. At the foot is a spring. The place was fortified by Rehoboam, and was celebrated as the birthplace of the prophet Amos, who was originally a herdsman (Amos i. 1). The ruins are a shapeless mass; the remains of a church (there was a monastery here in the middle ages) may still be recognized, and an octagonal font is to be seen.

At this bend we leave the valley and ascend the steep hillside to the E. At the top we again see Bethlehem. In 20 min. we descend to the spring of Khareitûn, named *Bîr el-'Aineizîyeh;* by the rock opposite lies the ancient ruined 'laura', or monkish settlement of *Khareitûn*, and before us opens a deep gorge. The whole scene is very imposing. We now descend on foot by a path to the right along the hills to the traditional **Cave of Adullam** (now called *El-Ma'ṣâ* or *Maghâret Khareitûn*), which has been identified since the 12th cent. with the fastness in which David sought refuge (comp. p. 125). In the Christian period it was occupied by St. Chariton (d. ca. 410), and later also by other hermits. The opening is partly blocked by fallen rocks. The cavern is a natural labyrinthine grotto formed by the erosion of water, and, as the explorer may easily lose his way, he should be provided with a cord of at least 220 yds. in length, or better with a guide. The temperature in the interior is somewhat high, and coat and waistcoat may be advantageously left at the entrance. The galleries are often so low as to be passable by creeping only, but they sometimes expand into large chambers. In many places the ground sounds hollow, as there are several stories of passages, one above another. The innermost passages contain niches cut in the rock, and the fragments of urns and sarcophagi found here indicate that the place was once used for interments. The inscriptions found in the inmost recesses are illegible.

From the *Wâdi Arṭâs*, and a little above the point at which we left it, a road ascends to the N.E. to the (1 hr.) —

Frank Mountain (2490 ft.), so called because the Crusaders here offered their last prolonged resistance to the Moslems. The Arabic name is *Jebel el-Fureidîs* ('paradise' or 'orchard').

The attempted identification with *Beth Haccerem* (Jer. vi. 1) fails of proof. Josephus says (Ant. xv. 9, 4, etc.) that Herod founded the castle of *Herodium* near Tekoah and about 60 stadia to the S. of Jerusalem. This distance and the further description of the castle seem to fit the present ruins. Josephus states that the hill was thrown up artificially, a statement which is correct, if the rounded top only of the hill be taken into account. He also informs us that Herod was buried here. Herodium was the seat of a toparchy. After the overthrow of Jerusalem it surrendered without a blow to the legate, Lucilius Bassus.

At the foot of the hill, on the W. side, are some ruins called *Ṣṭabl* (stable) by the natives, and a large reservoir, called *Birket Bint es-Sulṭân* (pool of the sultan's daughter), 81 yds. long and 49 broad, but now dry. In the middle of it rises a square structure, resembling an island. Remains of the conduit from the Arṭâs spring (p. 109) are also visible. On the N. we see traces of the great flight of 200 steps mentioned by Josephus. The summit of the hill, which rises in an abrupt (ca. 35°) conical form to a height of about 330 ft., may be reached in 10 minutes. The castle which once stood here has disappeared with the exception of the enclosing wall, of which the chief traces are the remains of four round towers mentioned by Josephus. The E. tower contains a vaulted chamber with a mosaic pavement. The large, regular, and finely hewn blocks of stone which lie on the plateau at the top and on the slopes of the hill are excellent specimens of the masonry used in the buildings of Herod (p. xcvi).

The *View is beautiful. It embraces to the E. the desert region extending down to the neighbourhood of the Dead Sea, with a profusion of wild cliffs, between which a great part of the blue sheet of water is visible. To the S. the view is intercepted by hills. To the S.W. are the ruins of Tekoah and the village of Khareitûn. To the W.S.W. is the weli of Abu Nejeim, and to the N.W. Bethlehem; to the right of it Beit Sâḥûr, and in the foreground Beit Taʿâmir (see below); on a hill rises Mâr Elyâs. To the N. are En-Nebi Samwîl and Abu Dîs. Farther off stretches the chain of hills to the N. of Jerusalem.

The Road to Bethlehem ascends to the N.W., at first along the *Wâdi eḍ-Ḍiyaʿ*. After 1/4 hr. we leave the abandoned village of *Beit Taʿâmir* (with traces of ancient buildings) on a hill to our right. After 25 min. the way begins to descend into the *Wâdi el-Ḳauwâs* to the S. of Bethlehem, and in 1/2 hr. more it reaches the floor of the valley, whence it ascends to *Bethlehem* (p. 101) in 1/4 hr.

12. From Jerusalem to Hebron.

Comp. Map, p. 92.

23 M. Carriage Road. Time required: for carriages 4 1/2 hrs., for riders 6 hrs. (comp. p. 19). Price for a carriage 30 fr., or if a night be spent out 40 fr. Dragoman advisable.

From Jerusalem to the *Pools of Solomon* (2 1/4 hrs.), see p. 108. Our route ascends gradually past the highest pool to the hill towards the S.W. ($^1/_4$ hr.), where we obtain a fine retrospect of Bethlehem and the Mount of Olives. As we proceed we see the ruins of Deir el-Benât on the right; to the left, far below, is the deep Wâdi el-Biyâr (p. 109). Our road runs in great windings along the slopes of the hills round the ravines of the lateral valleys of the Wâdi el-Biyâr. On the right is *Khirbet Beit Zakaryâ* (*Beth-Zachariah;* 1 Macc. vi. 32 et seq.), where Judas Maccabæus was defeated by Antiochus Eupator; on the left, Khirbet Beit Faghûr. After 40 min. we cross the *Wâdi el-Biyâr* near its head and come to a small plateau. On our right (12 M.) is *Khirbet Beit Ṣâwîr.* Farther on we reach ($12^1/_2$ M.) *Khirbet Beit Shaʿr*, on the right, with a new settlement; at some distance off, on the hill, is *Beit Ummar* (perhaps *Maʿarath*, Josh. xv. 59), and near it are the ruins of *Khirbet Jedûr* (*Gedor*, Josh. xv. 58). We descend into the broad *Wâdi el-ʿArrûb*, and in $^1/_4$ hr. ($14^1/_2$ M.) we reach the —

Bridge over the Wâdi el-ʿArrûb, where the coachman generally halts at a small café. To the right and left of the road are copious springs; immediately to the right (W.) of the bridge is a well-room. A portion of the water is brought by a subterranean conduit from the isolated ruin-strewn hill to the W. On this hill lie the extensive ruins of *Khirbet Ḳûfîn.*

About 10 min. below the bridge is a large but now dry reservoir known as *Birket el-ʿArrûb.* This reservoir (80 yds. long by $53^1/_2$ yds. broad) is of similar construction to Solomon's Pools, and is connected with them by the conduit mentioned at p. 109.

From the bridge the road ascends past a (10 min.) pool *(Birket Ḳûfîn)* partly hewn in the rock, the water from which used also to be conducted to the Birket el-ʿArrûb; it is dry in summer. On the S. side of the hill, a few paces to the right of the road, are several fine rock-tombs and small caverns. Above, to the left, is (17 M.) *Khirbet Kheirân.* After $1^1/_4$ M. more we reach (left) the spring of *ʿAin ed-Dirweh*, above which are a Mohammedan house and a praying-place. In the time of Eusebius the spring in which Philip baptized the eunuch was pointed out here (comp. p. 93), and it is so marked on the mosaic map of Mâdebâ (p. 152). The traces of an ancient church were formerly visible. A little way to the S. there are tomb-chambers in the rock. At the top of the hill are ruins called *Beit Ṣûr*, which answer to the ancient *Beth-Zur* (Josh. xv. 58; Nehem. iii. 16). At the period of the Maccabees Beth-Zur was a place of great importance. A little farther on (5 min.) the Mohammedan village of *Ḥalḥûl* (Josh. xv. 58) becomes visible on a hill to the left. The mosque of *Nebi Yûnus*, outside the village, is built, according to Moslem tradition, over the grave of the prophet Jonah. Later Jewish writers mention a tradition that the prophet Gad was buried here (2 Sam. xxiv. 11). There are rock-tombs in the neighbourhood.

A little farther on ($20^1/_2$ M. from Jerusalem) we perceive, about 440 yds. to the left of the road, the ruins of **Ḥaram Râmet el-Khalîl.* The S. and W. walls only are preserved (71 yds. and $53^1/_2$ yds.

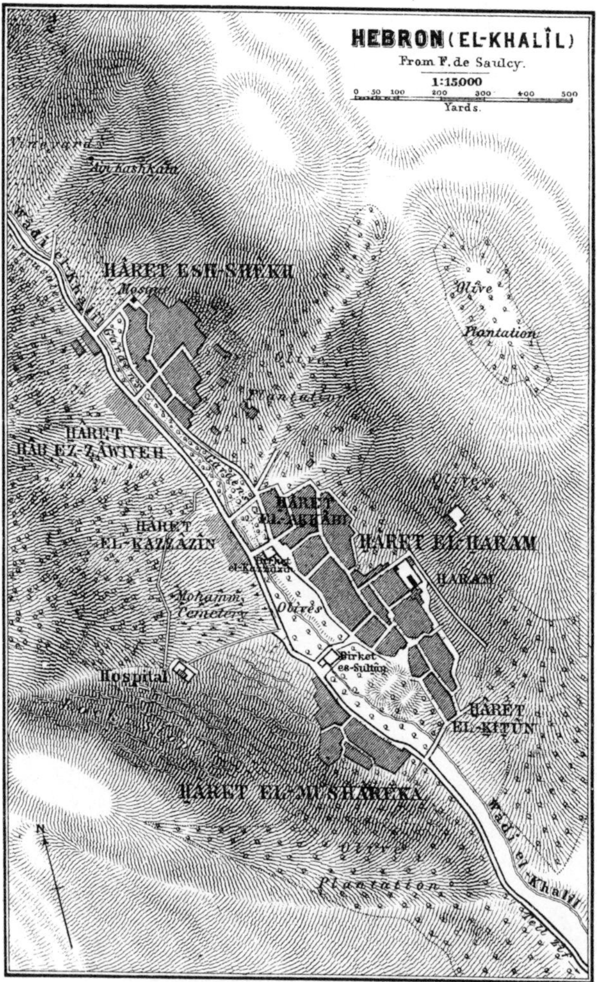

Wagner & Debes' Geograph. Estabi. Leipzig.

long respectively), and two or three courses of stone are still visible. The blocks are of great length (10-16 ft.) and are jointed without mortar. In the S.W. angle of the interior there is a cistern. What purpose the building served, and whether it was ever completed, cannot now be ascertained. Jewish tradition places here the *Grove of Mamre* (see p. 115), and the valley is still called the *Valley of Terebinths* (comp. p. 124). The earliest Christian tradition also looks for Mamre somewhere between Hebron and Beit Ṣûr (p. 112). About 60 paces farther to the E. is a large ruined church, probably the basilica erected by Constantine at the terebinth of Mamre. Near it are two oil-presses in the rock. A large cistern 5 min. farther to the S. is shown as the bath of Sarah.

Returning to the road, we come, a few paces farther on, to an indifferent footpath on the right, which leads past the ruins of the village of *Khirbet en-Naṣârâ* ('ruin of the Christians'), or *Rujûm Sebzîn*, and proceeds direct to (1/2 hr.) the Russian hospice, the tower of which is visible from afar. Following the road, we gradually descend the hill, pass the hospital of the Scots Mission (see below), and reach the small town of *El-Khalîl* (Hebron) in about 1/2 hr.

Hebron. — **Accommodation.** Russian Hospice, near Abraham's Oak (p. 115; good lodging but without board; during the season a letter of recommendation from the superintendent of the Russian Buildings at Jerusalem is necessary). In case of necessity male travellers can obtain accommodation in some Jewish Houses. The price should be fixed beforehand. — ***Turkish Post & Telegraph Office.*** — *Anglo-Palestine Co.'s Bank.* — It is advisable to take a Guide (6-12 pi.; more in proportion for a party), as the Moslems here are notorious for their fanaticism. Travellers are earnestly warned against that arrant beggar, the son of the deceased old sheikh Ḥamza.

The *Scots Mission (United Free Church)* has a hospital here (physician, *Dr. Paterson*). The *German Jerusalem Society* maintains a native teacher, who also conducts Protestant service in the Arabic tongue.

History. ***Hebron*** is a town of hoar antiquity. Mediæval tradition localized the creation of Adam here; and at a very early period, owing to a misinterpretation of Joshua xiv. 15, where Arba is spoken of as the greatest *man* among the Anakim (giants), Adam's death was placed here. The ancient name of Hebron was *Kirjath Arba* ('city of Arba'). In Numbers xiii. 22 it is claimed that Hebron was founded seven years before Zoan, *i.e.* Tanis, the chief town of Lower Egypt. Abraham is also stated to have pitched his tent under the oaks of Mamre, the Amorite (Gen. xiii. 18, xiv. 13). When Sarah died (Gen. xxiii.) Abraham purchased from Ephron the Hittite the double cavern of ***Machpelah*** as a family burial-place; and Isaac and Jacob were also said to be buried here. Hebron was destroyed by Joshua (Josh. x. 37) and became the chief city of the house of Caleb (Josh. xiv. 13). David spent a long time in the region of Hebron. After Saul's death David ruled over Judah from Hebron for 7 1/2 years. It was at the gates of Hebron that Abner was slain by Joab, and David caused the murderers of Ishbosheth, the son of Saul, to be hanged by the pool of Hebron. Hebron afterwards became the headquarters of the rebellious Absalom (2 Sam. iv. 12). It was fortified by Rehoboam, and repeopled after the captivity. Judas Maccabæus had to recapture it from the Edomites, and Josephus reckons it as a town of Idumæa. Hebron was next destroyed by the Romans. During the Moslem period Hebron regained much of its old importance, partly by its commerce, and partly as a sacred place owing to its connection with Abraham (comp. p. lxviii), to whom its Arabian name refers (see p. 114). The Crusaders called Hebron the *Castellum*, or

Praesidium ad Sanctum Abraham. Godfrey of Bouillon invested the knight Gerard of Avesnes with the place as a feudal fief. In 1167 it became the seat of a Latin bishop, but in 1187 it fell into the hands of Saladin.

Hebron, Arabic *El-Khalîl* (abbreviated from Khalîl er-Raḥmân, 'friend of God', *i. e.* 'the city of Abraham, the friend of God'), the capital of a Ḳaḍâ (p. lvii), contains 22,000 inhab., including 2000 Jews (with three synagogues). It lies 3040 ft. above the level of the sea, in the narrow part of a valley descending from the N.W. The environs abound in springs and are extremely fertile. The Jews make good wine from the grapes grown in the vicinity (comp. p. 116), and almond and apricot trees also flourish. The place has also some commercial importance and carries on a brisk trade with the Beduins. The chief branches of industry are the manufacture of water-skins from goats' hides, and glass-making. Glass was manufactured here as early as the middle ages, and the principal articles made are lamps and coloured glass rings used by the women as ornaments. A visit to the glass-furnaces is not uninteresting.

The present town is divided into seven districts, irrespective of the large Jewish quarters to the N.W. and S.W. 1. In the N.W., the *Ḥâret esh-Sheikh*, deriving its name from the beautiful *Mosque* (begun in 668, or A.D. 1269-70) *of the Sheikh 'Ali Bakkâ*, a pious man who died in 670 (A.D. 1271-72). Above this quarter is the aqueduct of the *Ḳashḳala* spring, near which there are ancient grottoes and rock-tombs. From the spring a path leads to the top of the hill *Hobâl er-Riyâḥ*. 2. *Ḥâret Bâb ez-Zâwiyeh*, adjoining the first quarter on the W. To the S. of the second quarter is (3) *Ḥâret el-Ḳazzâzîn* (of the glass-blowers), and to the E. (4) *Ḥâret el-'Aḳḳâbi* (water-skin makers). Farther to the S. are (5) *Ḥâret el-Ḥaram* and (6) *Ḥâret el-Mushâreka*, the latter on the slope on the other side. To the S.E. lies (7) *Ḥâret el-Ḳiṭûn*, or quarter of the cotton-workers. — Ancient Hebron lay to the W., on the olive-covered hill *Rumeideh*, to the N.W. of the Quarantine (see below). On this hill are ruins of old cyclopean walls and modern buildings called *Deir el-Arba'în*, 'the monastery of the forty' (martyrs); within the ruins is the tomb of Jesse (Isai), David's father. At the E. foot of the hill is the deep spring of Sarah, *'Ain Jedîdeh.*

In the bed of the valley to the S.W. of the Ḥâret el-Ḥaram are situated two large reservoirs: the upper one, called *Birket el-Ḳazzâzîn*, or Pool of the Glass-blowers, is 28 yds. in length, 18 yds. in width, and 27$^1/_2$ ft. in depth; the lower basin, constructed of hewn stones, is square in form, each side being 44 yds. long, and is called *Birket es-Sulṭân*. According to tradition, it was near the latter that David hanged the murderers of Ishbosheth (p. 113). Close to the Birket es-Sulṭân stands the new *Serâi*. The tombs of Abner and Ishbosheth shown in the town are not worth visiting. — On the hill of *Kubb el-Jânib*, to the S., is the *Quarantine Station.*

The only object of interest is the Haram, the sacred area which encloses the legendary site of the Cave of Machpelah (p. 113) and contains a mosque and the dwellings of dervishes, saints, and guardians. Up to a height of about 39 ft. the enclosing wall is built of very large blocks, all drafted, hewn smooth, and showing the marks of the Herodian period (p. xcvi). This wall is strengthened externally by square buttresses, sixteen on each side and eight at each end. The upper part of the wall is modern. At the four corners stood minarets, of which two still exist (N.W. and S.E.). The Moslems have also erected a second enclosing wall on the N., E., and S. sides. Two flights of steps, on the N. and S. sides, between this wall and the old one, lead to the interior court, which is 14½ ft. above the street-level. 'Unbelievers' may ascend to the seventh step of the flight on the S. side. Beside the fifth step is a large stone with a hole in it, which the Jews believe to extend down to the tomb. On Friday the Jews lament here as they do at the Place of Wailing in Jerusalem (p. 65). — No Europeans, except a few of high rank, have hitherto been admitted to the interior of the Ḥaram. From the elevation to the N.E. of the Ḥaram (by the mosque of *Ibn 'Othmân*) a sight of the court and the buildings within the walls may be obtained.

The Mosque, which occupies the S. side of the Ḥaram and is bounded on three sides by the old enclosing wall, is a building erected by the Crusaders in 1167-87, probably on the site of a church of the Justinian era, and has been restored by the Arabs. It measures 70 ft. from N. to S. and 93 ft. from E. to W. The interior is divided by 4 columns into a nave and aisles running N. and S. The capitals of these columns appear to be partly Byzantine, partly mediæval. The walls of the church are incrusted to a height of nearly 6 ft. with marble, above which runs a band with an Arabic inscription. Two openings in the floor of the church lead direct to the *Cave of Machpelah* beneath (p. 113), which is said to consist of various passages and chambers. Above ground are six shrines or cenotaphs, which are said to stand exactly over the tombs below. The cenotaphs of the Patriarchs are hung with green cloths, richly embroidered with gold, those of their wives with similar cloths of crimson. The cenotaphs of Isaac and Rebecca are inside the mosque, those of Abraham and Sarah in octagonal chapels in the porch to the N. of the mosque, those of Jacob and Leah in chambers at the N. end of the Ḥaram. — Outside the Ḥaram, at the N.W. angle, is a two-story Building of 1393, containing two cenotaphs of Joseph. A footprint of the Prophet Mohammed is still shown in a stone here. — The oldest Arabian buildings date from 1331, under the Mameluke Sultan Moḥammed Ibn Kilâwûn. — Comp. ZDPV. xvii (1894), pp. 115 et seq. & pp. 238 et seq. Good photographs of the Ḥaram may be obtained at Raad's in Jerusalem (p. 20).

Adjoining the Ḥaram on the S. side is a 'castle', now used as barracks and half in ruins.

The traditional *Oak of Abraham* or *Oak of Mamre* is in the garden of the ***Russian Hospice*** (p. 113), which we reach in ½ hr. by a road (practicable for carriages) diverging to the left from the Jerusalem road, and leading between vineyard walls. This fine old tree, which unfortunately is slowly dying, was highly revered as far back as the 16th century. For the earlier (Jewish) tradition, see p. 113. The trunk of the oak is about 32 ft. in circumference at the bottom. Behind the hospice stands a *View Tower* (key in the hospice), which commands a magnificent *View extending to the sea.

In the country to the W. of Jordan, the oak (*el-ballûṭ*, Quercus ilex pseudococcifera) does not, as beyond Jordan, develop into a large tree, but, as the young shoots are eaten off by the goats, it usually takes the form of a bush only. A few gigantic trees have been carefully fenced in, so as to allow them to grow up unmolested, owing doubtless to superstitious veneration.

13. From Hebron to Beit Jibrîn and Gaza.

Comp. Map, p. 11.

From Hebron to *Beit Jibrîn*, 4 hrs. on horseback; thence to *Gaza* ca. 9 hrs. — For this tour a guide is desirable. — Visitors to the tombs of Beit Jibrîn must first obtain the permission of the Ḳâimmaḳâm of Hebron (candles required).

We follow the Jerusalem road to the point where the route to the Russian Hospice diverges (1/2 hr.; see p. 115). Here we turn to the left (W.) and descend the *Wâdi el-Ḳûf;* on a hill to the right is *Beit Iskâhil*, perhaps the *Eshcol* ('valley of grapes') of Numbers xiii. 24 et seq., whence the Israelitish spies brought back the huge bunch of grapes. In 1 hr. we reach the spring of *'Ain el-Ḳûf*. The valley now expands, turns to the W., and receives the name of *Wâdi el-Merj*. On the (1/2 hr.) hill to the left lies *Terḳûmyâ (Tricomias)*, with a few antiquities. In 1 1/2 hr. the road skirts the base of another hill on the left, upon which is *Deir Nakhkhâs*. In 1/2 hr. we enter *Beit Jibrîn* from the N. E.

From Jerusalem to Beit Jibrîn, 8 3/4 hrs. To (2 1/4 hrs.) the Pools of Solomon, see p. 108. Before reaching the pools we diverge by a road to the right (W.), which leads viâ (1/4 hr.) *El-Khadr* (p. 108). In 35 min. we see *Ḥûsân* a little to the right; to the left opens the Wâdi Fûḳîn. After 1/2 hr. the road to Beit 'Aṭâb diverges to the right, while our route proceeds (l.) to the S.W. 3/4 hr. Hill with extensive ruins (on the left); 1/2 hr. *'Ain et-Tannûr*, deep down in the valley, with lemon-groves; 10 min. Ruins (to the left). We are now following an old Roman road. After 40 min. a road diverges to the right to Beit Nettîf (p. 124); we, however, descend to the left. 20 min. Roman milestone (prostrate); 1/2 hr. we cross the bed of the *Wâdi es-Sanṭ;* to the left a weli on a hill. In 1/4 hr. a road diverges to the left (which we do not follow); to the right, in the valley, the Tell Zakaryâ (p. 124) is visible. In 1/2 hr. our route enters the *Wâdi Zakaryâ* (left) and leads to the S. across a well-cultivated plain, with frequent traces of the Roman road. Beyond an ancient well, with reservoirs, we reach (1/2 hr.) Beit Jibrîn.

The village of **Beit Jibrîn** ('House of Gabriel'), with about 1000 Moslem inhab., lies between three hills, the *Tell Burnât* on the W., the *Tell Sandaḥanneh* on the S., and the *Tell el-Judeideh* on the N.

The Israelitish town, home of the prophets Micah (Micah i. 1) and Eliezer (2 Chron. xx. 37), was known as *Mareshah* (Greek *Marissa*) and stood originally about 1 M. farther to the S. on the Tell Sandaḥanneh, which overlooks the roads from Gaza to Hebron and Jerusalem. The old name reappears in *Khirbet Merâsh*, 1/2 M. to the S.W. The town was fortified by Rehoboam (2 Chron. xi. 8), and after the Exodus became an Edomite capital. Under the Ptolemies a large settlement of Phœnicians was established here. In the wars of the Maccabees it was a place of considerable strategic importance and was captured by Hyrcanus. The town, which was destroyed by the Parthians in B.C. 40, reappears in A.D. 68, under the new name of *Baithogabra*, as a fortress standing on the present site (see Bell. Jud. iv. 8, 1, where the name is erroneously given as Betaris). The town received various privileges coupled with the name *Eleutheropolis*, or *Lucia Septimia Severiana*, from the Roman emperor Septimius Severus in 202, on the occasion of his journey in the East (Roman coins still offered for sale). It was the seat of a Christian bishop as early as the 4th century. The Crusaders found the place in ruins; they called it *Gibelin.* Under Fulke of Anjou, in 1134, a citadel was erected here. In 1244 Gibelin was finally taken by Beybars (p. lxxxv). The fortress was restored in 1551. Comp. 'Excavations in Palestine during the years 1898-1900' and *J. P. Peters & H. Thiersch*, 'Painted Tombs in the Necropolis of Marissa' (1905; 2*l.* 2*s.*), published by the Palestine Exploration Fund.

The village occupies about one-third of the site of the ancient town. Ruins of old buildings are incorporated with most of the houses. A portion of the ancient wall, perhaps built by the Crusaders in 1134, still exists on the N. side; it was formerly flanked by a moat. To the N.W. and E. were forts. At the E. fort there still exist fragments of columns, a fine large portal, and a reservoir. The N.W. fort (small fee) stood on an eminence, and the ancient substructions are still easily distinguished from the later work. Over the door is an inscription dating from the year 958 of the Hegira (1551). The fortress was flanked with a tower at each corner. The interior contains a handsome cistern and many vaulted chambers now used as dwellings. On the S. side runs a gallery from E. to W., which was originally the aisle of a church. On the left and right are five piers, formerly enriched with columns in white marble and with Corinthian capitals. The arcades are pointed.

The chief objects of interest are the *ROCK CAVERNS (*'urâḳ* or *'arâḳ)* in the vicinity (comp. pp. xcv, 124). The caverns consist of round, bell-vaulted chambers, 20-50 ft. (in some cases even 100 ft.) in diameter, supported in some cases by pillars. They are 30-40 ft. in height. Each cavern is lighted from above by a well-like opening. Even if we allow for the softness of the material, a kind of grey chalk, the manner in which the chambers have been excavated is none the less admirable. Most of these caverns date back to the ancient Hebraic or some even earlier period. Their number and similarity lead to the inference that they were used as dwellings; some of them are connected with each other, and a few were cisterns; St. Jerome informs us that the *Hôrîm*, or dwellers in mountains and caves, once lived in this district, and that the Idumæans lived in caverns throughout the country from here to Petra, in order to escape from the intensity of the heat. Some of the caverns seem to have been used as chapels, as they have apses turned towards the E. and crosses engraved on their walls.

The following walk is the most interesting here. We descend from the fortress to the S. E., pass the tombs, and ascend a small water-course. In 5 min. we observe caverns below us. To judge from the niches hewn in them (five at the back, three on each side), they must once have been used as sepulchres. The niches are 2 ft. above the ground, and high above them are hewn numerous triangles (possibly for lamps). Some of the round openings above have been widened in the course of ages. After the falling in of the chambers there have also been formed open spaces in front of them, within which the pillars of the groups of chambers are still preserved. — Farther to the S. is a second group of more lofty grottoes. One of them contains a well, and at several places the ground sounds hollow. The walls are green with moisture and very smooth. Rudely engraved crosses, and inscriptions dating from the early period of Islamism (in Cufic characters), are sometimes observed. The marks of tools are clearly visible on the walls. Proceeding from one cavern to another, we ascend the valley as far as a ruined church, which in a straight line is only 1 M. from the village. It is still called by the natives *Mâr Hannâ*, or *Sandaḥanneh.* The substructions of this church date from the Byzantine period, but the ground-plan was altered by the Crusaders. The principal apse is well-preserved. The window-arches are round. The stones are carefully hewn, and the walls are massive. On each side of the entrance are pilasters, and under the N. aisle is a crypt with vaults. Opposite the church is the cavern *Mughâret Sandaḥanneh*, comprising several chambers, the largest of which is 100 ft. in diameter. Not far off, to the W., is the passage of *Es-Sûḳ*, a tunnel over 33 yds. long, with two cross-galleries, containing no less than 1906 small niches (columbaria), which served as receptacles for cinerary urns. — The whole chain of hills of Mâr Ḥannâ is honeycombed with caverns and tombs. The finest tomb lies on the E. side of the Wâdi el-Biyâḍ, opposite the Tell Sandaḥanneh. It was constructed ca. B.C. 250 for the head of the Phœnician colony. Adjoining the antechamber on the N., E., and S. are three chambers, with 41 loculi (Kôkîm, p. xcvi) for bodies hewn in the walls. They have gabled roofs, the only ones of the kind found in Palestine. The main chamber (E.) opens out into a large rectangular recess, with three niches for sarcophagi. Paintings form the chief decoration of the tomb. Above the loculi in the chief chamber is a broad frieze of hunting-scenes, beginning in the S.W. corner and running round the walls. First comes a man blowing a trumpet, next a rider attacked by a leopard, then various animals, each with an inscription in Greek. To the right and left of the portal to the main chamber are paintings of the three-headed Cerberus and a cock. The paintings betray the hand of a Greek artist and resemble those on vases of the 5th and 4th cent. B.C. — Somewhat to the S. lies another collection of tombs. They are less richly painted, but the figures of the two musicians are worthy of notice. These are the only tombs in Palestine thus decorated.

The road to Gaza crosses the range of hills to the W. of Beit Jibrîn, affording a fine retrospect of that village from (1/4 hr.) the top. After 35 min. we observe in the fields to the right the weli of the *Sheikh ʿAmr.* We now leave the mountains of Judah behind us and gradually descend their last spurs to the plain, in a W. direction. On the left, after 1/2 hr., rises *Tell el-Manṣûra*, with some ruins, and 1/2 hr. farther on we reach some caverns which have fallen in, known as *ʿArâḳ el-Menshîyeh.* Our route next turns towards the S.W. On the right (1/2 hr.) lies *ʿAjlân*, which the Septuagint confounds with Adullam, a mistake followed by Eusebius (see p. 110). In about 1 3/4 hr. from ʿArâḳ el-Menshîyeh we reach —

Tell el-Ḥasî, probably on the site of the Biblical *Lachish*, an important frontier-fortress in the direction of Egypt (2 Kings xviii. 14 et seq.) during the period of the Israelitish kings.

Lachish was besieged by Sennacherib (2 Kings xix. 8) and, according to Egyptian inscriptions, captured by him. According to Jeremiah (xxxiv. 7), Lachish was one of the last cities taken from the Jews by Nebuchadnezzar. The extensive and highly interesting excavations, which the Palestine Exploration Fund has undertaken here in the last few years, have brought to light many fragments of town-walls and fortifications of different periods (some very ancient), numerous clay vessels, etc. (comp. *Flinders Petrie*, 'Tell el Hesy'; *J. Bliss*, 'A Mound of Many Cities').

To the S.E. of Tell el-Ḥasî, 4½ M. up the *Wâdi el-Muleiha*, lies the *Tell en-Nejileh*, probably the site of the ancient *Eglon* (Joshua x. 3, 34, 35).

From Tell el-Ḥasî our route continues to descend the *Wâdi el-Ḥasî*. After 1¾ hr. we reach *Bureir*, where the first palms occur. To the right, after 40 min., we perceive the village of *Simsim*, in an olive-grove. Tobacco and sesame are grown abundantly here. Soon after we cross the wâdi to the S.W. After ¼ hr., on the left the village of *Nejd*, and on the right, in the distance, the dunes near the sea. The road next passes (25 min.) *Dimreh* on the right, and (¾ hr.) *Beit Ḥanûn*. We soon reach orchards with olives, sycamores, and palms, and in 1½ hr. more the town of —

Gaza or **Ghazzeh.** — Accommodation at the Latin Hospice (*Mr. Gatt*, a German), or at the Greek Monastery (introduction from Jerusalem desirable). The best place for pitching Tents is near the Serâi. — *Turkish Post Office; International Telegraph Office.* — British Consular Agent, *Knesevich.* — Money. At Gaza the mejîdi is worth 46 piastres, and other coins are also worth twice as much as at Jerusalem. — For admission to the Great Mosque (p. 121), it is necessary to have the permission of the Kâimmakâm (in the Serâi), who appoints a soldier (fee ¼ mejîdi, more for a party) to accompany the visitors.

History. In the country of *Peleshet*, *i.e.* the low plain between Carmel and the frontier of Egypt, we find in historical times the '*Pelishtîm*', or Philistines, a nation which did not belong to the Semitic race. Their invasion was made from the sea about 1100 B.C., when they took possession of the coast with its originally Canaanitish towns. Their origin is unknown. The Bible (Amos ix. 7, etc.) connects them with *Caphtor*, which has been supposed to be Crete. The Philistines adopted not only the civilization, but the Semitic language and the cult of the Canaanites; their principal divinities were Dagon (Marnas), a Canaanitish god, and the Syrian goddess Derketo (Atargatis). both deities in the form of fish. — The Philistines must early have established a constitution; Jewish history, at any rate, shows us a perpetual league of their five chief towns, Gaza, Ashdod (p. 122), Ascalon (p. 123), Gath (p. 124), and Ekron (p. 13). According to all accounts the Philistines far surpassed the Hebrews in culture; and in war-chariots and cavalry they were superior to the Israelites (1 Sam. xiii. 5). The heavy-armed soldiers wore a round copper helmet, a coat of mail, and brazen greaves, and carried a javelin and a long lance, while each had a shield-bearer, like the Greeks in the Homeric poems. The light-armed were archers. The Philistines possessed fortified encampments; they built lofty walls round their towns. They carried on a vigorous and extensive commerce, especially inland; and their wars with the Israelites were partly caused by their efforts to retain the command of the great caravan routes, especially that to Damascus. — In the last decades of the period of the Judges the Philistines contested the hegemony of Palestine with the Israelites, and, in fact, ruled over Israel for a long time. In what way this guerilla war was carried on, we may learn from the lively and vigorous narrative of the hero Samson (Judges xiii. et seq.). The first kings of Israel, Saul and David, effected their final deliverance from the foreign yoke, though several of the succeeding kings had to wage war with the Philistines. In the course of the great war between Egypt and Assyria the Philistian plain became strategically important, and its occupation therefore formed a constant source of strife between these nations, to the great disquiet of the Philistines. Some of the Philistines, too, were probably exiled at this period. After the Jewish captivity the kingdom of the Philistines had disappeared. In the wars between the Syrian and Egyptian diadochi Philistia again became the scene of fierce conflicts. During the Maccabæan period the Philistian-Hellenic coast-towns gave fresh proofs of their hereditary enmity against the Jews, but the Maccabæans succeeded in permanently subjugating the Philistian plain.

Gaza lay on the important route from Egypt to Babylonia, which was joined here by the trading-routes from Elath (p. 213) and Arabia. It was thus always a place of great commercial importance and a frequent object of contention. Its port was *Majumas*, which was raised by Constantine the Great to the dignity of an independent town under the name of *Constantia*. According to the Old Testament Gaza was one of the five allied Philistine cities (see p. 119), and it was here that Samson performed some of his remarkable exploits (Judges xvi.). The Israelites held possession of the town only during the most flourishing period of their empire (1 Kings iv. 24). Tiglath-Pileser III. of Assyria captured the town in 734 B.C., and it thereafter remained a part of the Assyrian, Babylonian, and Persian empires. Alexander the Great took it after a siege of two months; and it was long an apple of discord between the Ptolemies and the Seleucids. In 96 B.C. it was again taken and destroyed by Alexander Jannæus. Under Gabinius New Gaza was built some distance to the S. of the former town. It was presented by the Emperor Augustus to Herod, after whose death it reverted to the Roman province of Syria. Under the Romans Gaza peacefully developed its resources. Philemon, to whom the Epistle of that name was addressed, was traditionally first bishop of Gaza. Down to the time of Constantine the town was one of the chief strongholds of paganism, adhering to its god Marnas (see p. 119), whose statues and temples stood till the year 400, when they were destroyed by an edict of the emperor. On the site of the principal temple a large cruciform church was afterwards erected by Eudoxia, wife of the Emperor Arcadius. In 634 the town was taken by the Arabs under ʿOmar, and it was regarded as an important place by the Moslems, because Hâshim, Mohammed's grandfather, who had once traded with the place, had died and been buried there. The Crusaders found Gaza in ruins. In 1149 Baldwin II. erected a fortress here. In 1170 Saladin plundered the town, though unable to reduce the fortress; in 1187, however, the whole place fell into his hands. In 1244 the Christians and Moslems were defeated by the Kharezmians near Gaza. Since that period Gaza has been a place of no importance. In 1799 it was taken by Napoleon. — Comp. communications of *Gatt* in ZDPV. vii (1884). 1-14, 293-298; xi (1888). 149-159.

Ghazzeh, the seat of a Ḳâimmaḳâm (p. lvii) and containing a small garrison, has 40,000 inhab., including 1000 Greeks (who possess a church), 100 Latins (also with a church), and 150 Jews. The upper town lies on a hill about 100 ft. high; in the plain, to the E. and S., are the new quarters of the town. The walls of the upper town have disappeared. The ancient town was a good deal larger than the modern one, and to the S. and E. elevations of the ground are visible, marking the course of the old town-walls. The newer houses are largely built of ancient materials. The town lies in the midst of orchards. Owing to the abundance of water contained by the soil the vegetation is very rich. The town-wells are 100-160 ft. deep, but the water in most of them is brackish. — Gaza is a town of semi-Egyptian character; the veil of the Moslem women, for example, closely resembles the Egyptian. The bazaar, too, has an Egyptian appearance. The old caravan-traffic with Egypt (see above) is now almost extinct, but the market is still largely frequented by the Beduins, especially for dates, figs, olives, lentils, and other provisions. Gaza is, moreover, an important depôt for barley, wheat, and durra. The principal industries are the making of pottery and weaving; yarn to the value of 10,000*l.* is exported annually for the latter from Manchester to Gaza and Mejdel (p. 124). There is also a steam-mill owned by a German. — An unusually large proportion of the inhabitants suffer from ophthalmia, for the relief of which the English Church Missionary Society has established a hospital here. The same society has schools for Moslem and Christian boys and girls under the direction of the Rev. Dr. Sterling.

In the N.W. part of the upper town, near the *Bâb ʿAsḳalân* (Ascalon Gate), lies the *Jâmiʿ es-Saiyid Hâshim*, a building of some antiquity, in which Hâshim (p. 120) is buried. It was restored in the 19th cent., in part, however, with the old materials. — From this point we proceed to the E. to the *Serâi* (on the N.E. side of the upper town) dating from the 13th cent., with finely jointed masonry, now in great part fallen into decay. A little to the E., by the *Bâb el-Khalîl* (Hebron Gate), is the sanctuary of *Abu'l-ʿAzm* ('Father of Strength', *i.e.* Samson), with the *Tomb of Samson.* — To the S.W. of the Serâi rises the *Jâmiʿ el-Kebîr* or *Great Mosque* (adm., see p. 119; shoes must be removed). The court of the mosque is paved with marble slabs; around it are several schools. The mosque itself was originally a Christian church, consisting of nave and aisles, built in the 12th cent. out of ancient materials and dedicated to St. John. The Moslems erected an additional aisle on the S. side, and, in order to make room for the minarets, built up the apses. Over the three square pilasters and two half-pillars which bound the nave rise pointed arcades. On one of the beautiful columns (N.E.) is a bas-relief representing the seven-branched candlestick, with a Greek and Hebrew inscription. The W. portal is a fine specimen of Italian Gothic.

To the S.W. of this mosque is situated a handsome caravanserai, called the *Khân ez-Zeit* ('oil khân'). Proceeding to the S. through the *Ḥâret en-Naṣâra* and *Ḥâret ez-Zeitûn* quarters, with a mosque of finely hewn stones, we reach the former town-gate of *Bâb ed-Dârûn* (Dârûn = *Daroma*, the old Greek name for the S. part of Palestine); along this road pass the caravans to Egypt. — Continuing to the E., we reach the *Bâb el-Munṭâr*, the old S.E. gate. Here, tradition maintains, is the place whence Samson took away the gates of the Philistines (Judges xvi. 2 et seq.), which he then carried up to the top of the Jebel el-Munṭâr (see below).

A ride of 1/4 hr. to the S.E. of Gaza brings us to the *Jebel el-Munṭâr* (270 ft. above the sea), which is covered with tombs. The view hence repays the ascent: to the S., beyond the cultivated land, lies the sandy desert; to the E., beyond the plain, rise the hill-ranges of Judæa; to the W., beyond the broad, yellow sand-hills, stretches the sea; but the most picturesque object of all is the town itself, looking forth from its beautiful green mantle.

From Gaza to El-ʿArîsh, 13 hrs. From Gaza in 1 hr. 5 min. to *Tell el-ʿAjûl* near the *Wâdi el-Ghazzeh.* About 1 hr. to the S.E. of Tell el-ʿAjûl, near *Tell Jemʿa*, are the ruins of *Umm Jerâr* (probably the *Gerar* of Gen. xx. 1; xxvi. 1). After 1 1/4 hr. we reach *Deir el-Belaḥ* (the ancient *Dârûm;* the mosque *Jâmiʿ el-Khiḍr* stands on the site of an old chapel). We next reach (1 hr. 37 min.) *Khân Yûnus*, a large village with a fine mosque of the time of Sultan Barḳûḳ. In $1^1/_4$ hr. we reach *Tell Rifah*, or *Raphia*, on the Egyptian frontier; then ($2^1/_4$ hrs.) *Sheikh Zuweid*, ($2^3/_4$ hrs.) *Khirbet el-Borj*, and ($2^1/_2$ hrs.) the broad valley of *El-ʿArîsh*, the 'River of Egypt' of the Bible (Numb. xxxiv. 5; Isaiah xxvii. 12). In 20 min. more we reach the fortress and the quarantine-station. **El-ʿArish** (7500 inhab.), occupies the site of the ancient *Rhinocolura*. By the cistern in the court there is an Egyptian sarcophagus (a monolith of granite), now used as a trough. — The town is said to have been originally founded by an Ethiopian-Egyptian king as a place of banishment, and under the name of *Laris* it was an episcopal see in the first centuries of our era. Baldwin I. of Jerusalem died here in 1118. The *Hajar Berdawîl*, or 'Stone of Baldwin', is still pointed out. Napoleon took El-ʿArîsh in 1799.

From Gaza to Jaffa, ca. $45^1/_2$ M., by road (carr. in 9-10 hrs., 40-50 fr.; there and back in 2 days, 60-70 fr.). — The road leads to ($4^1/_2$ M.) *Beit Lahja* (the ancient Bethelia), leaving *Beit Hanûn* (p. 119) to the E. $11^1/_2$ M. *Barbara*, a large village; 15 M. *Mejdel* (excursion by donkey to Ascalon, see p. 124); $16^1/_2$ M. *Ḥamâmeh*, with 2000 inhab.; $18^1/_2$ M. *Misḳât Suleimâm Agha*, a khân.

23 M. **Esdûd**, a village with 5000 inhab., stands on the slope of a hill commanded by a still higher eminence on which the acropolis probably stood. European travellers will find a hearty welcome at the house of the German proprietor of a large steam-mill. Esdûd is the ancient *Ashdod* (Greek *Azotos*), which appears to have been the most important city of the Philistian Pentapolis (p. 119). Its position on the main route between Egypt and Syria lent it importance for both countries. About the year 711 B.C. it was captured by the Assyrians, and a century later it was taken from them by Psammetichus after a siege of twenty-nine years. The Maccabæans added Ashdod to the possessions of the Jews (1 Macc. x. 84), but Pompey restored its independence. Subsequently it formed part of the kingdom of Herod. Philip the evangelist preached the gospel here (Acts viii. 40), and bishops of Azotus are mentioned at a later period. At the entrance to the village, on the S. side, lies the ruin of a large mediæval khân, with galleries, courts, and various chambers. Ancient masonry and fragments of columns are also detected in the houses and mosques. About 3 M. to the W. is the old seaport of Ashdod, with the ruins of a castle.

Beyond Esdûd the road brings us to (25 M.) the bridge over the *Wâdi Sukreir*, and to (28 M.) the dilapidated *Khân Sukreir*.

$32^1/_2$ M. **Yebna**, a rather large village with two mosques, one of which (*El-Kenîseh*) was no doubt once a church of the Crusaders, and has a handsome portal. It is situated on the *Wâdi eṣ-Ṣarâr* (possibly the valley of *Sorek*, Judges xvi. 4) and corresponds to the ancient *Jabneh* or *Jabneel* (Josh. xv. 11), the Greek name of which was *Jamnia*. Jabneh possessed a seaport of the same name, the ruins of which lie at the mouth of the *Nahr Rûbîn*, 3 M. to the N.W. (see below). This seaport is said to have been burned by Judas Maccabæus (2 Macc. xii. 8), but the Jews did not obtain permanent possession of the town until the time of Alexander Jannæus. Pompey restored its independence; Gabinius rebuilt the town, which had fallen into decay; and Augustus presented it to Herod. At that time it was a populous town and, as a seaport, more important than Joppa. Even before the destruction of Jerusalem Jamnia became the seat of the Jewish Sanhedrin; a famous rabbinical school flourished here, and the town was afterwards intellectually the centre of the conspiracy against Trajan, A.D. 117. The Crusaders called the town *Ibelin*, and erected a large fortress here.

From Yebna our road leads to (33 M.) a bridge over the *Nahr Rûbîn* (Ruben), the lower course of the *Wâdi eṣ-Ṣarâr* (p. 14). $38^1/_4$ M. Jewish colony of *Rishon le-Zion* (p. 15). $42^1/_2$ M. *Yâzûr*, on the road from Jerusalem to Jaffa. Thence to Jaffa, see pp. 15, 8.

From Gaza to *Beersheba*, see p. 170.

14. From Gaza to Jerusalem viâ Ascalon.

Comp. Maps, pp. 11, 92.

From Gaza to *Ascalon*, $3^1/_2$ hrs. on horseback; thence to *Jerusalem* $15^1/_2$ hrs. Nightquarters may be found at Esdûd (p. 122) or at Mejdel (p. 124).

The best route is that along the coast, which we reach viâ the *Weli Sheikh Riḍwân* in 20 minutes. We then skirt the coast all the way to (ca. 3 hrs.) the —

Ruins of Ascalon (*'Asḳalân*). — Ascalon was one of the five principal towns of the Philistines, and a seat of the worship of the goddess Derketo (p. 119). From the time of Tiglath-Pileser III. (p. 120) the town paid tribute to the Assyrians; in the Persian period it belonged to the Tyrians, in the 3rd cent. B.C. to the Ptolemies, and from the reign of Antiochus III. onwards to the Seleucidæ. In 104 B.C. it succeeded in making itself independent, and it reckons its own chronology from that date. It enjoyed its greatest prosperity in the Roman period, as a kind of free republic under Roman protection. Herod the Great was born at Ascalon, and he caused the town to be embellished with baths, colonnades, and the like, although it was not within his dominions. The citizens, like those of Gaza, were bitter opponents of Christianity down to a late period. On the arrival of the Crusaders, Ascalon was in possession of the Fatimites of Egypt. On Aug. 12th, 1099, the Franks gained a brilliant victory under the walls of the town, but it was only after a siege of five months by sea and land that they at length compelled the place to capitulate. Saladin's victory at Ḥaṭṭîn brought Ascalon once more into the hands of the Moslems, and its walls were razed at the beginning of the Third Crusade. In 1191 Richard Cœur-de-Lion began to rebuild the fortress, but he was obstructed by the jealousy of the other princes, and in a subsequent truce with the Moslems it was agreed that the place should remain unfortified. In 1270 Beybars caused the fortifications to be demolished, and since then Ascalon has been a ruin.

Ascalon is correctly described by William of Tyre, the historian of the Crusades, as lying within a semicircle of ramparts, the chord of which was formed by the sea on the W., and sloping towards the sea. The top of the ramparts affords an interesting survey of the ancient site. Near the S.W. corner lay the small and bad harbour of Ascalon. Of the bastions which defended it a few remains still exist. On the side towards the sea stood a gate, the site of which is still called *Bâb el-Baḥr* (sea-gate). The W. wall is continued along the low cliffs on the coast. Large fragments of it have occasionally fallen. — In the S. part of the wall another gate, called that of Gaza, is still distinguishable, and there are also remains of towers. — The ramparts on the E. side were the most strongly fortified, the walls there being very massive and upwards of $6^1/_2$ ft. thick; fragments of columns built into them are sometimes seen projecting. On the hill, near the *Weli Moḥammed*, are the still tolerably preserved towers which defended the principal gate, that of Jerusalem; but the remains are deeply buried in sand. — Within the walls are luxuriant orchards, among which are found fragments of columns, statues, remains of Christian churches, and, most important of all, 40 cisterns of excellent water. The orchards belong to the inhabitants of *El-Jôra*, a village with 300 inhab., situated to the N.E. of the ancient

Ascalon. Sycamores abound, and vines, olives, fruit-trees, and an excellent kind of onion also thrive in this favoured district. This last was called by the Romans Ascalonia, whence the French échalotte and our shalot are derived.

From Ascalon (El-Jôra, p. 123) the road leads N.E. to (3/4 hr.) **Mejdel** (possibly *Migdal-Gad*, Josh. xv. 37), a place of 8000 inhab., surrounded by luxuriant orchards and possessing a well-stocked bazaar and a considerable weaving-industry (comp. p. 120). About 3/4 M. to the N. is a steam-mill, the proprietor of which, *Mr. Egger*, can generally provide accommodation (previous notice desirable). The mosque is partly built with ancient materials, and has an elegant minaret. — After 7 min. we turn to the E. from the main road. In 50 min. we reach *Wâdi Makkûs*, and (10 min.) leave *Jôlis* on the right (S.). We then reach (55 min.) the village of *Eṣ-Ṣawâfîr*, and then (5 min.) another of the same name. A third Ṣawâfîr lies farther to the N., and one of them perhaps answers to *Saphir* (Micah i. 11). We next reach (to the E; 1/2 hr.) the well-watered *Wâdi eṣ-Ṣâfiyeh.* The road passes (1 hr.) a water-course, and then (3/4 hr.) returns to the Wâdi eṣ-Ṣâfiyeh, but does not cross it. The plain here is always marshy in spring. In 20 min. we reach the foot of the Tell eṣ-Ṣâfiyeh.

The **Tell eṣ-Ṣâfiyeh,** which commands the outlet of the great *Wâdi es-Sanṭ* (valley of mimosas; probably the valley of *Elah* or *Terebinth Valley*, 1 Sam. xvii. 2; comp. pp. 18, 113), is perhaps identical with the ancient *Gath* of the Philistines (p. 119; the identifications with *Mizpah*, Josh. xv. 38, or *Libnah*, Josh. x. 29, are untenable). In 1138 King Fulke of Anjou built a castle here, which was named *Blanca Guarda* or *Specula Alba* from the conspicuous white chalk rocks. In 1191 the castle was taken by Saladin and destroyed. On the W. slope of the hill is a cavern (probably an old quarry), beyond which we traverse the miserable modern village. On the top (10 min.) a few substructions of well-hewn stones are all that now remains of the Crusaders' castle. The weli is also built of ancient materials. Excavations of the Palestine Exploration Fund have brought to light some curious fragments of pottery, possibly of painted Philistine ware. The view is very extensive.

Here we re-enter a region of Rock Caverns like those with which we became acquainted at Beit Jibrîn (p. 117). Some of these are at *Deir el-Buṭûm*, 20 min. to the S.E. of Tell eṣ-Ṣâfiyeh, others at *Deir ed-Dibbân*, 1/4 hr. farther, others again at *Khirbet Dakar*, 1/2 hr. to the W. of Deir ed-Dibbân.

About 1 hr. beyond Tell eṣ-Ṣâfiyeh we leave the village of *'Ajûr* on the hill to the right (E.), and soon obtain a fine view of the *Wâdi es-Sanṭ* (see above). After 1/4 hr. we observe to the left (N.) the *Tell Zakaryâ*, probably the site of the ancient *Aseka* (Josh. xv. 35; 1 Sam. xvii. 1). English explorations here have unearthed the remains of fortifications (dating partly from the pre-Israelitish period), pottery, terracottas, etc. We descend into the broad and well-cultivated floor of the valley. After 1 hr. we pass a small valley and the well *Bîr es-Safsâf* on the right. On the hill to the left is **Beit Nettîf** (hardly to be identified with the ancient *Netophah*, Ezra ii. 22), which we reach in 1/2 hr. more. The village contains about 1000 inhabitants and affords a very extensive View. Below the village the Wâdi eṣ-Ṣûr, coming from the S., unites with the Wâdi el-Mesarr, descending from the N.E. To the S. lies Ḍahr el-Juweiʿid, and a little towards the W. the extensive ruins of Shuweikeh, with ancient caverns (perhaps the *Socoh*, or *Shochoh*, of Joshua xv. 35 and 1 Sam. xvii. 1 et seq.). To the W. lies Deir ʿAṣfûr, to the N.W. Khirbet esh-Shmeili, Tibna (*Timnath*, Judges xiv. 5), and ʿAin Shems (p. 14). To the N. are Zânûʿa (*Zanoah*, 1 Chron. iv. 18) and Ṣarʿa (p. 14), a little to the right of which lies the small village of Khirbet Jerash. To the N.E., in the distance, is Beit ʿAṭâb (supposed to be the rock *Etham*, Judges xv. 8; a cave still exists there).

The site of *Adullam* (Joshua xv. 35, xii. 15; 1 Sam. xxii. 1; 2 Sam. xxiii. 13, 14) has been supposed to be identical with a spot 1 hr. to the S. of Shuweikeh, near the hill *Sheikh Madkûr* (comp. p. 110). Adullam, which has also been placed here by Eusebius, was probably a mountain-fastness, the reading 'cave' being erroneous.

From Beit Nettîf we descend in 25 min. to the outlet of the *Wâdi el-Mesarr*, and in 1/4 hr. we pass the ruin of a khân. We diverge to the left into the *Wâdi el-Leḥâm*, a small side-valley. In 1 hr. we reach the crest of the hill (fine view). We next pass (20 min.) the ruin of *Khirbet el-Khân*. We now follow the top of the hills and enjoy a magnificent view. Vegetation becomes sparse, and we enter a stony desert. After 1 hr. 10 min. we reach the watershed and keep to the left (N.E.); the road to the right (S.E.) leads past El-Khaḍr (p. 108) to Bethlehem. About 1/2 hr. farther on we begin to descend into the valley, passing to the left of the village of *El-Ḳabû*, and then (55 min.) turn to the right into the large main valley, the *Wâdi Bittîr*. Riding up the valley, we reach *Bittîr* (p. 14) in 25 minutes. Thence to Jerusalem, see pp. 93, 92.

15. From Jerusalem to Jericho, the Jordan, and the Dead Sea.

Comp. Map, p. 92.

By Carriage this excursion (there and back) takes 1 1/2 day (fare 60 fr.). There is a road as far as *Jericho* (4 hrs.), but beyond that driving is practicable in dry weather only. A dragoman may be dispensed with by male travellers, as there is hotel accommodation at Jericho. — Riders from Jerusalem to *Jericho* take 6 hrs., thence to the *Jordan* 1 1/2 hr., and thence to the *Dead Sea* 1 hr. The whole trip, including the return-journey viâ *Mâr Sâbâ* (p. 135), takes 3 days. For this the dragoman should be content with 70-80 fr. a head (exclusive of tents).

To *Gethsemane*, see p. 76. The road gradually ascends and then bends to the E. On the Mount of Offence, to the right, is the Benedictine convent. Farther on, in the small valley that descends on the left from the summit of the Mount of Olives, we are shown the site of the fig-tree which was cursed by Christ (Matt. xxi. 19). On the crest of the hill before Bethany, to the left, is the Passionist convent. In 40 min. after leaving Jerusalem we reach —

Bethany (Arabic *El-'Azarîyeh*), an entirely Moslem village consisting of about forty hovels, situated on a S.E. spur of the Mount of Olives. There are numerous fig, olive, almond, and carob trees.

Bethany was a favourite resort of Jesus. It was in the house of Simon the Leper that the woman anointed him with precious ointment (Mark xiv. 3; Matt. xxvi. 6). Bethany was also the scene of the resurrection of Lazarus, the brother of Mary and Martha, as related in John xi. At a very early period churches and monasteries were erected here. The Roman lady Paula (p. 106) visited a church on the site of Lazarus's grave. In 1138 Milicent, wife of Fulke, fourth King of Jerusalem (p. 74), founded a nunnery by the church of St. Lazarus, and in 1159 the building came into the possession of the Hospitallers. — The Arabic name is derived from *L*azarus or '*L*azarium', the Arabs having taken the L for the article. Both Christians and Moslems regard Lazarus as a saint. — Comp. *Fenner*, Die Ortslage von Bethanien (ZDPV. xxix, 1906, pp. 151 et seq.).

The *Tomb of Lazarus* (*Ḳabr el-'Azar;* candles necessary) lies hard by the mosque; the entrance, on the N. side, from the street, was constructed by the Christians in the 16th cent. after the Moslems had walled up the old E. entrance from the church. We descend by 22 steps into an antechamber with pointed vaulting, and thence by two more deep steps to the tomb-chamber proper. This was originally a cavern (with tombs), the rocky walls of which are now lined with masonry. — About 30 paces to the S.W. of the tomb is a ruined *Tower*, the so-called 'Castle of Lazarus', now generally known as the '***House of Simon the Leper***'. Milicent (see above) had the tower erected as a protection to the nunnery, but the lower part with its large drafted stones is older. The tower now belongs to the Greeks. — The house of Mary and Martha stands 33 yds. to the E. of the ruined tower. Here may be seen the ruins of buildings, which probably belong to the above-mentioned nunnery. The traditions regarding the sites of the houses of Simon the Leper (see above) and of Mary and Martha have varied considerably. Beyond Bethany, on the hill to the right, we see the village of *Abu Dîs*. Farther on, to the right of the road, stands a Greek chapel built on ancient foundation-walls and enclosing the *Stone of Meeting*. The stone marks the spot where Martha met Jesus (John xi. 20; comp. p. 80). The Arabic name of the place is ***El-Juneineh***, or 'little garden'.

We now descend into the *Wâdi el-Ḥôḍ*, or 'valley of the watering-place', so called after the (20 min.) *Ḥôḍ el-'Azarîyeh* (coffee-house), the only well between this point and the Jordan valley, and known since the 15th cent. as the '*Apostles' Spring*'. The water is not very good.

It was assumed that the apostles must have drunk of its water on their journey. Its identification with the 'sun-spring' of ***En-Shemesh*** (Josh. xv. 7) is doubtful. A well-house constructed in the 16th cent. has disappeared.

The route now descends the Wâdi el-Ḥôḍ. After 20 min. the ***Wâdi el-Jemel*** ('camel valley') descends from the right; 10 min. later the ***Wâdi el-Ḥârîḳ***, also to the right; after 35 min. we leave the Wâdi el-Ḥôḍ at the *Wâdi el-Mufâkh* (on the right), and enter the *Wâdi es-Sikkeh*. Farther on we cross the *Wâdi es-Sidr* (for the 'sidr' tree, see p. 129). About halfway to Jericho, 50 min. from the Wâdi el-Mufâkh (see above), lies the *Khân Ḥathrûr* (refreshments; Turkish post-office). This district is quite deserted, and tradition localizes the parable of the Good Samaritan here (Luke x. 30-37). Above the khân, to the N.E., are the ruins of a mediæval castle. From the khân we descend the *Talʿat ed-Dam* ('Ascent of Blood'), the 'going up to *Adummim*' of the Bible (Josh. xv. 7; xviii. 17). The descent into the (20 min. from the khân) *Wâdi er-Rummâneh* ('valley of pomegranates') is called *ʿAḳabet el-Jerâd* ('ascent of the locusts'). The road follows the valley, which now assumes the name of *Wâdi Talʿat ed-Dam*. After 20 min. the new carriage-road to *En-Nebi Mûsâ* (p. 134) branches off to the right. From the elevation to the left of the road, near ($3/4$ hr.) the fragments of an ancient aqueduct, we obtain a magnificent view into the deep *Wâdi el-Ḳelt* (see below), the lower portion of the *Wâdi Fâra* (p. 98), which contains water during the greater part of the year. Its identification with the valley of *Achor* (Josh. xv. 7) or with the brook *Cherith* (1 Kings xvii. 3, 5) is undoubtedly wrong. A cavern in the rock-wall to the left has been converted into the Greek *Monastery of St. George;* the substructions date from the ancient monastery of *Khoziba* (535). Here are also remains of mosaics. After $1/4$ hr. *Beit Jabr el-Foḳâni* (the 'upper') appears on the left. The two ruined houses, called *Beit Jabr* (the upper and the lower), perhaps occupy the site of the ancient castles of *Thrax* and *Tauros*, which once defended the pass. After 3 min. a footpath leads to the left to the Monastery of St. George (see above). The view gradually develops itself, and at length we perceive the Dead Sea and the plain of Jordan. In 10 min. more the *Wâdi el-Ḳelt* reappears, the S. side of which the road ascends. In 10 min. we reach, on the right, *Beit Jabr et-Taḥtâni* (the 'lower'; see above). — Entering the plain, we see, to the left of the road, the *Tell Abu ʿAlâiḳ* ('hill of the leeches'). The excavations of the German Oriental Society here in 1909 have brought to light the Palace of Herod and its terraces on the N. Opposite the hill, to the right of the road, we see the ancient *Birket Mûsâ*, or Pool of Moses (188 yds. by 157 yds.). It belonged to the ancient system of conduits which once irrigated this district and rendered it a paradise. It is the remains of a pool constructed by Herod. This is the site of the *Jericho* of the New Testament, which extended chiefly to the N. from this point, while the Jericho of the Old Testament lay near the ʿAin es-Sulṭân (p. 129). Somewhat farther on, to the S. of the Pool of Moses, we see the ruin of *Khirbet el-Kâkûn*. After 20 min. the road leads past the modern aqueduct, which carries the water from the Ain es-Sulṭân (p. 129) across the Wâdi el-Ḳelt (see above), and then crosses the valley by a bridge. In 5 min. more we reach the village of *Jericho* (p. 128).

Jericho. — **Hotels** (variously judged). JORDAN HOTEL, HÔTEL GILGAL, and HÔTEL BELLEVUE, pens. at all these (without wine) 10*s*. — RUSSIAN HOSPICE (introduction from the Archimandrite at Jerusalem necessary), good and clean; 3 fr. per day without board, which travellers must provide for themselves. — Travellers with tents pitch them to the E. of the village or beside the Sultan's Spring (p. 129), to which the road diverges at the aqueduct mentioned at p. 127, before entering the village. — *Turkish Post Office.*

The inhabitants of Jericho are obtrusive, and the traveller should be on his guard against thieves. The villagers usually crowd round travellers with offers to execute a '*Fantasia*', or dance accompanied by singing, both of which are tiresome. The performers clap their own or each other's hands, and improvise verses in a monotonous tone.

Travellers should not forget to take drinking-water with them when visiting the Dead Sea (p. 134).

History. The ancient Jericho lay by the springs at the foot of the Jebel Karanṭal (p. 129), that is to the W. of modern Jericho, and to the N. of the Jericho of the Roman period (p. 127). The Israelitish town (Joshua v, vi) at first belonged to the tribe of Benjamin, afterwards to the kingdom of Israel. The town was of considerable size and enclosed by walls. It is sometimes called the 'city of palms', and down to the 7th cent. of our era date-palms were common, though they have now almost entirely disappeared. Around the town lay a large and flourishing oasis of corn and hemp fields. It was specially noted for its balsam gardens. The balsam plant has now disappeared entirely, although the plants of South Arabia and India would still flourish in this warm climate. Here, too, flourished the henna (*Lawsonia inermis*), which yields a red dye. Antony presented the district of Jericho to Cleopatra, who sold it to Herod; and that monarch embellished it with palaces and constituted it his winter-residence (p. 127). He died here, but directed that he should be interred in the Herodium (p. 111). — It was at Jericho that the Jewish pilgrims from Peræa (E. of Jordan) and Galilee used to assemble on their way to the Temple; and Christ also began his last journey to Jerusalem from this point (Luke xix. 1). — As early as the 4th cent. the councils of the church were attended by bishops of Jericho. The emperor Justinian caused a 'church of the mother of God' at Jericho to be restored, and a hospice for pilgrims to be erected. *New Jericho*, on the site of the present village, sprang up in the time of the Crusaders, who built a castle and a church of the Holy Trinity here. The place was afterwards inhabited by Moslems and gradually decayed.

Jericho (Arabic *Erîḥâ;* ca. 820 ft. below the sea-level), the seat of a Mudîr, consists of a group of squalid hovels, the Serâi (government building), and a few shops. It is also one of the three seats of administration for the crown domains in the valley of Jordan, which extend from the Sea of Tiberias to the Dead Sea. The inhabitants, only 300 in number, seem to be a degenerate race, on whom the hot climate (p. 1) has had an enervating effect. The vegetation is thoroughly sub-tropical. In the garden of the Russian church are the remains of a large building (perhaps a church) with piers and mosaic pavement. The only other curiosity in the village is a building on the S.E. side, resembling a tower. It probably dates from the Frank period, when it was erected as a protection against the incursions of the Beduins. Since the 15th cent. this building has been said to occupy the site of the *House of Zacchaeus* (Luke xix. 1-10). In the 4th cent. the sycamore into which Zacchæus climbed was shown.

Everywhere the ground is overgrown with thorny underwood, sometimes taking the form of trees, such as the ***Zizyphus Lotus*** and ***Z. spina Christi*** (the *nebk* and *sidr* of the Arabs), the fruit of which ('jujubes', Arab. *dôm*) is well flavoured when ripe. The formidable thorns of these rhamnaceæ, from which Christ's crown of thorns is said to have been composed, are used by the peasants in the construction of their almost unapproachable fences. Among the other plants occurring here is the *Zakkûm* tree (*Balanites Ægyptiaca*), also called the pseudo-balsam tree, or balm of Gilead, with small leaves like the box, and fruit resembling small unripe walnuts, from which the Arabs prepare 'pseudo-balsam' or 'Zacchæus oil', quantities of which are sold to pilgrims. The 'rose of Jericho' (*Anastatica hierochuntica*) does not occur here (comp. p. 171). Near Jericho is also found the *Solanum sanctum* (Arab. *ḥadaḳ*), a very woody shrub, 3-4½ ft. high, with broad leaves, woolly on the under side. The fruit looks like an apple, being first yellow, and afterwards red, and containing black seeds. It is sometimes called the apple of Sodom (for the genuine apple of Sodom, see p. 171), and has been erroneously connected with the wine of Sodom mentioned in Gen. xix. 32.

A pleasant occupation for the evening is a walk to the *'Ain es-Sulṭân ('Sultan's Spring')*, about 1 M. to the N.W. The water of the copious spring (temp. 80° Fahr.) is collected in a pond. It supplies the power to a mill near by, and is conveyed by a conduit to the different gardens of the village. According to an early tradition this was the water which Elisha healed with salt (2 Kings ii. 19-22), whence it is called *Elisha's Spring* by the Christians. On the hills near the spring lay the Jericho of Old Testament times (comp. p. 127). The excavations of Professor Sellin and the German Oriental Society (1907-1909) have established the fact that there existed an outer and an inner course of walls and have unearthed part of the actual masonry, which presents a curious form of construction and rests on a foundation of huge squared stones.

Taking the road to the W., we reach the ruins of three mills called *Ṭawâḥîn es-Sukkar* (sugar-mills), in reminiscence of the culture of the sugar-cane which flourished here down to the period of the Crusaders. Proceeding to the N.W. from the uppermost mill (20 min. from 'Ain es-Sulṭân) for ½ hr., we reach the *'Ain en-Nuwei'imeh* and *'Ain Dûk*, the springs of the well-watered *Wâdi en-Nuwei'imeh*. Here probably lay the ancient castle of *Docus* or *Dok* (1 Macc. xvi. 15), where Simon Maccabæus was assassinated by his son-in-law.

A (10 min.) footpath diverging from the road to 'Ain Dûk leads past the plantations of the Greek monastery to the (25 min.) hermits' caverns on the *Jebel Ḳarantal*, used as a place of punishment for Greek priests. The grotto in which Jesus is said to have spent the 40 days of his fast (Matt. iv. 1 et seq.) is used as a chapel. The name of the mountain is an Arabic corruption of the name *Quarantana*, which was first applied to the hill in 1112. The Frankish monastery on the hill was dependent on Jerusalem.

Among the cliffs higher up (40 min.) there are the ruins of a 'Chapel of the Temptation', as well as several rows of hermitages, some of which have even been adorned with frescoes. These, however, are accessible only to practised climbers. The weird seclusion of the spot attracted anchorites at a very early period. Thus St. Chariton (p. 110) is said once to have dwelt here, and the hermitages were enlarged by Elpidius. — The summit of the hill, which can be reached more easily from the W. side (in 1½ hr.; guide necessary), commands a noble prospect. On the S. side the Karantal is separated from the hill *Nḳeib el-Kheil* by the deep *Wâdi Deinûn*. On the top of the hill are a Greek monastery and traces of Frankish fortifications.

From Jericho to Beisân. This excursion (15 hrs.), for which an escort is indispensable, can, on account of the heat, be made early in the season (Jan.-March) only. — The Jordan valley contains a number of artificial hills *(tells)*, in the interior of some of which bricks have been found. We cross (55 min.) the *Wâdi Nuweiʿimeh* (p. 129); on the left the rock *ʿOshsh el-Ghurâb* (raven's nest; perhaps *Oreb*, Judges vii. 25), with a little valley, *Meṣâʿadet ʿIsâ* ('ascent of Jesus'). Here, previously to the 12th cent., was shown the mountain of the Temptation. Then (50 min.) the *Wâdi el-ʿAujeh*, the (35 min.) *Wâdi el-Abyaḍ*, the (¾ hr.) *Wâdi Reshash*, and the (1 hr.) *Wâdi Fasâil*, or *Mudahdireh*. At the foot of the mountains lie the ruins of *Khirbet Fasâil*, the ancient *Phasaëlis*, a town which Herod the Great named after Phasaëlus, his younger brother, and presented to his sister Salome. Palms were once extensively cultivated here. A much-frequented highroad ascended the valley of the Jordan viâ Phasaëlis to Cæsarea Philippi (p. 264).

About 1 hr. beyond the Wadi Fasâil the valley of the Jordan contracts. The second peak to the left is the lofty **Ḳarn Ṣarṭabeh,** 1245 feet above the sea-level, 2225 feet above the Jordan valley, the great landmark of the valley of Jordan. According to the Talmud the Ḳarn Ṣarṭabeh belonged to a chain of mountains on which the time of new moon was proclaimed by beacon-fires. In ascending it from the S. we find remains of a conduit. The ruins which cover the top consist of large, drafted, rough-dressed blocks and probably belonged to the *Alexandreion*, a castle built by Alexander Jannæus and refortified by Herod.

To the N. of the Ṣarṭabeh the valley of the Jordan becomes better watered and more fertile. On the left extends the beautiful plain of the *Wâdi el-Fârʿa* (p. 224). In this wâdi lies *Karâwa* (the *Koreae* of Josephus), and farther up are the ruins of *Buṣeilîyeh*, probably the ancient *Archelais*, erected by Herod Archelaus, the son of Herod the Great. The best sugar-canes known in mediæval times were cultivated near Karâwa. Farther to the N. the Jordan is joined by the *Nahr ez-Zerḳâ* (pp. 138, 139), descending from the E.

We next reach (2¼ hrs. from Karn Ṣarṭabeh) the caverns of *Makhrûk*, the (1 hr. 20 min.) *Wâdi Abu Sidreh*, and the (¾ hr.) *Wâdi Bukeiʿa*. The road crosses the (55 min.) *Wâdi Tûbâs*, the (½ hr.) *Wâdi Jemel*, the (40 min.) *Wâdi Fiiyâd*, a branch of the *Wâdi el-Mâliḥ*, and then several other branches of the same large valley, and reaches (50 min.) *ʿAin Ferʿûn*, by the ruins of *Sâkût*. The route passes the *Tell Huma* on the right and leads to the (1 hr.) *ʿAin el-Beiḍâ*, a copious spring. The brook *El-Khazneh* is crossed (35 min.) near the ruins of *Berdela*, the (20 min.) spring of *Mâkhûs* and the (1 hr.) *Tell Maʿjera* (p. 224) are passed, and we at length reach (1 hr.) *Beisân* (p. 240). Where the *Nahr Jâlûd* flows into the Jordan there is a ford *ʿAbâra*, which has been supposed to be the *Bethabara* (house of the ford) of John i. 28 (p. 131).

From Jericho to the Jordan there are two roads. The shorter (1½ hr.) is suitable for driving in fair weather; it crosses the *Wâdi el-Ḳelt* immediately beyond the tower of Jericho, and leads in an E.S.E. direction across the uncultivated plain. In 1¼ hr. we see, at some distance before us, the Monastery of St. John (p. 131). Leaving this on the left, we descend along the steep clayey side of the old bed of the river, and in ½ hr. reach the bathing-place of the pilgrims in the **Jordan,** which is bordered here with tamarisks, willows, and large poplars *(Populus euphratica)*.

The second of the two roads mentioned at p. 130 is somewhat longer, but is suitable for driving in all weathers. It runs along the N. side of the Wâdi el-Kelt. After 1/2 hr. we come to a fine group of four tamarisks. Close by it are an ancient pool and the ruins of *Khirbet el-Etheleh*, probably the site of the Gilgal of the Byzantine period. The so-called *Tell Jeljûl*, not far distant, is thought by some authorities to be the ancient **Gilgal,** where, according to Joshua (iv. 19 & 20), the Israelites erected twelve stones in commemoration of their passage of the Jordan. [The Gilgal mentioned in 1 Sam. (vii. 16; xi. 14 et seq.) has not yet been identified.]

Hence we reach in 1 hr. the Greek monastery of *Deir Mâr Yuḥannâ* ('Monastery of St. John'), usually called *Kaṣr el-Yehûd* ('castle of the Jews'). This stands on the remains of a monastery of St. John which was in existence as early as the time of Justinian and, according to tradition, was erected by the Empress Helena over the grotto where John the Baptist dwelt. It was restored in the 12th cent.; a number of vaults, frescoes, and mosaics are still visible. From Ḳaṣr el-Yehûd we reach the bathing-place of the pilgrims in 1/4 hr.

The **Jordan** (Hebrew *Yardên;* Arabic *Esh-Sherî'a el-Ḳebîr*, *i.e.* the large watering-place) rises on Mt. Hermon (pp. 263, 264), 1705 ft. above the sea. It has two main collecting-basins, the upper at the Lake of Ḥûleh (p. 262), 7 ft. above the level of the sea, and the lower and larger one in the Lake of Tiberias (p. 254), 680 ft. below the surface of the Mediterranean Sea. Its main course, from the Lake of Tiberias to the Dead Sea, has a fall of 610 ft., and a length, owing to its numerous windings, of upwards of 185 M., while the air-line distance between the two lakes is little more than 60 M. The deep valley of the river is called *El-Ghôr* by the Arabs, while the Hebrews gave the name of *'Araba* (p. 176) to that part of the valley between the Lake of Tiberias and the Dead Sea. From time immemorial this has formed a natural boundary, as the paths descending to the river are all wild and rugged. Most of the N. part of the valley is fertile, while in the S. part barren tracts alternate with green oases. For the vegetation and climate, comp. pp. l, lii. Many of the tributary streams, particularly those on the E. side (comp. pp. 138, 139, 241), are perennial. In the course of time the river has worn for itself two channels. The older channel, which we first reach, takes 1/2 hr. to cross. The present and deeper channel averages only 100 ft. in width, but the river often overflows its banks in time of rain. The thicket *(ez-zôr)* which conceals the water from view harbours wild boars and many birds, and was formerly infested by lions (Jerem. xlix. 19). The water is of a tawny colour from the clay which it stirs up in its rapid course, and its temperature is high. It contains numerous fish. — In ancient days, as at present, the Jordan seems to have been crossed almost exclusively at its few fords (1 Sam. xiii. 7; 2 Sam. x. 17); but David and Barzillai were conveyed across it in a ferry-boat (2 Sam. xix. 18, 31). The most famous ford is that of *Maḥâdet Ḥajleh.* Another ford, *El-Ḥenu*, lies farther to the S.

Maḥâdet Ḥajleh, the bathing-place of the pilgrims, is supposed to be the scene of the *Baptism of Christ* (Mark i. 5-11). The miraculous division of the waters by the cloak of Elijah (2 Kings ii. 8), and the legend of St. Christopher, who carried the infant Christ across the river, are also localized at this ford. In the middle ages the spot was supposed to be somewhat farther up. We have, however, no trustworthy clue to the site of *Bethabara* (John i. 28), though the two monasteries of St. John (see above and p. 133) afford a proof that the baptism of Christ was at a very early period believed to have been performed here. Baptism in Jordan was as early as the time of Constantine deemed a special privilege. In the 6th cent. Antoninus found a great concourse of pilgrims here and records that both banks were paved with marble. The pilgrims were conducted, or rather hurried, into the water by Beduin guides, and quarrels among the Christians were not uncommon. Down to the present time the Greeks attach great importance to the bath in Jordan. The great caravan starts for the Jordan before Epiphany (Jan. 6th O. S.), and the encampment, on the bank of the river, lighted with torches, presents an interesting spectacle. After the water has been blessed before daybreak by a high church dignitary, men and women bathe together in their white garments. At Easter and other seasons also crowds of pilgrims are often encountered here. Many of the pilgrims fill jars from the river to be used for baptisms at home. — Caution is recommended to bathers, as the stream is very rapid and it takes a powerful swimmer to reach the opposite bank.

The Route from the Bathing Place to the Dead Sea (drinking-water, see p. 128) is practicable for carriages (p. 125) in dry weather only, since the clay-soil, coated with strata of salt and gypsum, is very soft after rain. The way leads through the bushes on the bank of the river, and then across the open country among curiously-shaped chalk-hills. In 1 hr. we reach the bank of the Dead Sea. The view of the sea and the mountains, which are usually veiled by a slight haze, is very beautiful. Seen from a distance, the water is of a deep-blue colour, but when close at hand it assumes a greenish hue. The promontory on the right is ***Râs Feshkhah.*** Farther to the S. is ***Râs Marsid,*** beyond which lies Engedi (p. 171). The Mouth of the Jordan ($^3/_4$ hr. to the E.) is not visible; at the N.E. corner of the Dead Sea is the influx of the *Wâdi es-Suweimeh* (perhaps the *Beth-jesimoth* of Numbers xxxiii. 49); to the left, at some distance, is seen the ravine of the *Zerḳâ Mâ'în* (p. 153). Comp. also the Map at p. 11.

The **Dead Sea,** called in the Bible the *Salt Sea* or *Sea of the Cadmonites* (*i.e.* 'Eastern people'), also named by the Greeks and Romans the *Sea of Asphalt* (*Asphaltitis;* comp. p. 133), is commonly called *Bahr Lûṭ*, or Lake of Lot, by the Arabs, Mohammed having introduced the story of the destruction of Sodom (p. 174) and the rescue of Lot into the Koran. Its surface lies 1290 ft. below the Mediterranean Sea, but its level varies from 13 to 20 ft. with the seasons. The Dead Sea is 47 M. long, and its greatest breadth is about 10 M. (both dimensions being about the same as those of the Lake of Geneva); its greatest depth (1310 ft.) reaches a point 2600 ft. below the level of the Mediterranean. On the E. and W. sides it is flanked by precipitous mountains, with often little or no space between them and the water. The shallow S. bay of the sea ($11^1/_2$ ft. only in depth) is separated from the main basin by a low peninsula (Arab. *El-Lisân*, 'tongue'; Josh. xv. 2). At the S.W. end of the lake are huge deposits of rock-salt (p. 174). It has been calculated that $6^1/_2$ million tons of water fall into the Dead Sea daily, the whole of which prodigious quantity must be carried off by evaporation. In consequence of this extraordinary evaporation the water that remains behind is impregnated to an unusual extent with mineral substances. The water contains 24 to 26 per cent of mineral salts (about the same as the Great Salt Lake of Utah), 7 per cent of which is chloride of sodium (common salt). The chloride of magnesium, which also is largely held in solution, is the ingredient which gives the water its nauseous, bitter taste, while the chloride of calcium makes it feel smooth and oily to the touch. Bathers should be careful not to get any of the water into their mouth or eyes. The average specific gravity of the water is 1.166. Fresh eggs float in it with a third of their volume above the water. The human body floats without exertion on the surface, and can be submerged only with difficulty; but swimming is unpleasant, as the feet have too great a tendency to rise to the surface. In spite of its high percentage of salt, organic life is not altogether lacking in the Dead Sea, as is proved by the existence of a species of small viviparous fish (Cyprinodon dispar). — The lake was navigated in the time of Josephus and in the middle ages. The ruined buildings on its bank were probably hermitages.

The subsidence that formed the whole Jordan depression dates from the end of the tertiary period. The Dead Sea could never have been connected with the Red Sea as was at one time supposed (comp. p. 176). This inland lake was, on the other hand, the collecting reservoir for the enormously copious rainfall of the first ice age, during which the water-level was about 1400 ft. higher than at present, or about 105 ft. above the level of the Mediterranean. By the discovery of lacustrine deposits and traces of fresh-water fauna at that height it has been proved that the Dead Sea at that time filled the valley of the Jordan as far as the Lake of Tiberias. It seems clear that the N. bank has considerably receded within the historic period (comp. ZDPV. xvii. 225 et seq.; comp. also p. 174), and recent observers maintain that the level of the water is again rising. — The earlier accounts of the Dead Sea were somewhat exaggerated, and our first accurate information about it is due to the expedition which the United States of America sent to explore it in 1848 (see Report by *W. F. Lynch*). Further explorations have been made by *De Saulcy*, the *Duc de Luynes*, and the Palestine Survey Expedition. Comp. also *F. M. Abel*, 'Une Croisière autour de la Mer Morte' (Paris, 1911; 8 fr.); *Blanckenhorn*, 'Entstehung und Geschichte des Toten Meeres' (Leipzig, 1896; 2 *M* 40 pf.) and 'Das Tote Meer und der Untergang von Sodom und Gomorrha' (Berlin, 1898; 1 *M*).

The Salt found in the Dead Sea and the argillaceous strata adjoining it has been collected since the earliest times (pp. 171, 174) and is considered particularly strong. Asphalt is said to lie in large masses at the bottom of the lake, but it seldom comes to the surface except when loosened by storms or earthquakes. Others, however, think that the asphalt proceeds from a kind of breccia (a conglomerate of calcareous stones with resinous binding matter) which lies on the W. bank of the lake, and finds its way thence to the bottom; and that, when the small stones are washed out, the bituminous matter rises to the surface. The asphalt (bitumen) of the Dead Sea was highly prized in ancient times.

The Route from the Dead Sea to Jericho (1½ hr.) leads through the plain to the N.W. About halfway we see, on the right (E.), the large *Monastery of St. Gerasimos* (also called by the natives *Deir Mâr Yuḥannâ Ḥajleh*), built on the ruins of an old monastery, probably also dedicated to St. Gerasimos. Traces of frescoes of the 12th and 13th cent. and some ancient mosaics are preserved. About 10 min. to the N.E. of the monastery lies the lukewarm spring of *'Ain Ḥajleh*. The ruins of *Ḳaṣr Ḥajleh* correspond to the ancient *Beth Hogla* (Josh. xv. 6).

From the Dead Sea back to Jerusalem viâ the Monastery of Mâr Sâbâ.

Riders from the Dead Sea to *Mâr Sâbâ* take 5 hrs., thence to *Jerusalem* 3 hrs. (or to Bethlehem 2¾ hrs.). — For this excursion the traveller must be provided with a guide from *Abu Dîs* (p. 126; inquire at the hotels in Jericho). The right of escorting travellers is in the hands of the sheikh of this village. It is customary to pay the sheikh 1 mejîdi per day, and to give the guide himself ½-1 mej. at the end of the journey. A letter of introduction to Mâr Sâbâ should be procured, with the aid of the consul, from the Great Greek Monastery at Jerusalem (p. 34), as otherwise the traveller will not be admitted. — It is advisable to arrive early at the monastery, as no one is admitted after sunset, even when duly provided with letters.

The road follows the bank of the sea. After 18 min. we leave the *'Ain el-Jehaiyir* to the left; the brackish water of this spring contains pretty little fish *(Cyprinodon Sophiae)*. We then leave the sea and ascend to the N.W., through the *Wâdi ed-Dabr*, deeply eroded by its brook, and partly overgrown with underwood, which abounds in game (partridges, wild pigeons, hares, etc.). After 35 min. we enjoy a fine view of the Jordan valley and the Dead Sea. The route then leads to the left, skirting a deep ravine, and affording several other points of view. To the right we soon perceive the pass of *Neḳb Wâdi Mûsâ*, and in 35 min. we enter the *Wâdi el-Ḳeneiṭera*. Along the wayside are numerous heaps of stone *(shawâhid)*, in token that *En-Nebi Mûsâ* or Tomb of Moses is now visible. This Moslem pilgrim-shrine, of which we have no notice earlier than the 13th cent., is visited every Good Friday by a great Moslem pilgrimage, accompanied by many fanatical dervishes.

We continue our ride through the valley. After 40 min. the *Jebel el-Kaḥmûn* rises on our right, and we reach the tableland of *El-Buḳei'a*, which ascends towards the S.S.W., and is frequented in spring by Beduins of the tribe of Ḥteim. The view hence of the Dead Sea, far below the mountain-spurs, is grand and beautiful. After 42 min. we cross the *Wâdi Kherabîyeh*, which like all these valleys descends towards the E. In ½ hr. we reach the rain-reservoir of *Umm el-Fûṣ*. After 20 min. we see other heaps of stones by the wayside (see above). After 35 min. more we lose sight of the Dead Sea, and descend by a bad path into the *Wâdi en-Nâr*, or Kidron valley, the floor of which is reached in 28 minutes. On the other side the path ascends and in 20 min. reaches the top of the hill near a watch-tower, where our goai, the monastery of *Mâr Sâbâ*, now lies before us.

Mâr Sâbâ. — Accommodation will be found by gentlemen in the monastery itself; ladies must pass the night in a tower outside the monastery walls. Visitors must knock loudly at the small barred door for the purpose of presenting their letter of introduction and obtaining admission. The accommodation is rather poor, but bread and wine are to be had, and there are kitchens for the use of travellers who bring their dragoman and cook. The divans of the guest-chamber are generally infested with fleas. For a night's lodging 3 fr. each is paid, besides 9-12 pi. to the servant, and 3-6 pi. to the porter. — The best place for pitching tents is opposite the monastery.

History. In the 5th cent. a Laura, or settlement of monks, was founded here by *St. Euthymius*, whose favourite pupil *Sabas* or *Saba* (born in Cappadocia in 439) joined him in this wilderness. As the reputation of Sabas for sanctity became known, he was joined by a number of anchorites, with whom he lived according to the rule of St. Basilius. In 484 he was ordained priest by Sallustius, the Bishop of Jerusalem, and raised to the rank of abbot of the order of Sabaites named after him. He died in 531 or 532, after having greatly distinguished himself in theological controversies against the Monophysites (p. lxi). In 614 the monastery was plundered by the Persian hordes of Chosroes (p. lxxxi), and in subsequent centuries its wealth repeatedly attracted marauders (796 and 842), in consequence of which it became necessary to fortify it. It was again pillaged in 1832 and 1834. In 1840 it was enlarged and restored by the Russians.

The monastery of *Mâr Sâbâ*, now occupied by about 50 monks, consists of a number of terraces adjoining and above one another, and supported by massive retaining-walls. Every available spot has been converted by the monks into a miniature garden. Figs ripen here much earlier than at Jerusalem, as the sun beats powerfully on the rocks. In the centre of the paved court stands a dome-covered *Chapel*, decorated in the interior with greater richness than taste, containing the empty tomb of St. Sabas. This sanctuary is the chief attraction for pilgrims, although the remains of the saint have been removed to Venice. To the N. W. of this detached chapel is the *Church of St. Nicholas*, consisting chiefly of a grotto in the rock, which was perhaps once a hermitage. Behind a grating here are shown the skulls of the martyrs slain by the troops of Chosroes. The *Monastery Church*, of basilica form, on the E. side, is uninteresting. The tomb of Johannes Damascenus (8th cent.), one of the last distinguished theologians of the early Greek church, is also shown here. — Behind the church lie the chambers of the pilgrims and the cells of the monks. The latter, in accordance with the rule of their order, lead an ascetic life, eating little else than vegetables, and fasting frequently. Their principal occupation is feeding wild birds of the country (pigeons, *Columba Schimpri*, and pretty little black birds with yellow wings, resembling the starling, *Amydrus Tristrami*). The monastery is supported by donations and by the rents of a few landed estates. One of the little gardens contains a palm-tree which is said to have been planted by St. Sabas. Its dates have no stones. The chief memorial of the saint is his grotto, on the S. side of the monastery. A passage in the rock leads to a cavern, where the saint and a lion lived peaceably together.

Those who happen to pass a moonlight night in the monastery will carry away the most distinct idea of its singularly desolate situation. On such a night the visitor should take a walk on the terrace and look down into the valley. The rock falls away perpendicularly into the ravine, the bottom of which lies about 590 ft. below the monastery, and at about the same level as the Mediterranean. The barren heights beyond the valley contain a number of old hermitages.

The ROAD FROM MÂR SÂBÂ TO JERUSALEM descends into the Kidron valley, or Wâdi en-Nâr (20 min.), and then ascends it on the left side. Beyond (7 min.) a Beduin burial-place (tomb of the *Sheikh Muzeiyif*) the route turns to the left. On the left (S.), after 7 min. more, we observe the *Bîr esh-Shems* ('sun spring'). In 40 min. we leave the Kidron valley, which here makes a circuit towards the S. (the path through the valley is good, but takes longer), and enter a lateral valley, which leads to the N.W. After 1/2 hr. we reach the watershed, whence a striking view of Jerusalem is obtained. Descending to the W., we regain (50 min.) the Kidron valley, the Greek monastery *Deir es-Sîk* lying on the hill on the left; on the right the *Wâdi Kattûn* descends from the Mt. of Olives. In 1/4 hr. we reach Job's Well (p. 84), and in 1/4 hr. more the Jaffa Gate.

FROM MÂR SÂBÂ TO BETHLEHEM, 2³/4 hrs. A tolerable path ascends to the N. from the upper tower of the monastery. After 25 min. the monastery-tower disappears. Far below, in the Wâdi en-Nâr, are seen the huts of the natives who live under the protection of the monastery. After 10 min. the Mt. of Olives comes in sight on the right. In 20 min. we gain the top of the hill, whence we have a fine view. About 10 min. to the right of the path lies the Greek monastery of *Deir Ibn ʿObeid* (or *Deir Dôsi*), erected on the ruins of an ancient monastery of Theodosius. After 4 min. we descend into the *Wâdi el-ʿArâis* (10 min.). After 1/2 hr. we have a view of Bethlehem, and on the right rises Mâr Elyâs. In 40 min. we reach the first fields and orchards of Bethlehem. The monastery of Mâr Sâbâ also possesses land here. We leave the village of Beit Sâhûr to the left and, passing the Latin monastery, reach (25 min.) *Bethlehem* (p. 101).

16. From Jericho to Es-Salṭ and Jerash.

Comp. Map, p. 11.

RIDERS from Jericho to *Es-Salṭ* require 8³/4 hrs.; thence to *Jerash* 8 hrs. (dragoman and tents necessary). An escort of 1 or 2 khaiyâls is obtained by applying to the consulate at Jerusalem. Charge, 1 mej. per day for each man.

HISTORY. Gilead, in the wider sense of the name, embraces the region inhabited by the Israelites to the E. of the Jordan between the Yarmûk (N.; p. 241) to the Arnon (S.; p. 154). This hilly region was bisected by the brook Jabbok (*Nahr ez-Zerḳâ;* p. 139). At the present day the name Gilead is applied to the mountains to the S. of the lower Nahr ez-Zerḳâ (*Jebel Jiʿâd*). — Gilead was a pastoral region and supported numerous flocks. The W. slopes are for the most part still wooded. The land is fertilized by a copious supply of water and a heavy dew-fall. The E. neighbours of the Israelites were the Ammonites, with whom they carried on perpetual war. Jephthah (Judg. xi) and Saul fought against them (1 Sam. xi), and David captured Rabbah or Rabbath Ammon (p. 145), their chief city (2 Sam. xii. 29). The

Ammonites do not disappear from history till the 2nd cent. B.C. — Gilead afterwards belonged to the northern kingdom, and it suffered severely in the campaign of King Hazael of Damascus (2 Kings x. 32, 33). After the return from the captivity a number of Jews settled in Gilead in the midst of a heathen population. Alexander Jannæus frequently waged war on behalf of Gilead. Under Herod and his successor Antipas the Roman influence began to gain ground, and the numerous Roman ruins prove that Roman culture afterwards took deep root in Gilead.

The road leads N.E. from Jericho to ($1^3/_4$ hr.) the Jordan, which it crosses by a bridge (toll for man and horse, 3 piastres). Beyond the river the road forks, the right (S.E.) branch leading to Mâdebâ (p. 151), that to the left (N.E.) to Es-Salṭ. On reaching the ($^1/_2$ hr.) *Wâdi Nimrîn* we turn to the right (E.) along it, leaving the great caravan-route, which continues through the *Wâdi el-Aḥṣeniyât.* After $^3/_4$ hr. we reach (to the right, on the S. side of the valley) the ruins of *Tell Nimrîn*, the *Beth Nimrah* of the tribe of Gad (Joshua xiii. 27; Num. xxxii. 3, 36), near which the 'Waters of Nimrim' (Is. xv. 6) are probably to be sought. Among the ruins is a tomb adorned with the figure of a rider with a sword. [From this point to ʿArâḳ el-Emîr, see p. 149.] Our route next ascends the *Wâdi Shaʿîb*, or upper part of the *Wâdi Nimrîn*, at first along the right bank; after $1^1/_2$ hr. we cross the stream and continue along the ridge on the left bank. In 1 hr. 50 min. we reach (l.) the *Weli Nebi Shaʿîb.* [Shuʿaib, the diminutive of Shaʿîb, is the name given in the Koran to the Jethro of the Bible, Exodus iii. 1.] The weli is hung with rags (comp. p. lxxv). About $^1/_4$ hr. later we again cross the stream and ascend the right side of the valley to ($^3/_4$ hr.) the spring *ʿAin el-Mukerfât*, on the left. The valley is well cultivated. In 35 min. we reach the spring *ʿAin Hazîr*, on the right, and in 35 min. more *ʿAin Jâdûr.* Above this spring is a large group of tombs, known as *Sâra*, dating from early Christian times. In 10 min. more we reach —

Es-Salṭ (2740 ft. above the sea), capital of the Ḳaḍâ (p. lvii) of *El-Belkâ*, with a Turkish *Telegraph Office.* English physician.

Owing to an erroneous statement by Eusebius, *Ramoth Gilead* (1 Kings xxii. 3, etc.; the *Mizpeh of Gilead* of Judges xi. 29) has been sought for here, though in reality it must have lain considerably farther to the N. On the other hand *Gadara*, mentioned by Josephus (Bell. Jud.; v. 7, 3) as the capital of Peræa, was probably situated in this neighbourhood. The name *Es-Salṭ* is, perhaps, derived from the Latin word *saltus* (wooded mountains). Es-Salṭ is mentioned as the seat of an early Christian bishop. The fortress was destroyed by the Mongols, but soon afterwards rebuilt by Sultan Beybars (p. lxxxv).

Es-Salṭ contains over 15,000 inhab., among them 400 Protestants (English mission-station, church, school, and hospital), 900 Latins (church, convent, boys' school, and girls' school managed by the Sœurs de Charité), 3000 Greeks (convent, two churches, boys' and girls' schools), and 11,000 Moslems (Government schools, elementary and high). The Moslem Arabs and the Christians have much in common with the nomadic tribes in their customs and language. Agriculture and vine-growing are the chief resources of the inhabitants, but some of them are engaged in industrial pursuits. The market is much frequented by the Beduins. The fields yield a considerable quantity of sumach, which is exported for dyeing purposes. The raisins of Es-Salṭ are famous. The chief portion of the town lies on the slope of a hill crowned with the ruins of a castle; the more modern parts also stretch across on to the hills opposite. On the S. side of the castle-hill is a grotto in which rises a spring. In this grotto there seems once to have been a church hewn in the rocks. It still contains some remains of sculpture and a passage descending to an artificial grotto below.

From Es-Salṭ a very interesting excursion may be made in rather less than 1 hr. to the **Jebel Ôsha'** (3595 ft.). This mountain affords a magnificent view, embracing a considerable part of Palestine. The Jordan valley, for a great distance, is stretched at our feet like a carpet. The river, of which a white strip only is visible at a few points, traverses the vast, yellowish plain to the Dead Sea. To the S.W. the Mt. of Olives is visible. Mts. Ebal and Gerizim opposite us present a very fine appearance. Mt. Tabor and the mountains around the lake of Tiberias are also visible, and the Great Hermon to the N. terminates the panorama. The scene, however, is deficient in life. — Near a fine oak on the top of the mountain is the weli of the prophet *Ôsha'* (Arabic for Hosea), which is about 300 years old. The tradition is probably of Jewish origin. The prophet Hosea belonged to the northern kingdom, and he may very possibly have been born in the country to the E. of Jordan. In chap. xii. verse 11 he speaks of Gilead. The weli contains an open trough, about 30 ft. long, which is said to have been the tomb of the prophet. The Beduins still kill sheep here in honour of Hosea.

The Route from Es-Salṭ to Jerash ascends the Nâbulus road to the N.W. (following the telegraph-wires), and after 1/2 hr. turns N. On reaching (10 min.) the summit of the pass, on which are the ruins of *Khirbet el-Ḳuḳ'ân*, we have a fine retrospect. We descend to the N.E. into the (10 min.) *Wâdi Ḳuṭṭein*, in which, 10 min. lower, the *'Ain el-Ḥarâmîyeh* ('robbers' spring') lies hidden among the woods and rocks. Our route now leads us through fine woods, consisting of massive oaks and other deciduous trees, pines, firs, etc., festooned with numerous climbing-plants; but unfortunately the inhabitants of the district are recklessly felling the trees. From the (1 hr.) farther edge of the wood we reach in 25 min. the Christian village of *Er-Remeimîn* (120 Latins, with a church, and 150 Greeks, with a chapel and a school). A steep descent of 1/4 hr. then brings us to a ford over the usually well-filled *Wâdi er-Remeimîn*. The road on the other side of the stream passes (1/2 hr.) a stone circle about 13 ft. in diameter, and in 1/4 hr. more reaches the top of the hill. We again descend, reaching in 25 min. a waterfall about 60 ft. high in the *Wâdi Salîḥi*. The cascade is enclosed in a frame of luxuriantly verdant creepers. By-and-by we quit the stream and ascend the hill of *Ḍahrat er-Rummân* (1/2 hr.), 1/4 M. beyond which lies the Turcoman village of *Er-Rummân* (1805 ft.). After 10 min. we cross the *Wâdi er-Rummân*, with its picturesque stream; 25 min. *'Ain Umm Rabî'a*, a copious spring of excellent water; 12 min. *'Ain el-Masṭaba* (1870 ft.), a feeble spring. Thence we reach in 1 hr. more the *Nahr*

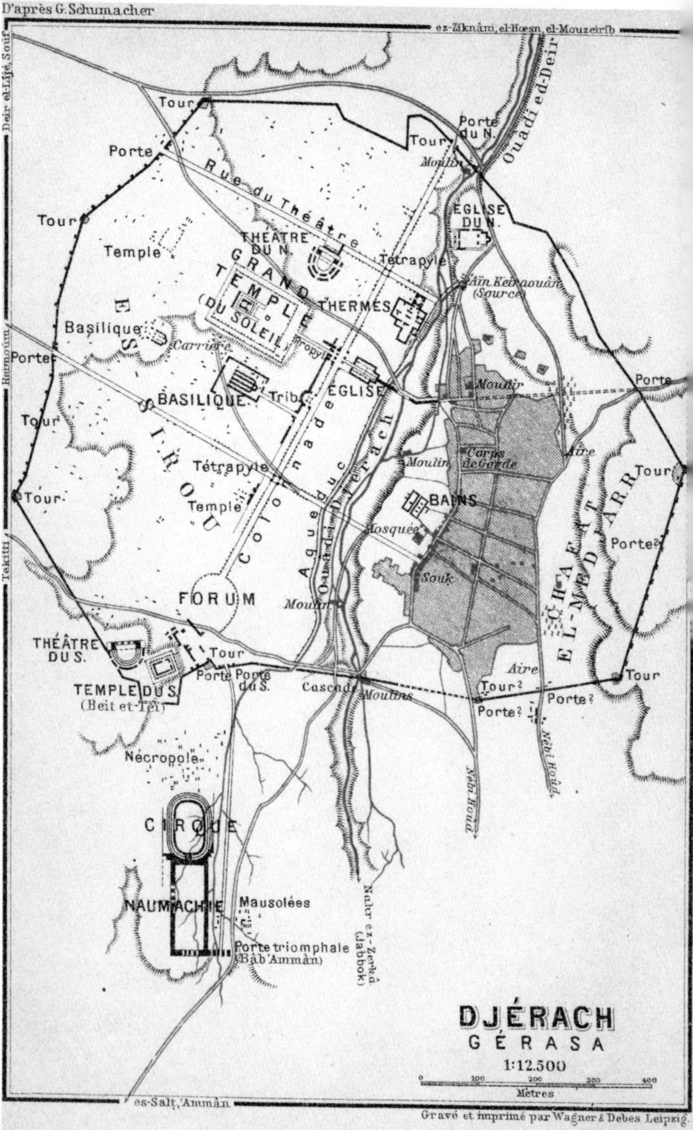

D'après G. Schumacher
ez-Ziknâni, el-Hoesn, el-Mouzeirîb
Deir el-Lifé, Souf
Ouadi ed-Deir
Tour
Porte du N.
Porte
Moulin
Rue du Théâtre
Tour
EGLISE DU N.
THEATRE DU N.
Temple
GRAND TEMPLE (DU SOLEIL)
Tétrapyle
THERMES
Aïn Keiraouân (Source)
Basilique
Carrière
Propyl.
Porte
BASILIQUE
Trib.
EGLISE
Moulin
Porte
Tour
Colonnade
Aqueduc
Ouadi Djerach
Corps de Garde
Moulin
Aire
Tour
Tétrapyle
Tour
Temple
BAINS
Mosquée
Porte?
Souk
FORUM
Moulin
THÉÂTRE DU S.
Tour
Aire
Porte
Porte du S.
Cascade
Moulins
Tour?
Tour
TEMPLE DU S. (Beit et-Teï)
Porte?
Porte?
Necropole
Nebi Houd
CIRQUE
NAUMACHIE
Mausolées
Porte triomphale (Bâb 'Ammân)
Nahr ez-Zerkâ (Jabbok)
DJÉRACH
GÉRASA
1:12.500
0 100 200 300 400
Mètres
es-Salt, 'Ammân
Gravé et imprimé par Wagner & Debes Leipzig.

ez-Zerkâ, a little below the influx of the *Wâdi Jerash* (785 ft.). The Nahr ez-Zerkâ, or 'blue river', is the *Jabbok* of the Old Testament (Gen. xxxii. 22; see p. 136). The banks are bordered with oleanders. The brook is generally well filled with water, and in rainy weather is often difficult to ford. — Crossing the river and riding due N. along the hills, we reach ($1^3/_4$ hr.) *Jerash.*

Jerash (Gerasa).

The best place for pitching TENTS is near the North Gate. A visitation of the ruins takes a full day.

HISTORY. *Gerasa* is first mentioned under Alexander Jannæus, who captured it. Its freedom was restored by Pompey; and it afterwards belonged to the Decapolis of Peræa. Its most prosperous period was early in the Christian era. Its buildings of the 2nd and 3rd centuries show how Roman influence had penetrated even to such remote towns as this. In the 4th cent. Gerasa was still considered one of the largest and strongest towns in Arabia, and it lay on a great Roman military road. The valley in ancient days was called *Chrysorrhoas*. The Arabian geographer Yâkût (at the beginning of the 13th cent.) describes Gerasa as deserted. The ruin of the town seems to date from the time of the Arabian immigration. There is now a settlement of Circassians here. — Comp. *Schumacher* on Jerash in ZDPV. xxv, 1902, pp. 109 et seq.

Jerash (1900 ft. above the sea), a village with 1500 inhab. and the seat of a Mûdîr (p. lvii), lies in the *Wâdi Keirawân* or *Wâdi Jerash* (here called also *Wâdi ed-Deir*), on the left bank of a copious stream, which is bordered with oleanders. The imposing ruins of the ancient town are upon the loftier right bank, but, as they are used as quarries for building-stone, they are rapidly disappearing. The town-walls, following the slopes of the hill, are partly preserved, and are about 3885 yds. in circumference. Material for all the ancient buildings was furnished by the limestone of the vicinity. There are but few traces of basalt and other costly materials.

We begin our inspection of the ruins with the large **Triumphal Gate** *(Bâb 'Ammân)* to the S. of the town, a handsome building with a total width of 83 ft. The central archway is 21 ft. wide, 39 ft. high, and 22 ft. in depth, and there are smaller gateways on each side. The columns on the S. side have calyx-shaped pedestals of acanthus-leaves above their bases. Above the side-gateways are square niches. The striking similarity of the gateway to Trajan's Arch at Rome indicates the middle of the 2nd cent. as the probable period of its erection. — To the W. the gate is adjoined by a large hollow, now filled up with alluvial deposits and brought under the plough. The lower part of this was a *Naumachia*, or theatre for the representation of naval battles, 170 yds. long and 60 yds. broad. The S. retaining-wall of this, $15^1/_2$ ft. thick, is still visible, with four sluice-gates for the admission of the water. The rows of seats for the spectators were parallel with the longer axis of the basin. An aqueduct connected the Naumachia with the spring of 'Ain Keirawân (p. 142). The N. wall of the Naumachia forms the S. boundary of a large *Circus*, measuring 295 ft. by 180 ft. Remains of four rows of seats are preserved here. — To the N. of the circus are remains of an extensive *Necropolis.*

The *Southern Gate* of the town, which is now almost entirely destroyed, appears to have resembled the outer gateway. On each side it was once evidently connected with the town-walls. A few paces to the W. of the town-gate stand the ruins of a **Temple** (now called *Beit et-Tei*), 98 ft. long by 66$^1/_2$ ft. wide. It was a peripteral temple, with 11 columns on the N. and S. and 8 columns on the W. and E. The bases of the columns, 11 ft. distant from the cella, are easily traced. The vestibule seems to have had two rows of columns with Attic bases and Corinthian capitals. The portal is 15$^1/_2$ ft. in width. The cella, the S. wall of which is still standing to a height of 33 ft., was 82 ft. long by 50 ft. wide. The mural pillars of the finely jointed wall have been deprived of their capitals. Above the wall is a simple and very slightly projecting cornice. The style of the whole building is noble.

Adjacent to the W. side of this temple is the **Southern Theatre**, measuring 288 ft. in its longer diameter, and containing 32 well-preserved rows of seats. The stage, now in ruins, had its back to the town-wall, so that the spectators must have enjoyed an admirable view of the handsome public buildings in their city. A broad passage, approached from below by five flights of steps and from above by nine, divides the rows of seats into a lower and an upper section. Eight small chambers or 'boxes' are ranged along this gangway or gallery, and on the S. it communicates with the outside of the building by four vaulted passages. In the front wall of the proscenium, once fitted up with great magnificence, there were three portals, the central of which was of rectangular form, while the others were vaulted. Along the inside of this wall ran a row of Corinthian columns, and between these columns were richly adorned niches. The acoustic arrangement is admirable. The theatre is unfortunately used by the Circassians as a convenient quarry.

The so-called **Forum**, to the N.E. of the temple and theatre, consists of a semicircle of 56 columns of the Ionic order opening to the S.W. As most of the columns are still erect and are still connected with each other by an entablature, they present a very striking appearance. Portions of the pavement are also still intact.

To the N.E. of this forum begins the **Colonnade**, fully $^1/_2$ M. in length, by which the whole town was intersected. Its width measured from the middle of the columns is 41 ft.; the intervals between the columns vary from 10 ft. to 15 ft. The Colonnade consisted originally of about 520 columns, of which 75 are still standing; the others have been overthrown by earthquakes and have of late been much mutilated by human agency. Including the base and capital, the columns are from 21 to 30 ft. high; the shafts are composed of drums from 3 to 5 ft. in height, and are all unfluted. Towards the middle of the town the columns are of the Corinthian order and have fine acanthus capitals; near the Forum and towards the N. gate they are, on the contrary, of the Ionic order and somewhat clumsy. All these differences in detail afford a presumption that the Colonnade was erected at a comparatively late period, and was constructed of materials already existing. Remains of a second row of columns on both sides of the street seem to show that arcades ran along the fronts of the houses, above which, on a level with the first story, there were probably open galleries.

At the intersection of the next cross-street, 220 yds. to the N. of the Forum, stood a *Tetrapylon* (p. xcvii), of which four pedestals, $6^1/_2$ ft. in height, with niches for statues, still exist. These supported a dome 32 ft. in diameter. — The cross-street here was also flanked by columns, only a few of which still remain. It descends to the S.E. to a broad flight of steps and to a *Bridge* crossing the brook in five arches, the central one of which is $37^1/_2$ ft. wide. The aqueduct mentioned at p. 139 crosses the street close by.

About 142 yds. to the N. of the Tetrapylon, to the left of the Colonnade, are the remains of a large building with a *Tribuna*, within the semicircle of which (11 yds. across) stood a fountain. The building had two stories, which were separated from each other by a cornice with brackets, and each of which was articulated by three semicircular and four rectangular niches; at the top is a rich cornice with 'interrupted' pediments. The interior of the building is filled with large hewn blocks, scattered in wild confusion.

Farther on we reach the *Propylaea* of the Great Temple, which still afford an idea of the grandeur of the original structure, in spite of their ruined condition. The style of this fine gateway is that of the Roman adaptation of the Corinthian order. The great portal, the architrave of which has fallen, stands between two window-niches with richly-decorated pediments. The W. side of the Propylæa is adorned with nobly conceived and well-preserved sculptures. To the right and left, between the pilasters, are niches ending above in the form of a shell; over these is a small gable with delicate ornamentation.

The **Great Temple**, which was probably dedicated to the sun, stands upon a terrace 527 ft. long and 344 ft. wide, which was enclosed by 260 columns. The temple itself is $87^1/_2$ ft. long by 66 ft. wide, and rises upon a podium 8 ft. in height, the flight of steps leading to which has disappeared. The portico has one row of six columns and one row of four columns, besides a column on each side at the end of the projecting temple-wall. Nine of these columns are in perfect preservation and make a very imposing appearance. Including their bases and their capitals, which are adorned with admirably executed acanthus foliage, they are 45 ft. high; their lower diameter is 5 ft. The portal, which was 16 ft. in width, has fallen in. The cella has a clear width of $36^1/_2$ ft. and is 56 ft. long. It is for the most part in a state of ruin and its floor is covered with rubbish; part of the enclosing walls, however, are preserved, with six oblong niches on each side. The image of the deity probably stood in the vaulted chamber opening in the rear wall. On each side of the door in the rear wall were steps leading to galleries. The Temple probably dates from the first half of the 2nd cent. A.D., and, in any case, it is earlier than the Colonnade (p. 140).

To the S. of the Temple is a *Basilica* (with nave and aisles) built out of old materials, and to the S.W. of it is a smaller *Church*; neither of these, however, is important. — A third *Church*, to the E. of the Propylæa, apparently also belonged originally to the precincts of the Temple of the Sun. The nave was 42½ ft. wide, and on its S. side there still stand seven columns, which were probably brought hither from the street leading to the second bridge. The semicircular apse of the nave is also recognizable.

About 165 yds. to the N. of the Propylæa is another street-crossing, also marked by a *Tetrapylon*. This, however, was round in the interior, and square on the outside only; it was formerly adorned with statues. The cross-street, of which only three columns remain, was adjoined on the W. by the North Theatre, and on the E., near the brook, by the Thermæ.

The **North Theatre**, which seems to have been intended for combats of gladiators and wild animals, possesses 17 tiers of seats with a total height of 39 ft. The corridor between the eighth and ninth row of seats is reached by five gangways, between each pair of which are a large niche and two smaller shell-shaped niches. The proscenium, which is now buried in rubbish, lay very low, and was adorned with detached columns.

The extensive ruins of the **Thermæ** are now called *El-Khân*. The entrance is formed by a well-preserved dome-structure about 55 ft. square. A staircase led to the bath proper, which consisted of a main building, 222 ft. long by 98 ft. broad, and of a side-building to the S., 138 ft. long by 38 ft. broad. The vaulting of the bath-chambers has fallen in. The water was brought by an aqueduct from the spring of *'Ain Keirawân*, situated to the N.E., beyond the brook.

There is another ancient *Bath* near the village mosque.

The great Colonnade ends at the *North Gate*, where we obtain a beautiful view. The direction of the wall, and the place where it crosses the brook, are distinctly traceable here. — On the E. bank of the brook are the enclosing walls of a fourth *Church*, which is rapidly being torn to pieces (ZDPV. xviii, 1895, pp. 127 et seq.). This building is 197 ft. long by 120 ft. wide; the nave was 42 ft. wide, and the aisles 28 ft. Internally the chancel has a semicircular ending, with shell-shaped niches, but the exterior is rectilineal. The only remains of the columns are nine bases of the Attic order and a few drums. On the W. this church possessed a colonnade with a portico 28 ft. in width. According to an inscription it was originally a sanctuary of Nemesis, dating from the time of Trajan.

To the N., outside the gate, lay the most important **Necropolis** of the ancient city. The road to the ($1^1/_8$ M.) springs of *Ez-Ziknâni* is flanked all the way on both sides by tombs, sarcophagi, and the like. The water of the springs is collected in two ponds, an upper (295 ft. by $157^1/_2$ ft.) and a lower ($157^1/_2$ ft. by 59 ft.), and was conducted to the town by an aqueduct. About 110 yds. farther on is the large mausoleum of *Es-Samûri* (26 ft. by 28 ft.), which possesses a fine portal and three noble Corinthian columns.

From Jerash to ʿAmmân ($8^1/_2$ hrs.). We descend the *Wâdi Jerash* to the *Zerḳâ* ($1^3/_4$ hr.; p. 139), beyond which we ascend the mountain and follow the Es-Salṭ route (see p. 138) to (1 hr. 40 min.) *ʿAin Umm Rabîʿa*. We then ascend a small valley to the left and reach the ($^3/_4$ hr.) spring of *ʿAin Umm Buṭmeh*. In 10 min. more we attain the summit; thence we descend to the S. and after $^1/_2$ hr. arrive at the plain of *El-Buḳeiʿa*. At first we cross this in a S. direction; then, where the path divides (the branch to the right leading to Es-Salṭ, p. 137), we take the path to the left and cross the plain in a S.E. direction. After 25 min. we see, on the right, *Rijm el-Hawi* and in $^1/_4$ hr. more we come to the ruins of *Khirbet el-Bâsha* (p. 148), with a spring. Thence another 10 min. brings us to the S.E. corner of the plain, whence we ascend a small valley to the Circassian village of *Suweiliḥ* (p. 147). Thence in 55 min. to *ʿAmmân* (p. 148).

From Jerash to *Derʿa* and *El-Muzeirîb*, see p. 160.

17. From Damascus to El-Maʿân by the Ḥejâz Railway.

Comp. Maps, pp. 155, 11.

The construction of the narrow-gauge railway ($3^1/_2$ ft.) from Damascus to (ca. 1120 M.) Mecca, connecting Syria with the Ḥejâz (*i.e.* Arabia Petræa), was begun in 1901 by order of Sultan ʿAbdu'l Ḥamîd II., chiefly to facilitate the annual pilgrimages to Mecca (p. lxxii). The undertaking, which may therefore be regarded as a pious one, was assisted by voluntary contributions from every point of the territory of Islam. The old government also levied special taxes and employed Turkish soldiers in the construction of the line. Under these favourable circumstances it was in 1908 already in operation as far as Medîna (823 M.). Since the advent to power of the Young Turk party, there seems, however, little chance of the continuation of the line to Mecca. — Passengers other than Moslems are not allowed to use the railway beyond El-Maʿân without special permission from the government. A branch-line from Derʿa to Ḥaifâ connects the railway with the coast (pp. 239-242).

At present three trains run weekly in each direction, leaving Damascus on Mon., Wed., and Sat. morning, and returning from El-Maʿân on Mon., Thurs., and Sat. afternoon. Fare from Damascus to (6 hrs.) *Derʿa* 62 pi. (1st cl.) or 25 pi. (2nd cl.), to (12 hrs.) *ʿAmmân* 111 pi. 20 paras or 50 pi., to (26 hrs.) *El-Maʿân* 230 or 109 pi. (Government Rate of Exchange; comp. the Table facing the title-page). Some of the trains at present have only one class, equivalent to our third class. Railway restaurants at Derʿa and El-Maʿân only. At Derʿa, ʿAmmân, and El-Maʿân horses or donkeys can be procured; otherwise, for trips to right and left of the line of railway, the traveller should send on horses in advance.

Damascus, see p. 298. The train starts from the new station near the Serâi (comp. p. 298) and first traverses the *Ghûṭa* (p. 300), running parallel to the French Ḥaurân Railway (p. 157) and at some distance from it. On emerging from the Ghûṭa we cross the low chain of the *Jebel el-Aswad* (p. 267) and then traverse the broad depression of the *Wâdi el-ʿAjam*, through which flows the *Nahr el-Aʿwaj*. The upper part of this stream is called the *Nahr es-Sâbirânî*, and is the ancient *Pharpar* (2 Kings v. 12), although the *Nahr Barbar* of the present day no longer flows into it. The snow-crowned summits of Mount Hermon remain constantly in view.

13 M. *El-Kisweh* (2425 ft.; p. 158), a considerable village on the Nahr el-Aʿwaj. To the left appears the barren range of the *Jebel el-Mâniʿ*, on the highest summit of which (3640 ft.) lie the ruins of the ancient castle *Ḳalʿat en-Nuḥâs*. — The line continues to the S.E. along the base of the mountain to (19½ M.) *Deir ʿAli*.

31 M. *El-Mismiyeh* (2030 ft.), the ancient *Phaene*, at one time a populous town and the seat of a bishopric. Several of the old houses are still well preserved, but the fine temple has unfortunately been entirely demolished, and its stones used for building-material. The town stands on the border of the *Lejâh (Lohf el-Lejâh)*, which the line now skirts in a S.W. direction.

El-Lejâh is the ancient district of *Trachon*, so called from its wild and broken aspect. The surface of the stony soil (lava) is generally level and may be compared to a troubled sea that has suddenly solidified. In former times the country was enlivened here and there with vineyards and plantations; a Roman road traversed it from El-Mismiyeh (see above) to Es-Suweidâ (p. 166). At the present day, however, El-Lejâh has a somewhat desolate appearance. The inhabitants of the Ḥaurân have nevertheless always had a predilection for this almost inaccessible region on account of the many hiding-places it offers. Its name signifies 'hiding-place', and the Druses also call it *Ḳalʿat Allâh* ('fortress of God'). The border of the Lejâh, which rises some 33 ft. above the plain of the Ḥaurân, is protected in many places by rough stone walls. For this reason it was not without great difficulty that Ibrâhîm Pasha (p. lxxxvi) was able to suppress the revolt here in 1838, and it is only quite lately that the Turkish government has acquired a firm hold on the country. The formation of the Lejâh is due to the descent from the mountains of streams of lava, chiefly from the *Tell Shîḥân* and the *Gharârat el-Ḳiblîyeh* (p. 169).

39 M. *Jebâb*; 43 M. *Khabeb*. The line makes a bend to the S.S.E. — 48½ M. *Maḥajjeh*; 53 M. *Shaḳra*.

56½ M. *Ezraʿ* (1990 ft.), the ancient *Zoroa*. The town lies 2 M. to the N.E. of the railway station. The fine Greek Orthodox Church of St. George, on the N.E. side of the town, was completed in 515; over the W. portal is an inscription. The Church of the United Greeks to the S.E. dates from the 7th century.

From Ezraʿ to El-Kanawât, ca. 8 hrs.' riding. We follow the S. border of the Lejâh in an E. direction, passing *Buṣr el-Harîrî* (probably the ancient *Bosor*, 1 Macc. v. 26) and traversing the *Wâdi el-Ḳanawât*. — *El-Ḳanawât*, see p. 166.

After leaving Ezraʿ the train turns southwards through the fruitful plain of *En-Nuḳra*, the great plain of the Ḥaurân and the granary of Syria. It derives its name, which means 'depression', from its position among peaks and ranges of hills, which give it the appearance of a round valley. — 66 M. *Khirbet el-Ghazâleh* (1885 ft.).

76½ M. **Der'a** or *Der'ât* (1800 ft.; *Railway Restaurant*, with bedrooms, pens. 10 fr.; Turkish telegraph), situated on the S. slope of the Wâdi ez-Zeidî (see below), is the seat of a Ḳâimmaḳâm, with 4000 inhabitants. It is the ancient *Edre'i* (Numb. xxi. 33 et seq.), and during the Christian period was the seat of a bishop. — In the bottom of the *Wâdi ez-Zeidî* lies a large reservoir, 64½ yds. long, 59 yds. wide, and 6½ ft. deep. On the W. side of the reservoir lies the *Ḥammâm es-Siknâni* (an ancient Roman bath in ruins); near it, the inaccessible mausoleum of *Siknâni*. At the S.E. end of the town stands a *Ruwâḳ*, or hall for prayer, 65½ yds. long and 31½ yds. wide, with a double colonnade running round it. This was erected in 1253 and had eighty-five columns of different kinds and three gates. In the court lies a sarcophagus with two lions' heads. At the N.W. corner rises a lofty tower (*El-Meidani;* view). Farther to the S., at the end of the road, a threshold is visible, with an inscription of the Emp. Gallienus (253-268). — The labyrinthine subterranean dwellings here, into which it is possible to crawl, are very interesting. The entrance is in the Wâdi ez-Zeidî.

Branch-line from Der'a to *Haifâ*, see R. 27. The first station on this line is (7½ M.) *El-Muzeirîb*, the terminus of the Ḥaurân railway (p. 158).

From Der'a the train runs towards the S.E., crossing the Wâdi ez-Zeidî and skirting the E. side of the *Jebel ez-Zumleh*. The last is a hilly district, nowhere rising to a greater height than 330 ft. above the plain (2300 ft. above sea-level), which stretches from N. to S. for a distance of about 37 M. It encloses on the W. the desert of *El-Ḥamâd* ('stony plateau'), a tract devoid of spring-water, covered only with a meagre desert-grass, and uninhabited. Geologically these hills, which contain vast deposits of flint in chalk-marl, represent the transition from the dolerites and lavas of the Ḥaurân to the calcareous formations of the Jebel 'Ajlûn (p. 156).

84½ M. *Naṣîb;* 100½ M. *Ḳal'at el-Mefraḳ*, where the line reaches the Pilgrim Route (*Derb el-Ḥajj*, p. 158); 115 M. *Khirbet es-Samrâ*. — 126 M. *Ḳal'at ez-Zerḳâ*, close to the spring of that name. The line here reaches the upper end of the *Wâdi ez-Zerḳâ* (Jabbok, p. 139), which it crosses immediately afterwards on a viaduct. We now ascend the valley, the upper part of which is called the Wâdi 'Ammân, and reach the station of (138½ M.) *'Ammân* (2420 ft.; scanty accommodation obtainable if necessary).

'Ammân (2745 ft.), one of the finest ruined cities in the district to the E. of the Jordan, is the seat of a Mûdîr and lies 3 M. to the W. of the rail. station. The government has established a colony of Circassians here, unfortunately not to the advantage of the ruins.

History. *Rabbath Ammon*, the capital of the Ammonites, was besieged and taken by Joab (2 Sam. xii. 26-31). Later, however, it appears to have again belonged to the Ammonites (Jerem. xlix. 2). Ptolemy II. (Philadelphus) of Egypt rebuilt it and added the name *Philadelphia*, and for several centuries it was a thriving place, belonging to the Decapolis. It never quite lost its original name, by which alone it was afterwards known to the Arabs.

The **Citadel** *(El-Ḳal'a)* of 'Ammân lies on a hill on the N. side, which towards the S.W. forms an angle, and towards the N. is separated from the rest of the hill by a (perhaps) artificial depres-

From an Original Survey by G. Armstrong — Wagner & Debes' Geogr. Estabt. Leipsic

sion. The citadel consists of three terraces, rising from E. to W. The gate is in the S. side. The thick enclosing walls are constructed of large, uncemented blocks. On the uppermost (W.) terrace the traces of a temple (bases of the columns of the pronaos) are still visible, and there is a well-preserved tower in the S. wall. All these buildings date from Roman times, but there is an interesting specimen of Arab architecture (*El-Ḳaṣr;* hardly a mosque) to the N. of the temple. The details of the work in the interior are magnificent. The citadel commands a fine view of the entire field of ruins.

The most important ruins in the valley below are as follows (from W. to E.). 1. On the left (N.) bank of the river, near the mouth of a lateral valley, which flanks the castle-hill on the W., is a *Mosque* of the time of the Abbasides; to the E. of this, near the river, is an almost completely destroyed *Basilica* in the Byzantine style, and close by it are the ruins of an Arab *Bazaar*. — 2. A little to the N.E. of the basilica are the remains of **Thermæ.** The S. wall is well preserved, and consists of a handsome apse connected with two lateral ones. Columns without capitals are still standing. At a great height are richly decorated niches, and holes for cramps indicate that the building was once decorated with bronze ornaments. A conduit running parallel with the river on its N. bank conveyed the water. Immediately to the N.E. of the baths is a piece of the old vaulting over the brook (comp. below) and somewhat farther down the stream, on the left bank, is a fine portico. — 3. Starting from the mosque (see above), we may follow the course of the ancient **Street of Columns,** which ran through the town parallel with the stream and on its left bank for a distance of about 990 yds. Only a very few columns now remain standing. — To the left (N.) of the street of columns and in the middle of the village are the remains of a *Temple* (or possibly a forum) of the late-Roman period. The fragments at the E. end of the street of columns seem to have belonged to one of the gates of the town. — 4. On the right (S.) side of the brook, well stocked with fish, lies the **Theatre,** in excellent preservation. A row of columns runs from the theatre to the Odeum (see below). Another colonnade seems to have run from its W. corner northwards to the river. Only a few remnants of the stage still exist. The tiers of seats are intersected by stairs. Of the lowest section five tiers of seats are visible, the second has fourteen, and the third sixteen tiers of seats. Between the second and third sections, and particularly above the third, are boxes for spectators. Words spoken on the stage are distinctly heard on the highest tier of seats. The theatre was constructed for about 4000 spectators. — To the N.E., in front of the theatre, are the ruins of a small *Odeum* (usually called so, although it was not covered). The proscenium had towers on each side; the one on the S. is still preserved. — 5. Descending the brook, the traveller notices on its banks, among the gardens, remains of Roman masonry. The whole stream was vaulted over here for a distance of 330 yds. — 6. There are also ruins of buildings on each side of the street of columns; in the neighbourhood are many burying-places and dolmens.

FROM 'AMMÂN TO ES-SALṬ, 5 hrs. (carriage-road under construction). Ascending from the castle towards the N., we come (10 min.) to the ruins of a building and to (1/4 hr.) *Rijm el-Aneibideh*, beyond which we ride towards the N.W. along the W. brink of the *Wâdi en-Nuweijîs*. In 1/2 hr. we pass *Khirbet Brikeh*, on the right, and (5 min.) *Rijm el-Melfû'a*, on the left. We cross a low saddle, and in 1/2 hr. reach, on the right, *Khirbte Ajbeihât* (*Jogbehah*, Numbers xxxii. 35). The route then (1/4 hr.) descends the wâdi to the W., passes (10 min.) the Circassian village of *Ṣuweiliḥ*

(p. 143), by the wâdi of that name to the left, and reaches ($^1/_4$ hr.) *Khirbet es-Ṣâfût*, with the remains of an ancient temple. Beyond a (10 min.) spring we descend the *Wâdi Harba*, and (10 min.) reach the plain of *El-Bukeʿa* (p. 143), the S. part of which we cross in $^1/_2$ hr., leaving *Khirbet el-Bâsha* (p. 143) to the right. In 10 min. we see *Birket Ṭawla* on a hill to the W., beside a pond. In 40 min. more we begin a steep descent to the

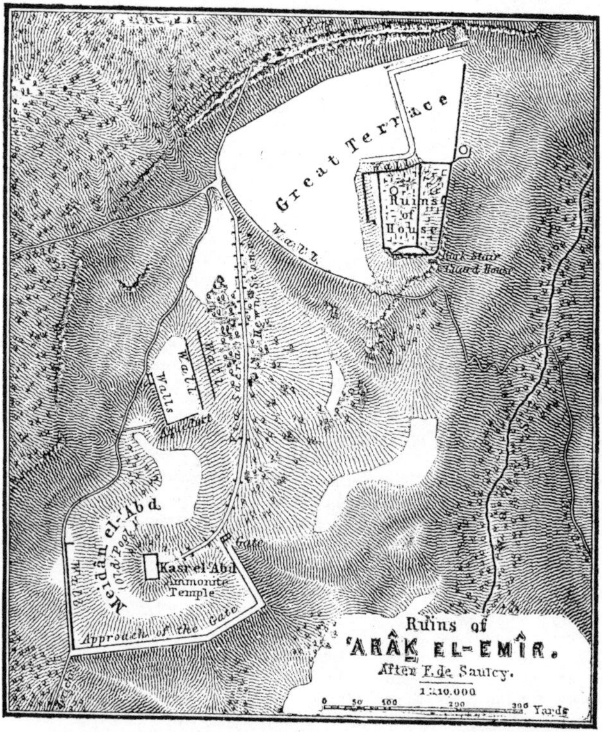

W. into the (10 min.) *Wâdi Saidûn*, which we cross. Ascending the opposite slope (10 min.), we turn to the W. at the top and proceed over stony hills for 25 minutes. Then another steep descent on the slope of the *Jebel Amrîyeh* brings us to a (13 min.) valley, which we follow to its junction with the (12 min.) *Wâdi Shaʿîb* (p. 137), about 10 min. above *Es-Salṭ* (p. 137).

From ʿAmmân to ʿArâḳ el-Emîr ($3^1/_4$ hrs.) and Jericho ($9^1/_4$ hrs.). The route ascends on the left bank of the brook to a spring, where there are remains of several buildings. An aqueduct conveys water hence to the town (17 min.). The numerous ruined villages show that this district must once have been richly cultivated. On the right lies *Kaṣr el-Melfûf* ('castle of cabbages'), on the left *ʿAbdûn*, then on the right *Umm ed-Ḍabʿa*. After the plateau has been traversed (1 hr.), *Ṭabaḳa* is seen on the left, and *Suweifiyeh* on the right; then *Ed-Demein* on the left. The road now enters the green and beautifully wooded *Wâdi esh-Shita*, or valley of rain. On the right is the ruin of *Khirbet Ṣâr;* then, *ʿAin el-Baḥal*. To the left, at the outlet of the valley (1 hr.), is a ruined mill; on the right, the ruin of *El-Aremeh*. About 1 hr. farther on is —

ʿArâḳ el-Emir (1465 ft.). — Josephus informs us (Ant. xii. 4, 11) that a certain Hyrcanus, in the time of Seleucus IV. (B.C. 187-175), built himself here a strong castle of white stone, surrounded by a fine park. The description of Josephus answers in the main to the ruins still extant here, and *Tyros*, the ancient name of the castle, is moreover recognizable in the name of the valley, *Wâdi eṣ-Ṣîr*. It is, however, probable that the castle and its animal-figures (see below) are of pre-Hellenic origin and were only restored by Hyrcanus. On his death it fell into ruins.

The principal building in the place is called *Kaṣr el-ʿAbd*, or castle of the slave, and stands on a platform in a half-isolated situation. In many places the substruction consists of a wall with abutments, composed of enormous blocks. The causeway leading to the castle is flanked with large blocks of stone, pierced with holes, in which a wooden railing was probably once inserted. The Kaṣr, the wall of which is preserved on one side only, is also built of large blocks. The upper part is adorned with a frieze in relief, bearing large and crude figures of lions. — The open space around the castle, once probably a moat, is now called *Meidân el-ʿAbd*.

On a hill to the left, farther to the N., are seen remains of buildings and an aqueduct, and a large platform (N.) is at length reached whereon stood a number of buildings, once enclosed by walls. On the hill beyond this platform runs a remarkable gallery in the rock, which has evidently been artificially widened. Portals lead thence into a number of caverns, some of which seem to have been used as stables, to judge from the rings in the walls. A few inscriptions in the ancient Hebrew character have not yet been definitely deciphered. Josephus mentions caverns of this description.

Beyond ʿArâḳ el-Emîr the road to Jericho (6 hrs.) leads to the N.W. over a low pass (1/4 hr.) and across a flat plateau to (1/2 hr.) *Wâdi en-Nâr*, into which there is a steep descent (10 min.). It then ascends (the ruin of *Ṣûr* remaining to the S.) to the top of the *Jenân eṣ-Ṣûr;* after 40 min. it descends a steep rocky slope (10 min.), and leads through the *Wâdi Jerîʿa*, a side-valley of the *Wâdi Nimrîn*, to (1 1/4 hr.) *Tell Nimrîn*. Thence to Jericho (3 hrs.), see p. 137.

From ʿAmmân to *Jerash*, see p. 143; to *El-Kerak*, see R. 18.

Beyond ʿAmmân the train leaves the valley and ascends in windings to the plateau. — 144 M. *El-Ḳaṣr* (3085 ft.); 155 M. *Lubbein*.

About 7 M. to the N.E. of (161 1/2 M.) *Jîzeh (Ḳalʿat Zîzâ)* are the ruins of *Meshîtâ (Meshetta)*, with a fine Omaiyade palace of the beginning of the 8th cent. (comp. p. lxxxii), the façade of which was taken to Berlin in 1904 as a present from the Sultan to Emperor William II. — The line now makes a bend to the E., in order to pass round the heads of two deep valleys, the *Wâdi el-Waʿleh* and the *Wâdi el-Môjib* (*Arnon*, p. 154).

173 1/2 M. *Ḳalʿat eḍ-Ḍabʿa*. Here the line again joins the Pilgrim Route, which it henceforth follows. The train slowly ascends across the desert.

183 1/2 M. *Khân ez-Zebîb* (2565 ft.); 202 1/2 M. *Kaṭrâneh;* 235 M.

Kalʿat el-Hesâ (2695 ft.), in the *Wâdi el-Hesâ* (p. 177); 246 1/2 M. *Jurf ed-Darâwîsh* (3145 ft.); 263 M. *Kalʿat ʿAneizeh* (3450 ft.).

285 M. **El-Maʿân** (3525 ft.; small Greek *Inn* at the station; Turkish telegraph). The town lies 1 1/2 M. to the W. of the station. El-Maʿân (ca. 3000 inhab.), the seat of a Kâimmakâm, is the ancient *Mâʿôn;* its inhabitants, the Mehunims, are perhaps identical with the Jewish-Arabian Minæans, and are mentioned in the Old Testament (2 Chron. xxvi. 7; Neh. vii. 52). The present town, which possesses no antiquities, consists of two quarters 1/2 M. apart: *Maʿân esh-Shâmîyeh* ('Northern Maʿân') and *Maʿân el-Kebîr* ('Great Maʿân'), the latter also called *El-Mûdîrîyeh* ('seat of government'). The houses are constructed of mud bricks, as is also the enclosing wall. There is abundance of water, and palm, fig, pomegranate, apricot, peach, and slender poplar trees flourish in the numerous gardens. The town is surrounded by a dreary desert. — To *Petra*, see p. 175.

From El-Maʿân the railway (but comp. p. 143) runs along the Pilgrim Route to the S.E. through the red sandstone desert (as far as El-ʿUlâ five water-stations only). From the watershed at (322 M.) *Batn el-Ghûl* ('Belly of the Monster'; 3830 ft.) the train descends in numerous curves, affording fine glimpses of the savagely fissured landscape. — Between (378 M.) *Dhât el-Hajj* (2265 ft.) and (430 M.) ***Tebûk*** (2540 ft.) mirages (Fata Morgana) are often seen. Tebûk is an oasis with some thousand date-palms, railway-buildings, a mosque, and a hospital. About 15 M. to the N.E. is the *Jebel Sharôra* ('Pulpit of the Prophet'). Farther on the train crosses the *Wâdi Ethîl* by a stone bridge. — 472 M. *Akhdar* (2895 ft.); 514 1/2 M. *Muʿazzam* (3215 ft.). — 593 1/2 M. *Medâin Sâlih* or *El-Hejr* (2560 ft.), one of the chief stations of the pilgrim-caravans, is the *Egra* of Ptolemy and possesses enormous Nabatæan rock-tombs very similar to those at Petra (see p. 180; comp. 'Mission archéologique en Arabie', by Jaussen and Savignac, Paris, 1909). — 609 M. *El-ʿUlâ* (2235 ft.), with 3500 inhab. and a very ancient grove of date-palms and lemon-trees. The last section of the railway, between El-ʿUlâ and (823 1/2 M.) *El-Medîna* (1970 ft.), was built by Turkish engineers and is accessible to Moslems only. The projected continuation of the line (comp. p. 143) will reach the Red Sea at *Sherm Râbigh* and then ascend S.E. to (296 1/2 M. from El-Medîna) *Mecca* (525 ft.).

18. From ʿAmmân to El-Kerak viâ Mâdebâ.

Comp. Map, p. 11.

Guide necessary (3/4-1 mej. per day). The guides do not always follow the same route. An Escort (1 or 2 khaiyâls) is obtained by applying to the Mûdîr in ʿAmmân (1 mej. per day for each man).

1. From ʿAmmân to Hesbân (5 hrs.) and Mâdebâ (6 3/4 hrs.).

ʿAmmân, see p. 145. We go up the main valley as far as the ruins of a bridge (1/4 hr.), and then ascend the hill to the left. The plateau is crossed in a S.W. direction and in 4 hrs. we reach *Khirbet el-ʿÂl*, situated on an isolated hill (the ancient *Elealeh*, which belonged to the tribe of Reuben, Numb. xxxii. 3, and was afterwards taken by the Moabites, Isaiah xv. 4). Hence, along a Roman road, we come in 35 min. to —

Hesbân (2950 ft.), the ancient *Heshbon*, which is mentioned in the Old Testament (Numb. xxi. 25 et seq.) as the city of Sihon, King of the Amorites. The town was allotted to Reuben, and afterwards came again into the possession of the Moabites (Jerem. xlviii. 45). In the time of the Maccabees, however, it had been recovered by the Jews.

The ruins lie on two hills, bounded on the W. by the *Wâdi Hesbân* and on the E. by the *Wâdi Mâ'în*. There are many cistern-openings among them. In the middle of the N. hill are the remains of a tower and to the S.E. of it are a large pool, hewn in the rock, and also a square enclosure built of large blocks. The greater part of the ancient town was built on the saddle between the two hills, where there is a large reservoir. On the S.W. hill are traces of a citadel, or possibly a temple, with shafts of columns. — The ruins of *Meshîtâ* (p. 149) lie about $12^1/_2$ M. to the E. of Ḥesbân.

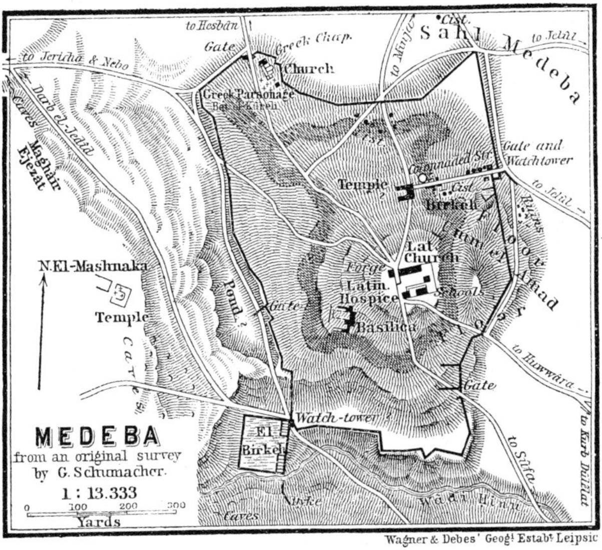

Wagner & Debes' Geog! Estab! Leipsic

From Ḥesbân we ride in $1^3/_4$ hr. direct to the S. to —

Mâdebâ (2540 ft.; accommodation at the house of the Greek priest; Turkish *Post & Telegraph Office*), which is the seat of a Mûdîr (p. lvii). — *Mâdebâ*, *Mâdaba*, or *Medba* was originally a town of the Moabites (Josh. xiii. 9). It was afterwards allotted to Reuben. According to the inscription on the 'Moabite Stone' (p. 153) the town belonged to Israel in the reign of Omri. In the middle of the 9th cent. B.C. it again came into the possession of the Moabites, and at a later period it is called a town of the Nabatæans (Arabs). Hyrcanus captured the town. In the Roman period it belonged to Arabia Petræa. During the Christian period it was the seat of a bishop.

The ruins of Mâdebâ have been occupied since 1880 by about 2000 Christians from El-Kerak. These are mostly Greeks (with a church and schools), but there are also about 350 Latins, who have a presbytery and a school (p. 152), on the highest point in the place. The modern village lies on a small hill, about 100 ft. in height of which 20-25 ft. consist of rubbish. The ancient town-walls embraced a considerably larger area. Close to the N. gate lies the Greek *Church*, built on the foundations of an old basilica with an atrium, dating from the 5th or 6th century. A *Mosaic Map*, discovered in the pavement, of which only a small fragment, representing Palestine, is preserved, is of great importance as the oldest existing map of the country; the representation of Jerusalem should be particularly noticed (comp. p. 29). For an inspection of the mosaic, permission must be obtained from the Greek Patriarchate (p. 34). Comp. also *Palmer & Guthe*, 'Die Mosaikkarte von Mâdebâ' (10 coloured plates; Leipzig, 1906). — From this point we proceed to the S. and then bend to the E. before reaching the mosque. A *Colonnaded Street*, about 150 yds. in length, led hence to the N. gate in the E. wall, which was flanked with a watch-tower. The scanty remains of the colonnade, consisting of a few columns near the gate, date from the early-Christian period. — On the S. side of this colonnaded street, a little to the W. of the gate, are the ruins of an old *Church of St. Elias*, concealed in part under the walls of the houses; in the crypt is a mosaic with an inscription. — Opposite, on the N. side of the street, are the remains of a *Church of the Virgin*, a circular building (originally, perhaps, a temple), with an apse on the E. side ($31^1/_2$ ft. in diameter). On the pavement are a Greek polychrome inscription and other mosaics of unusual beauty. — On the crest of the hill, where the ancient *Acropolis* lay, rise the *Latin Church* and presbytery, with a school for boys and girls. — To the S. of the village lies the *Basilica*, now almost completely destroyed, 156 ft. in length, preceded by a court 46 ft. wide. The nave, which ends in an apse, is 33 ft. in width, and is separated by columns from the aisles, each of which is 15 ft. in width. On the S. side is a wing with an apse, and possibly there was a corresponding wing on the N. The pavement was originally in polychrome mosaic. — A private house a little to the S.W. contains a fine mosaic pavement (animals, trees, a human head, and a Christian inscription in Greek). — Outside the walls, at the S.W. angle, is a large pool (*El-Birkeh*), 108 yds. long, 103 yds. wide, and now 10-13 ft. deep, to which a broad flight of steps descends. At its N.E. angle is a tower (or bath). The pool is no longer filled, as its water used to be a constant source of quarrels between the Beduins and the villagers. There was a second reservoir beside the W. gate, and a third near the E. gate. — On the slope of the hill to the W. of the village are numerous caves, some of which were human habitations. On the top of the hill two columns with fine capitals mark the ruins of a church or perhaps a temple (44 yds. by 38 yds.). On the shafts the Beduins have carved tribal symbols (*wasm*). The popular name for the ruins is *El-Mashnaka*, or 'Gallows', referring to the columns. — Comp. *Schumacher*, in ZDPV. xviii. (1895) 113 et seq.

From Mâdebâ to the Jebel Nebâ (and Jericho), $1^1/_2$ hr. The road leads over cultivated ground. From **Mt. Nebo** (2645 ft.) Moses beheld the whole of the Promised Land before his death (Deut. xxxiv. 1-4). The view hence is very extensive, including the mountains from Hebron as far as Galilee, the Dead Sea from Engedi northwards, the whole valley of Jordan, and beyond it even Carmel and Hermon. To the N. a view is obtained of the Wâdi 'Ayûn Mûsâ. On the top of the hill are some ruins and stone circles; on the N. slope are dolmens.

A steep descent (1 hr.) on the N. side of Mt. Nebo leads down into the valley of the Wâdi 'Ayûn Mûsâ, in which are the copious *'Ayûn Mûsâ*, or 'Springs of Moses'. Here also is a large cavern, with huge stalactites.

From the Springs of Moses we may proceed in 1 hr. more to the summit of the *Jebel Ṣiyâgha* (2290 ft.), which faces Mt. Nebo on the W. and commands a still finer survey of the plain of Jordan. On the summit is a large ruined church, perhaps originally dedicated to Moses (ZDPV. xvi., 1893, 164). — Hence to the *Wâdi Sha'ib* (p. 137) in 2 hrs.

From Jericho direct to Mâdebâ, $9^1/_2$ hrs. To the ($1^3/_4$ hr.) point where the road forks beyond the bridge over the Jordan, see p. 137. Here we turn to the right (E.S.E.); in 50 min. we reach some cultivated plots irrigated from the *Wâdi el-Kefrein*, which we cross 35 min. later. About $^1/_2$ hr. farther on (keeping always in the same direction) we reach the *Wâdi er-Râmeh*, also called *Wâdi Ḥesbân*. We now follow the valley towards the

E., passing *Tell esh-Shâghûr*, on the left. In 25 min. we pass a small lateral valley and beyond (10 min.) a mill begin to ascend the slopes of *ʿArkûb el-Maṭâbaʿ*, with its flint formations. We pass several dolmens and two Roman milestones. After $3^1/_4$ hrs. we reach the top of the *Tell el-Maṭâbaʿ*, on which are stone circles. Hence we gradually ascend towards the S.E. to the upper course of the *Wâdi Abu Neml*, which we follow to the (1 hr.) fertile tableland of *Arḍ ʿAbdallah*. The Jebel Nebâ (p. 152) is now in view; above, to the left, is the *Kabr ʿAbdallah*, or Tomb of ʿAbdallah. Passing the ruins of *Kafr Abu Bedd* and *Deir Shillikh*, we reach ($1^1/_4$ hr.) *Mâdebâ*.

---

2. From Mâdebâ to El-Kerak ($14^1/_2$-$22^1/_2$ hrs.).

From Mâdebâ to Dîbân. — a. The *Direct Route* ($5^1/_2$ hrs.) leads to the S. across the fertile plain, passing (25 min.) the ruin of *Et-Teim*, on the right, and in $2^1/_2$ hrs. reaching *Libb*. In $1^1/_3$ hr. more we cross the *Wâdi el-Waʿleh*, which has a copious stream well stocked with fish and is covered with luxuriant oleanders. Proceeding across the S. tableland for 1 hr., we see, to the right, the ruins of El-Kubeibeh and Abu Zîghân, and, to the left, Jûfra. In 40 min. more we reach **Dibân**, the ancient *Dibon*, in the tribe of Gad (Numb. xxxii. 34), afterwards recaptured by the Moabites (Is. xv. 2). Here the famous 'Moabite Stone' of King Mesha was found (p. 154).

b. Viâ Mâʿîn, Ḥammâm ez-Zerḳâ, and Mukaur (13 hrs.). From *Mâdebâ* the road leads S.W. to ($1^1/_4$ hr.) **Mâʿin**, the ancient *Beth-Baal-Meon* wosh. xiii. 17), or house of Baal Meon. It belonged to Reuben, and afterJards again to Moab (Ezek. xxv. 9). Eusebius informs us that this was he birthplace of Elisha. — From Mâʿîn to *Libb* (see above) $1^3/_4$ hr.

From Mâʿîn we proceed to ($1^1/_2$ hr.) *Râs Zerḳâ Mâʿîn*, and then descend the *Wâdi Zerḳâ Mâʿîn* to (3 hrs.) **Ḥammâm ez-Zerḳâ.** The bottom and sides of the ravine are covered with a luxuriant growth of plants, including palm-trees. The flora resembles that of S. Arabia and Nubia. At the bottom of the valley is seen red sandstone, overlaid with limestone and basalt. A number of hot springs (145° Fahr.) issue from the small side-valleys, all of them containing more or less lime, and all rising in the line where the sandstone and limestone come in contact. In ancient times they were in great repute, and the Arabs still use them for their healing qualities. The remains of an aqueduct are still to be seen here. Many attempts have been made to identify these springs with the baths of *Callirrhoë*, where Herod hoped to rid himself of his fatal disease. They are, however, more probably to be looked for at *Ḥammâm ez-Zârâ* (hot springs), about 3 M. to the S. of the mouth of the valley.

From Ḥammâm ez-Zerkâ we proceed up the valley for 2 hrs., then turn to the S. and reach (1 hr. 10 min.) **Mukaur**, the ancient *Machaerus* (2425 ft. above the level of the Mediterranean and 3705 ft. above that of the Dead Sea), which was fortified by Alexander Jannæus. The castle was destroyed by Gabinius, but was afterwards rebuilt by Herod the Great. Pliny calls it the 'second fortress of Judæa after Jerusalem'. It lay on the S. boundary of Peræa. Josephus informs us that John the Baptist was beheaded here (Ant. xviii. 5, 2; comp. p. 225). After the destruction of Jerusalem a number of the unhappy survivors found refuge in this stronghold for a time (Bell. Jud. vii. 6, 1-4). — The extensive citadel covering the entire hill, where a tower and a large cistern are still preserved, is interesting.

About 40 min. to the N.E. of Mukaur lies *ʿAṭṭârûs* (*Ataroth*, in Gad, Numb. xxxii. 3, 34). On a hill to the N. lie the ruins of a castle, near a terebinth-tree. The view from the ruins of the town is preferable; it embraces Bethlehem, Jerusalem, Mt. Gerizim, and the plain to the E.

From ʿAṭṭârûs we may follow the Mâdebâ-Dîbân road to ($1^1/_2$ hr.) *Libb* (see above) or we may proceed direct viâ the ruins of *Ḳureiyât* (*Kerioth* Jeremiah xlviii. 47), and thence along the Roman road, crossing the *Wâd Heidân* (the lower part of the Wâdi el-Waʿleh; see above) to *Dîbân*.

From Dîbân to El-Kerak (9-$9^1/_2$ hrs.). The route crosses the plain to the S., soon passing within a short distance of the ruins of *ʿArʿâir* (*Aroer;*

Josh. xii. 2), which lie to the left (E.) of the road. In 1/2 hr. we reach the verge of the precipitous ravine (2130 ft. deep) of the **Wâdi el-Môjib** (*Arnon*, Josh. xii. 1; see p. 136) and descend to the (1 1/4 hr.) river-bed. The remains of a bridge are seen. The road ascends the S. slope in about 1 1/4 hr. To the E. we see the ruins of a Roman fort, *Mahâdet el-Ḥajj*. On the S. side of the Môjib basalt is chiefly to be found, while on the N. side limestone is the prevailing formation. We proceed across the tableland, first to the S.W., then to the S., and in 40 min. reach the ruins of *Eriḥâ*, where there are numerous heaps of stones. In 40 min. more (traces of an ancient Roman road) we arrive at the ruins of *Shîḥân*, at the foot of the *Tell Shîḥân*, a hill of moderate height commanding a fine view, which extends to Beth-lehem and the Mt. of Olives. From Shîḥân the road leads in 1 hr. 10 min. to the ruins of *Beit el-Karm (El-Kaṣr;* occasionally called *Kaṣr Rabba)*, with columns and blocks of a ruined temple. On the left (E.) rise the hills of *Jebel eṭ-Ṭarfûyeh;* also on the left (10 min.) are the ruins of the old tower of *Misdeh*, adjoining which are the ruins of *Hemeimât*. After 20 min. we pass the foundations of a small Roman temple (left) and reach in 1/4 hr. more **Rabba**, the ancient *Rabbath Moab*, which was afterwards confounded with *Ar Moab*, and thence called *Areopolis*. The ruins are about 1 1/2 M. in circuit. A few only of the ruins, such as the remains of a temple and some cisterns, are well-preserved. Two Corinthian columns of different sizes stand together not far from the temple. — From *Rabba* the road leads towards the S. across a plain and past the ruined villages of *Mukharshît*, *Duweineh*, and *Es-Ṣuweinîyeh* to (2 hrs.) the *Wâdi ʿAin es-Sitt*. Thence an ascent of 20 min. brings us to El-Kerak.

El-Kerak (3115 ft.; scanty accommodation at the Latin convent; Turkish post and telegraph office) is the ancient *Kir of Moab*, *Kir Haraseth*, *Kir Haresh*, or *Kir Heres* (Isaiah xv. 1, xvi. 7, 11; 2 Kings iii. 25; Jeremiah xlviii. 31), one of the numerous towns of the *Moabites*. This warlike people were closely related to the Israelites (p. lxxvi), whom they compelled to pay tribute, until the Israelites under Ehud threw off the Moabite yoke (Judges iii. 12-30). Saul fought successfully against Moab. David, whose great-grandmother was a Moabitess (comp. the Book of Ruth), forced them to pay tribute. After Ahab's death the Moabites revolted. Their king at that period was Mesha, a monument to whose memory (p. lxxviii), was found in 1868 at Dîbân (p. 153). Jehoram, allied with Jehoshaphat, King of Judah, invaded Moab from the S., through Edom, but they were successfully resisted by the fortress of *Kir Haraseth* (2 Kings iii.). The Moabites as a separate nation disappeared in the 2nd cent. B.C. In the Christian period Kerak was the seat of an archbishop, but he derived his title, as at the present day, from Petra Deserti. In the time of the Crusaders Kerak was a frequent object of contention, as it commanded the caravan-route from Egypt and Arabia to Syria. In 1183 and the following years Saladin made a series of furious attacks upon Kerak, which was held by Rainald de Châtillon, and in 1188 he gained possession both of Kerak and Shôbek (p. 178). The Aiyubides extended the fortifications of Kerak, and frequently resided there. Later it became an apple of discord between the rulers of Egypt and Syria.

El-Kerak is the capital of a liwa of the vilâyet of Syria (p. lvii), and contains 3000 inhab., including a garrison. It consists almost entirely of wretched huts. The Greeks possess two old churches here, the Latins a school. Each of the Christian sects, as are also the Moslems, is under a sheikh of its own. The environs are fertile, and the inhabitants are chiefly employed in agriculture and cattle-raising. The trade of El-Kerak is wholly in the hands of merchants from Hebron. As a rule, the inhabitants are in bad repute on account of their cupidity.

The town lies upon a hill cut off on all sides by deep gorges; it is separated from the adjoining hill on the S. by a large artificial moat. The huge *Castle* on the S. side of the town now serves as barracks. A moat also skirts the N. side of the fortress, and on the E. side the wall has a sloped or battered base. The walls are very thick and well preserved. The extensive galleries, corridors, and halls constitute it an admirable

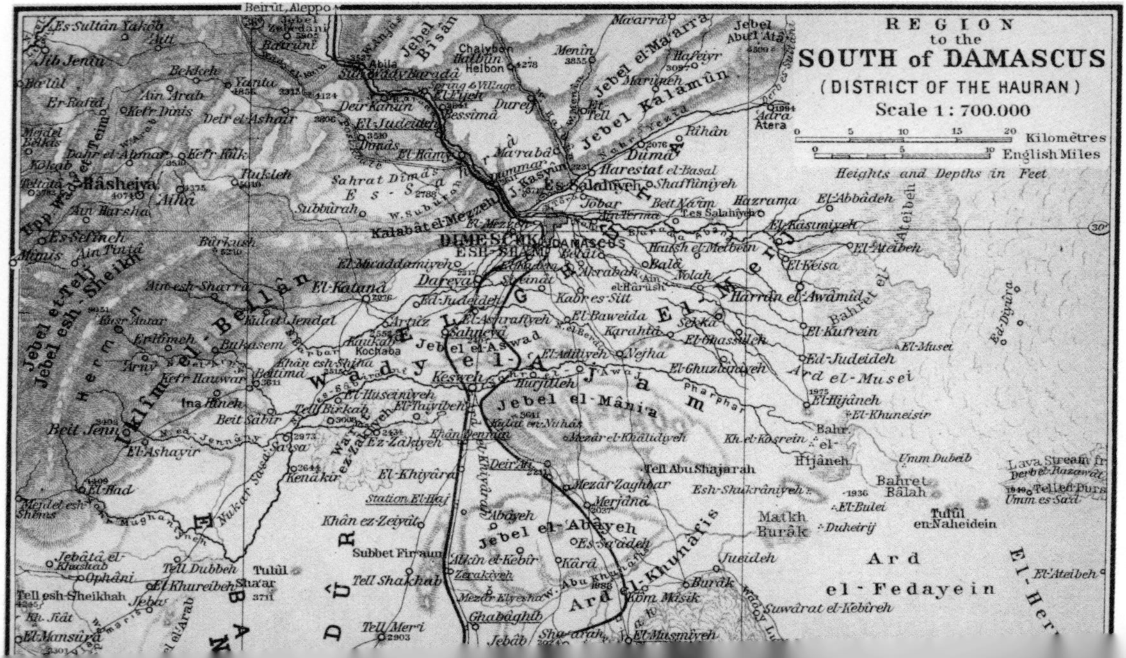

REGION to the
SOUTH of DAMASCUS
(DISTRICT OF THE HAURAN)
Scale 1: 700.000
Kilomètres
English Miles
Heights and Depths in Feet
Beirût, Aleppo
DIMESCHK
DAMASCUS
ESH-SHÂM
Jebel Kalamûn
Jebel el-Ma'arra
Jebel Bisân
Jebel esh-Sheikh
Jebel et-Telj
Hermon
Jebel el-Aswad
Jebel el-Mâni'a
Jebel el-'Abâyeh
Ard el-Musei
Ard el-Fedayein
Kalabât el-Mezzeh
El-Katanâ
Kesweh
Dâreya
Es-Salahiyeh
Harestat el-Basal
Dûmâ
Hazrama
El-'Abbâdeh
El-Kâsumiyeh
Harrân el-'Awâmîd
El-Kufrein
Ed-Judeideh
El-Hijâneh
Bahret el-'Ateibeh
Bahret Bâlah
Râsheiya
Beit Jenn
El-Had
Kh. el-Kosrein
Tell Abu Shajarah
Khân ez-Zeiyât
Subbet Fir'aun
Tell Shakhab
Station El-Haj
Pharphar
Lava Stream

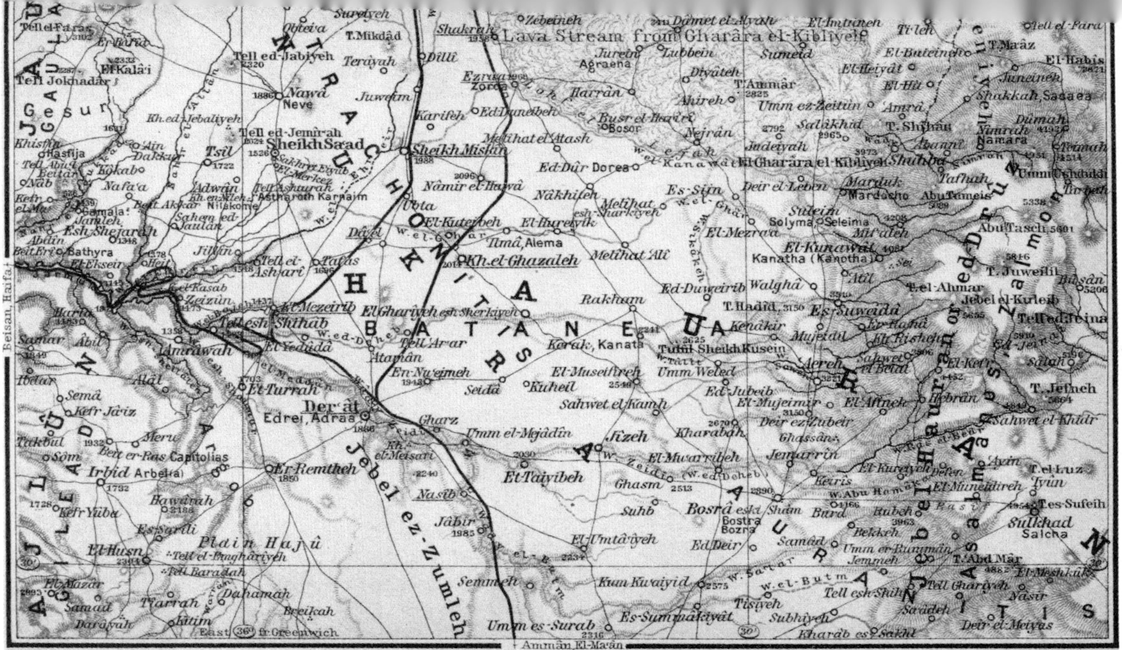

Dr H. Fischer del.

Geogr Estab! Wagner & Debes, Leipzig

example of a Crusader's castle. The upper stories are in ruins, but the approaches to them are still in good preservation. A staircase descends into a subterranean chapel, where traces of frescoes are still visible. In the interior of the fortress are numerous cisterns. Although the springs are situated immediately outside the town, large cisterns have been constructed within the town (particularly by the tower of Beybars). — The view from the top of the castle embraces the Dead Sea and the surrounding mountains. In the distance the Mt. of Olives, and even the Russian buildings beyond it, are visible. A survey of the valley of Jordan as far as the heights of Jericho is also obtained.

The town is surrounded by a wall with five towers, but the N. and E. sides of this have largely disappeared. The well-preserved tower at the N.W. corner, called *Burj eẓ-Ẓâhir*, bears an inscription and figures of lions of the kind common in Arabian monuments of the Crusaders' period. The lower parts of the wall, to judge from the stones composing it, are of earlier date than the upper. The town originally had three entrance only, consisting of tunnels in the rock. The tunnel on the N.W. side has an entrance-arch dating from the Roman period (notwithstanding its Arabic inscription). This tunnel, about 80 paces long, leads to the tower of Beybars (N.W.), whose name is recorded by an inscription adjoining two lions. The walls are provided with loopholes.

The present ***Mosque*** of El-Kerak was originally a Christian church, of which the pillars and arches are still extant. A Christian symbol, in the form of a sculptured chalice, has escaped destruction by the Moslems. — The ***Christian Church***, dedicated to St. George (El-Khiḍr), contains pictures in the Byzantine style. In one of the houses are remains of a Roman bath, including a fine marble pavement.

From El-Kerak to ***Petra***, see p. 177.

19. The Ḥaurân.

Comp. Maps, pp. 11, 224.

A visit to those parts of the Ḥaurân lying away from the railways (p. **143** & p. **157**) is generally undertaken for scientific purposes, rarely for mere pleasure. There are still numerous inscriptions to be found here: Greek, Latin, Nabatæan, Arabic, and some in the so-called Sabæan (South Arabian) characters. On the plain of the Ḥaurân, the company of one Khaiyâl will suffice (p. xxvi), but in the mountains it is necessary to have an escort of Druses. Information may be obtained at the consulates in Jerusalem or Damascus.

Literature. ***Wetzstein's*** 'Reisebericht über den Ḥaurân und die Trachonen' (Berlin; 1860). ***De Vogüé's*** 'L'Architecture civile et religieuse' (comp. p. civ) contains numerous illustrations. ***Schumacher's*** 'Across the Jordan' (London, 1886; out of print); 'Beschreibung des Dschôlân' (ZDPV. ix. 1886); 'Northern ʿAjlûn' (London, 1890; 6*s*.); 'Das südliche Basan' (ZDPV. xx. 1897). ***Von Oppenheim's*** 'Vom Mittelmeer zum persischen Golf' (2 vols.; Berlin, 1899; 20 marks); ***Rindfleisch***, 'Die Landschaft Ḥaurân in römischer Zeit und in der Gegenwart' (ZDPV. xxi. 1898). Records of the Princeton Archæological Expedition to Syria (New York; 1904). ***Chas. M. Doughty***, 'Travels in Arabia Deserta', Vol. I. (Cambridge, 1888; also abridged edition in 2 vols.: 'Wanderings in Arabia', London, 1912). — Map of the Jebel Ḥaurân, drawn by ***Dr. H. Fischer*** (ZDPV. xii.), 1889.

The **Haurân** corresponds to the district which in ancient days was called *Bashan* by the Hebrews. The Bible mentions an *Og*, King of Bashan, whom the Israelites defeated at Edrei (Numbers xxi. 33-35). The pastures and flocks of Bashan were celebrated (Ezek. xxxix. 18). The oak plantations of Bashan also seem to have made a great impression on the Israelites (Ezek. xxvii. 6; Isaiah ii. 13). At a later period (Ezek. xlvii. 16-18) the name of Ḥaurân, which originally belonged to the mountains only (the *Asalmanos* of the ancients), was extended to Bashan also, as at the present day. In the Roman period the country was divided into five provinces:

Ituraea, *Gaulanitis*, to the E. of these *Batanaea* (a name also applied to the whole, like Bashan), to the N.E. *Trachonitis* and *Auranitis*, including the mountains of the Ḥaurân in the narrower sense, and the present plain of *En-Nuḳra*, or 'the hollow' (p. 158). The Ḥaurân in the wider sense is now bounded on the N.W. by the district of Jeidûr, on the W. by the Nahr el-ʿAllân towards the Jôlân (N.), and by the Wâdi esh-Shellâleh towards ʿAjlûn (S.), on the S.W. and S. by the Belḳâ and the steppe of El-Ḥamâd (*i.e.* 'stony plateau'), and on the N. by the low chain of the Jebel el-Aswad (p. 267), beyond which lies the plain of Damascus. Towards the N.E., and beyond the 'Meadow Lakes' (p. 322), extends a remarkable hill-district, consisting of a series of extinct craters, in the centre of which is the *Ṣafâ*, with the ruin of the 'white castle'. To the S. and E. of this lies the *Harra*, an undulating plain of the dreariest description, entirely covered with sharp-edged fragments of lava. Jeremiah (xvii. 6) evidently had the Ḥarra in mind when he spoke of the punishment of exile to 'the parched places in the wilderness'. — The prevailing formation of the Ḥaurân is a granulous dolerite and a brownish red or blackish green slag, blistered and porous. The dolerite consists of thin slabs of crystal of greyish white labradorite, with small grains of olivine and augite. The soil in the district of the Ḥaurân is extremely fertile, and consists of soft, decomposed lava.

The larger villages only are surrounded with walls, and these are provided with numerous towers, the courses of stone in which are generally connected by means of the peculiarly shaped tenons known as 'swallow-tails'. The numerous Troglodyte dwellings are of great interest and certainly belong to hoar antiquity. The other houses are built of large, well-hewn blocks of dolerite which are jointed without cement. The doors consist of large slabs of dolerite, and the windows of similar slabs with perforations. The gates of the larger buildings and streets are adorned with sculptured vine-leaves and inscriptions. Only the best-preserved of the houses are now occupied. The staircases consist of slabs of stone let into the outer walls of the court. The windows and doors of the upper floor were open. The ceilings of the rooms rest on round arches, and those of the better sort are enriched with decorations. The cupboards, the seats, and even the square candlesticks are of stone. The large cisterns hewn in the rock, the vaulted reservoirs, and the artificial pools which are filled by the spring rains and afford drinking-water throughout the whole year, also date from a very early period.

The last period of culture in the Ḥaurân was during the early Christian centuries, after the adoption of Christianity by the Arab tribes of the district (*Jefnides* or *Ghassanides*). As far back as the year 180 we hear of a King ʿAmr I. who erected numerous monasteries. The influence of Græco-Roman culture is proved by many temples and mausolea in the style of the grave-towers of Palmyra. The numerous Greek inscriptions are not always spelled correctly, but are interesting from the fact that they are contemporaneous with the buildings themselves. The capital of the Ḥaurân was Boṣrâ (p. 162). The rise of Islam made an end of the empire of the Ghassanides. According to Arabic inscriptions, the land seems to have regained a share of its former prosperity in the 13th century. Nothing more is heard of it until 1838, when Ibrâhîm Pasha endeavoured to penetrate into the Lejâh. He did not, however, succeed in conquering this bleak plateau of lava, nor did Moḥammed Kibrisly Pasha fare better in 1850.

Both the N.W. district of the Ḥaurân and the 'Jebel' itself are now chiefly occupied by Beduins, but the slopes of the hills and the plain are inhabited by peasants who form the permanent part of the population. Since 1861 so many of the Druses have migrated to the Ḥaurân from Lebanon, that the district is sometimes called *Jebel ed-Drûz (Druse Mountains)*. A number of Christians, chiefly of the Greek Orthodox church, are also settled here. The climate of the tableland of the Ḥaurân, lying upwards of 2000 ft. above the sea-level, is very healthy, and in the afternoon the heat is tempered by a refreshing W. wind. The semi-transparent 'hard wheat' of the Ḥaurân is highly prized and largely exported. Wheat and barley in this favoured region are said to yield abundant harvests, but the crops sometimes fail from want of rain or from the plague of locusts. The fields are not manured, but a three or four years' rotation of crops is observed. The dung of the cattle is used for fuel, as the 'oaks of Bashan', which still grow on the heights, are gradually being exterminated. No trees grow in the plain, though it bears traces of once having been wooded. Fruit-trees are planted near the villages only. Thanks to the energetic action of the government, the villagers are no longer seriously oppressed by the Beduins. The native type of the Ḥaurân is so peculiar that it may be regarded as uniform, in spite of the fact that religious differences exist between the various tribes. The peasant of the Ḥaurân is taller and stronger than the Beduin, but preserves not only his language but also many of his virtues. Every village possesses its '*menzûl*' or '*meḍâfeh*' (public inn), where every traveller is entertained gratuitously, and the Ḥaurânians deem it honourable to impoverish themselves by contributing to the support of this establishment. As soon as a stranger arrives he is conducted to the inn. A servant or slave roasts coffee for him, and then pounds it in a wooden mortar, accompanying his task with a peculiar melody. Meanwhile the whole village assembles, and after the guest has been served, each person present partakes of the coffee. Now, however, that travellers have become more numerous, the villagers generally expect a trifling bakshish from Europeans. A sum of $^1/_2$-1 mej., according to the refreshments obtained, may therefore be given. The food consists of fresh bread, eggs, sour milk, grape-syrup ('*dibs*'), and in the evening of '*burghul*', a dish of wheat, boiled with a little leaven and dried in the sun, with mutton, or rice with meat.

1. From Damascus to Der'a (Ḥejâz Railway).

For this route ($76^1/_2$ M.), see pp. 143-145.

2. From Damascus to El-Muzeirîb.

a. By the Ḥaurân Railway.

63 M. Narrow Gauge Railway of the 'Société Ottomane du Chemin de Fer Damas-Ḥamâ et Prolongements' (opened in 1895; 3-4 trains weekly). To this company belong also the lines from Beirût to Damascus (R. 37) from Reyâḳ to Aleppo (R. 45), and from Ḥomṣ to Tripoli (R. 45). The train leaves *Damascus* at 6.30 a.m., reaching *Eṣ-Ṣanamein* in $2^1/_4$ hrs. (fares 38 pi. 10, 25 pi. 20 pa.), *Sheikh Miskîn* in $3^1/_2$ hrs. (60 pi., 40 pi.), and *El-Muzeirîb* in $4^1/_2$ hrs. (75 pi. 30, 50 pi. 20 pa.). The return-train leaves *El-Muzeirîb* at midday, reaching *Damascus (Meidân)* at 5 p.m. — *Rate of Exchange* for the railway-fares, see p. 280.

Those who intend to make excursions aside from the railway must take horses, tents, etc., from Damascus.

Damascus, see p. 298. — *Meidân*, the chief station of the French line, is situated in the S. part of the town (Pl. B, 8). The trains start, however, from the subsidiary station of *Beramkeh* (Pl. B, 4), whence we reach the main station in 13 min. after traversing the Ghûṭa (p. 300). The line runs parallel to the Ḥejâz Railway (R. 17), at a greater or less distance to the W. of it.

$3^1/_2$ M. *Dâreiya*, a place of some importance, as it was also in the middle ages. The Franks extended their ravages as far as this point.

6 M. *Ṣaḥnâyâ*, beyond which begins a continuous view of the snow-covered summit of Hermon. The line now crosses the low chain of the *Jebel el-Aswad* (p. 267) and the *Wâdi el-'Ajam* (p. 169), follows more or less closely the *Derb el-Ḥajj* or 'Pilgrim Route', and crosses the *Nahr el-A'waj* (p. 158).

12¹/₂ M. *El-Kisweh (Kessoué)*, also a station on the Ḥejâz Railway (p. 144). — 13 M. *Khân Dennûn.* We here enter the lava region. — Passing *El-Khiyâra*, in a fertile district, we reach —

20¹/₂ M. *Zerâkîyeh.* To the right rises the hill of *Ṣubbet Fir'aun*, with the ruins of *Ḳaṣr Fir'aun*; to the left is the *Jebel el-'Abâyeh*, with the *Mezâr Elyesha'* (shrine of Elisha).

24 M. *Ghabâghib*, with a large reservoir. As we proceed we see *Dîdi*, to the left, with the long *Tell el-Ḥamîr* behind it.

31¹/₂ M. **Eṣ-Ṣanamein**, the ancient *Ære*, is an excellent specimen of a Ḥaurân village (p. 156). In the centre of the village rises a well-preserved temple built of yellowish limestone, with Corinthian columns and a niche in the form of a shell. The doors and windows are admirably executed, and the decorations are very rich. According to inscriptions, it was dedicated to Fortuna. To the S. of the temple is a building with columns; on the E. side a vaulted gateway leads to a square chamber and to various rooms with a portico, Corinthian columns, and several arches. Outside (N.) of the village are two lofty grave-towers, built of yellow and black stones without mortar, and also richly decorated. There is another tower to the S.

At Eṣ-Ṣanamein begins the plain of *En-Nuḳra* (p. 156). — 36 M. *El-Ḳuneiyeh;* 39 M. *El-Kuteibeh.* — 50 M. *Sheikh Miskîn* (Turkish telegraph), a large and thriving village, is the seat of the Muteṣarrif (p. lvii) of the Ḥaurân. Excursions may be made hence to (1 hr.) *Sheikh Sa'd* (p. 159) and *El-Merkez* (p. 159).

55¹/₂ M. *Dâ'el.* — 59¹/₂ M. *Tafas.*

63 M. **El-Muzeirib** (1540 ft.) was formerly the rendezvous of the caravan of pilgrims (p. lxxii), which halted here for several days. El-Muzeirîb, unhealthily situated in a swampy district, is also a station on the Der'a-Ḥaifâ line (p. 242). It consists of a new and an old village. The new village, *Ed-Dakâkîn*, on the N. side of the hill, has a market for Beduins and the ruins of the *Ḳal'at el-Jedîdeh*, or 'New Castle'. The older village, *Kôm el-Muzeirîb*, is situated on the site of the former and more important town, on an island in the middle of the *Baḥrat el-Bajjeh*, a pool abounding in fish. One of the sources of the Yarmûḳ (p. 241) flows out of this pool. It is a bathing-place for pilgrims and is regarded as sacred. On the E. side of the village rises the large ruinous 'Old Castle' *(Ḳal'at el-'Atîḳa)*, which is said to have been built by Sultan Selîm (d. 1522). In the interior is a small ruined mosque.

b. By the Pilgrim Route *(Derb el-Ḥajj).*

16 hrs. As far as *Sheikh Sa'd* the road is good, and carriages may proceed even to *El-Muzeirib.*

From the *Bauwâbet Allâh* (p. 314) we reach *El-Ḳadem* in 20 min.; cross the *Wâdi el-Berdi*, with *El-Ashrafîyeh* to the right, in 1 hr.; and in 1 hr. 20 min. arrive at *El-Kisweh* on the *Nahr el-A'waj* (p. 157). Thence the route skirts the railway (see above). ¹/₂ hr.

Khân Dennûn; 25 min. *El-Khiyâra;* $1^1/_4$ hr. *Subbet Fir'aun* (p. 158), on the right; $^1/_2$ hr. *Mezâr Elyesha'* (p. 158), on the left; 40 min. *Ghabâghib;* $1^1/_2$ hr. *Dîdi* and *Tell el-Hamîr*, on the left; 20 min. *Es-Sanamein* (p. 158). Thence we proceed viâ *Inkhil* and *Obtei'a* to ($18^1/_2$ M.; in about 6 hrs.) the large village of **Nawâ**, the ancient *Neve*, the home of the celebrated Moslem theologian Nawâwi. The village has been entirely built from the ruins, but two ancient buildings still remain: the *Medâfeh* (public inn), possibly an ancient mausoleum, and a tower, 49 ft. high.

About $3^1/_2$ M. ($1^1/_4$ hr.) beyond Nawâ we reach **Sheikh Sa'd** (Turkish telegraph), a wretched village inhabited by negroes, who were established here by the son of 'Abd el-Kader. The village contains ruins and antiquities. On the S.W. end of the hill is the *Stone of Job (Sakhrat Aiyûb)*, within a Moslem place of prayer. At this block of basalt, about $6^1/_2$ ft. in height, Job is said to have been visited by his friends. The stone is a monument of Ramses II. (ca. 1300 B.C.) and bears an Egyptian inscription with a relief of Osiris and the king. The church of Job, which was visited by St. Silvia (end of the 4th cent.), probably stood here. — At the foot of the hill is the *Bath of Job (Hammâm Aiyûb)*, in which Job is said to have bathed after his cure, and which is venerated by the fellahin and Beduins for its healing virtue. A basaltic lion not far off is an example of Hittite art (p. 415). Adjoining it to the W. is the *Makâm Sheikh Sa'd*, formerly shown as the tomb of Job (*Makâm Aiyûb;* see below). Comp. ZDPV. xiv. 1891, 142 et seq.; xv. 1892, 196 et seq., 205 et seq.

El-Merkez (p. 158) lies about $^1/_2$ M. to the S. of Sheikh Sa'd. It has a locanda, where accommodation of a primitive character may be obtained. In the N.W. corner are the remains of the ancient **Monastery of Job** *(Deir Aiyûb)*, now converted into barracks. To the W. of the place is a building called *Makâm Aiyûb*, containing the tombs of Job and his wife.

Job, according to a popular tradition, was a native of Jôlân, and early Arabian authors and the mediæval Christians even point out his birthplace in the neighbourhood of Nawâ. The great veneration of the Haurânians for this shrine indicates that it must have had an origin earlier than Islamism. According to Arabian authors the monastery was built by the Jefnide 'Amr I. (p. 156), and it probably dates from the middle of the 3rd century.

About 1 M. beyond El-Merkez is the village of *'Adwân*, on the right; $1^3/_4$ M. farther on is the ruin of *Et-Tîreh;* and $2^1/_4$ M. farther on is a new bridge spanning the *Wâdi el-Ehreir*. On the left is the *Tell es-Semen*, where the Beduin tribe of the *Wuld 'Ali* encamp from the month of April on; a visit to the camp is interesting. Thence we ride to the S.W. to ($1^1/_4$ M.) the humble village of *Tell el-Ash'ari*, possibly the *Ashtaroth* of Joshua ix. 10. The pond *Bahrat el-Ash'ari* was perhaps an ancient naumachia, fed by the numerous springs of the neighbourhood. — 3 M. *El-Muzeirîb* (p. 158).

3. From Jerash to Derʿa or El-Muzeirîb (9-10 hrs.).

Jerash, see p. 139. Quitting the village by the left bank of the stream, we ascend the slopes of the *Jebel Kafkafa*. In $1^1/_2$ hr. we reach the top of a narrow ridge called *Tughrat ʿAṣfûr*, whence a route diverges to the left to *Sûf*. We next reach (1 hr.) the wide valley of the *Wâdi Warrân*. $1^1/_4$ hr. *Naʿeimeh*, a well-built village of some size (good water). 35 min. *Kitti*, a poor village. Thence we descend through a fertile district to (65 min.) *El-Ḥuṣn*, or *Ḥuṣn ʿAjlûn* (1935 ft.), with 1200 inhab., half of whom are Christian. The Latins have a school and pilgrim-hospice here, the Greeks a chapel, school, and hospice. There are few antiquities. To the N. is the castle of *Tell el-Ḥuṣn*, with traces of an ancient girdle-wall. Accommodation in the Latin or Greek mission-house.

The route proceeds hence in $^1/_2$ hr. to the prosperous village of *Eṣ-Ṣarîḥ*, where it divides. To the N.W. it leads to ($1^1/_2$ hr.) *Irbid* (see below), and to the N.E. to ($2^1/_4$ hrs.) *Er-Remtheh*, whence we may reach *Derʿa* (p. 145) in $1^3/_4$ hr. Between these runs a third road (to the N.), leading in $^1/_2$ hr. to *Ḥawârah*. After $2^1/_4$ hrs. we join the great pilgrim-route at *Eṭ-Ṭurra* (p. 161). In $^1/_4$ hr. we cross the *Wâdi el-Meddân*, the lower part of the Wâdi ez-Zeidî (p. 145), then in $^1/_2$ hr. the *Wâdi ed-Dheheb*, and in $^1/_4$ hr. more reach *El-Muzeirîb* (p. 158).

4. From Tiberias to Derʿa viâ Irbid.

About 15 hrs. To *Irbid*, 10-11 hrs.; thence to *Derʿa*, 4 hrs.

Tiberias, see p. 252. To *Bâb et-Tumm*, the ford of the Jordan (1 hr. 50 min.), see pp. 255, 256. From the ford we follow the right bank of the Jordan in 35 min. to *El-ʿAbâdîyeh;* after 55 min. we reach the mouth of the *Sherîʿat el-Menâḍireh* (p. 241) descending from the E., and in $^1/_2$ hr. more we come to the bridge of *Jisr el-Mujâmiʿ* (bridge-toll 3 pi.; railway from Haifâ to Damascus, see p. 241). Thence we ride to the S.E. to the ($^1/_2$ hr.) *Wâdi el-ʿArab*, which we ascend to the *Wâdi Zaḥar*. We then follow the latter (to the S.E.) viâ *Hôfâ* and *Zaḥar en-Naṣâra*, and, in 7 hrs. from Jisr el-Mujâmiʿ, reach —

Irbid, an important and newly built place with 2000 inhab., the chief town of the Ḳaḍâ of ʿAjlûn. Turkish telegraph-office. To the S. of the village is a large reservoir. Basaltic blocks with inscriptions are to be seen here.

From Irbid the road (an ancient Roman thoroughfare, uniting the Ḥaurân with the coast) leads N.E. viâ the *Wâdi esh-Shellâleh* to (3 hrs.) *Er-Remtheh* (see above), and thence to ($1^3/_4$ hr.) *Derʿa* (p. 145).

5. From Tiberias to El-Muzeirîb viâ Mukeis.

About 14 hrs. To *Mukeis*, 5 hrs.; thence to *Beit er-Râs*, 4 hrs.; from Beit er-Râs to *El-Muzeirîb*, $4^1/_2$ hrs. — The traveller may send on the horses in advance from Tiberias to Samakh, and perform that part of the journey by boat.

From Tiberias to the ford of *Bâb et-Tumm* (2 hrs.), see pp. 255, 256. On the opposite bank we proceed to the S.E. viâ *Samakh* (railway station, p. 241) to (1 hr.) the *Sherî'at el-Menâḍireh*, at the point where it enters the plain of Jordan. From this point we ascend the wild valley (3 M.) to the *Hot Springs of Gadara*, or *Amatha*, now called *El-Ḥammi* (railway station, p. 241). — About 1 hr. from the ford at the baths we reach —

Mukeis *(Mkeis)*, the ancient *Gadara*, a city of the Decapolis, the capital of Peræa, and a strong fortress as early as the reign of Antiochus the Great. Alexander Jannæus took the stronghold. Pompey restored the town to please his freedman Demetrius, a native of the place. Augustus presented the town to Herod the Great, but after that prince's death annexed it to the province of Syria. In the Jewish War it opened its gates to Vespasian. Numerous coins of the city of Gadara belonging to the Roman period have been found. Gadara afterwards became the residence of the bishop of Palæstina Secunda. The town was famed for its baths. The ancient name of Gadara is still preserved in that of the caverns of '*Jadûr Mukeis*', and the name of '*Jadar*' is mentioned by the older Arabian geographers.

Mukeis lies 1195 ft. above the sea-level, on the W. extremity of a mountain-crest rising between the valley of the *Yarmûk* (p. 241) on the N. and the *Wâdi el-'Arab* on the S. Approaching from the E., we first come to tomb-caverns with various chambers and doors in stone, still preserved, some of them with rudely executed busts on the architraves. Some of these chambers also contain sarcophagi, while other sarcophagi lie scattered along the slopes of the hill. These are richly adorned with garlands and busts of Apollo and genii; the lids are drafted at the corners and sloped sharply upwards. — To the W. of these caverns we come to a *Theatre*, the upper parts of which have fallen in. A good survey of the ruins is obtained hence. About 360 paces farther to the W. lies another and larger theatre, built of basalt and on the whole well preserved, though the stage is covered with rubbish. The aristocratic quarter of the town extended from the theatres towards the W., along the foot of the hill, on a level plateau about 1½ M. in width. Many fragments of columns with Corinthian capitals lie scattered about. Substructions of buildings are also traceable, and in many places the ruts of carriage-wheels are still visible on the basalt pavement. — Still farther to the W. lies a modern cemetery, and on the slope of the hill here we enjoy a charming view of the Jordan valley.

Beyond Mukeis we follow the ancient conduit *(Kanât Fir'aun)* which is visible at intervals along the route and comes from Der'a. It was constructed by the Ghassânide king *Jebeleh I.* After ½ hr. we pass on the right the ruined temple of *El-Kabû*. We continue to ride along the heights eastwards. For some time we have a view of Irbid on a long mountain-ridge to the S.E., while a little to the N. of it, on the highest summit, appears Beit er-Râs. After 40 min. we diverge to the right from the Roman road, which leads straight on to the E. to Irbid (p. 160). Our route descends to the (¼ hr.) spring of *'Ain Umm el-Jerein*, from which a descent of 20 min. more brings us to the *Wâdi Barûka*. Ascending the valley, we reach the top in about 1 hr., and see before us the hill on which lies Beit er-Râs, while Irbid is seen to the right. In 1 hr. more we reach **Beit er-Râs**, which probably corresponds to the ancient *Capitolias*, an important fortified town in a commanding position. The interesting ruins here are extensive and in some cases well preserved. Fine view from the *Tell el-Khaḍr*.

The route from Beit er-Râs to El-Muzeirîb (4½ hrs.) is an old Roman road leading due E. across the tableland. In ¾ hr. we reach the village of *Meru* and in about ½ hr. more the upper verge of the *Wâdi er-Râhûb*, on the height beyond which appears El-Emgheiyir. A steep descent of 20 min. is followed by an equally steep ascent of 20 min. on the other side of the valley. We then ride close by *El-Emgheiyir* and in ½ hr. cross the deep *Wâdi esh-Shellâleh*, and then the shallow *Wâdi esh-Shômar*, beyond which we reach (¼ hr.) *Et-Turra*, and in ¼ hr. more join the *Derb el-Hajj*, or great pilgrim-route (p. 158). Following the last, we cross the (¼ hr.) shallow depression of the *Wâdi el-Meddân*, below the ancient ruined bridge, and the (½ hr.) *Wâdi ed-Dahab* by means of a new bridge, and in ¼ hr. more reach the railway station of *El-Muzeirîb* (p. 158).

6. **From Der'a to Boṣrâ** ($7^1/_2$ hrs.).

From Der'a (p. 145) a broad road (an old Roman road, p. 161) leads E.S.E. to Boṣrâ. About $1^1/_4$ M. up the valley the conduit *Ḳanât Fir'aun* (p. 161) crosses the *Wâdi ez-Zeidî* by means of an aqueduct called *Jisr el-Meisari.* After $1^1/_2$ hr. we see (on the right) the round ruin-heap of *Gharz.* We next pass ($^1/_2$ hr.) *Umm el-Meyâdin*, on the right, at the junction of the *Wâdi el-Buṭm* and the Wâdi ez-Zeidî. The Roman road (a few remains) runs about 300 yds. to the N. of the village. Farther on are the lava ridge of *Nuḳaṭ el-Khaṭîb*, with traces of ruins, and ($^3/_4$ hr.) the prosperous village of *Eṭ-Ṭaiyibeh* (on the right). Here we once more cross the Wâdi ez-Zeidî, by means of an ancient bridge with two arches. About 1 hr. farther on we see the village of *Jîzeh*, on both sides of the valley (about 650 yds. to the N. of the road). In the E. part of the village is an old church (now used as a stable by the sheikh), and to the N. is an ancient (Christian) tower, near a ruined monastery. Boṣrâ, and beyond it the Tell eṣ-Ṣufeiḥ, near Salkhad, become visible. After 35 min. we observe some extensive ruins on the left, near the valley of *Khirbet el-Ḥarwâsi.* $^3/_4$ hr. *Ghasm*, with a ruined church, beyond which we pass the ruin of *Rujm el-Misrif* (perhaps a Roman customs-station). On the left lies *El-Mu'arribeh*, with a tower and fragments of a monastic-looking edifice to the N. Farther distant, to the N., lies the Christian village of *Kharaba.* We next pass ($1^1/_4$ hr.) *Ḥommâs* on the right, and in $1^1/_4$ hr. more reach —

Boṣrâ, also called *Eski Shâm* ('Old Damascus'), the ancient capital of the Ḥaurân. It is a poor-looking village with about 1000 inhab., including a garrison of over 100 men, and is partly enclosed by fortified walls.

Owing to its remarkably commanding situation *Boṣrâ* (Lat. *Bostra*) was probably a place of some importance at an early period. It is first mentioned in 1 Macc. v. 26. It belonged to the Nabatæan kingdom, which was formed into the Roman province of Arabia by Cornelius Palma in 105 (or 106) A.D. Boṣrâ became the headquarters of the Legio III. Cyrenaica and soon afterwards the seat of the governor. From the capture of the town dates the so-called Bostrian era, which began on March 22nd, 106, and was soon adopted throughout the province of Arabia in reckoning time. Trajan enlarged and embellished the town, which thereupon assumed the name *Nova Trajana Bostra* on coins and in inscriptions. In the reign of Alexander Severus (222-235) the town became a Roman colony; and under Philippus Arabs, who was born here, it was made the metropolis. When, probably under Diocletian, the province was divided into Palæstina Tertia (the S. half, with Petra for its capital) and Arabia (the N. half), Bostra or Boṣrâ was retained as the capital of the latter. — Boṣrâ was an important centre of the caravan-traffic. A road led hence direct to the Persian Gulf, and another to the Mediterranean (comp. above). It was frequented by Arabian merchants, including Mohammed's uncle, who was accompanied by the prophet himself (p. lxvi). At Boṣrâ dwelt the monk Baḥîra, who is said to have recognized Mohammed as a prophet. Even in the middle ages Boṣrâ was very important as a market and as a fortress. Baldwin III. vainly endeavoured to take the town. The town at length fell into decay, partly owing to earthquakes (especially one in 1151), and afterwards in consequence of the weakness of the Turkish government.

The town is intersected by two main streets, one running from E. to W., and the other from N. to S. Outside the town, near the N.W. corner, is an altar with an inscription. On the left, outside the well-preserved *West Gate*, is a small guard-house. A little way to the left, inside the gate, is a spring, adjoining which is a low-lying meadow, probably once a naumachia (comp. p. 139). In the vicinity are the small mosque of *El-Khiḍr* and an old tomb.

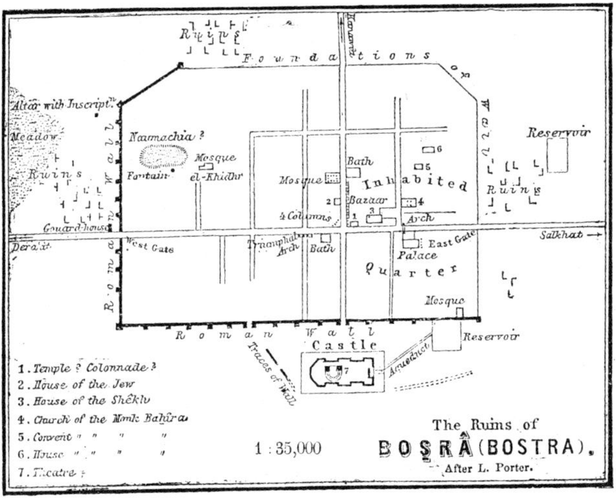

The Ruins of BOṢRÂ (BOSTRA).
After L. Porter.

The *Principal Street* of Boṣrâ, running from E. to W., seems to have been flanked by columns. At the entrance to the third street diverging to the right (S.) from the main street stands a Roman *Triumphal Arch*. The central arch of the three is about $42\frac{1}{2}$ ft. high. One of the pilasters bears a Latin inscription. A little farther to the E., on the right, are the remains of *Baths*. We now come to the point of intersection of the two main streets. We see on our left four large columns, the remains of a once splendid *Building*, with admirably executed Corinthian capitals. — On the opposite side of the street are remains of another beautiful *Building* (Pl. 1), which may have been a temple or a colonnade, of which two columns with bases of white marble are preserved; in the wall are three rows of niches.

On the right side of the cross-street leading to the N. we come to a series of open vaults, which once evidently formed the *Bazaar* of Boṣrâ. On the left is the so-called *House of the Jew* (Pl. 2), who was unjustly deprived of his original dwelling, which, however, was rebuilt after the mosque erected on the spot had been pulled down by order of the righteous-minded Caliph ʿOmar. Also on the left we next see a deserted *Mosque*, the foundation of which is ascribed to Caliph ʿOmar. The materials are ancient. One column bears the date 383 (of the Bostrian era), or A.D. 489. At the entrance is a kind of porch with columns, then a quadrangle having a double open passage on two sides. The arches rest on antique columns, seventeen of which are monoliths of white marble, while the others are of basalt. A handsome frieze runs round the walls. At the N.E. corner of the mosque stands a minaret, with a handsome stone door, the ascent of which richly rewards the visitor. The view embraces the Nuḳra (p. 156), an undulating plain, clothed with vegetation in spring; to the E. is the hill of Salkhad; to the S.W. rises the Jebel ʿAjlûn; and towards the S. extends the steppe in which, about 5 hrs. off, are the interesting ruins of Umm el-Jemâl (possibly Beth Gamul, Jeremiah xlviii. 23). — On the side of the street opposite the mosque are the ruins of a large bath.

Proceeding to the E. from the intersection of the main streets, we come to theq uarter of Modern Boṣrâ. Farther on the street is spanned by a Roman arch, to the right (S.) of which are the ruins of a large house with many fragments of sculptures and columns. The street which diverges here to the left leads to the old '*Church of the Monk Baḥîra*' (Pl. 4), a square building externally, but a rotunda internally. The dome has fallen in. According to an inscription on the gateway, the church was built in 407 of the Bostrian era (*i.e.* 513). A building a little to the N. of this bears a beautiful Arabic inscription. Near the church the *Monastery of Baḥîra* (Pl. 5) is also pointed out. The roof has fallen in. On the N. side is a vaulted niche, with a Latin inscription adjacent. Still farther N. the *House (Dâr) of Baḥîra* (Pl. 6) is shown; over the door is a Greek inscription. — Farther to the N., outside the town, is the mosque of *El-Mebrak*, or the 'place of kneeling', where the camel of ʿOthmân, which carried the Koran, or, according to other versions, the she-camel of Mohammed, is said to have knelt.

Outside the wall, on the E. side of the town, lies a large *Reservoir*, with tolerably preserved substructions. A larger reservoir near the S.E. corner of the town is in still better preservation. At its N.E. angle are the ruins of a mosque.

To the S. of the town rises the huge *Castle*, which was erected by the Aiyubide sultans during the first half of the 13th century. A bridge of six arches leads to a series of subterranean vaulted chambers, where visitors should beware of the cistern-openings in the ground. Beyond these we reach the platform inside the castle, where are still seen the six tiers of seats of the *Roman Theatre* that constituted the nucleus of the building (Pl. 7). The stage was bounded by a wall in two stories, behind each of which ran a passage. The theatre was about 79 yds. in diameter. The tiers of seats are partly concealed by the later buildings. Between the lower double stairs are doors from which passages descend to the 'vomitoria' (approaches to the stage and the auditorium). Around the highest tier of seats ran a colonnade, a few columns of which are still preserved. Descending passages also ran below the landings of the stairs. — The S. battlements of the castle command a fine view.

7. From Boṣrâ to Damascus.

Distances: to *Es-Suweidâ*, 3¾ hrs.; *El-Ḳanawât*, 2 hrs.; *Shuhba*, 2¾ hrs.; *Burâk*, 9½ hrs.; *Damascus*, 6½ hrs.

From Boṣrâ a Roman road leads due N. to (½ hr.) *Jemarrîn*. To the N. of this village a bridge (near which stands a watch-tower) crosses the *Wâdi ed-Dheheb* (the upper part of the Wâdi ez-Zeidî, p. 145). The road next reaches (½ hr.) *Deir ez-Zubeir*, probably once a monastery. ʿAereh is 1 hr. distant.

ʿAereh lies on an eminence between two water-courses. The ruins are extensive, but insignificant. The place derives some importance from being the residence of a Druse chieftain. The 'castle', fitted up in half-European style, was erected by *Ismaʿîl el-Aṭrash* (d. 1869), the chief sheikh of the Druses of the Ḥaurân.

Leaving ʿAereh, we descend the hill to the N. and cross a brook. In 1 hr. we reach the thinly peopled valley of *Mujeidil*, near which, to the left, lies the building of *Deir et-Treif*. We (½ hr.) begin to ascend. Beyond the building of *Deir Senân* we reach (10 min.) *Es-Suweidâ* (p. 166).

From Boṣrâ to Es-Suweidâ viâ Ḥebrân, 6 hrs. We ride towards the N.E., cross the *Wâdi Abu Ḥamâḳa*, and in ¾ hr. reach the *Wâdi Râs el-Bedr*. We then pass (¾ hr.) *Ghassân* on the left, *Deir el-ʿAbûd* to the right, then *Huzḥuz*, and (1 hr.) the Druse village of *El-ʿAfîneh*. To the E. of the village, near a Roman road, are the arches of an aqueduct which Trajan caused to be conducted hither from El-Kanawât. In ¾ hr. we reach **Ḥebrân**, a Druse village commanding a fine view. To the S. of the village are the fine ruins of a castle, adjoined by those of a church. According to a Greek inscription, the building was erected in 155 by Antoninus Pius, so that it was originally a pagan structure. In the middle of the village are the remains of another small church.

A pleasant route leads in 40 min. from Ḥebrân to *El-Kafr*, with a handsome meḍâfeh (public inn). The houses, and even the narrow lanes with pavements on each side, are admirably preserved. On the W. side of the little town is a handsome gate. Proceeding to the N. of El-Kafr, we soon reach (10 min.) the copious *ʿAin Mûsâ* or *Well of Moses*, which waters the village of *Sahwet el-Khiḍr*, situated 3¼ hrs. to the S.E. From the well we may ascend in 1 hr. to the top of the **Ḳuleib** (5635 ft.), one of the highest mountains in the Ḥaurân. The cone of this mountain contains a wide cleft, to which we ride across a plain covered with volcanic substances and thus reach the extinct crater, forming an extensive wooded basin. The actual summit can be reached on foot only and with some climbing. A little below it are several caverns, probably used for collecting rain-water. On the small height are the ruins of a temple. — From the base of the Kuleib to *Es-Suweidâ* is a ride of 2 hrs. The Beduins (*'Ajeilât*) of this district, as well as their dogs, sometimes molest travellers.

Es-Suweidâ (Turkish telegraph), the residence of the Ḳâim-maḳâm of the *Jebel ed-Drûz* (Druse Mountains, p. 156) and of the military commandant of the Ḥaurân (garrison), contains 4500 inhab. and is probably the ancient *Maximianopolis.* Nerva constructed a nymphæum and an aqueduct here. — Starting from the Meḍâfeh (public inn), we first come to a small *Temple.* A street leads hence to a *Gate* resembling a triumphal arch. Farther down, near the centre of the little town, lie the ruins of a large *Basilica* of the 4th or 5th century. We next come to a *Mosque*, occupying the site of an older public building. Near it is the so-called *Meḥkemeh*, or *Court House*, with a Greek inscription. Ascending the hill, we reach a large reservoir. Beyond the N. valley, on the road to El-Ḳanawât, we cross a Roman bridge and reach an interesting tomb, which rises on a basement with rude Doric half-columns and bears an inscription (perhaps of the 1st cent. A.D.).

El-Ḳanawât is reached from Es-Suweidâ by the direct road which leads to the N.N.W. in $1^1/_2$ hr. A slight digression ($^1/_2$ hr.) enables us to visit *'Atîl*, a Druse village which contains a small and elegantly-built temple, now occupied as a Druse dwelling, and dating, according to the inscription, from the 14th year of the reign of Antoninus Pius (A.D. 151). Passing an old church with a tower, we come to another temple, called *El-Ḳaṣr*, to the N. of the village.

El-Ḳanawât, perhaps the Biblical *Kenath* (Numb. xxxii. 42), and more certainly the *Kanatha* of classical writers, was, as is indicated by inscriptions, a flourishing town at an earlier date than Boṣrâ. Pliny and Ptolemy both include it in the Decapolis, and Eusebius includes it in the province of Arabia. Bishops of Kanatha are mentioned in connection with several councils. Coins of the town have been found with a veiled head of Isis on the reverse.

On the S. side of the town, outside the town-wall and to the left of the road to the Es-Suweidâ, stand the ruins of a small peripteral *Temple.* This rises on a terrace, 10 ft. in height, and, according to the inscription, was dedicated to Helios.

Continuing hence to the N. into the valley, we reach the lanes of the LOWER TOWN of El-Ḳanawât. It lies on the left bank of the brook, which was formerly crossed by several bridges. The streets are still well paved at places and most of the houses are in good preservation. — On the right slope of the valley is a handsome *Theatre*, with nine tiers of seats. It is almost entirely hewn in the rock, and is ca. 21 yds. in diameter. — Farther up are the ruins of a small *Temple*, perhaps a *Nymphaeum*, situated over a spring. Steps hewn in the rock lead hence to a massive *Tower*, which was perhaps connected with the military defences of the defile below. The substructions are older than the Roman period. A little to the N. of this building rises a large round tower (perhaps sepulchral), 82 ft. in circumference.

The Upper Town, on the left bank, contains the principal part of the ruins of El-Ḳanawât, presenting an extensive scene of desolation. Near the remains of a mill the town is entered by a beautifully preserved ancient aqueduct, adjoining which are fragments of huge walls, probably ante-Roman. The principal building, known as the *Serâi*, is an aggregate of several structures. On the S. side there is first a smaller building, which consists of two independent

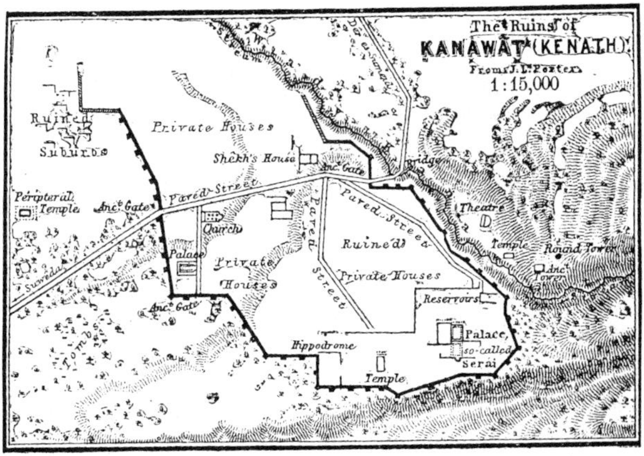

edifices crossing each other; the older had an apse with three arches towards the E. Another building with an apse towards the N. was then erected across this older portion; and to this belongs the large S. façade with its three portals. To the N. of this building is a long edifice which also has a fine colonnade on the W. side. Three gates led into the vestibule, borne by 18 columns, of the *Church*. On each side of this hall is a small gallery, covered with three arches above. A beautiful and most elaborately executed central portal, with a cross, leads into the church, which is 82 ft. in length. On the E. side is a large apse $14^1/_2$ ft. in depth. — To the S. of this point stands a *Temple*, a 'prostylos', with a portico of four huge columns about 33 ft. high. Near this temple lie fragments of numerous roughly executed statues, and there seems to have been a *Hippodrome* here. Beyond the well-preserved S.E. wall of the town, which is furnished with towers of defence, we soon reach several *Sepulchral Towers* concealed among oaks. We then re-enter the town by a gate at the S.E. corner. On the left side of the broad paved street is the ruin of a handsome house, once adorned with a colonnade, and on the right are the remains of a large church of a late period.

At *Seï̂* (*Siâh*), ³/₄ hr. to the S.S.E. of El-Ḳanawât, stands a ruined temple, resembling in style the Herodian Temple at Jerusalem, and indeed recording in its inscriptions the names of Herod and Herod Agrippa. The gazelles, lion's head, saddled horse, and other architectural enrichments, and the rather stiff capitals, are well worthy of inspection. The temple was dedicated to *Baʿal Samin* (god of heaven).

From El-Ḳanawât to *Ezraʿ*, see p. 144.

Our route now leads across a little-cultivated plain and passes below the (2 hrs.) village of *ʿAin Murduk;* it then ascends to the N.E. in the direction of the two curious old craters of the *Gharâra.* This name, signifying a heap of grain, is derived from a Moslem legend, according to which the grain which Pharaoh had forcibly taken away from the peasants and heaped up here was miraculously turned into stone. Our route passes the S. crater and brings us to Shuhba, ³/₄ hr. after leaving ʿAin Murduk.

Shuhba, the ancient *Philippopolis*, is still in part surrounded by walls and also contains a few Roman antiquities. The streets, some of which are 25 ft. wide, are paved with long slabs, and were probably once flanked by colonnades. At the intersection of the two main streets are the remains of a *Tetrapylon* (p. xcvii), and about 120 paces to the S. of this are the ruins of large *Baths*, containing lofty chambers adorned with sculptures. Some of the pipes and five arches of the aqueduct, by which the water was conducted to the bath, are still preserved. The hooks or cramps on the walls were used to secure the marble incrustation. About 230 paces to the E. of the intersection of the streets stand five columns, being remains of the colonnade of a *Temple*, of which a few fragments of walls are the only other trace. Near these are the outer walls of an *Amphitheatre*, which was built against the slope. Between the theatre and the principal street stands a small *Temple* with a kind of crypt, now filled with rubbish. — Proceeding towards the sheikh's dwelling, we now come to a curious building, buried 14 ft. deep in the ground. In the centre of the building is a round apse about 13 ft. wide, with niches on each side for statues. In front of the building is a large open space. The purpose of the building is unknown.

From Shuhba to Burâḳ viâ Shaḳḳâ (11 hrs.). The route first crosses the *Wâdi Nimra* (see next page) and then runs towards the N.E. On the left, after 40 min., is seen *El-ʿAṣalîyeh.* On the hill to the right (S.) lies *Ṭafḥâ.* In 40 min. more we reach the large village of **Shaḳḳâ**, the ancient *Sakkaia* (Ptolemy). Among the ruins are several towers of different periods, but few buildings are preserved. Towards the N.E. are the ruins of a basilica of the 2nd or 3rd cent., with a nave and aisles. On the E. side of the inhabited quarter of the town are remains of a monastery of the 5th century (Arab. *Deir esh-Sharkîyeh*), traces of the semicircular apse of the church of which may be distinguished. To the N. of Shaḳḳâ rises a square tower (*El-Burj*), in three stories. The upper parts of the building are more modern than the lower. A number of mummies and skulls have been found here. According to the inscription, the tower was erected by a certain Bassos, in the year 70 of the Bostrian era (A.D. 176). — From Shaḳḳâ we ride to the N.W., past *Tell ʿIzrân*, to (3/4 hr.) *El-Hît*, situated in the *Arḍ el-Betheniyeh*. The village contains several towers and a reservoir, and it is also passed by a large subterranean conduit from the Wâdi el-Luwâ (see below), running from S. to N. — To the N.W. of El-Hît we next reach (1/2 hr.) the village of *El-Heiyât*, occupied by Roman Catholics, before entering which we observe to the E. of the road a large building with stone doors and a terrace affording a fine view. In 2 hrs. more from this point we reach *Lâhiteh* (see below).

The direct route from Shuhba to Damascus at first follows the great *Wâdi Nimra*, called *Wâdi el-Luwâ* in its lower part, which separates this district from the *Lejâh* (p. 144). The *Gharârat esh-Shemâlîyeh* ('the northern') rises to the left, and after crossing the valley we pass, likewise on our left, the volcanic *Tell Shîḥân* (3740 ft.). The W. side of the crater of this hill is broken away, so that it somewhat resembles an easy chair without arms. From its extensive crater and from the *Gharârat el-Ḳiblîyeh* vast lava-streams once poured over the Lejâh. In 50 min. we reach the village of *Umm ez-Zeitûn*, with the unimportant ruins of a temple.

The route skirting the Lejâh is exposed to danger from the Beduins. Little water is to be found, and the heat is often oppressive. A few fields and many traces of former cultivation are passed. The villages on each side of the route present few attractions. On the right are *ʿAmrâ* and *El-Hît* (see above), on the left (25 min.) *Es-Suweimira* and (20 min.) *El-Muraṣraṣ*. We next pass (20 min.) *Umm el-Ḥâretein* and *Sumeid*, farther to the W., (1/4 hr.) *El-Imtûneh*, (25 min.) *Rijm el-Iʿs*, (10 min.) *El-Ḳuseifeh*, (25 min.) *Lâhiteh*, (25 min.) *Ḥaḍar*, (20 min.) *Er-Ruḍeimeh*, (25 min.) *Suwârat eṣ-Ṣaghîreh*, (1/2 hr.) *Dhekîr*, (1/2 hr.) *Deir Nîleh*, and (40 min.) *Khalkhaleh*. In 2 hrs. more we reach *Suwârat el-Kebîreh*. To the N.E. lies the extensive tract of *Arḍ el-Fedayein*. After 1/2 hr. we cross the *Wâdi el-Luwâ* (see above), and in 50 min. more (9 1/2 hrs. from Shuhba) we reach —

Burâḳ, formerly a thriving place, but now very thinly peopled. Many old houses in the style peculiar to the Ḥaurân (comp. p. 156) are still well preserved, and there is a fine reservoir.

Beyond Burâḳ we at first traverse a poorly cultivated plain, and then gradually ascend a dreary range of hills. These hills belong to the *Jebel el-Mâniʿ* (p. 144). After 2 1/4 hrs. we pass, to the left, the *Tell Abu Shajara*, or 'hill of the tree', a name derived from the solitary terebinth which grows here. Beyond the pass a beautiful view is revealed of the dark-blue plain of Damascus. Descending hence, we reach (1 3/4 hr.) the valley of the *Nahr el-Aʿwaj* (p. 157), and near it the Moslem village of *Nejhâ*, which, situated in the *Wâdi el-ʿAjam*, presents fewer of the characteristics of the Ḥaurân. We now enter the plain of *El-Merj*. To the right (E.) we see the hills of the Ṣafâ (p. 322). Jebel el-Aswad (p. 267) rises on the left. After spending two days among these inhospitable deserts the traveller will be better able to appreciate the eager delight with which Orientals welcome the view of the fruitful and well-watered plain of Damascus. After $1^1/_3$ hr. we reach the village of *Kabr es-Sitt*, or 'tomb of the lady', so called from the fact that *Zeinab*, a granddaughter of Mohammed, is buried here. After 35 min. we pass the village of *Babbîla* and in $^1/_2$ hr. more reach *Damascus* (E. gate. p. 315).

20. The Desert of Judah to the S.W. of the Dead Sea.

Comp. Maps, pp. 11, 92.

Extreme caution is advisable in selecting a DRAGOMAN. Tents are indispensable. The necessary escort of one or two Khaiyâls is obtained through the dragoman, who is responsible for their keep and pay.

The **Desert of Judah** is mentioned in the Old Testament either under that name (Ps. lxiii. 1), or under the names of its parts (1 Sam. xxiv. 2 and other places). It consists of an arid plateau about 12-20 M. broad and 60-70 M. long, with small conical hills and intersected by deep ravines. — The country to the S. of Hebron (Heb. *negeb*) contains many ruins, and there are many caverns in its hills. The ground is soft white limestone, through which the water penetrates and, where it is not collected in cisterns, runs away below the surface of the beds of the valleys. Near Yuṭṭâ, Dûra, and Yekîn the ground falls some 490 ft., forming a plateau about 2620 ft. above the sea-level. This plateau is crossed by the great valley extending from Hebron to Beersheba and then to the W. to Gerar.

1. Beersheba.

FROM GAZA TO BEERSHEBA, 9 hrs. (carriage-road in summer). To the ($^1/_4$ hr.) *Jebel el-Munṭâr*, see p. 121. Leaving the summit of the mountain to our right, we ride in a continuous S.E. direction across the extensive and tolerably level plateau, from which only a few hills rise here and there. In about 3 hrs. we reach the *Tell Abu Hareireh*, near which is the *Weli* of that saint. The district is cultivated by the Beduins. Crossing the *Wâdi esh-Sherî'a* almost immediately, we enter a more monotonous and barren region. After about $3^1/_2$ hrs. we arrive at the springs (brackish) and ruins of *Khirbet Abu Rukeiyik*. About 2 hrs. more bring us to —

Bir es-Seba', the ancient *Beersheba*, the wells of which play a prominent part in the history of the patriarchs (Gen. xxi. 28-32). Beersheba was the southernmost town belonging to the Israelites, whence arose the proverbial phrase 'from Dan to Beersheba' (Judges xx. 1, etc.). In the days of Eusebius it was a considerable market-village with a Roman garrison; and bishops of Beersheba are occasionally mentioned. By the 14th cent., however, the town was deserted. Extensive ruined remains are to be seen on the N. side of the *Wâdi es-Seba'*, the lower part of which is named *Wâdi el-Ghazzeh*, the upper part *Wâdi el-Khalîl*. The seven old wells, which still supply good water, lie on the N. side of the valley, where it forms a curve. They are all 5-9 ft. in diameter and ca. 45 ft. deep. The town, which has lately been resettled, is the seat of a Kâimmakâm; it contains 800 inhab., a Serâi, a mosque, a post and telegraph office, and a khân. It lies a little to the S.W. of the old town, whence building-materials have been taken for its construction. The ten or twelve shops here supply the simple requirements of the neighbouring Beduins, who visit the place in considerable numbers.

FROM BEERSHEBA TO HEBRON, $8^1/_4$ hrs. The road ascends the *Wâdi el-Khalîl*, with *Bîr es-Sakâti* and *Bîr el-Mokenneh* to the right, leaving *Bîr Lekîyeh* to the left. Beyond the (3 hrs.) poor village of *Tâtereh* we re-enter the mountainous region. In $1^3/_4$ hr. more we reach *Ed-Dâharîyeh*, which is perhaps the *Kirjath-Sepher* or *Debir* of Judges i. 11. Thence we may ride to Hebron direct in $3^1/_2$ hrs., or in $4^1/_2$ hrs. with a détour to the E. viâ *Yuṭṭâ*, the *Juttah* of Josh. xv. 55 but hardly the 'city of *Judah*' of Luke i. 39.

2. Engedi.

From Bethlehem to Engedi, 9 hrs. A guide from the *Ta'âmireh* Beduins or the *Beni Na'im* is necessary and may be found either in Bethlehem or Jerusalem. — To the *Frank Mountain*, see pp. 111, 110. Leaving this on our left, we descend the *Wâdi ed-Dîya'*, which farther on takes the name of *Wâdi Khareitûn*, to the (1/4 hr.) *Wâdi el-Hamdeh*, which opens on the right. We now ascend the ridge towards the S.E. for 1/4 hr. and then ride across the high plateau of *Kenân Eskeir*. At (1 hr.) its other end we pass two isolated hills, and after crossing several valleys we enter (1 3/4 hr.) the *Wâdi Hasâsâ*. Descending this wâdi, we pass in 25 min. the cisterns of *Bîr Sukeirîyeh* and *Bîr Hasâsâ;* after 1 1/4 hr. the road leaves the valley and passes over the hill of *Râs en-Nuweita* into the (1 hr.) *Wâdi esh-Shakîf*. Hence we continue to the S.S.E. over the hilly plateau, and in 1 1/2 hr. reach the culminating point of the *Pass of Engedi* (655 ft. above the sea-level, 1945 ft. above the Dead Sea; magnificent view). The descent (3/4 hr.) on the other side to Engedi is very toilsome.

From Hebron to Engedi, 7-8 hrs., a fatiguing route. The road ascends the *Jebel Jôbar* (fine restrospect from the top) and in 1 1/2 hr. reaches *Tell Zîf* (*Ziph*, 1 Sam. xxiii. 24), on the left; after 40 min., cisterns; 1 hr., *Wâdi Khabra* (little water), which we follow (2 hrs.). Then we ascend in 1 1/2 hr. to the top of the *Pass of Engedi* (see above).

Engedi (680 ft. below the Mediterranean and 605 ft. above the Dead Sea) is now called *'Ain Jidi*, both names signifying 'goat's spring'. The precipitous cliffs on one side and the sea on the other, the warmth of the atmosphere, and the strange-looking vegetation combine to produce a wonderful effect. To the wilderness of Engedi David once retired, and it was in a cave here that he spared the life of the sleeping Saul (1 Sam. xxiv. 1 et seq.). The 'camphire of Engedi' (henna, see p. 128) is mentioned in the Song of Solomon (i. 14). According to Josephus there were once beautiful palm-groves here, and in the time of Eusebius Engedi was still a place of importance. The water of the spring is warm (80° Fahr.), sweetish, and impregnated with lime, and contains small black snails. The natives assert that the water comes under the mountain from Se'îr (?) near Hebron. The *seyâl (Acacia seyal)*, from which gum-arabic is obtained, occurs here; likewise the *sidr* (p. 129), and the *'oshr (Calotropis procera)*. This tree bears the genuine apple of Sodom (comp. p. 129), a yellow, apple-like fruit, described by Josephus; on being squeezed it bursts, and only fibres and bits of the thin rind remain in the hand. Among the smaller plants the nightshade *(Solanum melongena)* is very common. — By the spring, and to the E. of it, are a few remains of old buildings. The ancient Engedi probably lay below the spring. The gradual slope towards the Dead Sea was converted into terraced gardens.

3. Masada.

From Engedi to Masada, 4 1/2 hrs. (water should be taken). — We descend from the spring towards the S. and cross the (1/2 hr.) *Wâdi el-'Areijeh* at the ruins of *Kasr el-'Areijeh;* on the slopes of the hill are vestiges of ancient vineyards. Masada comes in sight to the S. We next reach (20 min.) a sulphur-laden spring, and 40 min. later we cross a line of hills which stretch to the sea; beyond these to the left lies the *Birket el-Khalîl* ('Pool of Abraham'), so called after a Moslem legend, where salt is obtained by evaporation from the water of the Dead Sea. In 1/4 hr. more we cross the *Wâdi el-Khabra*. In the valley and in the littoral plain is found the so-called *Rose of Jericho (Anastatica Hierochuntica)*, but the plant is neither a rose, nor does it now grow near Jericho. It is a low annual herb of the cruciferous order, soft and herbaceous at first, but whose branches become woody with age. It owes its name *anastatica* (the arising) to a peculiarity of its woody branches, springing from the crown of the root, which are curved inwards when dry, but spread out horizontally when the plant is moistened. This phenomenon has given rise to a superstitious belief in the virtues of the plant, and it is accordingly gathered in great quantities and sent to Jerusalem, where it is sold to pilgrims. Another similar plant to be found here is the ***Asteriscus aquaticus***, which was perhaps considered in earlier times to be the Rose of Jericho. Wild barley and a few saline plants are also found here. The chief of these is the *Salsola kali*, Arabic *Kili*, a plant with a flat, glossy, reddish stalk, and small glass-like leaves, which the Arabs burn in order to obtain alkali (*al-ḳali*). The fauna of the region includes the mountain-goat of

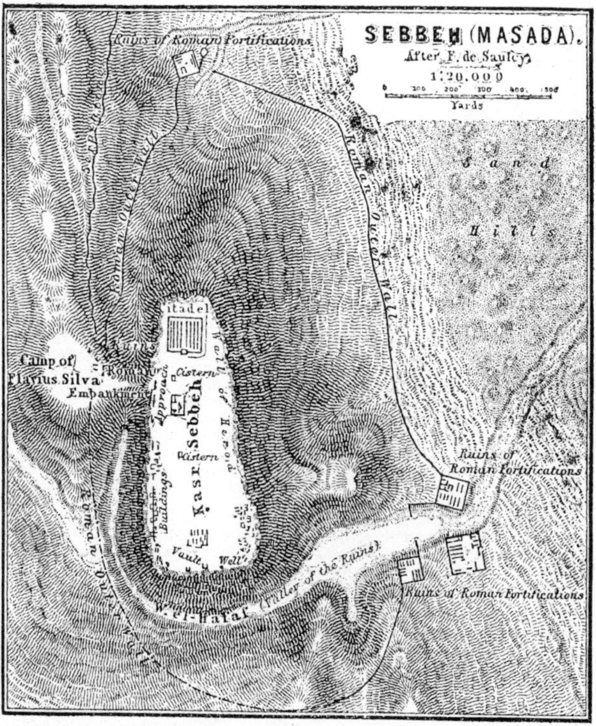

Sinai, and also the cony (*Hyrax Syriacus*, Arab. *wabr*; p. lvi), a very curious little animal of the cloven-footed family, with a brown coat. The flesh of the latter is much esteemed, but it was forbidden to the Israelites (Levit. xi. 5; Psalms civ. 18; Prov. xxx. 26).

After 3/4 hr. we reach the *Wâdi Mahras*, with seyâl-trees (p. 171); then (20 min.) the *Wâdi Khasheibeh*; (1/4 hr.) the *Wâdi eṣ-Ṣafâṣif*; and (25 min.) the *Wâdi Seyâl*. Beyond it we proceed direct to the hill of Masada. On the way we cross several deep crevices in the clayey soil, and in 40 min. reach the N.E. angle of the Roman enclosing wall, which runs entirely round the crown of the isolated hill. Following the wall to the S., we come in 20 min. to the Roman fortifications in the *Wâdi es-Sebbeh* (or *Wâdi el-Hafâf*), at the S. foot of the hill. The ascent to the top may be made in 1 hr. by a very difficult footpath.

The hill of **Masáda** (*i.e.* a mountain-stronghold; 1705 ft. above the Dead Sea), now called *Es-Sebbeh*, is stated by Josephus (Bell. Jud. vii. 8, 3) to have been fortified by Jonathan the Maccabæan. It was re-fortified by Herod the Great, who enclosed the whole of the plateau at the top of the hill with a wall constructed of white stone, seven stadia in circumference, 12 ells high, and 8 ells thick, and furnished with 37 towers, each 50 ells high. He also built a strong and sumptuous palace on the W. slope, with four corner-towers, each 60 ells high. The only access was by an artificial stair called 'the serpent'. The enclosed space, the soil of which was very rich, was used for cultivation. After the destruction of Jerusalem, the Jews still offered an obstinate resistance to the Romans on this spot. The latter (under Flavius Silva) then built out from the rock to the W. of the castle an embankment 200 ells in height, on which they brought their besieging engines close to the wall. The defenders thereupon erected within the outer wall a second one of wood and earth, and when this was destroyed by fire, they slew themselves with their wives and children, rather than surrender.

Ascending the hill, we reach (1/2 hr.) the ruins of Roman towers, and in 1/4 hr. more cross a slope of loose stones which formed part of the Roman embankment. Through a well-preserved mediæval gateway, consisting of a pointed arch with Beduin inscriptions, we enter upon the spacious plateau on the top of the hill. This plateau is 600 yds. long and 200-250 yds. wide, and falls off abruptly on almost every side. The enclosing wall is still preserved at places. The other remains are not extensive. On the N. side of the hill stands a square tower; and 39 1/2 ft. higher, but still 19 1/2 ft. below the level of the plateau, rises a round tower. From the N. wall branch off a great many side-walls, which were perhaps built during the last siege. To the W. and S. are large cisterns. In the centre of the plateau are the remains of a Byzantine chapel (?). To the S. of the chapel is a tomb-cavern with an inscription. To judge from the remains, it would seem that Masada was still inhabited after the catastrophe mentioned above. The archway on the W. side looks as if it belonged to the Crusaders' period. The ruins to the N. and W. of this arch, however, seem to belong to the palace of Herod, while those on the S. side of the plateau are now a shapeless mass. — The View of the wild and desolate mountainous region round the town is very imposing. Not a trace of a human habitation is to be seen. The colouring of the Dead Sea and the mountains, except when the midday heat envelops everything in a white haze, is singularly vivid, and we obtain almost a bird's-eye view of the S. end of the sea. Exactly opposite to us lies the pointed promontory of El-Lisân (p. 132); to the S. the eye ranges as far as the Jebel Usdum (p. 174), and opposite rise El-Kerak and the mountains of Moab. Immediately below the fortress to the S.E., as well as on a low chain of hills to the W., the camps of the Roman besiegers are still distinctly traceable; that on the W. was Silva's.

4. Jebel Usdum and El-Kerak.

From Masada to Jebel Usdum, 6 hrs. From the fortifications in the *Wâdi es-Sebbeh* (see above) the route leads S. along the upper edge of the littoral plain of the Dead Sea, which is intersected by clefts and ravines. After 1/2 hr. we reach the large *Wâdi el-Hafâf*, which we follow to (35 min.) the sea. Thence we turn S. again to (50 min.) the *Wâdi Rabad el-Jâmûs*, with tamarisks. After 1/2 hr. we reach the *Wâdi el-Ḳedr*. The coast-road is now quitted. After crossing a hill, our route lies along the slope of the mountain to the (50 min.) *Wâdi Hathrûra;* hence we reach in 20 min. the *Wâdi Mubaghghak*, with the ruined mediæval fort of that name, where good water and a convenient camping-place are found. There are two reservoirs here, which were once fed by a conduit from the mountains. — We follow the shore to ($1^1/_4$ hr.) the *Wâdi ez Zuweira*, through which runs the road from Hebron. The littoral plain gradually broadens. — The road to the *Wâdi Nukhbâr* (see below) runs straight to the S. through the *Wâdi el-Muhauwât;* the N. summit of the *Jebel Usdum* is reached to the S.W. in 20 minutes. The route along the E. side of the mountain has become impracticable owing to the rise in the level of the waters of the Dead Sea. The pillar of salt which passed for that into which Lot's wife was changed (see below) has fallen into the water. Nevertheless, it is perhaps worth while to ride for a short distance along the E. side of the mountain, as far as a little cavern rich in salt crystals. The whole of the S. bay of the Dead Sea is shallow (5-13 ft.).

The name of **Jebel** or **Khashm Usdum** echoes that of the Biblical *Sodom* (Gen. xviii, xix), though it is probable that this is due to artificial revival rather than ancient tradition. It is an isolated hill, about 7 M. in length, the highest point of which is about 590 ft. above the level of the Dead Sea. The sides are so steep and crevassed that it is difficult to ascend it. The base of the hill, up to about 100 or 150 ft., consists of pure crystallized salt, which is seamed with perpendicular fissures. These, under the influence of the weather, frequently give rise to needle-rocks, columns, etc., in which the popular imagination recognizes human beings turned to stone. Thus probably arose the tradition of the transformation of Lot's wife into a pillar of salt (Gen. xix. 26; Wisdom x. 7), which Josephus says was to be seen in his days. The salt is covered with a layer, 400-450 ft. thick, of chalky limestone and clay. The present condition of the salt-deposit is due to some convulsion of nature; formerly it was much more extensive, reaching perhaps as far as the peninsula of *El-Lisân*, where rock-salt was also found.

From Jebel Usdum to El-Kerak, 15 hrs. From the N. point of the mountain we ride along its W. side, and in $^1/_2$ hr. reach the end of the littoral plain and the entrance of the *Wâdi Nukhbâr*, forming a deep depression in the marly soil, which we now ascend. After $^3/_4$ hr. the valley contracts to the dimensions of a narrow and winding gorge, with almost vertical walls. In $^1/_4$ hr. we reach the surface of the stratum of marl, and now ride to the S. through the *ʿAraba* (p. 176). After 40 min. we descend into the ($^1/_4$ hr.) *Wâdi el-Amʿâz*, which we follow for 10 min. to the point where it debouches into the *Sebkha*, the marshy depression at the S. end of the Dead Sea. This district is inundated at flood-time, but when the water is low it is possible to cross it in a due E. direction to (2 hrs.) *Eṣ-Ṣâfiyeh*, with wretched reed huts in the *Ghôr eṣ-Ṣâfiyeh*. When the water is high, we are obliged to make a détour to the S. along the border of the Sebkha, past *El-Feifeh*, $4^1/_2$ hrs. from its beginning; thence to the *Ghôr eṣ-Ṣâfiyeh* in 2 hrs. Besides reeds we observe the ʿOshr tree (p. 171) and the *Salvadora Persica*, a tree averaging 25 ft. in height.

After $1^1/_2$ hr. we reach the plain of *El-Melûḥa*, with a brook, and in 40 min. the mouth of the *Wâdi Guweiyeh*. In $^1/_4$ hr. we leave the plain of El-Melûḥa, and in $^1/_2$ hr. reach the promontory near the *Wâdi Kheslân*. After $^1/_4$ hr. we reach the heap of stones *(rujûm)* marking the tomb of the *Sheikh Ṣâliḥ*, whom the Beduins invoke to aid them in their predatory expeditions. 13 min. *Wâdi en-Numeira;* 48 min. *El Muraḳsed;* 14 min. *Wâdi Berej*, on our right. After $^1/_2$ hr. we reach cultivated land. We then reach the *Wâdi ed-Derâʿa*, or *Wâdi el-Kerak*, which frequently contains water. Some ruins here are popularly called sugar-mills, and in the adjoining large and beautiful oasis of *El-Mezraʿa*, with numerous ʿOshr trees (p. 171), are encampments of Ghôr Arabs. The peninsula of *El-Lisân* is a flat, clayey plain, ca. 100 ft. in height, and without a vestige of life.

The path now ascends the wild and grand *Wâdi el-Kerak* to the plateau of *Derâʿa* (55 min.); after 52 min. we reach a cultivated plain. In 14 min. we have *Tell ed-Derâʿa* on our right; in 9 min. more we cross the beautiful brook *Seil ed-Derâʿa*. Continuing to ascend the Wâdi el-Kerak, in $3^1/_2$ hrs. we reach the spring *ʿAin es-Sakka*. In another hour we find ourselves below El-Kerak, and after 35 min. more of steep climbing we reach the N.E. corner of the town of *El-Kerak* (p. 154).

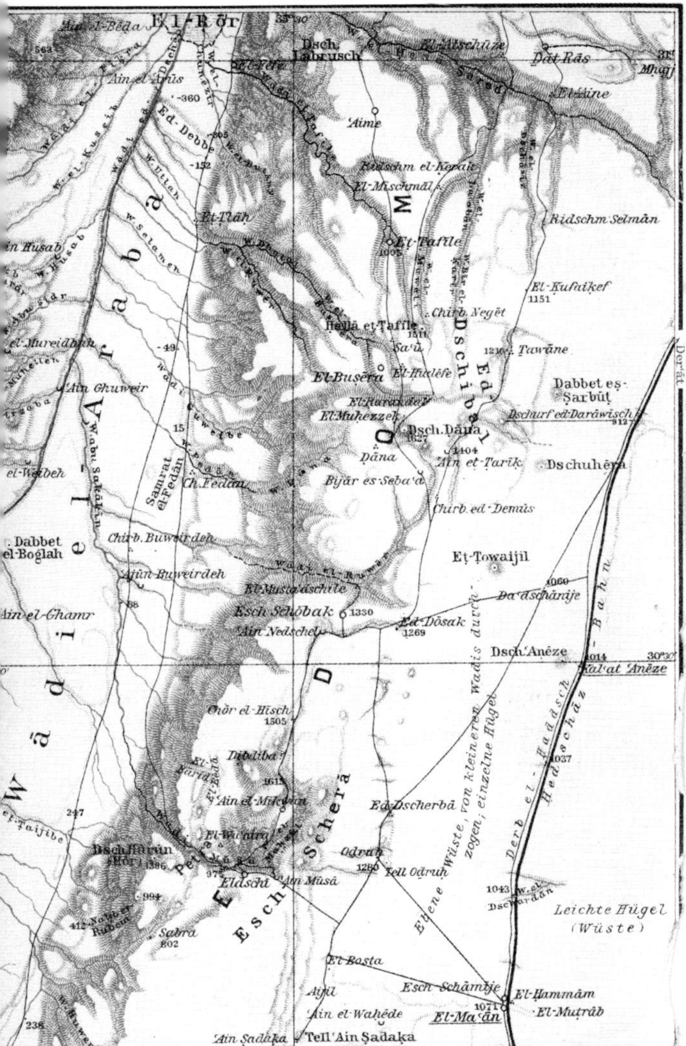

Brünnow, Provincia Arabia Bd. I. — Wagner & Debes, Leipzig

Km. 1:700,000 — Engl. Mei.